BUILDING AND CONSOLING A NATION

THE YIDDISH HISTORIANS IN THEIR OWN WORDS

SELECTED WRITINGS NEWLY
TRANSLATED INTO ENGLISH

BUILDING AND CONSOLING A NATION

THE YIDDISH HISTORIANS IN THEIR OWN WORDS

SELECTED WRITINGS NEWLY TRANSLATED INTO ENGLISH

Translated, Edited, and Introduced by Mark L. Smith

Including
a Conversation with Series Editor **Michael Berenbaum**
and Foreword by **Samuel H. Kassow**

ACADEMIC STUDIES PRESS
BOSTON
2026

Library of Congress Cataloging-in-Publication Data

Names: Smith, Mark L. (Mark Lee), 1957- editor translator
  writer of introduction | Kassow, Samuel D. writer of foreword
Title: Building and consoling a nation : the Yiddish historians in their
  own words : selected writings newly translated into English /
  translated, edited, and introduced by Mark L. Smith ; foreword by Samuel
  H. Kassow.
Description: Boston : Academic Studies Press, 2026. | Includes
  bibliographical references and index. | English translations from the
  Yiddish.
Identifiers: LCCN 2025047721 (print) | LCCN 2025047722 (ebook) | ISBN
  9798897831289 hardback | ISBN 9798897830725 paperback | ISBN
  9798897830732 adobe pdf | ISBN 9798897830749 epub
Subjects: LCSH: Jews--History--Historiography | Jewish historians | Yiddish
  literature--Translations into English
Classification: LCC DS115.5 . B95 2025 (print) | LCC DS115.5 (ebook)
LC record available at https://lccn.loc.gov/2025047721
LC ebook record available at https://lccn.loc.gov/2025047722

Copyright © Mark L. Smith, 2026

ISBN 9798897831289 hardback
ISBN 9798897830725 paperback

ISBN 9798897830732 adobe pdf
ISBN 9798897830749 epub

Book design by Lapiz Digital Services
Cover design by Ivan Grave

Published by Academic Studies Press
1007 Chestnut Street
Newton, MA 02464, USA
www.academicstudiespress.com

With Gratitude

For Publication

In appreciation to the following sponsors for supporting publication of this book:

Professor Michael Berenbaum, Director, Sigi Ziering Institute,
   American Jewish University
California Institute for Yiddish Culture and Language (CIYCL)
Central Yiddish Culture Organization (CYCO)
Conference on Jewish Material Claims Against Germany (Claims Conference)
Friends of Jewish Renewal in Poland / Beit Polska
Sady and Ludwig Kahn Chair in Jewish History, University of California,
   Los Angeles
Memorial Foundation for Jewish Culture
Toronto Workmen's Circle Foundation

For Open Access

In appreciation to the Conference on Jewish Material Claims Against Germany (Claims Conference) for supporting Open Access for this translation and publication project. Through recovering the assets of the victims of the Holocaust, the Claims Conference enables organizations around the world to provide education about the Shoah and to preserve the memory of those who perished.

Contents

Note on Languages and Usage   vii

A Conversation with Series Editor Michael Berenbaum   xv

Foreword
Samuel H. Kassow   xxiii

Introduction to the Yiddish Historians and Their Work
Mark L. Smith   vii

Part One
Jewish Autonomy

1   Autonomy in Jewish History
    by Simon Dubnow, 1934   3

2   The Jewish Parliament in Lithuania and Belorussia in Its Legislative Activity, 1623–1721
    by Israel Sosis, 1928   9

3   A Budget of the Council of Four Lands in 1726
    by Raphael Mahler, 1940   17

4   The Financial Collapse of the Central and Provincial Autonomy of the Jews in Old-Time Poland, 1650–1764
    by Ignacy Schiper, 1932   27

5   The Central Representative Bodies of the Jews in the Grand Duchy of Warsaw, 1807–1816
    by Artur Eisenbach, 1938   35

6   The Warsaw *Kehila* under the Leadership of Dr. Ludwik Natanson, 1871–1896
     by *Jacob Shatzky, 1953*   42

7   Jewish "Autonomy": The Nazi-Imposed Jewish Councils
     by *Isaiah Trunk, 1949*   50

Part Two
On the Jewish Street

8   Yiddish Theater in the German and Slavic Ghettos during the Sixteenth Century
     by *Ignacy Schiper, 1927*   63

9   The Structure of the Jewish Guilds in Poland, Lithuania, and Belorussia in the Seventeenth and Eighteenth Centuries
     by *Mark Wischnitzer, 1928*   71

10 Two Communities in One City: The Jews of Lemberg from Medieval to Modern Times
     by *Meir Balaban, 1930*   79

11 The Young Historians Circle in Warsaw, 1923–1939
     by *Raphael Mahler, 1967*   88

12 Varied Were the Ways (of Jewish Resistance against the Nazis)
     by *Mark Dworzecki, 1946*   94

13 The Wooden Synagogues in Poland before the Holocaust
     by *Rachel Wischnitzer, 1962*   102

14 The Soup Kitchen and the Yiddish Theater in the Warsaw Ghetto
     by *Rachel Auerbach, 1977*   107

Part Three
In the Non-Jewish World

15 Jewish-Christian Relations in Płock in the Sixteenth and Seventeenth Centuries
     by *Isaiah Trunk, 1938*   115

16 What Types of Taxes Did the Jews of Lublin Pay in the Former
    Independent Poland?
    by Bela Mandelsberg, 1930   121

17 Jewish Home Industry in Old-Time Poland
    by Emanuel Ringelblum, 1935   127

18 The "New Settlements" in 1808: How Belorussian Jews
    Responded to the First Order to Settle in Agricultural Colonies
    in Russian Ukraine
    by Simon Dubnow, 1932   132

19 Jewish Cantonists—Young Boys Recruited for Military Service in
    Tsarist Russia, 1828–1956
    by Saul Ginsburg, 1933   137

20 Antisemitism and Pogroms in Ukraine, 1917–1918: On the History of
    Ukrainian-Jewish Relations
    by Elias Tcherikower, 1923   146

21 On the Causes of Jewish Defenselessness against the Nazis and
    the Strength of Jewish Resistance
    by Isaiah Trunk, 1953   157

Part Four
Yiddish Literature

22 The *Brantshpigl (Burning Mirror)*, 1596—The Encyclopedia
    of the Jewish Woman in the Seventeenth Century
    by Maks Erik, 1926   165

23 On the Sources of the *Mayse-bukh* (Book of Stories), 1602
    by Israel Zinberg, 1926   173

24 Three Hundred Years of the *Tsene-rene* (Bible Stories for Women), 1616
    by Jacob Shatzky, 1928   180

25 The Tales of Rabbi Nachman of Bratslav (1815): Hasidism and
    Yiddish Literary Creativity
    by Shmuel Niger, 1932   185

26 On the History of Yiddish Literature in the Nineteenth Century: Haskalah Period
    by Meir Wiener, 1939   195

27 Four Unknown Yiddish Plays from the Mid-Nineteenth Century
    by Max Weinreich, 1930   205

28 Yiddish Literature under Nazi Occupation
    by Nachman Blumental, 1946   214

Part Five
Press, Post, Communications

29 Life and Language as Reflected by Yiddish Testimony in the Responsa Literature from the Beginning of the Fifteenth to the End of the Seventeenth Century
    by Zalman Rubashov, 1929   225

30 The Jewish Postal Service in Tsarist Russia during the Early Nineteenth Century
    by Saul Ginsburg, 1932   232

31 The First Yiddish Newspaper in the Russian Empire, *Kol mevaser*, and Its Time, 1862–72
    by Israel Zinberg, 1913   241

32 The Attitude toward Yiddish of the Russian Authorities in Vilna during the 1860s: On the History of Yiddish Bookselling in Vilna
    by Pinchas Kon, 1929   252

33 Ghettos and Concentration Camps Seeking Contacts: A Chapter of Jewish Resistance
    by Mark Dworzecki, 1949   257

34 Unknown Letters by Zelig Kalmanovich in the Vilna Ghetto to Isaac Giterman in the Warsaw Ghetto
    by Joseph Kermish, 1983   264

35 Inscriptions on Walls, Sacred Texts, and Other Books during the Holocaust
    by Nachman Blumental, 1966   276

Part Six
Education

36 Joseph Perl as a Pedagogical Leader and His School in Tarnopol
   125 Years after Its Founding
   by Philip Friedman, 1940 — 288

37 Yehuda-Leib Gordon as a Fighter for the Haskalah in Jewish Schools in
   Lithuania in the Mid-Nineteenth Century
   by Nadzieja Jaffe, 1938 — 298

38 The Rise of Yiddish Secular Schools in Poland during World War I
   by Chaim-Solomon Kazdan, 1947 — 306

39 Jewish Schools in the Vilna Ghetto as Spiritual Resistance
   by Mark Dworzecki, 1948 — 313

40 The Jewish Vocational and Higher School System
   in the Warsaw Ghetto, 1940–42
   by Esther Goldhar-Mark, 1949 — 322

41 The School System and Education for Holocaust Survivors
   in the Displaced Persons Camps in Germany
   by Philip Friedman, 1948 — 331

42 Four Years of the Chair for Holocaust Studies, Bar-Ilan University, Israel
   by Mark Dworzecki, 1963 — 343

Part Seven
Book Reviews

43 The History of the Jews in Russia (1914)
   Reviewed by Zelig Kalmanovich — 351

44 Saul Ginsburg. Historical Works (1937)
   Reviewed by Moyshe Shalit — 358

45 Isaiah Trunk. The History of the Jews in Płock (1939)
   Reviewed by A. Valdman — 363

46 Jacob Shatzky. In the Shadow of the Past (1947)
   Reviewed by Samuel Rollansky — 368

47 Philip Friedman. Auschwitz (1950)
    Reviewed by Julien Hirshaut   372

48 Mark Dworzecki. White Nights and Black Days: Jewish Camps
    in Estonia (1970)
    Reviewed by Israel Kaplan   377

49 Nachman Blumental. Words and Sayings from the
    Holocaust Period (1981)
    Reviewed by David Shtokfish   383

Note on Languages and Usage

All translations and transliterations are my own. In general, I have followed the standards of the YIVO Institute for Jewish Research in transliterating Yiddish. The few exceptions include well-known terms and names such as *yizkor* (rather than *yisker*) and Sholem Aleichem (rather than Sholem Aleykhem).

For Yiddish personal names, I have taken the dual approach of using the conventional English spelling in the text and the transliterated Yiddish spelling in the notes. Thus, "Simon Dubnow" appears in the text, and "Shimen Dubnov" appears in the notes.

I have made every attempt to transliterate Polish, Ukrainian, and Lithuanian personal names correctly. For names in all other languages, I have used the most common online spelling to assist the reader in finding further information, rather than following any recognized system.

For well-known Polish cities, I have used their common English names (Warsaw, Lodz, Bialystok, and Chelm), and for others, their correct Polish spellings. For all cities in general, their historical spelling is followed by the current spelling and country information in brackets. Where not noted, such pre-independence Ukrainian city names as Kiev and Odessa refer to present-day Kyiv and Odesa, respectively.

Many of the selections were written before the term "Holocaust" became widely used in English, so I have left the Yiddish term *khurbn* (destruction) untranslated, except in titles.

Throughout the translations, words in [brackets] are my editorial comments to the reader.

A Conversation with Series Editor Michael Berenbaum

Berenbaum: Can you tell us briefly, Mark, *af eyn fus*—while standing on one foot, as our tradition would say—what is the essential point of this book?

Smith: Above all, Michael, I've attempted to recreate or at least open the door to a world of Jewish thought that was once almost mainstream but which no longer exists, except in the minds of a few specialists. I came upon it by accident. Jewish history had been the subject of my "leisure reading" since childhood. My uncle, my mother's brother who had once been a Jewish educator, would bring me important books on Jewish history. Cecil Roth, for example, then Ben-Sasson and others, but all in English. Only later, when I began to read Jewish history in Yiddish, did I discover that, by contrast, the Yiddish works were not written *incidentally* in Yiddish but were part of a cultural system that existed *entirely* in Yiddish.

B: Isn't this to be expected, in any language or culture?

S: You might think so, but it collides with two preconceptions that are common among American Jews of Ashkenazi descent, even those who are students of Jewish history. The first preconception is that their own half-remembered or imagined view of Yiddish language and culture captures the whole of it, that surely they know what it is *not*. The second—perhaps because we live in an age when English is the lingua franca of Jewish scholarship—is that, since the content of Jewish historical writing in English is largely independent of language, the same should be true in other languages, including Yiddish. The combination is an unawareness of scholarly writing in Yiddish and the assumption that, if such writing exists, it would be as language-neutral as works in English, apart from some expected "homey" turns of phrase.

B: How has this affected your work?

S: When I coined the expression "Yiddish historians" to describe my group of scholars, the people who "got it" tended to be those closest to Yiddish intellectual life—and also those farthest removed. Among the latter, for example, my teacher Saul Friedländer (whose work is "limited" to French, Hebrew, German, and English), referred to me early on as "Mark Smith, who is working on the Yiddish historians." And, of course, my heart leaped at such validation. Yet from those in the middle ground, with an indistinct or partial Yiddish cultural inheritance, I have had such responses as, "But isn't your emphasis on Yiddish an unnecessary conceit; couldn't you just as well refer to these historians more generally as 'East European'?" (to which I might have replied: "Your themes are so universal, M. Proust, why do you need all that Frenchiness?"). Or, regarding the postwar period, "Surely you don't mean to suggest that Jewish nationalism continued to exist in Yiddish after the Holocaust?" These are blind spots that seem to arise among people with overly certain attitudes toward Yiddish.

B: But isn't this the very point of your work? That your group of historians undertook the task of giving historical consciousness to the Yiddish-oriented national movement that arose in Eastern Europe between the world wars—and which continued as long as Yiddish remained a spoken vernacular (outside of Hasidic Jewish communities)? Your argument is that these historians used Jewish sources of information wherever possible, often solicited from the Jewish public and, in turn, wrote about the history of Ashkenazi Jewry—for an educated lay audience of Yiddish speakers—in their own national language.

S: Precisely. The Yiddish national-cultural context is the main theme of this book and of my previous book on the Yiddish historians of the Holocaust. This combination is what has not been recognized. Historians who chose to work significantly in Yiddish created a distinct school of historical thought that is found in their Yiddish writings and was conducted through a worldwide conversation among themselves and their readers. Despite their many disagreements about politics and historical method, they shared a research agenda that focused on the "internal" aspects of Jewish life, including the economic, legal, literary, religious, and social organization of Jewish communities, with a largely a positive view of Jewish history—in contrast to prior and contemporaneous Jewish, and non-Jewish, historians who studied primarily Jewish oppression and suffering.

B: Isn't it unusual to anthologize the works of historians? Why is this necessary for the historians who worked in Yiddish in particular?

S: As far as I know, this book is unique. It would be hard to think of another language in which professional historians wrote the history of their own people and that *thereafter* fell into disuse among that very audience. Typically, the suppressed languages of literate colonized peoples, the Irish or Welsh for example, have become a vehicle for scholarly work during a stage of national revival, not at a stage followed by linguistic decline. As a result, Yiddish may well be unique in having a body of modern, professional scholarship that has become increasingly unreadable by its own populace and others. I have undertaken the mission of making these historians' Yiddish writings more widely known. I have often pointed out that, in the original 1971 edition of the *Encyclopaedia Judaica*, edited by Cecil Roth, the article on Jewish historiography devotes less than half a sentence to the historians who worked in Yiddish before World War II, and nothing at all to those who wrote in Yiddish after the Holocaust.

B: When I was managing editor of the second edition of the *Judaica* in the early 2000s, you agreed to write a few of the articles on our wanted list, and when you sent them to me, you asked if we could add an entry for historian Isaiah Trunk. You noted that, alone among his contemporaries, such as Ringelblum, Mahler, and Friedman, he had been omitted from the first edition.

S: And you were kind enough to have the courage of my convictions! I said it was impossible to do him justice in the usual five hundred words, and you agreed to provide the space needed. Consequently, his entry is the most complete for any of those I call "Yiddish historians." As an aside, I should say that I've been a lifelong "encyclopedia person." For my first birthday, my mother, who is responsible for both my love of Yiddishkayt and general learning, gave me a set of the *World Book Encyclopedia*—which she would show and read to me. When I graduated from high school, I used some prize money I had won to buy a set of the recently published first edition of the *Encyclopaedia Judaica*. And then, thanks to you, I had the honor of beginning my published output on the Yiddish historians with an entry in your second edition of the *Judaica*.

B: It was a most important addition, and, speaking of the term "Yiddish historians," please repeat briefly how you define the term. After all, it's less common to group historians by language than by nationality or school of thought.

S: Most Jewish historians of Eastern Europe began their work in other languages, such as Russian, Polish, or Hebrew, and turned deliberately to Yiddish for national and popular purposes. Most of them can also be included in more than one national or language community. Few wrote exclusively in Yiddish. I've used the term "Yiddish historian" for those who wrote to a significant degree for a Yiddish-speaking audience as part of a consciously national-Yiddish culture. I've also included scholars who were not specifically historians, recognizing that professional boundaries were less defined in the past than today.

B: What sacrifice did these historians make in terms of prominence, prestige, and reputation—fame—writing for their own people, when non-Jewish university-trained historians could not read their work?

S: The situations before and after World War II are mirror images. Before the Holocaust, Jewish historians in Eastern Europe struggled for inclusion in mainstream academia. Polish historical journals, for example, would publish reviews of Polish works by Jewish historians, often very critical of their statements on Polish-Jewish relations or the role of Jews in Polish economic history, but virtually never articles by Jewish historians themselves. Many Jewish historians were able to expand in positive directions by turning to Yiddish and writing for their own people. If prewar Eastern Europe had been like postwar America, there might have been no Yiddish national movement. But that is the very point of your question as we enter the postwar period. Such historians as Jacob Shatzky and Isaiah Trunk, respectively, would come to regret their choice or begin to publish in English. What had been liberating before the war became confining after the war. A major theme of my book on the Yiddish historians of the Holocaust is that their works would achieve great influence, especially on topics related to internal Jewish life under German occupation, but only a generation or two after the fact, with their eventual translation or a turn to publishing in English.

B: And why did they make this sacrifice? Who were their readers? And given what happened, especially in the post–World War II era, was their sacrifice in vain?

S: After the Holocaust, the surviving scholars who experienced the catastrophe at first hand felt a personal commitment to their fellow survivors, both to research every aspect of the Jewish experience of Nazi domination and, especially, to answer the ultimate Jewish question of the Holocaust—how could this have happened to us? The topic most widely studied among all Yiddish historians came to be that of resistance, particularly the unarmed resistance without which there would have been no survivors. They succeeded at times in expanding their readership, but they would never have abandoned their chief constituents. These included survivors as well as Jews who left Eastern Europe before the war but retained ties to family and community. I am certain they would have considered their commitment a holy task, not at all in vain. Yet it is the sense today that "all is vanity" in regard to Yiddish historical writing that impels me to attempt to rescue it from obscurity.

B: In your book on the Yiddish historians of the Holocaust you stressed what was their unique contribution to the historiography of the Holocaust. Could you also tell us, what has been their unique contribution to our understanding of Eastern European Jewish history?

S: Their unique contribution was a view of the Yiddish-speaking Jews of Eastern Europe as a national group defined, within the larger Jewish context, by a shared history and culture that transcended the boundaries of their home countries. In geopolitical terms, this takes account of a region in which Jewish settlement was at times more stable than the boundaries of the countries in which they found themselves. These historians fashioned a Jewish history of shared culture and internal relations that was more portable and independent of physical landmarks than earlier or parallel schools of Jewish history. Even the exception, of focusing on a specific location to establish the age and utility of a given Jewish community, was in the service of national self-defense.

B: The idea of surveying the entire historical output in a given language seems daunting. How did you know where to begin, or to continue looking, or most of all, when to stop?

S: I was fortunate to begin collecting Yiddish books in the early 1990s when they were still in used bookstores and, more often, in the libraries of older Yiddish readers then being disbursed. I collected and read widely, both in literature and nonfiction, but found that history remained my field—and that Yiddish had become my language. Blessed is the historian who is seized by his subject. With time, I collected articles written by historians in the dozens of well-known and obscure Yiddish journals and periodicals, as well as *yizkor* books, that I could find at my own university libraries—UCLA and American Jewish University—or while traveling, or by request, particularly from YIVO and HUC. Well before anything became available online, I had a file drawer with folders labeled for each historian, all later joined by digital files. These include not only the historians' original works, but their reviews of each other's works—a conversation that extended, over the decades, from St. Petersburg to Warsaw, Berlin, Paris, New York, Tel Aviv, Jerusalem, even Lincoln, Nebraska, and, on occasion, to Latin America and South Africa. Ultimately, I succeeded in collecting all of these historians' books, and, with regard to articles, eventually stopped coming upon pieces that were new to me.

B: So, in a sense, you recreated the process pioneered by Simon Dubnow and his followers, of first gathering an archive of materials on which to base your work—and collecting almost indiscriminately until you had done your best to exhaust the field.

S: That captures the process exactly. I called it "preventive research," not knowing what would become important, but attempting to collect everything I might need. As I gathered an increasing storehouse of materials, I tried to let them speak to me, to tell me what themes were broadly shared, which individuals had specialties or areas of divergence. Finally, I felt I had arrived at some understanding of how these historians conceived of the study of Jewish history. That is, of course subjective, and readers are free to come to their own assessments.

B: How does this book of translations relate to your previous book on the historians who wrote Holocaust history in Yiddish?

S: There are two direct connections. First, in writing the book on Holocaust historiography, I regretted that the earlier, formative, period of Yiddish historical work could be discussed there only as an introduction to the main subject. This book redresses that omission by covering the entire period of modern historical writing in Yiddish, from the early to late twentieth century. Second, it serves as a companion volume in offering at length the historians' own words that are quoted only briefly in the prior book. It allows them to breathe again, and it allows readers to evaluate for themselves the interpretations in my prior work.

B: It's uncommon for a historian to follow this organizational scheme, of preparing a book of translations to follow an original monograph. Was this always your intent, or how did it arise?

S: You're the first to ask this question. I had intended to write a comprehensive history of the Yiddish historians throughout their active period but, as a practical matter, came to focus on the Holocaust period. This translation project began in 2006, in speaking with my teacher David Myers, when I said it was a shame these historians weren't more accessible in English—and he gave me a telling look that we both knew portended a project in the making. Bringing it to completion has enabled me to fulfill the obligation I have felt toward these historians since I first began to read their works.

Foreword
Samuel H. Kassow

The last decades of the nineteenth century saw the beginnings of a cultural revolution that transformed East European Jewry. In addition to the rise of new political movements like Zionism and Bundism, this national awakening also saw the rise of a modern Yiddish literature, of a new Yiddish theater, of a daily Yiddish press with a circulation in the hundreds of thousands. North America and Latin America also became centers of Yiddish culture as millions of Yiddish-speaking Jews left Eastern Europe. A new "Yiddishland" emerged that spanned the globe. Long reviled and despised as a deformed jargon, the Yiddish language finally began to gain respect.

By the end of World War I, Yiddish was also becoming a language of scholarship. The founding of YIVO (Yiddish Scientific Institute) in Vilna in 1925 gave Yiddish scholars a home and a base. New centers of Yiddish research also appeared in Soviet Kiev (now Kyiv), Moscow, and Minsk. The year 1925 also saw the beginning of the Hebrew University in Jerusalem. The simultaneous rise of all these new scholarly institutions reflected a growing belief that the Jewish people needed their own universities and research centers to train not only physicians and scientists but also humanists and historians. And since many Jewish historians saw their task as a national mission, it was only natural that many would turn to Yiddish.

This wonderful anthology of historical writing in Yiddish, expertly compiled by Mark Smith, demonstrates the remarkable range of Yiddish-language historical scholarship, especially in the years between the two world wars. And even after the murder of millions of Yiddish speakers, even after the Nazi destruction of the Vilna YIVO and Stalin's assault on Soviet Yiddish culture, Yiddish scholarship continued for many decades after World War II and produced remarkable results, especially in the study of the Holocaust. The widely held view that serious Holocaust scholarship only began to emerge in the 1960s and 1970s was wrong. As soon as the war ended in 1945, scholars writing in Yiddish, including Isaiah Trunk, Philip Friedman, Artur Eisenbach, and others, began their groundbreaking studies of the Jews under Nazi occupation.

It is hardly coincidental that this anthology begins with an excerpt from Simon Dubnow's many writings on the role of autonomy in Jewish history. Although Dubnow (1860–1941) himself wrote most of his books and articles in Russian, he nonetheless helped set the agenda for the historians who followed in his footsteps. Indeed, while some of the historians featured in this first section—such as Raphael Mahler and Israel Sosis—were quite critical of Dubnow's largely positive evaluation of Jewish communal bodies during the Polish Commonwealth, they acknowledged that it was his work that laid the conceptual groundwork for their own study of East European Jewish history.

Dubnow belonged to a generation of Jewish intellectuals who came of age at a time of deepening antisemitism and growing doubts about European liberalism. Repelled by both religious orthodoxy and assimilation, barred from pursuing his education in a Russian university, the young Dubnow struggled to find a way forward. And then he had a eureka moment. The solution to his personal crisis of identity lay in the study of Jewish history. History could take the place of religion as the pillar of a new secular Jewishness:

> It was in the study of history that I found something that could serve as an antidote to both religious and philosophical dogmatism. I found myself thinking that I was both a religious and a philosophical agnostic, unable to accept the idea that either religion or philosophy held the key to understanding the puzzle of reality. Yet even so I could still find out how people in the past lived over the course of centuries and how they searched for truth and justice. I lost my own faith in personal immortality. But history taught me that there was a collective immortality.

That collective immortality was the history of the Jewish people. History, Dubnow believed, could harmonize universal culture and Jewishness, his sense of self and his belonging to the Jewish collective.

Dubnow changed the agenda of modern Jewish historiography by foregrounding the Yiddish-speaking centers of Eastern Europe, unlike the great Heinrich Graetz, who minimized their importance; by shifting emphasis from the history of the "Jewish Question," legislation governing the Jews, to the internal history of Jewish communities; by stressing the centrality of Jewish agency in Jewish history as a counterbalance to suffering and helplessness; and by underscoring that, however important the role of religious thinkers and philosophers, it was the Jewish people as a whole, its "will to live," that moved Jewish history forward. Remarkably, Dubnow argued, the Jews accomplished what few other nations could have done: they survived the loss of their homeland and political sovereignty, becoming a Diaspora nation whose vitality derived not from military power but from deeply ingrained spiritual resources that revealed themselves through the Jewish religion, through the ongoing development of Jewish self-government, and through a remarkable ability to adapt to changing circumstances. As one key Jewish center succumbed, another arose to take its place. From the Land of Israel to Babylonia, to Egypt to North Africa to Spain to the lands of medieval France and the Rhineland to the vast plains and forests of Eastern Europe, the history of the Jewish Diaspora was a history of shifting centers. And perhaps, Dubnow averred, as he watched harried Jews boarding a ship for America in the port of Libau (today Liepāja, Latvia), perhaps a new center was already beginning to take shape before his very eyes.

From the very beginning of his career as a historian, Dubnow realized that he was embarking not only on a personal scholarly quest but on a national enterprise of the highest importance. In 1891 he appealed to Russian Jewry to collect documents, community chronicles, and build archives. A people that didn't know its own history, or that didn't care about its own history, was a people that lacked the self-respect and the discipline to fight for its rights. Should the Jews leave the writing of their history to strangers and enemies? From the very beginning, therefore, the writing of Jewish history in Eastern Europe was part of a national endeavor. YIVO, for instance, depended on a large network of *zamlers* (collectors) who roamed far afield to collect materials to build new archives. Official state archives might suffice if one were writing a history of legislation affecting Jews. But to study the living Jewish people, the language, folklore, social psychology, and history of the millions of Jews in Eastern Europe, one needed to build archives from the ground up. And only a mass movement of *zamlers* could do this.

In large part because of Dubnow, St. Petersburg became the key center of East European Jewish historiography until the Bolshevik Revolution of 1917. Needless to say the main language of this historical scholarship was

Russian, not Yiddish. At the same time, Meir Balaban and Isaac Schiper, based in Habsburg Galicia and writing mostly in Polish, began to publish research that, like Dubnow's, regarded the Jews as a people, not as a mere religious grouping or as future "Poles of the Mosaic persuasion." On the eve of World War I, the first important contacts developed between St. Petersburg and these Galician historians, but they were cut short by the war.

The dislocations and turmoil of World War I, the rise of an independent Poland, the hopes and expectations sparked by the Balfour Declaration, and the Bolshevik Revolution all encouraged a new interest in Jewish history. Dubnow's leitmotif of Jewish autonomy in the Diaspora gained new relevance after the Allies forced the new nation-states in Eastern Europe, including Poland, to accept the Minorities Treaties. With millions of Jews once again under Polish sovereignty, Polish Jewish history also assumed new importance. Polish nationalist historians portrayed Jews as alien parasites who exploited the Polish peasantry, crippled the growth of a Polish middle class, and hastened the demise of the Commonwealth. In turn, Jewish historians in interwar Poland used history as a weapon to defend Jewish honor and to underscore that far from being alien interlopers, Jews had been in Poland for centuries and worked hard to build and defend the country. Trunk's history of the Jews of Płock is but one example of this genre, as is Emanuel Ringelblum's study of Jewish economic occupations in the eighteenth century and Friedman's work on Jewish regionalism. Close links developed between YIVO and the new Jewish Landkentnish (geographic) Society, organized in 1926 to encourage Jewish tourism in Poland. The goal was not just recreational skiing, hiking, and sailing but also to encourage the study of local history, the photographing and cataloguing of old synagogues and ritual objects, and the collecting of folklore. Implicit in this activity was the conviction that the Jews were deeply rooted in the Polish lands. As part of its mission the Landkentnish Society stressed the importance of Yiddish, and its bilingual journal carried Yiddish articles by leading Jewish historians as well as by architectural historians like Szymon Zajczyk.

Jewish historians including Balaban, Schiper, Ringelblum, Friedman, and Mahler wrote historical articles for the Jewish press in Yiddish and Polish. Polish Jews eagerly read historical novels like Sholem Asch's *Kidush hashem* (*Sanctification of the Name*, 1919) and Joseph Opatoshu's *In poylishe velder* (*In Polish Woods*, 1938). Historians became involved in the ideological and cultural battles that roiled Polish Jews. Controversies over religion vs. secularism, Yiddish vs. Hebrew, and Zionism vs. Diaspora Nationalism sparked intense and endless debate. Arguments about whether the old Jewish communal councils in the Commonwealth were guardians of national unity or organs of class exploitation, far from being mere scholarly disputes, had real political relevance. And what explained the remarkable survival of the Jewish people over the centuries? Was it religion? Persecution? Or, as Ringelblum and Mahler argued, did one have to look to economic factors? Was Yiddish culture a recent by-product of political radicalism, or was it, as Schiper maintained, rooted in a centuries-old popular culture? In addition to these issues, the traumatic pogroms that claimed up to one hundred thousand Jewish lives between 1918 and 1921 led Jewish historians like Eliyahu Tcherikower to collect documents, organize a pogrom archive, and prepare the publication, in Yiddish, of an extensive record of the massacres. Tcherikower's work played a key role in the Paris trial of Sholom Shwartzbart, who was acquitted of the murder of Ukrainian leader Semyon Petlyura. This investigation of the pogroms was the forerunner of the *khurbn-forshung* (destruction research) that would be conducted by historians like Friedman, Trunk, and Mark Dworzecki after the Holocaust. It served as a potent reminder that writing history was an important weapon of Jewish self-defense.

A younger generation of historians emerged in interwar Poland who, unlike Tcherikover and Dubnow, had received university doctorates. Mahler and Ringelblum, two of the leading historians of this cohort, were also devoted adherents of the Left Labor Zionists (Linke Poyle Tsien), a radical Marxist-Zionist political party that prioritized the development of Yiddish culture. They were also influenced by Balaban and especially by Schiper whose emphasis on Jewish economic history dovetailed with their own research priorities. In 1923, two years before the founding of YIVO, Ringelblum and Mahler organized the Young Historians Circle, which later joined the historical section of YIVO. and published two important journals of historical scholarship in Yiddish. As we see from Mahler's article in this anthology, this circle included many students enrolled in Meir Balaban's seminar on Jewish history at the University of Warsaw. Prominent up-and-coming younger members of the circle included Trunk, Eisenbach, and Bela Mandelsberg. While Mandelsberg perished in the Holocaust, Trunk and Eisenbach would play prominent roles as postwar Jewish historians.

Although the Berlin- and, later, Paris-based Tcherikower nominally headed YIVO's historical section and edited the three volumes of *Historishe shriftn* (Historical writings, 1929–38), the largest ever journal devoted to the publication of historical scholarship in Yiddish, the real base of YIVO's historical activity was in Warsaw, where Schiper, Balaban, Ringelblum, Mahler, and others enjoyed good working relations with key Polish historians at the University of Warsaw.

YIVO historians were not a homogenous group. Alongside Marxists like Mahler and Ringelblum, there were non-Marxists like Friedman, or Jacob Shatzky, who served as a key link between YIVO and the growing American Jewish community. But they all supported scholarship in Yiddish, as well as Dubnow's conviction that history had a national mission. This commitment found its highest expression in the underground archive (Oyneg Shabes) that Ringelblum organized in 1940 in the Warsaw ghetto.

After the war, Shatzky (along with Friedman, Trunk, Max Weinreich, and Lucjan Dobroszycki) revived YIVO's scholarly tradition in the United States. Between 1947 and 1956, Shatzky published his greatest work of scholarship, the three-volume *Di geshikhte fun yidn in varshe* (History of the Jews of Warsaw), one of the works excerpted here in translation. His death in 1956 prevented him from completing the project.

Mark Smith deserves our deepest appreciation for making the many contributions of these scholars available to the English-reading public and for reminding us of these wonderful historians who loved and served their people with such devotion.

Introduction to the Yiddish Historians and Their Work

Mark L. Smith

1. The Yiddish Historians

When I began to read Jewish history in Yiddish, I found that I had entered a world that was *eygnartik*—to use a Yiddish word that means, in this case, unique in itself. I discovered a community of scholars with shared goals and common interests, who carried on a lively conversation across the continents, and an equally lively critique of each other's works. At that time—around the year 2000—this community was almost within reach; most of these historians were still within the living memory of their students and other active scholars. That is, alas, no longer true.

With the eventual decline of secular Yiddish-language scholarship and its audience, little memory of the thousands of historical works written in Yiddish remains to be transmitted outside that cultural world. Most of their works are still untranslated and known only to specialists.

Yet, we might ask, why read Jewish history in Yiddish? Or, more to the point, why, in the early twentieth century, did certain Jewish scholars in Eastern Europe turn to writing in a language that was barely respectable—for journals so newly established they had no scholarly reputation, to advance an enterprise that could offer no professional advancement?

The answer lay in the excitement of a new venture, close to the heart. Never before in Jewish history had professional Jewish historians turned to writing the history of their own people—in their own daily *Jewish* language—for a readership consisting of the people themselves. Their goal was to construct the creation narrative for a borderless, Yiddish-speaking Jewish nation in Eastern Europe and its worldwide dispersion.

My own purpose is to make Yiddish historical scholarship accessible to the nonspecialist. My previous book, *The Yiddish Historians and the Struggle for a Jewish History of the Holocaust*,[1] attempts to recreate the world of those survivors who wrote Holocaust history in Yiddish as professional historians. In a sense, it was a sequel to a book not yet written, namely, the story of Yiddish historical writing *before* the Holocaust. It briefly traced the rise of historical writing in Yiddish before the Holocaust and then discussed the Yiddish historiography of the Holocaust as a continuation of that tradition. The present volume covers the entire period of modern historical writing in Yiddish, spanning most of the twentieth century. It is an anthology of forty-nine works, translated into English for the first time, each preceded by an introduction intended to provide historical context. The following is a brief overview.

★ ★ ★

Today, in the twenty-first century, when the spirit of the times demands that the Ashkenazi narrative of Jewish history be given less emphasis in favor of neglected parallel histories, the Yiddish historians should be introduced as revolutionaries in their own context. The rise of every historiographical movement is a reaction against the prevailing historiography, and theirs was the protest movement of its time on behalf of the Yiddish-speaking Jews of Eastern Europe whose culture and language had been neglected or disparaged in nineteenth-century Germany by the historians of the *Wissenschaft des Judentums* tradition, in particular Heinrich Graetz.

The Yiddish historians' goal was to write the history of a living people, and they addressed themselves to their readers in their own language. Their style is professional but not impersonal. They join their readers in the collective narrative, using such expressions as: "When one speaks among us Jews," "the dim caverns of our past," "a radical turning point in our 2,000-year history," "the mental and spiritual life of our folk masses," and, as Meir Balaban promised, "I will draw the Yiddish reader into the circle of our past in Poland."[2]

Like the historians of many subjugated groups, Jewish historians who found their calling in writing about the Jews of Eastern Europe did so not only to reach their chosen audience but to place themselves and their readers at the center of their own history. Jewish historical writing in Eastern Europe followed the pattern typical of such groups, with works written first by outsiders in foreign high-culture languages (chiefly Russian and Polish), then by insiders writing in those same languages as a mark of cultural emulation, and finally, by insiders demanding the use of their own national language. In Poland, however, this last stage gave rise to traditions in two languages, Polish and Yiddish.

A Polish Jewish tradition of historical scholarship flourished before the Holocaust among historians who promoted a Polish Jewish national consciousness.[3] Within the Ashkenazi frame of reference, it was a *particular* view of Jewish history in contrast to the *universal* view of the Yiddish historians. The *particular* view has become better known, but it was the minority position in its time.[4] The majority of historians who wrote Ashkenazi Jewish history during the interwar period were partisans for a *universal* Ashkenazi diaspora nationalism, as expressed through Yiddish language and culture. A few historians participated to some degree in both efforts. And yet, no matter how earnestly the Polish Jewish view may have been held by certain Jewish historians, for those who left Poland—whether before or after the Holocaust—it evaporated upon their departure, and they turned to writing almost exclusively in Yiddish and the languages of their new countries.

A third competing vision for the Jewish future was promoted by Zionism, with its Hebrew orientation. In addition to their support for Diaspora nationalism, most historians who wrote in Yiddish in the early twentieth century were also Zionists and were capable in Hebrew. Prior to the Holocaust and the creation of the State of Israel, however, they considered the possibility of a revived Hebrew-speaking nation remote, and they presumed that most Jews would remain in the Diaspora with Yiddish as their common language.

Modern historical writing in Yiddish can be dated from an article published in 1903 by Saul Ginsburg, one of the founders and editors of *Der fraynd* (The Friend), the first daily Yiddish newspaper in Russia. It is the earliest Yiddish historical work I have found that is written, albeit somewhat quaintly, with the voice and craft of the modern historian: "In a few days, it will be two hundred years since St. Petersburg was founded, and we consider it not unwarranted to acquaint our readers with a few facts about the history of Jews in the Russian capital city."[5] Ginsburg assembles his materials, uses them to recount a few key episodes, and footnotes them to their sources. Gone are the pathos and legendary incidents employed by premodern Hebrew-Yiddish historians like his contemporary Ezriel Nathan Frenk in Poland. Absent are the drama, predestination, and hand of the Almighty to be found in works by Graetz—but present is the living Jewish history of Eastern Europe. His obvious purpose is to demonstrate the contributions of Jews to early St. Petersburg (or more precisely, Jewish converts who found high positions with Peter the Great) when, in his own time, the city was still legally closed to nearly all Jews.

Before Ginsburg and other historians could offer more than occasional works in Yiddish, they required readers accustomed to historical writing in Yiddish, beyond the journalism and literature that had become widespread in the last third of the nineteenth century. Such an audience for historical writing arose through ancillary genres: works by journalists and other non-historians on natural history,[6] non-Jewish history,[7] and also Jewish history,[8] all based on secondary sources rather than original research, as well as Yiddish translations of works by historians such as Simon Dubnow and Graetz. Dubnow, widely recognized as the father of Jewish historical scholarship in Eastern Europe, opened his first translated volume, published in 1909 in Vilna, with the statement: "It has already long been my fervent wish to convert my *General Jewish History*, written in Russian, and give it to the Jewish people in their own living language" (using the term *mgayer zayn* for "conversion to Judaism").[9] By 1926, Ignacy Schiper, one of the founding figures of Jewish historical writing in Poland, introduced his own first book in Yiddish more confidently: "The strong interest that the Jewish reading public evinced in recent years regarding serious scholarly works in Yiddish made clear to the author that the time for which he had waited so long had become ripe" (see Selection 4 in this volume).[10]

The timeline of Yiddish historical writing begins with a few important works in the years immediately before World War I, finds its greatest accomplishments between the world wars, and sees a resurgence in productivity for more than twenty years after the Holocaust from within the survivor community. Geographically, Yiddish historical works were written before World War I primarily in St. Petersburg; between the world wars largely in Poland, the Soviet Union, and the United States; and after the Holocaust chiefly in Poland, Israel, the United States, and (for local history) Argentina.

Institutionally, the principal center of Yiddish historical writing was the Yiddish Scientific Institute (YIVO), founded in 1925 in Berlin but located in Vilna (then in Poland; today Vilnius, Lithuania), with a major branch in New York (also founded in 1925) and smaller branches in Paris (1927) and Buenos Aires (1928).[11] YIVO served as a shadow university for scholarship in Yiddish, assembling a library and archives, holding academic conferences, offering a graduate student program, and, most widely known, publishing journals and books in Yiddish. In 1940, the New York branch was transformed into the YIVO headquarters, which it remains. It is worth noting that, of the nine founding members of YIVO, their places of origin were Ukraine (three), Lithuania (three), Latvia (two), and Poland (one).[12] Many of the selections in this volume are by scholars associated to some degree with YIVO. One of them, Warsaw-born historian Jacob Shatzky, a co-founder of the New York branch, affirmed YIVO's transnational mission in 1932: "YIVO is not Vilna, and not even Poland. YIVO is a matter for all Jews in the entire world."[13]

Other important centers of Yiddish scholarship also operated in Eastern Europe, two before the Holocaust in Soviet Minsk and Kiev (at the official Belorussian and Ukrainian academies, founded in 1921 and 1926, respectively), and another in postwar Poland at the Central Jewish Historical Commission (founded in 1944 in Lublin and reorganized in 1947 as the Jewish Historical Institute in Warsaw). They all enjoyed relative freedom of academic inquiry until the imposition of Stalinist dictatorship in the Soviet Union in 1929 and in Poland in 1949. In each, the change was marked by denunciations of suspected Jewish nationalists and attacks on former colleagues in the West.[14] In prewar Minsk and Kiev, even scholars who had attempted a materialist and class-conscious approach to their work were ultimately denounced, purged, and exiled or executed in the 1930s. In postwar Warsaw, scholars learned the art of falsifying scholarship to satisfy imposed masters and safely continue their work. Much valuable historical research was produced in each of these locations under extreme conditions, but it belongs to a different tradition of writing (and reading). As a result, selections for this volume are limited to those centers' early periods.

The term "Yiddish historians" refers to writers of Jewish history who chose to work to a significant degree in Yiddish. None wrote exclusively in Yiddish, and all functioned in multilingual settings. For Jewish historians to work in languages other than Yiddish was not remarkable; it was the choice of Yiddish that carried both meaning and hardship. Approximately three dozen scholars chose, to a notable degree, to participate in the Yiddish national project by writing Jewish history. Most were educated as historians, but, in an era when professional boundaries were less formal than today, some had been trained in fields as diverse as law, chemistry, and medicine, while others came from related disciplines (such as literature or art) and wrote on the historical aspects of those fields. All the figures who appear in this volume were connected to one or more of the others as a teacher, student, colleague, critic, or participant in common institutions, research projects, or publishing venues. Through their writings, they conducted a worldwide conversation with each other and their readers in a network of scholarly and lay Yiddish journals published in Europe and America.

The cradle of Yiddish historical writing in prewar Poland was the *Yungerhistoriker krayz* (Young Historians Circle) founded by Mahler and Ringelblum in 1923 in Warsaw, which published four volumes of historical research, all in Yiddish, before World War II. Mahler later composed a memorial essay about the group that was published in Israel in both Hebrew and Yiddish. It now appears here in English as a further introduction to these historians and the emergence of historical writing in Yiddish (see Selection 11).

Yet it should also be noted that only one of these historians, Balaban, was able to obtain a university position in Jewish studies before the Holocaust. Most of the others worked as teachers in Jewish secondary schools. In prerevolutionary St. Petersburg, Zinberg was a chemical engineer at a manufacturing plant, and Ginsburg was the secretary of the Society for Promotion of Enlightenment Among the Jews. After the Holocaust, Isaiah Trunk and Joseph Kermish were chief archivists at YIVO and Yad Vashem, respectively, and Philip Friedman served as director of the Jewish Teachers Seminary and People's University in New York (the only institution in America that granted doctorates for dissertations written in Yiddish and Hebrew). Mark Dworzecki was a medical doctor in the Israeli health service, who ultimately succeeded in creating and then holding the world's first chair in Holocaust history, at Bar-Ilan University in 1959 (see Selection 42).

In their methods, they were positivist historians who believed that sufficient spade work would reveal the past. Their ideal research paper was one "based on archival sources" that would add another "tsigl tsu dem binyen" (brick for the edifice) of historical knowledge. For them, such bricks resembled the missing pieces of a puzzle rather than building blocks to be arranged in novel interpretations. None attempted a grand history (in the manner of Graetz or Dubnow); all were committed to smaller studies that would facilitate an eventual synthesis. Perhaps because they were studying a past so closely related to their present, they had no doubt that truth could be objectively ascertained, and they would likely have been puzzled by the postmodernists' allegations of subjectivity and ineffability. Yet they were not primitives, as Elias Tcherikower once labeled the medieval Yiddish and Hebrew chroniclers. They were historians of their own day. Some like Raphael Mahler and Emanuel Ringelblum were committed to Marxist economic materialism; others like Friedman and Balaban were decidedly not. Ginsburg quoted Herder; Trunk and Nachman Blumental cited Ranke. Several wrote important works on Jewish historiography (as noted below). Most held a doctorate or master's degree in history and were among the Yiddish intellectual elite before and after the Holocaust. They were frequently invited to write for leading nonacademic journals and to speak on the radio and at significant public events. The Hebrew translation of Dworzecki's history of the Vilna ghetto received the first Israel Prize in social science in 1952. The English version of Trunk's study of the Jewish Councils received the National Book Award for history in 1973.

Before the Holocaust, the chief characteristics of the Yiddish historical tradition were that it was a modern secular enterprise of historical scholarship, focused largely on the positive internal aspects of Jewish history (rather than on antisemitism or Jewish legal rights and disabilities), dedicated to strengthening Jewish peoplehood, and drawing in part on popular sources of historical information—with a reciprocal obligation to serve an educated lay readership. Their writings were often directed at a general audience, in popular as well as scholarly publications, and their academic journals were supported largely by lay readers around the world. For example, in 1935, when there existed only a few hundred Yiddish-oriented scholars in history and other disciplines combined, the principal YIVO journal, *YIVO bleter* (Pages), published in Vilna, had 1,231 subscribers, nearly two-thirds of whom lived in the United States, followed by Poland, Argentina, South Africa, Lithuania, and Australia.[15]

The Yiddish historians' positive approach to Jewish history predated the well-known appeal by Salo Baron in 1928 to "break with the lachrymose theory" of Jewish history.[16] For example, the imperative for such an approach was recognized by Jacob Shatzky in a 1925 Yiddish essay on Jewish memoir-writing. He notes that only extraordinary events such as wars, pogroms, or expulsions inspired people to write memoirs, and he asks, "To whom would it have occurred to write a memoir about an age of quiet, peaceful, secure Jewish collective life? Have we then not had such times? Certainly, we have, in nearly every country." And turning to his most familiar locale, he concludes: "Such a form of golden age existed among the Jews in Poland, with their own parliament, with a disciplined organization that had a broad, deep, rich scope in every aspect of life—where is that picture immortalized in memoirs by a Polish Jew of the time?"[17] A deliberately anti-lachrymose approach was announced by Elias Tcherikower, the founding head of YIVO's Historical Section, in his 1929 preface to the first volume of YIVO's *Historishe shriftn*

(Historical writings), in which he declares that its articles "resound not with persecutions and evil decrees—without which it is altogether impossible to imagine Jewish history—but principally with the rise of the major Jewish communities and their representative bodies, with internal life and the social conditions among Jews in various countries."[18]

Writing Jewish history also had urgent practical purposes. As Ringelblum wrote in his introduction to Trunk's 1939 history of the Jews of Płock, "This book appears at a time when the rights of the Jewish population in Poland are being disputed. . . . From the pages of Trunk's book we learn the importance of Jewish participation in the economic development of the city."[19] Such instrumental use of Jewish history made the historian, in Shatzky's words, "the ammunition supplier" in the fight for Jewish rights in interwar Poland, providing facts and arguments to prove the antiquity and value of the Jews' presence in Poland (see Selection 46 and the Introduction to Selection 24).

A subtler purpose is found in the study of Old Yiddish texts: they provide the literary pedigree for a modern Yiddish-speaking nation. Works such as the *Brantshpigl*, *Mayse-bukh* and *Tsene-rene* from the turn of the seventeenth century (see Selections 22–24) are lifted from their former status as incidentally Yiddish writings—in a sea of multilingual Jewish creativity—to serve as links in a historical chain of specifically Yiddish national expression.

That so few of the authors represented in this volume are women reflects four phenomena: The older generations of Yiddish historians born between 1860 and 1900 included no women. In the younger generation active before the Holocaust, women typically published (or were published) less often than men. In the same group, a greater proportion of women died at the hands of the Germans (among the Young Historians Circle in Warsaw, for example, twelve of the twenty-four men survived but only two of the eleven women).[20] And, in the postwar period, women who might have had independent careers subsumed them to those of their husbands (for example, Ada June Friedman, wife of Philip Friedman and herself the holder of a doctorate in history, completed his final book under the name Mrs. Philip Friedman). Included here are works by two of the more accomplished women of the prewar period, Bela Mandelsberg and Dina Jaffe (Selections 16 and 37), both of whom were killed by the Germans, and by three women who continued their careers in the postwar period, Rachel Wischnitzer, Rachel Auerbach, and Esther Goldhar-Mark (Selections 13, 14, and 40).

The absence of works from the Orthodox sector is explained by the traditional Jewish reluctance, still prevalent in the early twentieth century, to engage in historical writing—as either a waste of time or an imitation of non-Jewish values. Although most of the Yiddish historians had varying degrees of traditional religious education, all embraced the writing of Jewish history as a modernizing, secular project. The outstanding exception was Rabbi Shimon Huberband, a close colleague of Emanuel Ringelblum in the Warsaw ghetto, whose complete writings (in Yiddish) were preserved and have previously been published in both Hebrew and English translations.[21]

Before World War II, there were only two significant exceptions to the Yiddish historians' positive approach to Jewish history: a series of articles by Ginsburg on the cantonists, the Jewish boys forced to serve in the Russian army during the mid-nineteenth century; and works by Tcherikower on the pogroms in Ukraine after World War I (see Selections 19 and 20, respectively). In a well-known address to YIVO in 1941, Tcherikower discussed the difficulty of applying modern historical methods to recurring catastrophe, but without proposing concrete solutions. It happens that both historians found a safe refuge in the United States, but died before the advent of Holocaust historiography, Ginsburg in 1940 and Tcherikower in 1943.[22]

During the Holocaust, Yiddish historians met varying fates. Zinberg had already died in Soviet captivity during the Stalinist purges. The best-known victims of the Germans were Dubnow, who was killed in the Riga Ghetto, and Ringelblum, conductor of the secret Oyneg Shabes project in the Warsaw ghetto. Schiper was killed at Majdanek, and Balaban died a so-called natural death in the Warsaw ghetto. Among Ringelblum's associates, Rachel Auerbach was one of the few survivors. Several historians, including Mark and Rachel Wischnitzer, escaped from Europe to America. Regarding the survivors who became Holocaust historians: Friedman and Kermish each survived underground during the German occupation with the help of Christian friends; Trunk and Blumental fled east to the Soviet Union; Dworzecki survived the Vilna ghetto and several concentration camps. Dworzecki would later say of the survivors that non-Jews returned to their *families*, but Jews "returned only to their people."[23]

After the Holocaust, the survivors and intellectual heirs of the prewar Yiddish historical tradition continued to study the internal aspects of Jewish history, but with a new subject: the German occupation. Transformed into *khurbn-forshung* (catastrophe research), as Friedman called it, the prewar tradition reemerged as an imperative to write about everyday life in the ghettos and camps.

Most defiantly, their topic was Jewish life and the struggle to sustain it, rather than Jewish death and its perpetrators. The "question of questions" for which they felt the public demanded answers was: "How could this have happened to us?" In one of their most lasting contributions to Holocaust historiography, they fashioned a vigorous defense, in studying the many impediments to Jewish resistance (see Trunk, Selection 21), and also a daring offense, in redefining resistance to expand its scope from the limited instances of armed revolt to the widespread efforts of the unarmed Jewish masses to remain alive under Nazi occupation (see Dworzecki, Selection 12). Regarding the accusation that Jews "went as sheep to the slaughter," Blumental responded: "Are sheep not a symbol of purity and innocence!? And when slaughterers lead the sheep into the slaughterhouse, are the slaughterers or the sheep guilty!?"[24]

For these historians, the Holocaust became a new period of Jewish history—admittedly more frightful and painful—but one to be investigated with the same methods and research agenda as prior periods. Choosing to write in Yiddish about the Holocaust served the vital purpose of retaining a close connection both with the murdered subjects of their research and with the survivor audience who considered them uniquely capable of answering the urgent questions of their shared experience.

★★★

Returning to the original question—Why read Jewish history in Yiddish?—it is in Yiddish that these historians reveal their priorities for using the past to support the existence of a Yiddish-speaking Jewish nation in the present. Not surprisingly, the priorities of Jewish historians differed by language.

The telling comparisons are between works in Polish and Yiddish, whether before or after the Holocaust. Works in both languages emphasize Jewish autonomy and Jewish-Christian relations, and both use history to argue for Jewish rights on the basis of the age of Jewish settlement and Jewish contributions to the economy, but Polish writing more often leans toward political and economic history, while Yiddish writing focuses more on cultural and social history. Especially notable is that studies of fixed artifacts such as buildings, monuments, cemeteries, and the physical aspects of Jewish quarters are found chiefly in Polish (consistent with a Poland-centered approach to Jewish history), while portable cultural expressions such as literature, theater, and communications are more common in Yiddish (consistent with a pan-Ashkenazi approach to Jewish history).[25]

In the early postwar period, Holocaust research in Polish focused more on German crimes, while works in Yiddish concentrated almost exclusively on Jewish life and resistance.[26] These distinctions hold true between historians as well as within a given historian's own works in Polish and Yiddish.

There are also topics that appear first, and perhaps only, in Yiddish. Pre-Holocaust examples include Ginsburg's discussion of the Jewish postal service in tsarist Russia during the Napoleonic wars that ran more quickly and reliably than the government postal service (Selection 30); and Mahler's revelation that the supposedly beneficent Council of Four Lands devoted only an infinitesimal portion of its budget to social welfare (Selection 3). Post-Holocaust examples include the pioneering plea by Dworzecki, noted above, for recognition of unarmed forms of Jewish resistance (Selection 12); and Friedman's detailed overview of the educational programs for survivors in the Displaced Persons camps of postwar Germany (Selection 41).

Historians who wrote in Yiddish could be assured of addressing an exclusively Jewish audience with a special attachment to Jewish history and Yiddish culture, expressed (at times subtly, at times overtly, in the works in this volume) by a sense of shared history and destiny. Most of these nuances translate adequately into English, so that one may indeed "read Jewish history in Yiddish"—*in English*—which is the principal purpose of this volume.

Yet there is also the problem of the untranslatable. In writings on the Holocaust, for example, one finds the expression "Hitlers treyfen'm moyl." Simply translated, it is "Hitler's un-kosher mouth," which conveys almost nothing of the meaning. For Yiddish-speaking survivors, the very presence of Hitler's name in a postwar Yiddish work is a triumph of survival that would go unnoticed in English translation. The meaning of *moyl* is aptly conveyed by "mouth," but the problem lies in *treyfen'm* (from the everyday word *treyf*, meaning unclean, forbidden, not kosher). In English, the phrase "Hitler's un-kosher mouth" is at best a trivial curse. In Yiddish, *treyf* conveys scorn, revulsion, bitterness—and, of course, powerlessness to alter the course of evil—yet, remarkably, by means of this homey and familiar word, *evil is domesticated*. And that is what cannot be translated. Unlike many translation projects, this volume is not intended to supplant the original writings but to open the door to a less-explored cultural world. Perhaps it will find readers who are moved to encounter Yiddish historical writing in its original language.

2. About This Volume

The anthologies of Yiddish literature that have appeared continuously since the early twentieth century—both in Yiddish and in English translation—could form the core collection of an ample library of Yiddish works ranging from prose and poetry to plays, essays, folklore, and memoirs, but the shelf reserved for historical scholarship would hold only expectation. Fulfilling that expectation is, at least in part, my hope for this volume. Such an anthology of Yiddish historical writing has no precedent, whether in Yiddish or in English.[27] It may well have no precedent in the history of any people or language. Yiddish presents a unique confluence of circumstances that both demands and enables such a retrospective—a populace widely literate in its ancestral language, a nascent nationalist movement, and a recently professionalized cadre of historians motivated to produce secular scholarship in the popular vernacular, followed by the relatively rapid decline of each of those circumstances.

In less than a century, Yiddish historical scholarship produced dozens of books and thousands of articles that might today be called a closed canon yet to be canonized. There is no list of Yiddish historical works widely recognized as "essential" texts. I have attempted to select as many pieces as possible that I believe should be considered uniquely significant—and which, for the purpose of this volume, convey a concise point or story in a manner likely to be accessible to the non-specialist. More than merely a sampler that displays disparate pieces, the intended result is a mosaic that attempts to present an image, however rough, of the field of Yiddish historical work as it was envisioned by its creators.[28] The six topic areas of this volume are the categories into which the majority of the Yiddish historians' writings seem naturally to fall. I call them: Jewish Autonomy; On the Jewish Street; In the Non-Jewish World; Yiddish Literature; Press, Post, and Communications; and, lastly, Education. Nevertheless, I am aware that the resulting image is inevitably an invitation to see the field as I have come to understand it.

Yiddish historical work ultimately embraced two moods—hope and loss, building and then consoling a nation. Both moods are incorporated into this volume, without interruption, which is the manner adopted by the Yiddish historians of the Holocaust. Their writings stress continuity, both of their own lives and of the community. Friedman's bibliography of his own works, for example, merely skips a few blank years between his studies of prewar Jewish history and his writings on the Holocaust. These historians' studies of life in the Jewish ghettos trace the ongoing political, economic, social, cultural, and religious trends that prevailed before the German invasion. Accordingly, each of the topic areas in this volume begins with earlier centuries and concludes with writings on the Holocaust.

To avoid the usual dilemma of choosing between depth and breadth, I have aimed for depth *within* breadth by adopting a specific geographic boundary: in the interest of thematic unity, coverage is limited to the Yiddish-speaking heartland of Eastern Europe; to do justice to other locations, entire volumes could be devoted to the Yiddish historians' studies of new immigrant communities in Western Europe, the United States, Latin America and elsewhere in the Yiddish-speaking diaspora.[29]

The only respect in which the selections in this volume are unrepresentative is that the Yiddish historians seldom wrote short works suitable for an anthology. Many of the selections come from longer articles or books. To permit a broader selection of pieces, most of the works on pre-Holocaust topics have been abridged, while greater length has been allotted to Holocaust works, as they are more likely to remain uniquely valuable in their content and expression. Because many of these works were not intended to stand on their own, the titles of some have been revised to provide adequate context, but the original titles appear in the notes. Within each selection, citations have been expanded, corrected, and modernized to the extent possible, all without comment.

As a basic principle, selections are limited to Yiddish works not previously published in English, which has influenced the choices for only three historians, Philip Friedman,[30] Joseph Kermish,[31] and Isaiah Trunk.[32] I have also avoided the various town histories commissioned from Yiddish historians for *yizkor* books, in part because most are too general for an anthology of scholarly writing and also because English translations of many *yizkor* books have already appeared (and continue to appear) online.[33]

A topic area of a different character—perhaps of greater interest to specialists—could have been added for the Yiddish historians' writings on Jewish historiography (or as Friedman termed it, "historiosophy"), covering issues in Jewish history-writing. All such works appeared after the Holocaust, although not all pertain to the Holocaust. For the interested specialist (conversant in Yiddish), a few works are listed here by the chief authors: Friedman,[34] Mahler,[35] Shatzky,[36] Tcherikower,[37] and Trunk.[38]

Selecting the works for this volume required two layers of review, both because the Yiddish historians did not live in the age of peer review and because much new research has since appeared. Their principal forum for comment arose only after a work had been published—in the lively, and often critical, literature of published reviews. Commenced as correctives, such reviews often became original scholarly works of their own. An example in this volume is the review essay by Israel Zinberg (Selection 23).

The first layer of review has therefore been to avoid works whose fundamental conclusions would have been rejected by peer reviewers in their own time. An example is the chapter on Jewish antiquities in Ignacy Schiper's *Cultural History of Jews in Poland during the Middle Ages* (1926) in which he claims that the old synagogues of Kraków and Sandomierz demonstrate that "among Jews, there was no lack of accomplished architects who realized their ideas in the form of monumental, gothic buildings" (a problem of both logic and fact, as it was well known that urban Polish synagogues, like many Polish churches, were often designed by Italian Christian architects).[39] Aware that Schiper has been praised and also criticized for his deductive leaps, I chose selections from his works that were either closely sourced (as in Selection 4) or reviewed approvingly by his contemporaries (as in Selection 8).

The second layer of review has been to avoid works in which a basic assumption has been refuted by more recent scholarship. Although mindful that any work may become dated a century later, I have tried to avoid works that would now be considered unreliable or obsolete. An example is the long history of writings that assume the existence of a Jewish *shpilman*, a wandering bard presumed to have performed medieval and early modern Yiddish epic works, analogous to the German Christian *Spielmann*. This error, apparently originating in an assumption by the lesser-known Leo Landau in 1912, received approval from a chain of eminent "peer reviewers" (including Schiper, Maks Erik, and Max Weinreich) who expanded it in their own works, until the theory was ultimately disproved by Chone Shmeruk in 1979 (as discussed by Zehavit Stern in 2019).[40] Therefore, among the articles on Old Yiddish literature selected for this volume, there are none that reflect the *shpilman* theory. On the contrary, Zinberg (in Selection 23) indicates his skepticism about the theory as he emphasizes instead the Jewish origins of Old Yiddish texts.

On the following pages, each of the selections is preceded by a short introduction that touches briefly on the author's biography and connections to Yiddish scholarship.[41] The order of the selections within each topic area follows the chronology of historical events. It may surprise the reader to find prewar and Holocaust writings joined seamlessly in each section, but—as noted above—the continuity of Jewish life was one of the principal themes of the Yiddish historians of the Holocaust, and I believe it is authentic to maintain that point of view.

Examples of the public reception of the Yiddish historian's works are found in the final section, which offers book reviews by contemporary figures in the world of Yiddish letters. To a perhaps surprising degree, their responses as non-professional observers confirm the historians' intentions, whether stated or implicit: to discover and present the formative history of a living people—drawing where possible on Jewish sources of information—for an audience of educated lay readers—to help in building and fortifying a Yiddish-speaking nation—and, when all was lost, to console its surviving remnant.

Ultimately, this volume strives to be more than a vehicle for bringing old scholarship to new readers. It is a memorial to a scholarly endeavor—"vos iz nishto mer" (that exists no more), to use a common Yiddish phrase for losses sustained—that I hope will find renewed life with a new audience, both in this volume and by opening a door to the original Yiddish writings.

Notes

1. Mark L. Smith, *The Yiddish Historians and the Struggle for a Jewish History of the Holocaust* (Detroit, MI: Wayne State University Press, 2019).

2. These come, respectively, from the following selections in this volume: 30 (Ginsburg), 29 (Rubashov), 21 (Trunk), 22 (Erik), 31 (Zinberg), and 10 (Meir Balaban, *Yidn in poyln* [Vilna: B. Kletskin, 1930], 7).

3. See Natalia Aleksiun, *Conscious History: Polish-Jewish Historians before the Holocaust* (London: Littman, 2021).

4. Its half-dozen leading figures included (chiefly) Meir Balaban and Ignacy Schorr, (arguably) Ignacy Schiper and Emanuel Ringelblum, and (at times) Philip Friedman and Raphael Mahler.

5. Shoyl Ginzburg, "A bletl yudishe geshikhte tsum 200-yorigen yubileyum fun peterburg," *Der fraynd* 108 (St. Petersburg), May 27, 1903, 2–3 (signed "G—g").

6. Two examples (repeating the path of non-fiction Hebrew literature of the *Haskalah*): Ab. Kahan, "Darvinismus" [Darwinism], *Di tsukunft* [The future] 1, no. 1 (New York, January 1892): 22–38, and his subsequent articles in nos. 2, 3, and 5; Y. Blumshteyn, "Darvin un zayn teorye" [Darwin and his theory], *Leben un visenshaft* 1, no. 4 (Vilna, August 1910): cols. 47–84, and no. 5 (September 1910): cols. 41–62.

7. For example: Filip Krants, *Di geshikhte fun di groyse frantsoyzishe revolutsyon* [The history of the great French revolution] (New York: Literarisher farlag, 1903); Ab. Kahan, *Historye fun di fereynigte shtaaten* [History of the United States] (New York: Forverts, 1910).

8. For example: P. Viernik, *Di yidishe geshikhte* [Jewish history] (New York: Hebrew Publishing Co., 1901).

9. Shimen Dubnov, *Algemeyne yidishe geshikhte* (Vilna: Hed ha-Zman, 1909), I.

10. Yitskhok Shiper, *Virtshaftsgeshikhte fun di yidn in poyln beysn mitlalter* [Economic history of the Jews in Poland during the Middle Ages] (Warsaw: Ch. Brzoza, 1926), 9–10 (Introduction, dated March 1924).

11. For the history of YIVO, see Cecile Esther Kusnitz, *YIVO and the Making of Modern Yiddish Culture: Scholarship for the Yiddish Nation* (New York: Cambridge University Press, 2014). On the Paris branch, see Nick Underwood, *Yiddish Paris: Staging Nation and Community in Interwar France* (Bloomington: Indiana University Press), 2022.

12. According to Kusnitz, *YIVO*, 62, the founders of YIVO were (with birthplaces added here in brackets): Shtif [Rivne], Tcherikower [Poltava], Lestschinski [Horodishche, near Kiev], Menes [Grodno], Steinberg [Dvinsk], Weinreich [Kuldīga], Zilberfarb [Rivne], Eliashev [Kovno], and Efroykin [Kovno].

13. Yankev Shatski, "Yidishe visnshaft in amerike" [Jewish scholarship in America], *Literarishe bleter* 9, no. 37 (Warsaw, September 9, 1932): 588.

14. See Mark L. Smith, "Soviet-Jewish Scholars and the Fascist Accusation," *East European Jewish Affairs* 53, no. 2–3 (2023): 408–25, https://doi.org/10.1080/13501674.2025.2477239.

15. Kusnitz, *YIVO*, 167.

16. Salo W. Baron, "Ghetto and Emancipation: Shall We Revise the Traditional View?," *Menorah Journal* 14 (New York, June 1928): 526.

17. Y. Shatski, "Idishe memuarn literatur" [Yiddish memoir literature], *Di tsukunft* (New York, September 25, 1925): 484.

18. E. Tsherikover, ed., Preface to *Historishe shriftn fun yivo* I (Warsaw, 1929): unnumbered page (saying also that publication began in 1927 but was not completed until 1929).

19. Emanuel Ringelblum, Introduction to Yeshaye Trunk, *Geshikhte fun yidn in plotsk, 1237–1657* (Warsaw, 1939), V–VI, unsigned but credited to Ringelblum by Trunk in his "Emanuel ringelblum—der historiker 1900–1944," *Di tsukunft* (April 1965): 156.

20. See Mahler's memoir (Selection 11 in this volume). Another one of the eleven women died before the war.

21. Joseph Kermish and Nachman Blumental, eds., *Kidush ha-Shem—Ketavim mi-yeme ha-Sho'ah by Shimon Huberband* (Tel Aviv: Zakhor, 1969); *Rabbi Shimon Huberband, Kiddush Hashem: Jewish Religious and Cultural Life in Poland During the Holocaust*, trans. David E. Fishman, ed. Jeffrey S. Gurock and Robert S. Hirt (Hoboken, NY: KTAV/Yeshiva University Press, 1987).

22. E. Tsherikover, "Yidishe martirologye un yidishe historyografye," *YIVO bleter* XVII, no. 2 (March–April 1941): 97–112; "Jewish martyrology and Jewish historiography," *YIVO Annual of Jewish Social Science* I (1946): 9–23.

23. Mark Dvorzhestki, "Neshome-problemen fun der sheyres-hapleyte" [Psychological problems of the survivors], *Almanakh fun di yidishe shrayber in yisroel* (Tel Aviv: Farband fun yidishe shrayber un zshurnalistn in yisroel, 1962), 343.

24. Nakhman Blumental, "Apikursishe gedanken: tsum yortog fun geto-oyfshtand" [Skeptical thoughts: On the anniversary of the ghetto uprising], *Lebns-fragn* 147 (Tel Aviv, March 1964): 5.

25. For example, comparison of the Polish and Yiddish sections of Balaban's bibliography shows this very division of topics between the language of first publication and subsequent translation (i.e., Jewish antiquities, Polish 1920, Yiddish 1921; Yiddish press jubilees, Yiddish 1923, Polish 1924); see Israel M. Biderman, *Mayer Balaban: Historian of Polish Jewry* (New York: Dr. I. M. Biderman Book Committee, 1976), 310, 312, 319.

26. The only exception was Joseph Wulf. See Mark L. Smith, "Joseph Wulf and the Path Not Taken: The Turn from Writing Jewish History in Yiddish to Writing Nazi History in German," *Holocaust and Genocide Studies* 37, no. 1 (Spring 2023): 125–39, https://doi.org/10.1093/hgs/dcad024.

27. YIVO published two related anthologies consisting of reprints from the English-language *YIVO Annual*, including translations of articles by a half-dozen Yiddish historians (depending on how "Yiddish historian" is defined): Joshua A. Fishman, ed., *Studies in Modern Jewish Social History* (KTAV and YIVO: New York, 1972); and Deborah Dash Moore, ed., *East European Jews in Two Worlds: Studies from the YIVO Annual* (Evanston, IL: Northwestern University Press and YIVO, 1990).

28. The absence of a topic area for socialism and the workers' movement, so prominent in Yiddish writing generally, requires explanation. Among the Yiddish historians, only Tcherikower concentrated on these topics. Of his two principal contributions, the more valuable pertains only to the United States, which is outside the present scope: Elias Tcherikower, ed., *Geshikhte fun der yidisher arbeter-bavegung in di fareynikte shtatn* [History of the Jewish Labor Movement in the United States] (New York: YIVO, 1943, 1945). The other is the third volume of YIVO's *Historishe shriftn* (Vilna: YIVO, 1939), also edited by Tcherikower, in which many of the pieces are memoirs, historical documents, or articles by non-historians or nonspecialists in the field, with two principal articles by Tcherikower that have been largely eclipsed by later research. Despite his long connection with the topic, I believe he is better served by quoting from his pogrom history, on which his reputation was based.

29. Such an expansion would also have enlarged the list of historians to include Julius Brutzkus, Nathan Michael Gelber, Abraham Menes, Zosa Szajkowski, and Bernard Weinryb.

30. Many of Friedman's Holocaust studies may be found in the posthumous volume of translations edited by his widow: Ada June Friedman, ed., *Roads to Extinction: Essays on the Holocaust* (New York: Conference on Jewish Social Studies / JPS, 1980).

31. Several of Kermish's chief areas of research (including the underground press in the Warsaw ghetto, resistance in all its forms, daily life in the ghetto, and the survey conducted by Ringelblum's *Oyneg shabes* project on "Two-and-a-Half Years in the Ghetto") appear in his section introductions to the collection: Joseph Kermish, ed., *To Live with Honor, To Die with Honor! . . . : Selected Documents from the Warsaw Ghetto Underground Archives "O.S." [Oneg Shabbath]* (Jerusalem: Yad Vashem, 1986).

32. Three major works written in Yiddish by Trunk appeared in English: *Judenrat: The Jewish Councils in Eastern Europe under Nazi Occupation* (New York: Macmillan, 1972), published only in English; *Jewish Responses to Nazi Persecution: Collective and Individual Behavior in*

Extremis (New York: Stein and Day, 1979), of which the Yiddish original of the first portion only appeared in his *Geshtaltn un gesheenishn [naye serye]* [Figures and events [new series]] (Tel Aviv: Y. L. Perets, 1983), 274–314; and *Łódź Ghetto: A History*, trans. and ed., Robert Moses Shapiro (Bloomington: Indiana University Press, 2006), of which the Yiddish original was *Lodzsher geto* (New York: YIVO and Yad Vashem, 1962).

33. See the JewishGen Yizkor Book Project, accessed April 16, 2025, https://www.jewishgen.org/yizkor.

34. Filip Fridman, "Di forshung fun unzer khurbn" [The Study of Our *Khurbn*], *Kiem* (Paris, January 1948): 47–54; "Fun antihistoritsizm tsum superhistoritsizm" [From anti-historicism to super-historicism], *Kiem* (March 1948): 28–32; and "Di elementn fun undzer khurbn-forshung" [The elements of our *khurbn*-research], *Hemshekh* 1 (Munich, April 1948): 4–10; continued as "Di memuaristik" [Memoir-writing], *Hemshekh* 2 (1949): 26–34.

35. Rafoel Mahler, "Fuftsik yor yidishe geshikhts-visnshaft" [Fifty years of Jewish historical scholarship], *Yidishe kultur* 12, no. 9 (New York, October 1950): 19–22; continued in no. 10 (November 1950): 20–24; "Aktuele problemen fun der yidisher historyografye" [Actual problems of Jewish historiography], *Di tsukunft* (New York, March–April 1968): 162–64.

36. Yankev Shatski, "Problemen fun yidisher historisher forshung," *Problemen* 3–4 (Paris, February 1950), reprinted in *Shatski-bukh* (New York: YIVO, 1958), 227–32; and "Problemen fun yidisher historyographye," *Di tsukunft* 60, no. 3 (New York, March 1955): 121–26, reprinted in ibid., 233–48.

37. E. Tsherikover, "Yidishe martirologye un yidishe historyografye," *YIVO bleter* XVII, no. 2 (March–April 1941): 97–112; "Jewish martyrology and Jewish historiography," *YIVO Annual* I (1946): 9–23.

38. Yeshaye Trunk, "Vi azoy forsht men di geshikhte fun di khorev gevorene kehiles in poyln?" [How should one study the history of the destroyed Jewish communities in Poland?], in *Almanakh yidish*, ed. Yankev Pat et al. (New York: Alveltlekhn yidishn kultur-kongres, 1961), 275–86, reprinted in Yeshaye Trunk, *Geshtaltn un gesheenishn [naye serye]*, 108–23.

39. Yitskhok Shiper, *Kultur-geshikhte fun yidn in Polyn beysn mitlalter* (Warsaw: Ch. Brzoza, 1926), 226.

40. Zehavit Stern, "The *Shpilman* Theory and the Invention of the Jewish Bard," in *Worlds of Old Yiddish Literature*, ed. Simon Neuberg and Diana Matut, *Studies in Yiddish* 13 (Cambridge: Legenda, 2020), 291–308.

41. Two sources of information that include most of the Yiddish historians are the *YIVO Encyclopedia of Jews in Eastern Europe*, accessed April 16, 2025, https://yivoencyclopedia.org, and the *New Lexicon of Yiddish Literature*, trans., Joshua Fogel, *Congress of Jewish Culture* [blog], accessed April 16, 2025, https://yleksikon.blogspot.com.

Part One

JEWISH AUTONOMY

1
Autonomy in Jewish History
by Simon Dubnow, 1934

SIMON DUBNOW (1860–1941, see also Selection 18 below) was born in Mstislav, Belorussia (today Mscislaŭ, Belarus). His contemporaries and followers considered him the founder of East European Jewish historical scholarship. In St. Petersburg, he helped to create the Jewish Historical-Ethnographic Society and was a professor at the Institute of Jewish Studies (officially, Higher Courses in Oriental Studies). After the Bolshevik Revolution, he continued his work in Berlin, then in Riga, Latvia, where he was murdered during the liquidation of the ghetto by the Germans.

Dubnow is both the expected and paradoxical choice to begin a collection of Yiddish historical writings—expected because he became widely known to the Yiddish-speaking public through the Yiddish editions of his works; paradoxical because he wrote no original historical studies in Yiddish. He turned only late and with skepticism to the possibility of composing scholarly prose in his native vernacular. His ten-volume *World History of the Jewish People* was written in Russian and his three-volume *History of Hasidism* in Hebrew. His output in Yiddish consists of reminiscences, reportage, school texts, commentaries on historical documents, and prefaces to works by others, with the notable exception of the brief essay below.

Long before the other articles in this section, "Jewish autonomy," were conceived by their authors, Dubnow set forth his theory of autonomy in Jewish history, commencing with his "Letters on Old and New Judaism" in 1897 (in Russian). Three of his principal contentions were that 1) Jews continued to constitute a spiritual, non-territorial nation through the millennia of dispersion from ancient Israel, 2) the Jewish nation has been led throughout its history by a succession of geographic centers, and 3) until the most recent times, Jewish communities largely sought and attained self-governance. These three concepts—"Diaspora nationalism," "hegemonic centers," and "autonomy"—underly his approach to Jewish history and are central to the essay presented below. They also inform his political program of "autonomism" in advocating for Jewish national rights in the countries of Eastern Europe.

It is not surprising that Dubnow was invited to contribute the entry on "Autonomy in Jewish History" for the first volume of the Yiddish encyclopedia published in Paris by the Association Simon Dubnow, named in his honor.[1] As the younger historian Isaiah Trunk noted, "It is the tremendous historical service of our great historian Simon Dubnow" that he "introduced autonomism into Jewish history as one of its fundamental pillars."[2] Dubnow's essay summarizes for the Yiddish reader the central points noted above, drawn from his earlier works in other languages. The opening paragraphs build toward his chief interest: Jewish communal autonomy in Poland and Lithuania, which his influence led succeeding generations of Jewish historians to study, as illustrated by the further articles in this section.

In the first paragraph, Dubnow's use of the Yiddish word *landsmanshaftn* (hometown associations of Jewish immigrants from Eastern Europe) is a deliberate anachronism likely intended to give the general reader a sense of familiarity in reading about ancient history.

Autonomy in Jewish history has been a constant social factor because the Jewish people have lived among foreign peoples since the oldest times and were able to maintain their national characteristics only through *self-legislation* (the literal translation of the Greek word *autonomia*), namely, through their own social and cultural institutions. The Diaspora, the dispersion of the Jewish people across the world, had already begun in the period of the people's youth, at the time of the Babylonian Exile. In Babylonia, the exiles who were driven from Judea stayed together, separated from the surrounding peoples by their religion and lifestyle. They organized themselves into *landsmanshaftn*, groups of people from one city ("People of Beth-El," "People of Bethlehem," etc.), and each group was led by its elders. When the larger portion of the Babylonian exiles returned to Judea, those who stayed behind continued to live autonomously, based on privileges they received from the Persian government, and their representatives, Ezra and Nehemiah, later created a firm national organization in the motherland of Judea itself.

The "great Diaspora," which developed in the entire Mediterranean area of Asia and Africa in the period of Greco-Roman rule, created a large network of autonomous Jewish communities (called in Greek, "sunagoge," gathering, society, but not a synagogue or house of prayer, which had a different name). Each community selected its council of elders ("Gerousia"), just as the Greek city selected its city council ("Boule"). In the large commercial city of Alexandria, Jewish self-rule was concentrated in the hands of a top leader who carried the title of "ethnarch"—ruler of the people. The well-known Greek geographer of the first century, Strabo, wrote that the ethnarch "led the Jewish people and enforced their laws like the ruler of a free state."[1] When the Greek citizens in various cities of Asia Minor attempted to disrupt the Jewish community's autonomy, the Jews appealed to the ruler of Rome (Julius Caesar, and later, Caesar Augustus), and the city leaders received a strict order from above: do not interfere in the affairs of the Jewish community, and "let them live according to the laws and customs of their elders."[2]

After the Romans destroyed Judea and a second spiritual center was created in Babylonia, under Persian (later, Arab) rule, Jewish autonomy developed there in a centralized form. Over all the communities stood the "Rosh ha-Golah" ("Resh Galuta" in Aramaic or "Exilarch" in Greek), the head of the Diaspora. He was the official intermediary between the government and the Jewish communities in collecting state taxes, appointing judges and officials in the communities, interceding with the king about Jewish affairs, etc. He was assisted by the spiritual leaders of the people, the "roshei yeshiva" (academic deans) in Babylonia who created the Talmudic legislation, and later the "Geonim" who adapted the new laws to life.

When the leading (hegemonic) centers moved from Asia to Europe, autonomous forms of organization developed there too, in the manner of each country. In Arab and Christian Spain, the bridge between East and

West, the role of exilarch was played at first by Jewish financiers or diplomats at the royal court (Hasdai ibn Shaprut, Shmuel ha-Nagid, and others); but the king often conducted matters himself with the communities. For him, each Jewish community council was a sort of finance department that was required to satisfy the community's entire tax obligation and often pay large sums in advance for future years. There are thousands of letters from the King of Aragon, Jaime I, and his successors (thirteenth to fourteenth centuries) to the Jewish communities in Barcelona, Zaragoza, and many others, about such financial matters, but also about various subjects pertaining to Jewish autonomy. The community was called in Spanish "Aljama" (from the Arabic word "al-Jamā'a" [the gathering]). The rabbis had broad authority as judges, not only in financial matters but also in criminal matters; they could sentence to prison, corporal punishment, and even death. In 1432, a large meeting of Castilian Jews organized a constitution for the community leadership (in the city of Valladolid).

Varied forms of autonomy existed in Italy, France, Germany. In the ghetto of Rome, the large community council (*Congrega*) consisted of sixty members, who selected from among themselves three "agents" ("factori" in the sixteenth century). In France and Germany, the rabbis stood at the head of the communities, together with the secular "parnosim" [elected officials]. At meetings of the community representatives, statutes or regulations were enacted for the entire country (the councils in the Rhineland cities of Speyer, Worms, Mainz—*Takanot Shum* ["Enactments of SHU"M," the Hebrew acronym for the cities' names], in the thirteenth century, and others). The German kings attempted several times to appoint their official rabbis as community representatives, especially for fiscal purposes—to collect taxes, but the communities did not recognize such "Judenmeisters" as rabbis and considered them ordinary officials. As intermediaries with the government, the communities had their *shtadlonim* [intercessors/lobbyists]. One of them, Yosel Rosheim of Alsace, was the greatest intercessor with the German kings in the first half of the sixteenth century, at the time of Luther's Reformation.

The broadest autonomy was created by the Jewish communities in Poland. The Jewish community council, called the *kahal*, was like a government for the Jewish city alongside the Christian city government. The *kahal* was chosen once each year, during the intermediate days of Passover, and, in the larger cities, consisted of a few tens of members, who selected from among themselves an executive of seven "eldest and best" (*roshim* and *tovim*); the other members of the *kahal* functioned as treasurers for taxes, charity, and social assistance. A larger community, together with the surrounding smaller communities, would unite in one circle (*galil*) and several *glilim*—in one *medinah* or *eretz* [country or land], areas corresponding to the administrative subdivisions of Poland. There were five *medinot*: Great Poland (with its capital, Posen), Little Poland (with the capitals, Kraków and Lublin), Podolia and Galicia (capital, Lwów), Volhynia (capital, Ostróg), and Lithuania, with its large communities of Brest, Grodno, and Wilno. Each of these lands had its council or regional parliament—a periodic gathering of its communal leaders (*va'ad ha-medinah*). By the end of the sixteenth century, together they formed a central council of all the lands: *Va'ad ha-Aratzot*, a sort of Jewish parliament or congress (in official Polish records it was called *Kongres Żydowski*), which would assemble once each year, and less often later, at the large fairs in Lublin and other cities. In 1623, Lithuania separated from the land-union and created a council for itself of its large cities; thus, the Polish union consisted of four lands, and its central body was called *Va'ad Arba' Aratzot*, the Council of Four Lands. Both councils existed until 1764, when the Polish government disbanded them because it no longer needed them for financial purposes—apportioning the Jewish taxes among the communities and collecting and delivering them to the financial official of the government.

Jewish autonomy developed in this manner as long as Europe was governed by the principle of a "class-state," a state founded on ranks of higher and lower classes—officials, nobles, townsfolk, peasants, workers. In that period the Jews everywhere were not only a separate people with a separate religion but also a separate *class* of traders or artisans who were excluded from the Christian civic organizations. But the French Revolution of 1789 and the far-reaching democratic movements created the modern "legal state," which is founded on the principle of civic freedom. There, where the Jews were emancipated or fought for emancipation, they rejected the old national autonomy and proclaimed themselves a religious group, cult, or synagogue community in the style of the dominant nation. The Emancipation Proclamation of the French Revolution (1791) specifically demanded that the Jews renounce their "privileges" in the *kehilot*, and Napoleon created his "consistory system" that made the *kehila* a colorless organization of official rabbis. The *assimilation* movement greatly assisted the destruction of Jewish autonomy.

Only the Jewish national movement at the end of the nineteenth and beginning of the twentieth centuries, which opposed the stream of assimilation, revived the idea of Jewish autonomy in a modern form suited to the modern democratic state order. The new principle of "protection of national minorities" that developed after the World War also placed the issue of Jewish autonomy on a new international basis.

Introduction Notes:

1. Sh. Dubnov, "Oytonomye in der yidisher geshikhte," *Algemeyne entsiklopedye* [General encyclopedia], vol. 1 (Paris: Association Simon Dubnow, 1934), cols. 236–39.

2. Yeshaye Trunk, "Yidishe kiem-problemen in likht fun undzer geshikhte" [Problems of Jewish existence in light of our history], in *Oyfn sheydveg: hayntstaytike problemen fun yidishn natsyonaln kiem: ershter zamlheft* (Munich: Fraye tribune, 1948), 53.

Article Notes:

1. Joseph Flavius, *Antiquities*, book 14, chapter 7.
2. Ibid., 14, 10; 16, 6.

2

The Jewish Parliament in Lithuania and Belorussia in Its Legislative Activity, 1623–1721

by Israel Sosis, 1928

ISRAEL SOSIS (1878–1967) was born in Balta, Podolia (today in Ukraine). Following studies in sociology and history at universities in Berne and Paris, Sosis was associated with Dubnow and his organizations in St. Petersburg until the early 1920s. In contrast to Dubnow, who rejected communism and left the Soviet Union in 1922, Sosis joined the Communist Party in 1921 and found his career in Soviet institutions. In 1924 he was appointed head of the Historical Commission of the Jewish Section at the Institute for Belorussian Culture in Minsk, where he also became coeditor of the journal *Tsaytshrift* (Periodical) in which his article below appeared. It was the first scholarly journal in Yiddish to be published by a state authority, and its first volumes (1926 and 1928) illustrate the relative freedom of academic inquiry that was possible under the Soviet New Economic Policy, before the imposition of Stalin's dictatorship in 1929.

For this section, his article below offers a view of the overall functioning of an autonomous Jewish council during the period of its successful operation.[1] Like his other early works, many of which deal with Jewish social and economic history in Lithuania and Belorussia, it avoids the overtly Marxist bias of his later works. Sosis rejects Dubnow's idealist, "whole Israel" approach to Jewish history (which emphasized national unity over class distinctions), but at this early date was not compelled by official Soviet policy to seek only social conflict and economic determinism in Jewish history. Nevertheless, his collegiality with Dubnow and his failure to distance himself early enough from the "objective" norms of "bourgeois" historiography in the West led to his denunciation as a "non-Marxist" and his expulsion in 1931 from the Communist Party and academic Jewish studies.

An example of Sosis's less-than-total commitment to Soviet orthodoxy is found in his use of language, which is not evident in English translation. At a time when Soviet anti-Jewish and anti-Zionist policies required that words of Hebraic origin in Yiddish be spelled phonetically rather than traditionally, his writing offers an unusual abundance of words and sentences quoted verbatim from primary sources in Hebrew (rather than in Yiddish translation), in a seeming attempt to display both his competence in Hebrew and independence in skirting the prohibition on the use of Hebrew orthography in Yiddish writing.

It is the destiny of Lithuanian-Belorussian Jewish historiography to be the beneficiary of a great good fortune: The minute-book (*Pinkas*) of the Jewish parliament (*Va'ad ha-Medinah*—Council of the Land), which spread its activity across Lithuania and Belorussia over the course of almost 140 years, has been preserved complete. We have no other historical monument of this type in the field of Jewish history in Germany and Poland, where the forms of communal self-rule that also evolved in Lithuania and Belorussia were first created. Little specific information remains from the earlier community assemblies that took place in the German lands in the Middle Ages.[1] From the Jewish parliament in Poland (*Va'ad Arba' Aratzot*—Council of Four Lands), which existed for more than 200 years from the middle of the sixteenth century to the beginning of the 1760s, no *pinkes* [for the generic term, Sosis uses the Yiddish form of the word] remains extant (aside from a series of individual regulations), which would have had colossal significance for the history of the Polish Jewish population.[2] For this reason, the surviving Lithuanian *pinkes* has special historical value.

But only in recent years has the complete *Pinkas ha-Medina* been made available to the Jewish historian. So long as the *pinkes* lay in the archives, it was impossible to draw upon it exhaustively and analyze the enormous, rich material that is located there and is tied to various events of the seventeenth and eighteenth centuries. Ordinarily, the Jewish historian took from the *pinkes* what he needed *to supplement* his material and his old historiographic views. Often the decisions of the Lithuanian *va'ad* were brought forth in an absolute, static form.[3] Doing so ignores the fact that the regulations of the *va'ad* underwent a *long evolution* and changed in accordance with the social contradictions that also characterized Jewish history in Lithuania and Belorussia.

Publication of the Lithuanian *Pinkas ha-Medinah* had begun as early as 1909 (in Russian translation), as a supplement to *Evreiskaia Starina* [the journal *Jewish Past*, edited by Dubnow], but it was finished at last—although not completely (after a hiatus during the World War)—during the time of the civil war and remained unknown even for many specialists. Not until 1925 in Berlin (under Dubnow's editorship) was the entire *Pinkas ha-Medinah* published with all the very important appendices and necessary scholarly apparatus.[4] Only recently could this rare historical memorial become what it fully merited—the *point of departure* for new studies in the field of social development among Jews in Lithuania and Belorussia.

But it was not only this objective fact—the late publication of the Lithuanian *pinkes*—that delayed its availability for research. There were also subjective reasons.

In his introduction to *Pinkas ha-Medinah*, Dubnow pointed out the already long well-known fact that publication of this *pinkes* had begun (in St. Petersburg, under the editorship of Dr. Abraham Harkavy) sixty years earlier, in 1865–1866. But work was halted immediately because the Jewish *shtadlonim* [intercessors/lobbyists] in St. Petersburg feared—from the perspective of "Lamah yomru ha-goyim?" [the traditional question, "What will the nations of the world think?"]—that the *pinkes* would confirm that Jews had a *kahal*, a *va'ad*, and constituted a "state within a state"!

Conversely, in the late 1890s and at the beginning of the twentieth century, a special interest in the former "national autonomy" was awakened in Russian Jewish circles because the slogan of future national autonomy achieved great popularity among the Jewish nationalist intelligentsia (and also the "Bund" [General Jewish Labor Party]). This interest had the effect of finally bringing the *pinkes* to publication. It was not by chance that Dubnow, the theoretician of Jewish national autonomy, published the *Pinkas ha-Medinah* (previously as a supplement to *Evreiskaia Starina* and, in 1925, in Berlin).

But the political-nationalist aspect led Dubnow to idealize the former autonomy of the *kahal* and drew his attention away from the social conflicts that were connected with the organization of the *kahal* and *va'ad*. Dubnow was, above all, inspired by the idea that the *va'ad* was a ring in the historical chain of Jewish national autonomy, without which the Jewish people could not have existed after the destruction of its political independence. "The secret of national survival ('*kiyum ha-uma*')," says Dubnow, is tied to the onetime prophecy: "The scepter shall not depart from Judah" [Genesis 49:10]. In his opinion, this Jewish state never ceased to exist but had only assumed newer and newer forms, and one of those is the autonomy of the *kahal* with its *va'ad*. Antisemites claim that this is a state within a state, to which Dubnow replies in the name of the Jewish people [*Knesset Yisrael*]: "Yes, correct. We are indeed a state within a state . . ."[5]

In an institution that was created on the basis of Jewish lack of rights and national separateness, Dubnow sees the exemplar of national independence.

Dubnow, as a historian, sees in the Lithuanian *va'ad* what he wishes to see as an ideologue of national autonomism, but the bare prose that permeates the entire Lithuanian *pinkes*, the communal conflicts, the various social interests, etc.—those remain foreign to him. But in just this respect are the minutes of the Lithuanian *va'ad* of interest. For the seventeenth and largest part of the eighteenth century, they can serve as the chief source of social history for the Jews in Lithuania and Belorussia. In time, with the addition of further research on non-Jewish sources, particularly the Lithuanian *Metrica* [chancellery books of Lithuanian dukes], beginning in the seventeenth century, light will be shed on a whole series of questions that are touched upon in the Lithuanian *pinkes*.[6] In that respect, great significance (for the social history of Jews in Poland in general) will also be found in the responsa collection that we are preparing for publication (I have used some of these *shayles-utshuves* [rabbinic "questions-and-answers" to issues of Jewish law] for the current work). . . .[7]

In the work I present here, I dwell extensively on the social aspects and social conflicts that are connected with the activity of the Lithuanian *va'ad*—to the limited extent that they have been studied so far. I therefore do not touch upon a whole series of general and organizational questions about the *kahal* and *va'ad*, because they have already been much discussed.

***

The economic isolation of Lithuania and Belorussia (in comparison with Poland) also caused Jewish communal life to develop slowly there and, for a long time—until the beginning of the seventeenth century—to be under the hegemony of the Polish *va'ad*, which already existed, as mentioned above, in the sixteenth century.

The further strengthening of Lithuanian-Belorussian Jewry in the economic and cultural arena, the growth of such commercial cities as Brest, Pinsk, Grodno, and Vilna, the significant role of Jewish finance-capital in these cities—all of this, together with general influences (the economic peculiarity of the Lithuanian state, its autonomy in a number of political areas), laid the ground for the rise and enduring existence of the Lithuanian *va'ad*.

The new documents that were recently published (as appendices to the Lithuanian *pinkes*) show that, between these two Jewish parliaments, controversies and conflicts often arose. The Lithuanian *va'ad* distrusted the Polish *va'ad* and strongly emphasized its independence from it.

From what do these unfriendly relations between the two central bodies of the Jewish communities in Poland and Lithuania-Belorussia derive?

As we will see, certain social conflicts existed not only in each Jewish community—between the rich, middle class, and poor—but also between the richer, privileged *kehilot* and poorer Jewish communities: the former attempted to extend their hegemony over the latter (as detailed in coming chapters). Therefore, so long as the Lithuanian Jews were poor and culturally backward (in comparison with Poland, which was already renowned for its [Hasidic] "dynasties," famous rabbis, and yeshivas), they also had to submit to the hegemony of Polish Jewry in the field of central communal leadership. However, with the development of the abovementioned Lithuanian-Belorussian commercial and cultural centers, with their rich Jewish families, rabbis, and yeshivas, the Polish *va'ad* lost its earlier authority in the eyes of the newly rich and powerful who established themselves in the Lithuanian state. Between them and the wealthy Polish Jews, competition strengthened in the economic field, which also penetrated communal relations—insofar as the national duties of the community heads often blended with their private interests (as I will demonstrate).

For a long time (already in the sixteenth century) the delegates to the Polish *va'ad* were the actual representatives of Jewish national interests in all of Poland. To the extent that they had close relations with the Polish government, to the Sejm [Polish parliament] (as great financiers or ordinary

Jewish *shtadlonim*), they would often have advance knowledge of these or those harsh decrees or false accusations against the Jews and undertake certain measures against them. This necessitated large sums of money, which were obtained from the entire Jewish population in the form of special taxes. In apportioning this tax obligation, Lithuania had little influence: the Polish Jewish delegates dominated. On this ground, a split emerged between the Polish *va'ad* and the delegates from the large Lithuanian *kehilot*, who founded the Lithuanian *va'ad* in 1623. But conflicts also later arose between the Lithuanian and Polish *va'adim*.

In 1633, this type of conflict ended with a definitive judgment proclaimed by learned leaders. The Polish delegates had given out a certain sum as a gift to the king and for other expenses in connection with a false accusation against a Jew, and they demanded that the Lithuanian region should also participate in this. The court of arbitration ruled that the Lithuanian Jews were required to participate materially in the gift to the king but not in the gifts that the Polish Jewish delegates gave the president (*Marszałek*) and deputies of the Sejm because the Lithuanian Jews also gave gifts to the deputies from Lithuania. Regarding the other general expenses, it was established that the Polish Jewish leaders were obligated to include (in proportion to the sum of money) the leaders from Lithuania as well.[8]

In 1644, a conflict was again settled between both *va'adim*. The subject was again a false accusation. The demands of the Polish *va'ad* were partially satisfied, partially rejected—specifically, their demand that the Lithuanians participate in the expenses incurred in sending an emissary to Rome (in connection, it appears, with a blood libel), because he was sent without the knowledge of the Lithuanian leaders. . . .

Such conflicts—about taxes, decree-expenses, etc.—between both parties (Polish and Lithuanian *va'adim*) repeated themselves in 1656, 1668, 1670, and 1678. The Polish delegates would demand compensation for old debts, for expenses incurred by the Polish *va'ad* on behalf of *Klal-Yisrael* [the Jewish people as a whole] to prevent decrees expelling all the Jews. The leaders of the Lithuanian *va'ad* contended that they wanted no such partnership with the Polish *va'ad* and no connection to their expenses. It ended with new compromises by the court of arbitration. But relations between both *va'adim* remained unregulated.

In 1681 a court of arbitration again took place between the Polish and Lithuanian *va'adim*. The former submitted an extensive list of expenditures they had made for general interests: to rescind the expulsion from Mazovia (the Polish region that includes Warsaw), for trade fair expenses, to support the Jewish delegates in Warsaw, to compensate the *shtadlonim* in Warsaw, for gifts to the king and his princes during sessions of the Sejm, to prevent harm to Jews in various respects, to rescind the head tax [on Jews], and to fight the frightful false accusation leveled against the entire Jewish community in connection with a general expulsion, to help the poor, etc. The Lithuanian Jewish delegates, for their part, contended that they had never taken upon themselves any obligation regarding the Polish *va'ad*, that they had not entered into a partnership or combination with it, that all previous regulations in that regard were only temporary and not for the sake of partnership or unification; they, the Lithuanians, wanted, on the contrary, to separate themselves entirely from the Polish *va'ad* . . . and for the Polish *va'ad* to participate in the expenses of the Lithuanian region that also pertained to all Jews and to a general expulsion and various false accusations.

The court of arbitration in 1681 again made a certain compromise regarding the old claims by the Polish *va'ad* against the Lithuanian *va'ad*, but, together therewith, set out clearly the future relations between them. It was established that both Jewish parliaments had equal rights: the leaders of the Polish *va'ad* had no greater standing and no greater significance and power in comparison with the Lithuanian *va'ad* in any respect—not in honor, nor in money, nor in other matters; between both *va'adim* there was no unification or partnership. Even in the expenses related to rescinding a decree to expel all the Jews, there was no partnership. If such a danger did indeed arise, each party would intercede on its own behalf to rescind the decree; in this respect, the leaders of the Polish "four lands" would raise the money—for the king and the princes of Crown Poland, and the Lithuanian leaders would intercede separately with their money for the king and the princes of the Lithuanian state. If the expulsion pertained solely to Poland or solely to Lithuania, each *va'ad* was required to help the other independently in the indicated manner (at the same time, each should serve as a check on the other). However, if the danger did not consist of a general expulsion, but only a partial expulsion that affected only a few communities or regions, there was no obligation by one party with regard to the other.[9]

[Further sections of Sosis's article deal with such topics as the tax burden, social differentiation, monopoly rights of merchants, rights of residence and commercial activity, relations with non-Jews, help rendered by the *va'ad* during the Chmielnicki pogroms, and issues of family life, economic life of women, and religious education, among others.]

Introduction Notes:
   1. Y. Sosis, "Der yidisher seym in lite un vaysrusland in zayn gezetsgeberisher tetikayt, 1623–1721, loyt zayne protokoln" [The Jewish parliament in Lithuania and Belorussia in its legislative activity, 1623–1721, according to its minutes], in *Tsaytshrift* II–III (Minsk, 1928): cols. 1–27 (1–7 quoted).

Article Notes:
   1. The relevant regulations were set forth in their Hebrew original in the recently published English book on Jewish autonomy in the Middle Ages, L. Finkelstein, *Jewish Self-Government in the Middle Ages* (New York: Jewish Theological Seminary, 1924), 225–32, 265–74, 283–317. We find there also rabbinic regulations regarding community life (119–21, 149, 153, 154, 175–76, 191, 193, 195, 205–16). The very rare traces of community life in the *early* Middle Ages are scattered in B. Dinur's book *Toldot Yisrael*, vol. 5, *Yisrael Bagola* [History of Israel, vol. 5, Israel in the Diaspora], vol. 1 of 2 (a collection of historical materials and documents), published by "Dvir" in Tel Aviv, Palestine, 1926. In the subject index, see the section "The Community, its Foundations and Organization," second part, 458.
   2. Regarding the Polish *va'ad* and community life in general, see also—besides the bibliography in vol. 11 of *The History of the Jewish People* (Russian), published by Mir (510–12)—the recently published work by Dr. L. Lewin, *Die Landessynode der grosspolnischen Judenschaft* (Frankfurt a. M.: Kauffmann, 1926). Some information about the community in medieval Poland is given by Y. Schiper in his book *Di kultur-geshikhte fun di yidn in poyln beysn mitlalter* (Warsaw: Brzoz, 1926), 128–34.
   3. For example, the relevant articles in vol. 11 of *The History of the Jewish People*, noted above.
   4. Sh. Dubnov ed., *Pinkas ha-medinah o Pinkas Va'ad ha-kehilot ha-rashiyot bi-medinat Lita: Kovets takanot u-fesakim mi-shenat 383 'ad Shenat 521* (Berlin: 'Ayanot, 1925).
   5. Ibid., beginning. See also the prospectus of the *Encyclopaedia des Judentums* (which is being published in Berlin in German and Hebrew), 1926, Dubnow's article "Autonomy." See also Dubnow's introduction to his *World History of the Jewish People*, latest edition (in Russian, German, and Hebrew, in ten volumes; meanwhile available in German in five volumes [Berlin, 1925–27]).
   6. Prof. [Alexander] Bershadskii, as is well known, assembled his three-volume *Russian-Jewish Archive* (in Russian) principally from a great number of documents from the *Lithuanian Metrica*, but only up to 1569. The richness of these archival materials demonstrates how important a thorough study of the *Metrica* is for us with regard to later historical periods. So far as we know, these periods are also little discussed in the fourth volume of Bershadakii's *Archive*, which is still in manuscript (and from which I will later quote the most important documents belonging to the period of the Lithuanian *va'ad*).
   7. The *shayles-utshuves*, collected by Y. Ravrebe and B. Shulman, were prepared for publication by the Jewish Historical Commission of Invayskult [Jewish Bureau of the Byelorussian Academy of Science, Minsk] under the direction of I. Sosis.
   8. *Pinkas ha-Medinah*, 278.
   9. Ibid., 284–88.

3
A Budget of the Council of Four Lands in 1726
by Raphael Mahler, 1940

RAPHAEL MAHLER (1899–1977, see also Selection 11 below) was born in Nowy Sącz, Austrian Galicia (today in Poland), and received his doctorate in history from the University of Vienna in 1922.

Mahler's career encompassed three major Jewish centers and periods: Warsaw until 1937, New York until 1951, and Tel Aviv thereafter, during each of which he published widely in Polish, English, Hebrew—and in Yiddish, the only language common to each of these periods. His interests ranged from Polish Jewish history in general to the Karaites, Hasidism, the Haskalah, and Jewish historians. In his approach to each of these, he was a committed Marxist who sought economic and class explanations for the social and cultural phenomena of Jewish history. An example is the article below that explores the financial basis of the institutions of Jewish autonomy in eighteenth-century Poland and dismisses as negligible their contribution to Jewish economic welfare—but without, as other historians would contend, considering their role in national, religious, and cultural cohesion.[1] (All of the budgets he mentions appear as tables in the Yiddish original.)

The finances of the *Va'ad Arba' Aratzot* [Council of Four Lands] present not only an important chapter of the history of Jewish autonomy in old-time Poland, but a thorough study of this subject would also shed much light on the political, social-economic, and cultural history of Polish Jewry.

A detailed history of the unceasing disputes between the Jewish communities and the autonomous Jewish provinces and especially between the smaller and larger communities—the process of disintegration of provincial autonomy—would reveal to us important aspects of the social struggle waged by the exploited small-town Jews against the hegemony of the urban communities of the time. A detailed calculation of the salaries of the *parnosim* [elected trustees of the *va'ad*] and *shtadlonim* [paid intercessors/lobbyists] who controlled the apparatus of autonomy, an accounting of how the autonomous bodies sank continually further into debt to rabbis and secular magnates, and an accounting of the philanthropic expenses of the *va'adim* [councils], would further illuminate another side of the contradictions among old-time Polish Jews. The history of intervention by nobles and government officials in the internal matters of the *va'ad*, statistics about the "gifts" that the officials received both regularly and each time they came in contact with Jewish leaders, would again add much to the picture of the political situation of Polish Jews. The correspondence between the representatives of the *Va'ad Arba' Aratzot* and provincial *va'adim* with the officials of the Polish finance ministry, the manner, the ways and means of intercession, are likely to further illuminate the lifestyle and the cultural conditions of Polish Jews at that time.

The first substantial studies of the finances of the Jewish autonomy, published by Dr. Ignacy Schiper, are a beginning and a guide to the work that ought to be done in this field.[1] As a contribution to this work, we present here a detailed budget of the *Va'ad Arba' Aratzot* in the eighteenth century and in connection therewith a series of details that will clarify the role of the Jewish head tax in Polish state finances, the means of collecting the head tax, and the relations between the leaders of the *va'ad* and the officials of the treasury. Above all, analysis of the budget itself will clarify certain aspects of the political situation of the Jews in Poland at that time. . . .

Among the materials about the Jewish head tax in the seventeenth and eighteenth centuries,[2] we found a copy of a detailed budget of the *Va'ad Arba' Aratzot* for the year 1726. . . .

The Jewish Head Tax and the Means of Collecting It

The total Jewish head tax in Crown Poland as stated in the budget—220,000 złoty—was increased in 1717 to this amount (as is known) and was not increased further until 1764. How enormous a sum the Jewish head tax represented, not only in view of the remarkable impoverishment of the Jewish masses but even in proportion to the state income from other taxes, can be seen in the following figures:

The *Kwarta* tax, the most important tax in the former Polish kingdom— set at one-fifth [originally "one-quarter"] of the income from crown estates leased by the nobility—for all of Crown Poland, amounted to 273,228 złoty in 1746, and 263,540 złoty in 1747. Jews, who bore the burden of direct and indirect state taxes and municipal taxes equally with the Christian city-dwellers and, in addition, were obligated to pay a group of special Jewish ordinary and extraordinary taxes, also had to raise a sum for the Jewish head tax that reached not much less than the actual state income from the *Kwarta*. At the same time, the nobility was generally exempt from all taxes, and the *Kwarta* was paid only by those nobles who received nearly gratis leases of royal villages. The nobility was even free from the general head tax that the Sejm [parliament] would enact in times of special need in the state finances. The Jews kept the Sejm well supplied with donations each time the Jewish head tax was increased so that, in return, the Jews would not be subject to the Sejm's periodic increases in the head tax on the population as a whole. The Sejm itself, however, would quickly break its promise. In 1676, the Sejm proclaimed expressly that Jews were required to pay the general head tax equally with everyone, and in 1717 declared explicitly that the decision of 1676 remained in force.[3]

The remarkable burden of taxes on the Jewish population becomes still more striking when one considers the entire state budget of Poland. In 1748, the so-called "nonpermanent" revenue of Crown Poland (i.e., the entire revenue from *Kwarta*, Jewish head tax, grape tax, and tariffs!) amounted to 896,398 złoty. The Jewish head tax therefore reaches nearly one-fourth of the entire sum of the nonpermanent budget.[4] Even after the financial reforms of 1764, when all taxes were sharply increased, the entire budget of Crown Poland amounted to about 10 million złoty per year, the Jewish head tax brought in about 800,000 złoty per year.[5] Jews, therefore, supplied

8 percent of the entire budget with the Jewish head tax, notwithstanding that they continued to pay all other direct and indirect taxes.[6]

Such tax exploitation was carried out with respect to the Jewish population at a time when the Jews had to endure every manner of limitation in commerce and craftwork on the part of municipal governments and Christian guilds. Such obligations were demanded from those who could not dare to live legally in the larger cities of Poland, or in the best case had to suffocate in a crowded, restricted Jewish quarter—and, in the villages and small towns, were at the mercy or the favor or disfavor of the local landowner. In such circumstances, it is no surprise that the organizations of Jewish central, provincial, and local autonomy fell into ever greater debts in order to assemble the annual Jewish head tax and other taxes for the state treasury.

The state apparatus would indeed make use of every forcible means of collecting the Jewish tax regularly.

As is known, the Jewish head tax was collected in the following manner:

Once the central *va'ad* calculated the apportionment of the total sum among the various autonomous provinces, the regional *va'adim* would meet and apportion the sum of taxes set for the given province among the various communities. All of these calculations of apportionment, both by the central *va'ad* and the provincial *va'adim*, were initiated by the administrative office of the royal finance minister. The administrative office would entrust to a military regiment the assignments of tax sums apportioned to the various communities. Three times a year, in January, May, and August, the military regiment would send deputies to the indicated community to seize the installments of head tax.

In the collection of taxes by the regimental deputies, abuses and even severe repressions often took place against the Jewish population:

In 1666, the *Va'ad Arba' Aratzot* complained to King Jan Kasimir that the soldiers who received assignments from the finance minister for 26,000 złoty of the *va'ad*'s state tax forced the Jews to pay through killing and the destruction of their property. The *va'ad* was obligated to pay this sum in installments over three years, accepting sanctions on itself in the event they failed to keep their promise. The sanctions were: one could seize and imprison every Jew; evict Jews from their houses, confiscate all their property, and seal synagogues.[7]

[In subsequent paragraphs, Mahler provides further examples of actions taken in specific locations to collect Jewish taxes.]

Salaries and Gifts for State Officials

In the budget for the *va'ad* in 1726, immediately after the line item for the Jewish head tax, appear these expenses: 12,000 złoty for the head finance minister; 1,080 złoty for his clerks and officials; 700 złoty for the chief finance minister's chief clerk; 1,000 złoty for the clerk and notary public for the *Kwarta*; totaling 14,780 złoty in the budget for payments to state officials.[8]

Especially notable is the enormous sum of 12,000 złoty for the "annual salary" of the Polish finance minister, "the great finance minister of the Crown." Undoubtedly, this "custom" for Jews to pay a salary to the finance minister is as old as the Jewish head tax, which, as is known, was introduced in 1549 and probably still earlier. The annual salary for the finance minister was apparently increased in the same proportion as the Jewish head tax. . . . [with further details]

Regarding the finance minister's clerks, in addition to the "annual salary" that was officially listed in the budget of the *va'ad*, one must take into account the official payments made by the provincial *va'adim* when submitting their allocated portion of the tax. In the documents for the years 1726 to 1739, it is indicated that the Jewish region of Podolia regularly paid 36 złoty to "honorable sirs, clerks of the finance minister, for accepting the tax apportionment." Incomparably more than the province of Podolia, the largest Jewish autonomous province, Raysn (Eastern Galicia and the Bratslav region) . . . gave the finance minister's clerks a payment of 600 złoty each year when submitting their accounting of the tax apportionment. . . .

A "voluntary gift" (*donum charitativum*) was also received from the *Va'ad Arba' Aratzot* by the government minister who represented the finance ministry at the congress of the *va'ad*. In 1762, at the meeting of the *va'ad* in Police, the sum of 370 złoty was set for the government minister who was present as an emissary from the finance minister.[9]

Expenses for Intercession and *Kozubalec*

The expenses of the *va'ad* for intercession amounted to a still larger sum than the "annual salaries" and gifts for state officials. In the budget for 1726, we have the following line items for this category:

1. Expenses for the Warsaw Sejm: 10,116 złoty and interest on this sum—2,419 złoty (lines 16, 17).

2. A second expense for intercession in the budget for 1726 in the amount of a still greater sum, 10,725 złoty owed, and 2,791 interest (lines 18, 19), paid for the "Radom Commission" (i.e., during the meeting of the finance tribunal in Radom).
3. A payment for intercession in the sum of 1,760 złoty "for expenses of the Lublin Jews for the honorable deputies" (line 7), . . . meaning here the deputies of the nobility to the Crown Tribunal in Lublin.
4. In the category of bizarre line items . . . we must also include the sum of 143 złoty that appears in the budget of the *va'ad* as an expense for the *Kościelnys* (church staff) in the Chelm and Lublin districts (line 27). Here it should be noted that Jewish communities in Poland in the seventeenth and eighteenth centuries regularly needed to pay the church each year a specified sum of money or products in kind (mostly pepper, ginger, and other spices) or both together.[10] We also know that Jews would pay *Kozubalets*[11] not only to the students of Jesuit colleges, when they would pass by the colleges or the church; the community as a whole would also pay an annual assessment and give "gifts" to the staff and professors of academies (Kraków),[12] and the staff of the *palestre* (school for lawyers),[13] and the like.
5. The need for constant intercession extended so far that the *va'ad* also budgeted (line 39) the very significant sum of 300 złoty for—the jeweler of the finance minister, by the name of Meir. . . . [ellipsis in original]

Expenses of the Va'ad for Its Own Officials and Functionaries

Included in the budget of the *va'ad* for 1726 are such salaries for the officials and functionaries of the central body as: the four general clerks of the *va'ad* (1,600 złoty), pension for the widow of general clerk Hersh (400 złoty), clerks of the *va'ad* (150 złoty), the *shtadlan* of Piotrków (200 złoty), the *shamash* [sexton] of the *va'ad* (75 złoty), the *shamash*, clerk, and servants of the head of the *va'ad* (214 złoty).

As we see, the largest expense for officials is for the four general clerks, at 400 złoty per year. . . . The four general clerks also receive, aside from their salaries, a very large per diem (line 42): for wagons and food during the meeting of the commission of the *va'ad* in Rychwał (dwelling place of the finance minister),[14] they received 1,210 złoty, i.e., more than 300 złoty each. . . .

Expenses for Social Help and Religious Purposes

The expenses of the *va'ad* in 1726 for social help and religious purposes were thus: for the poor in 1726 (1,908 złoty, line 21), support for the Jews in Maków [Mazowiecki] (200 złoty, line 35), for the Jewish hospital in Jarosłów (60 złoty, line 38), and for building schools (*batei midrash* [study halls]) (400 złoty, line 32); in total, 2,568 złoty.

That supporting the poor was a regular annual expense of the *va'ad* is evident from line item 20, where 1,280 złoty is listed as the expense for the poor in the previous year, 1725. The sum that the *va'ad* gave out for this purpose would, it appears, always remain in the range of 1,000 to 2,000 złoty: in 1739 the *va'ad* budgeted 1,500 złoty for the poor. . . .[15] The support for the Jews of Maków was undoubtedly allotted for rebuilding after a fire. . . . Support for building schools and study halls in various Lithuanian cities was already recorded in the oldest rules of the Lithuanian *va'ad*, in 1628.[16] The *va'ad* of Crown Poland also considered such support to be a regular obligation. . . . [details reported in subsequent paragraphs]

In all, the expenses of the *va'ad* in 1726 for social and religious purposes amounted to 2,568 złoty, a quite modest sum in itself, not to mention in proportion to other expenses.

Structure and Character of the Budget of the *Va'ad* in 1726

After analyzing the various line items of the budget, let us now consider the budget as a whole, both as it reflects the financial situation of the central autonomous body and for what purposes its expenses were set.

The enormous expenses of intercession and bribes, the very significant salaries and per diems for its own officials, must have led to a remarkable increase in the debts of the *va'ad*.

The budget of the *va'ad* for 1726 indicates such claims, whose repayment was not foreseen in the previous year [listing various items of indebtedness]. . . . The total of all claims amounts to approximately

122,750 złoty. If we also include the remainder of 3,179 złoty in anticipated revenue that, per the accounting of the *va'ad*, was not expected to be received in the prior year, the total indebtedness of the central *va'ad* at the end of 1726 was approximately 126,000 złoty!

The financial structure of the budget itself characterizes best the extent of expenses set to cover new debts and payment of interest on old debts in respect to the ongoing expenses of the year.

The gross budget of the *va'ad* for 1726 amounts to 291,527 złoty. The net budget of the *va'ad*, after accounting for 220,000 złoty head tax, therefore amounts to 71,527 złoty. . . . Of that net budget of 71,527 złoty, i.e., more than 66 percent, altogether two-thirds, was allotted to paying debts and interest, and only one-third was dedicated to paying ongoing expenses of the budget year! The financial decline of the *va'ad* becomes clearly evident! To cover ongoing expenses, each year the *va'ad* had to sink ever further into new debts!

Let us see how the net budget of the *va'ad* is structured after accounting for the expenses. . . . [listing the various line items] The *va'ad* spent approximately 40 percent of its annual net budget on intercession. Close to 30 percent went to unspecified debts. More than 20 percent amounts to annual salaries for state officials. Of the remaining 10 percent, 6.7 percent went for its own operating expenses and 3.6 percent to social help and religious purposes. . . .

Sixty percent, an entire three-fifths of the central *va'ad*'s own expenses (not including the head tax) went to protecting the Jewish population from the ruling officialdom and the ruling class of nobles. This proportion itself speaks to the lack of rights of the Jewish population in former Poland!

Regarding the significance of the central autonomy for the Jewish population in former Poland, it was reduced to the level of a negligible 3.6 percent for social purposes. The other nearly 96½ percent of the net budget was thus devoted entirely to purposes connected with the Jews' tax obligations to the state and not with the needs of the Jewish population—because not only were the debts (close to 30 percent!) not spent for other things such as covering the costs of intercession and long-standing state taxes. Even the expenses of supporting the central *va'ad* (6.7 percent) were a result of the burden of Jewish taxes paid to the state: one needed to pay the Jewish general clerks to calculate the taxes; because of the duty to apportion the taxes among the various provinces, the commissions of the *va'ad* had to hold meetings that lasted for months and cost a fortune in per diems.

But all this relates only to the net budget of the *va'ad*. Regarding the full budget of the *va'ad*, in which the head tax alone amounts to 200,000 złoty, the expenses of the central autonomous body for positive purposes, for social help (including even the subsidies for building schools!), amount to not even one-hundredth (precisely 0.8 percent!)!

Here the true nature of the Jewish central autonomy in former Poland reveals itself. It was nothing more than an auxiliary apparatus of the nobility and state to extract special taxes from the Jewish population. The costs of supporting that apparatus imposed a new, heavy load on the shoulders of the impoverished Jewish masses.

Introduction Notes:
1. R. Mahler, "A budzhet fun vaad arba arotses in 18tn yorhundert" [A budget of the Council of Four Lands in the eighteenth century], *YIVO bleter* XV, no. 1–2 (January–February 1940): 63–86 (abridged and tables omitted).

Article Notes:
1. See the works by Dr. Y. Shiper: Ignaz Schipper, "Beiträge zur Geschichte der partiellen Judentage in Polen um die Wende des XVII. u. XVIII. Jahrhunderts bis zur Auflösung des jüdischen Parlamentarismus (1764)," *Monatsschrift für Geschichte und Wissenschaft des Judentums* 56 (N. F. 20), no. 7/8 (July/August 1912): 458–77; Y. Shiper, "Poylishe regestn tsu der geshikhte funem vaad arba arotses" [Polish abstracts of the Council of Four Lands], *Historishe shriftn fun yivo* I (1929): cols. 88–114; and especially Yitskhok Shiper, "Finantsyeler khurbn fun der tsentraler un provintsyeler oytonomye fun yidn in altn poyln, 1650–1764," *Ekonomishe shriftn fun yivo* II (1932): 1–19 [see Selection 4 below].

Certain interesting details about the expenses of the *va'ad* in the seventeenth century are found in Israel Heilprin, "Heshbonot va'ad arba' aratzot b'Polin (mi-Pinkas Tiktin)" [Accounts of the Council of Four Lands (from the Pinkas of Tiktin)], *Tarbits: Le-Made'i Ha-Ru'ah* 6 (1935).

2. The shelf mark of these materials: A. G. Dział: Skarbowe. Akta ogółowe pogłównego żydowskiego Nr. 2, 22–24.

3. *Volumina legum* 4 (St. Petersburg: Jozafata Ohryzki, 1860), 36, 142.

4. The so-called "permanent budget" or "precise pay" of Crown Poland, which was applied exclusively to the military, was instituted in 1717 in the sum of close to five million. This sum was to be covered by the general head tax and the winter-tax for the military (*hyberne*).

5. The figures for revenues from the *Kwarta* and for the state budget in Poland in the eighteenth century are taken from T. Korzon, *Wewnętrzne dzieje Polski za Stanisłwà August, 1764–1794* [Internal history of Poland under Stanisław August], vol. 3 (Kraków: L. Zwoliński, 1897), 130, 134.

6. Regarding taxes that Jews paid in the former Poland, see: Y. Schiper's article "Jewish Taxes" in *Istoria jewrejskawo naroda* [History of the Jewish nation], vol. 11 (Moscow: Mir, 1914). The accounts of the *va'ad* for the region of Tiktin from 1694 indicate that the Jews also paid the winter-tax for the military, *hyberne*. See: I. Heilprin, *Accounts*, 531.

7. M. Bersohn, *Dyplomataryusz dotyczący żydów w dawnej Polsce na źródłach archiwalnych osnuty: (1388–1782)* [A diplomatic treatise on Jews in old-time Poland based on archival sources] (Warsaw: Nicz, 1910), 210–11 (document no. 370).

8. In the budget of the *va'ad* for 1739, which was published by Dr. Schiper, a summary line item shows 14,000 złoty for annual salaries of state officials.

9. See Y. Shiper, "Poylishe regestn . . . [Polish Abstracts . . .]," *Historishe shriftn fun yivo* I (1929): 108.

10. See, for example, our article on Jews in Hrubaszów, *Encyclopaedia Judaica* 8 (Berlin: Eschkol, 1931), 262–63.

11. Yitskhok Rivkind noted correctly that the etymology of *Kozubalets* is "Kvassabilis" (that which trembles), i.e., the charge for playing dice. R' Zalman Zvi of Aufhausen in his *Yudisher Teriak*, "Dice and Kozibales" (Hanau: Zelikman, 1615). See Y. Rivkind, "Mas ha-Kubiya" ["The dice tax in connection with the tax of disgrace. A chapter in Jewish persecution"], *Zion* 1 (1935): 37–48.

12. M. Balaban, *Historja i Literatura Żydowska ze szczególnem uwzględnieniem Żydów w Polsce* [Jewish history and literature with special emphasis on Jews in Poland], vol. 3 (Lwów: Zakładu Narodowego im. Ossolińskich, 1924), 174.

13. H. Kołłątaj, *Stan oświecenia w Polsce w ostatnich latach panowania Augusta III (1750–1764)* [The state of enlightenment in Poland in the last years of August III's reign] (Warsaw: Gebethner i Wolff, 1905), 118.

14. The meeting of the *va'ad* took place in Jarosłów in 1725. Thereafter, the executive of the *va'ad* met in Rychwał to make the accounting of taxes for the various provinces.

15. Y. Shiper, "Finantsyeler khurbn," 2 (table 2).

16. *Pinkas Medinat-Lite* (1628), rule 98.

4

The Financial Collapse of the Central and Provincial Autonomy of the Jews in Old-Time Poland, 1650–1764

by Ignacy Schiper, 1932

IGNACY SCHIPER (1884–1943, see also Selection 8 below) was born in Tarnów, Austrian Galicia (today in Poland), and received his Juris Doctor degree from the Jagiellonian University in Kraków in 1907. A member of the older generation of Polish Jewish historians, he was a transitional figure in the emergence of historical writing in Yiddish. His principal interests were economic and cultural history. The first found expression in his *Economic History of the Jews of Poland in the Middle Ages*, which he published in Polish in 1911 and reissued in Yiddish in 1926. In the preface to the Yiddish edition, he declares:

> For twenty years the author occupied himself with scholarly Jewish historical research, and for nearly as long lasted the *Goles* (exile, Diaspora) of his works that were published in Polish, German, Russian, and English and which, because of language, could not be integrated into the consciousness of that broad circle of Jewish readers for whom they were originally created.... The strong interest that the Jewish reading public evinced in recent years regarding serious scholarly works in Yiddish made clear to the author that the time for which he had waited so long had become ripe.[1]

Schiper's second principal interest found expression in his *Cultural History of the Jews of Poland in the Middle Ages*, published in Yiddish in 1926 with the explanation that the first half had appeared previously in Polish, but that the remainder was newly composed in Yiddish. This turn to Yiddish occurred partly at the urging of his student, Emanuel Ringelblum, who was also his chief translator. Thereafter, Schiper wrote almost exclusively in Yiddish, which influenced the members of the *Yunger historiker krayz* (Young Historians Circle), organized in Warsaw by Ringelblum, to do the same during the 1920s and 1930s. During his final years, which he endured in the Warsaw ghetto, he attempted to continue his prewar studies until he was deported and killed at Majdanek.

The following article presents the results of Schiper's original research on the causes and consequences of the financial collapse that ultimately led the Polish government to abolish the institutions of Jewish autonomy.[2] (All of the financial documents mentioned in the article are available in the original article—in both Yiddish and in German translation.)

The Financial Decline of the Central Jewish Federation

In the frightful decade 1648–1658, when Poland was inundated by the "Flood" (the Cossack Uprising and the wars with Sweden, the Muscovites, etc.), the financial backbone of Polish Jewry was broken. The reconstruction that was undertaken by the Jewish autonomous bodies when the "Flood" was over could only be conducted with the help of credit. The treasuries of the communities and "lands" [of the Council of Four Lands] stood empty, the debts were altogether immense, and outside help was impossible because Western Jewry had not yet recovered from the wounds of the Thirty Years War and was overburdened by the tens of thousands of refugees from Poland who wandered the whole world.

Seeking financial support for reconstruction, the autonomous institutions of Polish Jewry had to find local capital and, to the extent it was possible, also think about foreign loans.

Detailed budgets of the central federation are first known to us from the first half of the eighteenth century, and, when we consider the entries for expenses, we find it is possible to separate them into the following principal types: a) the head tax that had to be paid each year to the state treasury; b) salaries and gifts for high officials; c) salaries for employees of the central federation; d) extraordinary expenses (for all manner of protection from danger); e) expenses connected with convening the *Va'ad Arba' Aratzot* or its commissions; f) other expenses (for charitable purposes, support for school systems, etc.). According to the magnitude of the entries, we may estimate that two tasks constituted the chief difficulty, namely: collecting the head tax and assembling the large sums associated with the activity of the general *shtadlan* (intercessor/lobbyist).

Finding coverage for these unavoidable expenses so soon after the "Flood" was a matter that surpassed the financial abilities of the destitute Polish Jews, and at the same time it also became clear that the financial collapse of the central federation did not arise from the debts incurred in the eighteenth century but mainly from debts incurred in . . . the period from 1666 to 1697. . . .

As we see, in these three decades, the central federation borrowed a total debt of 126,676 złoty and 12,120 thalers, of which 100,676 złoty came from Catholic clerics and the rest from secular capitalists (26,000 złoty and 12,120 thalers). How much the central federation borrowed at the same time from their "own people," namely, from wealthy Jews and from Jewish communities, is not known, but one can suppose it also drew on this source. For the loans the federation received from Catholic clerics, they paid 8 percent and more. Thus, for example, we are informed that the loan of 15,026 złoty, which it received in 1697 from the Dominicans of Targowica, included interest of 3,000 złoty from the prior loan of 1677, and that the federation therefore paid 8 percent. But we also have information that it once cost the general *shtadlan* as much as 30 percent when he urgently needed money. The debts and interest increased, and the longer it continued, the harder they were to pay. The difficulties are best illustrated for us by the budget of the Jewish central federation that is extant from 1739 and was assembled by the finance commission of the *Va'ad Arba' Aratzot* [Council of Four Lands] in agreement with the commissioner of the Polish treasurer. . . .

Of the debts [noted above] only two were paid in 1739, namely, 26,000 złoty and 12,120 thaler, which had been received from secular capitalists, while continuing to pay interest for the debts incurred between 1677 and 1697 from Jesuits and Dominicans. For the first time, we catch a glimpse of the monetary claims by individual Jews against the central federation—that is to say, a debt of 14,192 złoty was recorded in the extant budget from the following year as having been incurred from Jews. Besides this, debts to Jews were also recorded, from which the annual interest amounted to 1,699 złoty. . . . On debts to Jews, the federation paid as much as 30 percent (4,260 złoty interest on capital of 14,192), from which one can presume that the interest of 1,699 złoty was for a loan amounting to 5,633 złoty. Together with the indicated 14,192 złoty, the federation therefore owed various Jews 19,855 złoty.

In the following year, in 1740, the debt burden of the central federation increased with fresh debts that were incurred from Jews and Christians. They were undertaken for the sake of the expenses of the *Va'ad Arba' Aratzot* incurred in 1739, as well as for the protection money that had to be paid while a session of the Sejm [Polish parliament] took place in Warsaw.

In 1741, the budget of the central federation, including the federation's debts, amounted to nearly a half-million złoty, and debt service was projected at 304,576 złoty. The central federation suffered from the deficit, which came to 169,830 złoty, until its demise in 1764. It was unable to reduce the debt but instead constantly had to incur new debts. In the tragic year of 1764, when the Polish Sejm passed a resolution to put an end to the existence of the central federation and the "lands," the debts and obligations of the central federation, according to the records of the liquidation court, represented 183,843 złoty.[1]

The Financial Ruin of the Autonomous Lands (*Aratzot*) (1650–1764)

In the period under discussion, the financial distress of the autonomous lands was much greater than that of the central federation. The most important source that illustrates for us the financial ruin of the lands is the minutes of the liquidation court that the Polish Sejm ordered in 1764 to establish the debts of the central and provincial autonomous bodies of the Polish Jews and find a means of taxation for liquidating the debts. On the basis of these records, which we found in the Warsaw main archives, and also with the help of other, secondary sources, we will attempt here to further reconstruct a picture of the financial decline.

We will separate the materials according to the lands as they existed just before the demise of the provincial autonomy. . . . [followed by detailed discussions and tables of the debts of each of the four lands]

The Financial Collapse of the Central and Provincial Autonomy of the Jews

Summary

On the basis of the figures we presented here, . . . it is possible to assemble the following picture of the financial need that prevailed in the central and provincial autonomous organizations of Polish Jews in the period when its fate was set by the famous resolution of the Polish Sejm of 1764.

The debts of the central and provincial autonomy amounted to more than 2.5 million Polish złoty. Of this, the lands owed 2,312,746 złoty, and the central federation 188,843 złoty.

Of the 2.5 million debt, more than 1.5 million was owed to Christian clerics and secular powers. Of the nearly 900,000 złoty owed to Jewish creditors, almost 400,000 was owed to communities, and the rest to individual proprietors, salaried employees, yeshivas, etc. Of the 872,477 złoty in *claims from clerics, nearly half stemmed from the second half of the seventeenth century.*

Of the 872,477 złoty that the central federation and the lands owed to Christian clerics, the Jesuits and Dominicans alone claimed 472,743 złoty, 54 percent of the total sum. . . .

Of the debts to the nobility, which altogether amounted to 737,468 złoty, nearly 90 percent was claimed by six [noblemen, listed by amount]. Their composition reveals to us a detail that is very interesting for cultural history. It shows, namely, that the lands were able to borrow large sums only from the magnates of the eastern borderlands of Poland, i.e., from the Potockis, Osolińskis, Lubomirskis, Czackis, etc., who generally ruled in the Ukrainian Polish provinces.

★ ★ ★

The millions in debt of the central and provincial autonomies that we have dealt with here at length are a reflection of the financial ruin that prevailed in the eighteenth century in the communities. According to incidental information that has reached us, the debts of the communities in the same period surpassed by *several* fold the indebtedness of the lands and of the central federation. . . . Small communities, for example, Wronki, Inowrocław (Lesle), Drohobycz, were much more indebted than other smaller lands. In the four largest communities—Poznań, Liso, Kraków, and Lwów—the debts amounted to almost as much as the debts of all the lands combined.

The largest debts, which lay like a heavy weight on the Jewish autonomy, had already provoked unrest among the non-Jewish creditors in the eighteenth century. An interesting illustration of the mood that prevailed among the clerics and magnates in connection with the Jewish debt problem is given to us by the Sejm debates in 1746 and 1748, when a proposal to raise the Jewish head tax was debated. The majority of speakers came out against the proposal, expressing a fear that an increased tax burden would cause Jews to start to leave the country, which would place a question mark over the possibility of collecting not only the taxes but also the cash debts. Thus, Duke Czartoriski complained during the debates in 1746 "that as soon as one imposes heavy taxes on the Jews, they will incur new debts and then disappear from the towns."[2] In 1748, the marshal of the Sejm again warned that "at present one should not drive the birds (=Jews) from the country" (by imposing larger taxes).[3]

The opposite view was held by Duke Lubomirski. In a speech during the same session, he pointed out that "there is no basis for fearing that the Jews will flee from Poland because of taxes," and he brought as an example the Arians [dissenting Christian sect]. When the Polish republic imposed high taxes on the Arians, they, to be frank, all emigrated to Prussia . . . [ellipsis in original], but with the Jews it is entirely different because we are not indebted to the Jews like we were to the Arians, but instead we lend sums to the Jews. The proof: the large claims that the nobility and the clerical orders have against the communities, *which have led us to endeavor earnestly to protect the Jews so they will not run away from us.*"[4] Other deputies expressed the view that one could demand greater taxes from the Jews if one set aside the regime of the community heads because it "ought to be known that, from the sums that the community heads demanded from the communities and subcommunities, they themselves become rich, while the communities fall into great despair."[5] It would therefore be worthwhile—thought the majority of the deputies at the Sejm of 1746—that "to secure the taxes and the claims that exist against the communities and village Jews, one should transform the Jews into *annexi glebae*"[6] (i.e., "bound to the land" that lies *directly* under the control of the authorities, instead of the direct control of the autonomous Jewish bodies). Such a resolution, according to the Polish constitution, required unanimity, but it was not possible to reach a unanimous resolution, and "it remained as of old, that the Jews should belong *ut antea* (exactly as before) to their autonomous organizations.[7] Unanimity also eluded the subsequent Sejms. There were always one or more deputies who made use of the famous right of *liberum veto* and the matter was not able to move forward. Regarding those deputies, one would hear such expressions as: "Whoever speaks in favor of the Jews, already received something in hand." Yet, regarding the Jews' opponents as well, it was said, "Whoever speaks against the Jews, he *hopes* to receive something in hand. . ."[8] [ellipsis in original] With the help of bribery the Jews were once again able to rescue the autonomy. But with time it became ever more difficult to create "gifts" for the deputies and to secure their *protektsia*. Ultimately, the "silver bullets" were lacking and the Jews lost the battle they had conducted for the existence of the central and provincial autonomy. In 1764, in the Polish Sejm there was finally unanimity in favor of ending the Jewish central federation, as well as ending the autonomous "lands." At the same time, it was decided to collect the head tax from the Jews directly through state agencies. Regarding the debts, it was resolved "that all the heads of the lands must attend the quarter-annual term of the finance commission that would take place in February 1765 and bring with them all documents, bank notes, and record books related to the debts in order to establish—when necessary, also through oaths—the size of the claims and a means shall be devised for how the Jews will cover the debts."[9]

The finance commission of the Sejm, which became a sort of liquidation tribunal for the purpose of liquidating the central and provincial bodies of the Jewish autonomy, actually began its work not in February, but in May 1765. In the treatment that we have conveyed here to the public, we used *for the first time* the enormous material that was assembled by the commission during the proceedings with the heads of the communities and creditors.

Introduction Notes:

1. Yitskhok Shiper, *Virtshaftsgeshikhte fun di yidn in poyln beysn mitlalter* [Economic history of the Jews in Poland during the Middle Ages] (Warsaw: Ch. Brzoza, 1926), 9–10 (introduction, dated March 1924).

2. Yitskhok Shiper, "Finantsyeler khurbn fun der tsentraler un provintsyeler oytonomye fun yidn in altn poyln, 1650–1764," *Ekonomishe shriftn fun yivo* II (1932): 1–19 (1–7 and 17–19 quoted; abridged and tables omitted).

Article Notes:

1. *Likwidacja długów*, etc., Warsaw main archive [verbatim].

2. Władysław Konopczyński, *Dyaryusz Sejmu z r. 1746* [Sejm diary of 1746] (Warsaw: Towarzystwo Naukowego Warszawskiego, 1912), 175–76.

3. Idem, *Dyaryusz Sejmu z r. 1748* (1911), 230.

4. Ibid., 231.

5. Konopczyński, *Dyaryusz Sejmu 1746*, 248.

6. Ibid., 158–59.
7. Ibid.
8. Ibid., 176:"Kto mówl za Żydem, musial coś wziąć, kto przeciwko niemu, spodziewa się co wziąć" [Whoever spoke for the Jew had to take something, whoever spoke against him expected to take something].
9. *Volumina legum* 7 (1860), fol. 44–50.

5
The Central Representative Bodies of the Jews in the Grand Duchy of Warsaw, 1807–1816
by Artur Eisenbach, 1938

ARTUR EISENBACH (1906–1992) was born in Nowy Sącz, Austrian Galicia (today in Poland). He studied Polish Jewish history at the University of Warsaw, but did not complete his doctorate, and was active in the Young Historians Circle founded by Emanuel Ringelblum (his brother-in-law). He survived the Nazi occupation in the Soviet Union (losing his wife and daughter) and upon his return to Poland in 1946 joined the Central Jewish Historical Commission. For a decade, he devoted himself to Holocaust research and then returned to the general study of Polish Jewish history, serving from 1966 to 1968 as director of the Jewish Historical Institute in Warsaw.

Before the Holocaust, Eisenbach's chief interest had been an intended dissertation on the history of the Jews in the Grand Duchy of Warsaw, the regime controlled by Napoleon in central Poland. Portions of his work were published in various Yiddish journals. The article that follows is the chapter that describes the attempt by Jews to reestablish aspects of the former communal autonomy during the Napoleonic period.[1]

In this study, we will present the efforts by the representatives of the Jewish population in the Grand Duchy of Warsaw (1807–1815) to reconstitute the central and provincial bodies of Jewish autonomy.

During the short existence of the new Polish state, reestablishing these bodies of the Jewish communities was never envisioned. The provincial and state *va'adim* [councils] that arose in the period of the Grand Duchy of Warsaw are linked—both in their organizational forms and in their authorities—to the tradition of the *Va'ad Arba' Aratzot* [Council of Four Lands], but at the same time they already bear the stamp of changed social and political conditions. . . .

On July 6, 1764, the Polish Sejm [parliament] abolished the central and provincial bodies of Jewish autonomy—the *Va'ad Arba' Aratzot* and *va'ade ha-galil* [regional councils]. Of the manifold branches of Jewish autonomy in Poland, only the first level, the local community, continued to exist and retain its former authorities in all matters of internal Jewish life.

However, the traditional ties between the local Jewish communities were still sufficiently strong that, despite the formal liquidation enacted by the parliamentary decision mentioned above, when necessary, delegates from the communities assembled in joint meetings to consider the newly created situation. Thus, we know, for example, that after the First Partition of Poland in 1772 provincial *va'adim* were held among representatives of the Jewish communities from the territories that were taken by Prussia. The *va'adim* were held in Złatów, Schneidemühl, and Chodecz, and the leaders there were engaged in apportioning collection of the Jewish tax.[1]

During the Four-Year Parliament (1788–1792), when the deputies were engaged in developing projects for reforms regarding the Jewish Question, an illegal meeting was convened of representatives from Lithuanian communities in Želva on August 24, 1791. From the appeal published by the Lithuanian *va'ad*, we discover that it had undertaken relevant steps regarding the matter of Jewish reforms and attempted to raise the necessary funds for lobbying.[2] We also have information that, at the same time that the Lithuanian *va'ad* took place, representatives of the Jewish communities in Crown Poland assembled in Warsaw and conducted negotiations with the private secretary of King Stanisław Poniatowski, Scipione Piattoli, regarding the proposals for Jewish reforms. They attempted through him to convince the king and the Sejm deputies that, in the proposals introduced in the Sejm, the interests of the Jewish population should be taken into consideration. . . .

In preparing proposed laws for taxes for the first Sejm in the Duchy of Warsaw, the government resolved to centralize the various Jewish taxes and in their place introduce one general tax for the Jewish population, which would be easier to collect in such a manner. First, the government council set the overall amount of tax the Jews would need to pay at 2,400,000 złoty per year, later raised to 3,300,000 złoty per year.[3] Based on experience from the Austrian provinces [of partitioned Poland], the finance minister proposed introducing a kosher slaughter tax in the entire duchy in an amount that would bring in the anticipated amount of tax. Assuming that 40,177 Jewish families lived in the Duchy of Warsaw,[4] and that each family consumed an average of eight pounds of meat each week, altogether 16,713,632 pounds per year, and counting a charge of 6 groszy for a pound of meat, the revenue from the kosher meat tax would amount [at 30 groszy per złoty, at that time] to 3,342,726 złoty. Annually, apart from the revenue from slaughtering fowl,[5] the finance minister's proposal was adopted by the government council at the meeting of March 1,[6] and it was validated on March 18, 1809, by the plenum of the Sejm.[7]

According to the royal decree of March 25, 1809, the kosher meat tax would be issued by means of a public auction for the *arenda* [leasehold] in each department.[8] The leaseholder would also take care of collecting the tax. The overall amounts of tax set for the various six departments (according to the number of Jewish families in each department),[9] actually exceeded the ability of the impoverished Jewish population to pay at that time (the average annual [total] tax amount of each family amounted to 84 złoty and was over four times greater than in the Austrian provinces). In nearly no department was it possible to reach the auctioned sum. These difficulties in leasing out the slaughter tax were influenced in large measure by the concurrent political conditions, the war between the Napoleonic Duchy of Warsaw and Austria, and the resulting uncertain fate of the duchy itself.

These difficulties in leasing out the Jewish tax had already been anticipated by the government in the decree of March 25, 1809 (art. 5), which said explicitly that if "the amount anticipated by the calculated consumption was not reached" in the auction of the slaughter tax, the amount would be imposed on the Jewish population of the given department. In actuality, this decision converted the indirect consumption tax into a direct tax on the Jewish population. According to the later executive orders of the finance minister,[10] the prefects, on the basis of statistical tables, apportioned the annual sum among the various regions (*powiats*) in accordance with the number of Jewish families. The subprefects in turn, together with the heads of each *kehila* [community], divided the amounts among the individual Jewish families. The leaders of the *kehila* would take up collecting the tax. Consequently, they were personally responsible to the government for the entire amount of tax that fell on all members of the given *kehila*. In making the *kehila* leadership responsible for the taxes, the finance minister allowed them to excommunicate "recalcitrant" members of the community. According to article 7 of the decree of May 31, 1809, the *kehila* leadership was permitted to put in *herem* [excommunication] anyone who refused to pay the slaughter tax. . . . [quoting the actual text in Polish] In addition, the local administrative government was to come to the aid of the *kehila* in all necessary cases.

In giving the *kehila* the right of excommunication along with responsibility for the slaughter tax, the government in effect restored the old Jewish *kehila* and its fields of authority. While the Prussian government was entering into direct contact with the Jewish population in all matters and abolished the guarantee by the *kehila* for the taxes of its members, the government of the Duchy of Warsaw—contrary to its general policy as a centralized state—reintroduced the guarantee of the *kehila* and allowed it to make use of the *herem*. This fact not only strengthened the government and prestige of the *kehila* but also stimulated, as we will see later, the organization of the central body of Jewish communities in the country. . . . [followed by fifty pages on specific developments]

Closing Remarks

On the basis of the materials presented above, we come to the conclusion that at the time of the Duchy of Warsaw there existed central and provincial autonomous bodies which, according to their organization, were similar to the analogous institutions in old-time Poland.[11]

The ground floor of the autonomous structure was formed by the *kehilot* and their leadership. All the *kehilot* of a region (*powiat*) maintained close contact. Aside from the larger *kehilot*, just as in old-time Poland, there existed sub-*kehilot* (*przykahałki*). The *kehila* leadership represented the Jewish population of the given "parish," which usually included a city with ten or so surrounding villages. All *kehilot* of a region were represented—with regard to government agencies and internal Jewish relations—by one or two regional delegates, who necessarily must not come from the regional city. The Jewish delegates from the various regions would meet or communicate with each other about electing department delegates (ordinarily two, in some cases four to six delegates) who would represent the Jewish population of the entire department. We also encounter delegations of groups of departments, such as from the four Galician or Western departments. A meeting of delegates from all departments would take place only at a nationwide *va'ad*, which was the highest Jewish representative body in the country. At its meetings, various questions (chiefly financial) were considered, and it intervened and negotiated with the central state agencies about various matters pertaining to the Jewish population. On the basis of research to date, it is possible to ascertain that such general *va'adim* took place almost every year: those planned for fall 1809, summer 1810, two in 1811 (summer and winter), and the last about which we have information, in spring 1814.

These *va'adim* should not, however, be considered a continuation of the institution of *Va'ad Arba' Aratzot* with all its areas of authority. Formally, the central and provincial autonomous bodies had been abolished by the decision of the Sejm in 1764 (they actually ceased to exist much later). Here we are just in the stage of crystallizing a new form of Jewish representative body, central and provincial, that needed to be suited to the changed political conditions and the centralized character of the state.

In fact, the initiative to restore these autonomous bodies always originated with the Jewish representatives and not governmental spheres, and only for the sake of legalization purposes was the effort made to have the finance minister convene a meeting of the delegates to the department.[12] On the other hand, fiscal interests aroused in the government an interest in supporting these autonomous bodies and thereby helping the Jewish oligarchs reestablish their authority over the Jewish masses. In old-time Poland, the main factor that led to the emergence of Jewish autonomy, besides fiscalism, was the nature of social positions in the Polish state. Like the clerics, nobility, and (non-Jewish) city-dwellers, the Jews also had various autonomous bodies that organized all inner Jewish life. Conversely, in the Duchy of Warsaw, the constitution enforced a (formal) leveling of all social positions that gave equality of political and civil rights to all classes. The centralized character of the Duchy of Warsaw, in contrast with the decentralization of old-time Poland, did not prepare the ground for restoring the central body of Jewish autonomy, even in limited form. Only for fiscal purposes was the authority of the *kehila* now broadened and a central, Jewish representative body created.

Naturally, on that account at the same time, the character and authority of the nationwide *va'ad* had to change. Although it constituted a central representative body for the entire Jewish population, represented it before departmental and central state agencies, intervened in its name with the king and ministers on economic and political questions, and met during the deliberations of the Sejm and influenced the course of its negotiations, it nevertheless had limited areas of authority in comparison with the authorities of a "Council of the Land." It had broader rights only in tax questions and, since the beginning of 1812, also the right to distribute the overall amount of recruiting tax set by the finance minister. The departmental delegates were thus enlisted as auxiliary agents in the finance administration and consequently came in regular contact with the finance minister, just like the former trustees with the treasurer in old-time Poland. Besides this, as we already know, the *kehilot* were also enlisted as auxiliaries in the general administration and had the duty to keep books of statistics of the Jewish population.

Was the form of these central and provincial Jewish bodies affected by external, particularly French, influences? Influences from French legislation can be ascertained not only in the July Constitution, Napoleonic Civil Code, and in the organization and names of the administrative government agencies but also in the proposal about reforming the Jewish Question. The Great Sanhedrin of Paris (from February 9 to March 9, 1808) and the regulations in Napoleon's decree of March 17, 1808, regarding the organization of the Jewish consistories found a resounding echo in the Duchy of Warsaw. Bielowski had already made the giving of certain rights to Jews dependent on whether they would adopt the laws of the Paris Sanhedrin in his proposal for a Polish constitution.[13] The Polish "Jacobins" suggested sending a few secularly inclined Jews to Paris, who would, after acquainting themselves with the works of the Sanhedrin, work on reforming the Jews. . . .[14]

Thus, it is possible to ascertain influences of French legislation about the Jews on the Jewish Question in Poland. Nevertheless, they affected only the Polish statesmen who developed proposals for reforms on the Jewish Question and had no direct influence on the form of the provincial and central Jewish representative bodies. Those influences one must seek in the Jewish autonomous institutions of the former independent Poland.

Introduction Notes:

1. A. Ayzenbakh, "Di tsentrale reprezentans-organen fun di yidn in varshever firshtentum (1807–1815)," *Bleter far geshikhte* II (Warsaw, 1938): 33–88 (33–41 and 85–88 quoted; abridged and table omitted).

Article Notes:

1. Louis Lewin, *Die Landessynode des Grosspolnischen Judenschaft* (Frankfurt a. M.: Kauffmann, 1926), 64.

2. E. N. Frenk, *ha-Ironim veha-Yehudim be-Polin* [The townspeople and the Jews in Poland] (Warsaw: Ha-Zefirah, 1921), 107–8.

3. *Akta Rady Stanu X. W.*, vol. 228, fol. 3; *Protokoły posiedzeń Rady Stanu X. W., Akta Ogólne*, vol. 85sz., fol. 35 sesja z dn. 1 lutego [March] 1809 r.

4. The actual number of Jewish families was much smaller. In other apportionments, a number of 39,777 Jewish families was taken as the basis for all calculations. *A. S. Koszerne* K. 5, t. I, fol. 12.

5. *Akta Radt Stanu X. W.*, vol. 228, fol. 1. Report of the finance minister of February 14, 1809, on Jewish taxes.

6. Ibid., 6, 9, 13.

7. M. Handelsman, *Dziennik posiedzeń izby poselskiej sejma r. 1809* [Journal of the session of the Chamber of Deputies of the Sejm 1809] (Warsaw: Towarzystwa Naukowego Warszawskiego, 1913), 25.

8. *Dziennik Praw Księstwa Warszawskiego* [Journal of Laws of the Duchy of Warsaw] t. II, st. 34. *Akta Rady Stanu X. W.*, vol. 228, fol. 30.

9. The apportionment of the overall amount of tax among the various departments was set by the royal decree of April 20, 1809: *A. A. D. Ak. Rady St.*, vol. 228, fol. 24.

10. *Akta Rady Stanu X. W.*, vol. 228, fol. 49, 53; *A. S. Koszerne*, K. 5, t. I, fol. 11, 13. Formal decrees of the finance minister of May 13 and August 30, 1809.

11. Y. Shiper, "Der tsuzamenshtel fun 'vaad arba' arotses'" [The composition of the Council of Four Lands], *Historishe shriftn fun yivo* I (1929): 72–73.

12. It occurred in former times as well that the finance minister convened the *Va'ad Arba' Aratzot*. See Y. Shiper, "Poylishe regestn tsu der geshikhte fun vaad arba arotses" [Polish abstracts on the history of the Council of Four Lands] *Historishe shriftn* I (1929), 97 (re the year 1753).

13. G. Bielowski, "Projekt do Konstytucji narodu polskiego' [A draft for the constitution for the Polish nation], (Warsaw: n.p., 1807), quoted from M. Handelsman, *Studja Historyczne* (Warsaw: E. Wende i Spółka, 1911).

14. Szaniawski Józef Kalasanty, *Korespondencya w materyach obraz Kraiu i Narodu polskiego roziaśniaiących* [Correspondence in matters that illuminate the image of the country and the Polish nation] (Warsaw: Gazety Warszawskiey, 1807), 19.

6
The Warsaw Kehila under the Leadership of Dr. Ludwik Natanson, 1871–1896
by Jacob Shatzky, 1953

JACOB SHATZKY (1893–1956, see also Selections 24 and 46 below), historian of Polish Jewry, was born in Warsaw and received his doctorate for a dissertation on nineteenth-century Polish Jewish history from the University of Warsaw in 1922. In 1925, he settled in New York, where he was a founder and leading member of the American Branch of YIVO (Yiddish Scientific Institute, in Vilna) and in 1929 was employed as director of the library of the New York Psychiatric Institute. When YIVO transferred its headquarters to New York in 1940, Shatzky became head of the YIVO Historians' Circle. He worked almost exclusively in Yiddish and focused chiefly on the history of Yiddish-speaking Jews in Poland and the Ashkenazi diaspora, reflected in such topics as Yiddish literature, theater, press, education, Dutch Jewry, Latin American Jewry, and Jewish historiography.

Shatzky's magnum opus was his *History of the Jews of Warsaw*, published in Yiddish in three volumes from 1937 to 1953 (leaving unfinished a fourth and final volume). The work covers political, social, economic, and cultural aspects of Warsaw Jewry from the early fifteenth to late nineteenth centuries and is especially noteworthy for integrating multiple currents of events, influences, and personalities. An example is the chapter quoted here on the Warsaw *kehila* during the late nineteenth century, which is centered on the chief rabbi of the time.[1] In his review, Isaiah Trunk stated: "Shatzky shows us historical events through the lens of living and active people.... He sketches them and illuminates them with a deep, inner connection as if he were their contemporary (and he is indeed a fellow Varsovian). He penetrates deeply into the thoughts and actions that can be understood and evaluated correctly only if one thinks with the mentality of the period."[2]

The years when authority in the *kehila* lay in the hands of adherents of the Enlightenment, and some *misnagdim* [non-Hasidic Orthodox Jews] who went along with them, were the years of greatest growth and impressive activity, which no one denied. This was due above all to the chairman himself, Dr. Ludwik Natanson (1822–1896).

Among the seven sons of Zelig Natanson, Ludwik Natanson was the pride and joy of the family. The others were great businessmen and wealthy, powerful figures. He, however, was a prominent doctor and one of the very few community leaders who impressed both Jews and Poles.

Born in 1822, Ludwik Nathanson completed his secondary education at the Warsaw school for official state rabbis. In 1838 he left to study at the surgical-medical academy in Vilna. When it closed, he went to Dorpat [Tartu, Estonia] to continue his studies, which he completed in 1843. He settled in Warsaw and in 1847 became the founder and editor of *Gazeta Lekarska*, which was the best medical journal in Poland. The fact itself that a twenty-five-year-old doctor published a professional journal and considered this work to be an obligation to "patriotic medicine" greatly increased his prestige. The journal, which Natanson published until 1864, consumed much time and still more money. A man with a strongly developed sense of community, Natanson was one of the few social doctors in Poland. This clearly manifested itself in the years 1848–1852 when the cholera epidemic raged in Warsaw. He played a large part in fighting the epidemic and distinguished himself in the world of medicine. The Polish medical profession awarded him the best it could give: in 1863 he was chosen president of the Polish Medical Society.[1] As a communal worker, Natanson was a pragmatist. He had little regard for simple charity. He contended that the chief goal was to extricate Jews from panhandling and begging. Schools should be built for handicrafts and above all dedicate themselves to making the poorer Jewish classes in Warsaw productive. In the election for the *kehila* in 1871, of the 400 persons who paid a minimum of 15 rubles tax each year [to be eligible to vote], 308 participated. Such a small number of votes showed how easy it was to achieve victory. The government censor eliminated all strata except the adherents of the Enlightenment [*maskilim*] and the progressive *misnagdim*.[2]

The following were elected to the *kehila* executive: Dr. Ludwik Natanson; Mathias Berzon; Shmuel Portner (1809–1876); a banker, Leser-Levy; a collateral lender, Józef Poznanski; Jakub Lewenberg; and Hilary (Hillel) Nussbaum (1820–1895). Ludwik Natanson was elected chairman, and he occupied that position for twenty-five years until his death (1896).

The new executive was later considered to be thoroughly assimilated, but this is not correct. Some of the members were ordinary wealthy propertied Jews, only superficially Polonized. Besides Natanson, it was Hillel Nussbaum, the "Patriot of the 1863 Uprising" [and well-known early Polish Jewish historian], who gave the Jewish community a legitimizing stamp of Polishness.

In any event, the Polish press strongly approved of the new executive of "non-fanatics." This was apparent in the celebratory swearing-in ceremony for the new executive that took place on June 22, 1871, in the beautiful town hall chamber. It was said that not since 1861, when the celebratory declaration of "Polish Jewish Brotherhood" took place at the merchant association, had Warsaw seen such a representative ceremony.

Yet the holiday ended, and everyday life revealed a not-so-happy picture. The treasury of the *kehila* was empty and the debts frightfully large, with *kehila* officials owed several months' salary. It was determined that, even with an increased budget of 50,000 rubles, for which credit was due to Natanson's *shtadlones* [lobbying], the debts amounted to twice that much. The executive finished 1871 with an income of 17,000 rubles and a deficit of 35,000. Individual contributions from the trustees themselves succeeded in reducing the deficit. Above all, these leaders of the *kehila* refused their personal privilege as trustees of not paying the wealth tax. This gesture made a good impression, and it was noted that the wealthy trustees of the previous executive had not done so. . . .

In the course of this long regime, no opposition appeared. The press was loyal to the regime. Nahum Sokolow's *Ha-Tsefirah* [progressive Hebrew newspaper in Warsaw] coddled the *kehila* and always pleaded in its favor for the sake of the several *maskilic* ["enlightened"] raisins in the administrative cake [a pun by Shatzky, pairing "coddled" (*gekekhlt*) with "cake" (*kukhn*)]. No matter how undemocratic the composition of the regime may have been, no one denied the trustworthiness of its personnel and the substance of its results. The first shot at the *kehila* fortress was fired by a Hasid, one Zalman Krakoyer. In 1888 he brought an action against the *kehila* executive before the city president, contending that the proxies were not legal and the wealth tax threshold that entitled one to vote was unjust. The *kehila* won the trial in substance but lost in one detail. The city president ruled that the voters were not permitted to bring more than five proxies. With regard to lowering the wealth tax threshold so that more people could vote, the *kehila* won its argument.[3] The large Orthodox bourgeoisie did nothing to organize itself into an opposition. The Hasidic–*Misnagdic* conflict was truly constant. The press did not sympathize with Orthodoxy, not even the German Jewish press of the Frankfurt type that often wrote about *kehila* life in Warsaw. From those writings, the pious Jew in Warsaw would receive no pleasure, because the manner in which Natanson conducted the *kehila* was exactly to the liking of the pious Jews in Germany. They were greatly impressed with the sense of order and the organizational forms of the *kehila* departments. The same was true of the Russian Jewish press.[4] In truth, the number of new payers of the wealth tax rose each year, but a smaller portion had a desire to pay the minimum of fifteen rubles that entitled them to active and passive voting rights. To be a paying member of the community felt like a large expense, which was not much liked even by those who sought honor and wanted strongly to sit among the respectable fathers of the *kehila* executive.

The antidemocratic character of the governing body of the *kehila* also did not satisfy the more democratic assimilationists. The plutocratic spirit of the *va'ad ha-kehila* [community council] shocked them. Hillel Nussbaum, himself a former trustee, strongly opposed the system of choosing wealthy Jews: "It is generally not necessary," he wrote in 1879, "that the composition of the community should require men with money, because it is simply not the obligation of the members to give money from their own pocket . . ."[5]

Nussbaum contended that rich people should not occupy all the places in the *kehila* executive. "Progressive people of the average type" should be admitted—independent people who can allow themselves to give a few hours a day for the good of the *kehila*. Consequently, he proposed that truly progressive people should be chosen, but they ought to be popular figures—those to whom poor people at that time could have easier access.

There was a bit of truth in Nussbaum's analysis. The functional mechanism of the *kehila* regarding philanthropy was properly established, but it lacked the popular Jewish spirit. Even among the democratically minded "progressives," that spirit could not be found because they were far from the language and customs of the great Jewish folk masses. The ordinary Jewish person had no direct access to the leaders of the *kehila*. He would have to go through side channels by reaching out to the more pious communal workers, who were, in general, incidental rings in the bureaucratic chain of the *kehila*.

Sokolow, while he criticized the *kehila* leadership and demanded reforms, held that the "Polish European façade" of the *kehila* ought to remain because the *kehila* was *the* governing body of Polish Jewry. What disturbed him was that it lacked warmth when it came to doing kindnesses for the ordinary Jew.[6]

The *kehila* administration grew so much, with so many functions, that it became necessary to rely on paid officials. Despite their best intentions, the volunteer members of the charity section could not review so many requests and satisfy everyone.

In 1884, the *kehila* had 4,440 payers of the wealth tax. Of them, 200 paid between 60 and 150 rubles, 540 between 20 and 50 rubles, 1,700 between 5 and 15 rubles, and 2,000 between 2 and 4 rubles per year. In this way, 3,700 members of the *kehila* belonged to the middle and poorer classes and only 740 to the rich and wealthy classes. Only the 740 had a say in electing the trustees—indeed, twice as many as in 1871, but still a small minority. In 1891, this group of electors consisted of 1,206 members; in 1897 there were 1,350. The assimilationist group, however, always had a majority in this sector.[7]

Gradually, an opposition began to emerge, not, indeed, from among the pious but from the Lithuanian Jews. Yet it remained half silent, because there were not many Polish speakers among them. Many Lithuanian Jews from a generation earlier had assimilated and were already considered among the "Poles of the Mosaic faith."

The opposition had instances of impulsive excitement, but it was far from having a determined and internally harmonized program. The impressive activity of Natanson's regime covered many sins and deflected many demands and complaints. The growth of the *kehila* institutions spoke much more clearly. The Hebrew press—*Ha-Tsefirah* in Warsaw, *Ha-Magid* [in Prussia], and *Ha-Melitz* [in St. Petersburg]—seldom criticized the actions of the *kehila*. In 1881, the Warsaw statistician Zalewski asked Dr. Ludwik Natanson to appeal to the Jews to declare themselves Poles in the one-day census [of the Russian Empire]. Natanson raised the matter at a meeting of the *kehila*. A resolution was adopted to support the request of the Polish statistician. Consequently, they asked that those who were not willing to declare adherence to Polish nationality should at least refrain from listing any other nationality, Jewish included.

As a child of a period in which Jewish intelligence was more intelligence than Jewish, Natanson believed that Jews were not a nation. The Hebrew press did not criticize him for this, although it had already written widely and often about "Jewish national problems."

In the process of identifying himself with Jewish life, Natanson showed considerable comprehension of the principal problems of social need and constructive help. Like all positivists, he believed that the impediment to becoming "mit laytn glaykh" [not less than others; an equal among equals] lay in the Jews themselves, and he considered the Jewish problem to be purely social. In that respect, he was no innovator. Nevertheless, he became influential with his fervor and naturally democratic disposition, with his courage and firm attitude toward antisemitism and other occurrences in the life of the general community.

This was apparent in December 1881 during the pogrom. The head of the Warsaw *kehila* distinguished himself with his great personal virtues and steadfastness of character. The chief of police turned to him with a request that he "hold the Jews in check" because they had supposedly attacked Christians. Natanson replied to his letter by saying that the complaints had absolutely no basis.[8]

The greatest accomplishment of Ludwik Natanson's regime was the Jewish institutions that were built and that gave Jewish Warsaw the reputation it deserved. The people called Natanson "Warsaw Pharoah," yet he built Pithom and Ramses not with Jewish slaves but with Jewish money, which he was highly effective in extracting from the stingiest of the wealthy. He increased by tenfold the number of legacies, i.e., large donations left through wills as endowments for specific purposes. In his time (1878), the Great Synagogue on Tłomackie Square and the workshops for Jewish artisans were constructed. He planned the new hospital in the Czyste district of Warsaw, although he did not live to see it completed. Thanks to him, the spacious building of the *kehila* on Grzybowska Street was built, and the old building on Orle Street was given to the union of Jewish trade workers. The celebratory dedication ceremony for the cemetery building on Gensze Street and the *tahara* room [for ritual cleaning of the dead before burial] took place in July 1878. For this, Natanson obtained large sums from several individuals.

At the same time, the cemetery in the Praga neighborhood received a new *tahara* room. In 1870, he had abolished the Praga *kehila* and incorporated it into the Warsaw *kehila*. Heading the Praga *kehila* were Jews of the old generation who did not understand that a suburb of Warsaw needed to conduct itself in the same manner as the capital city itself. The *mikve* [ritual bath] was in frightful condition; the cemetery was nearly in ruins, without a fence or *tahara* room, which had burned down in 1874. In the course of three years, with a mighty hand [*yad hazakah*, the biblical term used in confronting Pharoah], Natanson conducted the necessary reforms and in this way silenced the pious opposition. He saw to the restoration of the historic synagogue on [Szeroka] Street, built by Rabbi Szmul Zbytkower. The old *mikve* was rebuilt, and Jewish Praga was raised to the same level as Warsaw. . . .[9]

Ludwik Natanson was also much occupied with education for Jewish children. In 1874 he attempted to obtain permission for a Jewish teachers' seminary. In 1878 he created the *realshul* [science-oriented secondary school] for the *kehila*, called Dickstein's School after its director, Samuel Dickstein. Ten years later, Natanson liquidated the school rather than accede to the government's demand that all studies be conducted in Russian [rather than Polish and Hebrew]. In 1879 he created the artisan workshops, which, starting in 1887, were located in a specially built structure. . . .

The twenty-five years of the Natanson regime were years when, from a provincial *kehila*, Jewish Warsaw was transformed into a metropolis. . . .

Introduction Notes:

1. Yankev Shatski, *Di geshikhte fun yidn in varshe*, vol. 3 (New York: YIVO, 1953), 118–29 (abridged).

2. Yeshaye Trunk, review of ibid., *YIVO bleter* XXXIX (1955): 299–300.

Article Notes:

1. Z. Kramsztyk, *Gazeta Lekarska* [Medical journal] XVI (1896): 631–34; J. Szwaicer, *Medycyna* XXIV (1896): 598–603; *Ateneum* III (Warsaw, 1878): 188–89; Wł. Konic, "Dr. Ludwik Natanson," *Głos Gminy Żydowskiej* [Jewish community bulletin] (1937): 4, 5; *Lu'ah*

Ahi'asaf [Ahi'asaf yearbook] V (1897). Ludvik Natanson married twice. His first wife was the daughter of Meir Berzon and died very young in 1849. His second wife was Natalya Epshteyn (1834–1891).

2. *Izrealita* (1871), 19. A list of revenues for 1871 appears in ibid., 29.

3. *Ha-Tsefirah* (1888), 131; *Niedielnaja chronika Woschoda* (1888), 17; *Israelita* (1888), 16.

4. Sliozberg, *Dela minuvshikh dnei: zapiski russkogo Evreia* [The deeds of bygone days: Notes of a Russian Jew], vol. 2 (Paris: n.p., 1933), 61.

5. Hilary Nussbaum, *Z teki weterana warszawskiej gminy starozakonnych* [From the portfolio of a veteran of the Warsaw Jewish community] (Warsaw: K. Kowalewskiego, 1880), 46–50.

6. N. Sokołów, *Zadania inteligencji żydowskiej* [Tasks of the Jewish intelligentsia] (Warsaw: J. Filipowicza, 1890).

7. *Ha-Asif* (1884/1885): 142–46; *Ha-Tsefirah* (1891), 57.

8. See the chapter [in the same book]: "The Rise of Antisemitism and the Pogrom of 1881."

9. According to Shloyme Grosglik's report in *Księga jubileuszowa Kurjera Porannego 1877–1902* [The anniversary book of Kurjer Poranny] (Warsaw: Kurjera Porannego, 1903), 219–25; W. Konic, *Głos Gminy Żydowskiej* [Jewish Community bulletin] (1937), 5; Jakub Platow (1800–1868) willed 12,000 rubles for a fence and *tahara* room in Praga, *Czas* 14 (1868).

7
Jewish "Autonomy": The Nazi-Imposed Jewish Councils
by Isaiah Trunk, 1949

ISAIAH TRUNK (1905–1981, see also Selections 15, 21, and 45 below) was born in Kutno, Poland. He received his master's degree in Jewish history from the University of Warsaw in 1929 and was active in the Young Historians Circle. During the Nazi occupation of Poland, he took refuge in the Soviet Union, where he was sent to a labor camp in the Soviet Far East for refusing Soviet citizenship, and on his return to Poland in 1946 became a member of the Central Jewish Historical Commission. After a brief period in Israel at Ghetto Fighters House, his principal postwar career was as a researcher and then chief archivist at YIVO in New York. In 1969, he earned his doctorate at the Jewish Teachers Seminary and People's University in New York with a dissertation, written in Yiddish, on Jewish life in the Nazi ghettos.

One of Trunk's continuing interests was Jewish autonomy in its various forms both before and during the Holocaust. This culminated in his major work *Judenrat* (1972) on the Nazi-imposed Jewish Councils in the ghettos (written in Yiddish but published in English), which received the National Book Award for history. Trunk viewed all instances of Jewish autonomy as being imposed for the benefit of the ruling power, and he traced commonalities among the benefits as well as detriments for the Jews from the medieval to Nazi periods. Although it has often been said that the study of Jewish life during the Holocaust, and especially Jewish leadership, emerged only in the early 1960s in response to the Eichmann Trial and the criticism of Jewish leaders by Hannah Arendt, Bruno Bettelheim, and Raul Hilberg, such a contention ignores the pathbreaking work of all the post-war Yiddish historians, particularly Trunk who began publishing studies of the *Judenrat* as early as 1949.

As his research progressed over the years, Trunk revised his assessment of the *Judenrat*. His tone became more tempered, and his view of *Judenrat* members became less categorically negative. This latter change may also reflect his emigration in 1950 from Communist Poland, where official Cold War policy linked the *Judenrat* to capitalism, fascism, anti-communism, and Western imperialism.

Three versions of Trunk's early work on the *Judenrat* are combined below for comparison. The first, with paragraphs marked [A], appeared in 1949 in the journal of the Jewish Historical Institute in Warsaw.[1] The second, marked [B], was a new article published in 1956 in the Bundist journal in New York.[2] The third appeared in Trunk's 1962 volume of collected writings,[3] in which he repeated with slight revision the central part of [A], marked here [A+], while replacing the introduction and conclusion with paragraphs from [B], and adding new material at the end, marked here [C]. He draws his connection between medieval and Nazi-imposed Jewish "autonomy" in the last of the [B] paragraphs.

Part 1. The *Judenrat*

Let us try to clarify what sort of role the Germans assigned the *Judenräte* [plural of *Judenrat*, Jewish Council] in their extermination policy for the Jewish population. The Germans well considered their diabolical plan to exterminate the Jewish population and understood how to harness the victims to the mechanism of destruction. The plan provided that the victims themselves should assist in their own deaths to spare the hangman undue effort and exertion. As the direct or indirect accomplice in this self-extermination, they skillfully employed both human degradation and humiliation and—to the point of bestiality—the human instinct for self-preservation. [A]

In this diabolical plan for self-extermination, the *Judenräte* and the Jewish police were assigned a fitting role. To our greatest pain and shame, we must affirm that the *Judenräte* and Jewish police, with few exceptions, carried out the role conceived for them. Over time, they became the spokespersons for the German authorities in the ghetto. [A]

The *Judenräte*, in their descent, underwent a certain evolution. The schema of this evolution is roughly as follows: At first, the *Judenräte*, which consisted mostly of former *kehila* [community] trustees (at least in the places where they remained), were considered by the Jewish population as legitimate heirs of the prewar *kehilot*. The Germans even bestowed on them immeasurably more functions than those of the prewar communities. The *Judenräte* received judicial and police functions regarding the ghetto residents. Moreover, in certain ghettos (i.e., Lodz and Theresienstadt), the Germans issued Jewish banknotes with the signature of the head of the *Judenrat*—implying a genuine "autonomy" that was supposed to recall the old-time autonomy in the Jewish ghettos of Germany and Poland during the Middle Ages (the Nazi propaganda even skillfully employed this trick abroad, presenting the ghetto system in Poland as a return to the old-time, wide-ranging *kehila* autonomy). [A+]

But the *Judenrat*, less than anything, represented the interests of the Jewish population (this was absolutely not part of the German plans), and their actual task was to cooperate with the German authorities in executing their orders. In the first phase, when the plan for total extermination had not yet been put in motion and the German government temporarily satisfied itself with stealing Jewish property, fragmentary murder-*Aktionen* [round-ups], and the strength of Jewish workers in slave labor, the *Judenräte*, with good or bad intentions, cooperated with the German government in confiscating Jewish property, in assembling card files of able-bodied workers, and in expulsions for forced labor, etc. [A+]

Naturally, in this first phase, ethically demoralized and corrupted members of the *Judenräte* already used their privileged position for private interests. One must bear in mind that in the *Judenräte* the upper hand was more and more gained by unscrupulous powerful people, morally depraved persons (naturally, the German authorities happily promoted and favored such persons in the *Judenräte*). Those who were morally untainted and protested had either fled—in the first period, refusing this "honored" position or fleeing elsewhere was a frequent occurrence—or later, by the course of events, necessarily retreated into the background. There are instances in which chairmen of the *Judenräte* committed suicide, for example, engineer Czerniaków in Warsaw.[1] [A+]

When the Germans, in a calculatedly refined manner, introduced the atmosphere of "who shall live and who shall die" into the ghetto, the *Judenräte*, using their privileged position, received the possibility of becoming masters of death and life in the ghetto. For the reward of saving themselves and their relatives, they delivered into the hands of the executioners hundreds and thousands of their own brothers and sisters. Once embarked on this course, the *Judenräte* rolled continually down that sloping plane to the end. [A]

The system of deception, which the Germans brought to perfection, naturally also drew into its net (and captured) those not-so-few *Judenrat* members who were easily fooled, even if still morally untainted. [A]

There were, of course, exceptions to the schema sketched above. It is sufficient to mention the *Judenrat* in Piotrków,[2] which transformed itself into a den of anti-Nazi conspiracy; the head of the council in Zduńska Wola, Dr. Lemberg,[3] the expansive activity of the *Judenrat* in Baranowicze, particularly of the chairman, Yehoshua Izykson, and his assistant, Genia Mann,[4] and others. [A]

But these exceptions cannot change our evaluation of the actual, objective role of the *Judenräte* as an expositor of German authority, particularly the behavior of the *Judenräte* in the period when there could not have been the slightest doubt about the German extermination plan, which, in the overwhelming majority of cases known so far,[5] underscores still more clearly their openly negative, often criminal, role in the Jewish ghettos. [A]

It is clear that with the introduction of the *Judenräte* the Nazi Germans intended to create an instrument in the Jewish community that would serve their extermination policy regarding the Jewish population, and they had absolutely no intention that the Jews should have their own leadership with regard to the German authority, let alone that this leadership should represent Jewish interests. Everywhere in the occupied countries, the Nazis sought and found partners among the local population, who—some consciously with clearly bad intentions, others perhaps with good intentions—collaborated with the Nazi occupation authority. They made no exception in this case either for the Jewish sector. [B]

Certainly, the Hitlerian goals in making use of collaborators among other peoples were different from making use of Jewish collaborators. There, the Nazi Germans had clearly *tactical-political* purposes: to politically dominate, morally disarm and rule the local population and eliminate the top level of the anti-Nazi movement, while, in their diabolical plans, the Jewish collaborators were required to perform a special role, the role of *self-extermination*, in the sense of helping the German authorities carry out their annihilation *Aktionen*, of which, in their final result, the Jewish servants of the Hitlerian extermination machine also became victims. [B]

There is still another difference. While collaboration with the Nazis by other peoples was *voluntary*, whether for the sake of a shared National Socialist ideology or for the sake of the possibility of being able to give vent to their own Jew-hatred and own lust for murder and robbery, among Jews it was usually *imposed*. In the majority of cases, particularly in the smaller *kehilot*, the Gestapo itself nominated the members of the *Judenräte*, and the nominees knew very well what it meant to oppose an order of the Gestapo. Naturally, we are excluding here the Jewish Gestapo collaborators and informers, who willingly and for the sake of material gain served the German authority. But this distinction between Hitlerian goals and the fact of imposition does not change the character of the *Judenrat* and its executive agency, the ghetto police—objectively, independent of the good intentions that the *Judenrat* as a whole, or certain of its members, invested in this cooperation—as a collaborationist institution. This is one aspect of the problem: the *political countenance* of the *Judenrat*. [B]

The second aspect is their *class-countenance*, particularly in the large and larger ghettos. The question is the extent to which the activities of the *Judenräte* were expressions of the interests of certain ghetto social classes, which the councils represented, as well as their attitude toward other social groups in the ghettos. [B]

The third aspect is the *ethical countenance* of the *Judenräte*, the question of at what social-moral level the *Judenräte* stood, particularly in the last extermination phases of the ghettos, before and during the various *Aktionen*, and what sort of role was performed by the *Judenräte* together with the ghetto police during these *Aktionen*. [B]

There is still another point that is characteristic of the *Judenräte*—the matter of *apparent power*. After a hiatus of hundreds of years (since the Middle Ages), a Jewish representative institution received so many economic and judicial-administrative functions regarding the Jewish population. This ostensible Jewish "autonomy" became a source of deep-reaching demoralization in the *Judenräte*, where all the authority complexes of power-hungry people played out. One must take into consideration that the *Judenräte* were a small ring in a system of power filled with lawlessness and cruelty and that this unfortunate small ring was also often infected with this poisoned atmosphere of power. [B]

[In the 1963 version of Trunk's article, the paragraphs marked "A+" appeared at this point, before the following partial reappraisal.]

It would be too superficial, simplified and, in any event, not correct if we were to see in all *Judenrat* members morally depraved persons whose only purpose was to save themselves, their families, and relatives at the expense of others whom they sent to death. A sort of *Judenrat ideology* was created, a tactical program of how to "save" the Jews in the ghettos. This "ideology" was preached by its representative bearers, for example, Barash in Bialystok, Gens in Vilna, and Rumkowski in Lodz. [B]

Of what does it consist? It was based on three fundamental assumptions: that the useful work that the ghetto performed for the German war industry was a solid foundation for its existence; second, to save even a portion of the Jews, the most valuable, those who had a greater chance of surviving, one must agree to hand over the other portion, those less valuable, who had little or no chance of surviving; third, the path of resistance led to nothing and could only bring misfortune on the ghetto. This *Judenrat* ideology has barely been touched in our Holocaust literature. It is an important key to understanding many motives and inner workings behind the actions of the *Judenräte*. [B]

Part 2. "Rescue through Work"

At a meeting in the Bialystok ghetto at the beginning of winter 1942, Barash said more or less as follows: "With difficulty we have succeeded in saving the ghetto from the disasters that befell our brothers in the neighboring cities. We were protected by our successful and productive work. See the factories, the ordered and organized life, each person working and living, no one among us dying of hunger as in other places. With our own initiative and energy, we have created something out of nothing, and this protected us and will continue to protect us in this difficult war."[6] [C]

Rumkowski, in his public appearances in the Lodz ghetto, would also continually emphasize that only on account of intensive work could the ghetto exist. This program of "Rescue through work" was realized in the Lodz ghetto with a robust outcome, such that at the end of 1943, the productive work of the ghetto engaged 85 percent of the adult population and even children. [C]

The same was preached and done by Gens in the Vilna ghetto. [C]

Regarding this "work ideology," one must note that it could find a *certain support* in the attitude of certain German economic and military circles to the extermination of the Jews. It is a well-known fact that these circles, in a certain period of the war, when victory was already doubtful, and especially when the Nazi war industry began to fill a large void in the foreign workforce, started to become skeptical of the senseless—from their standpoint—extermination of the almost free slave labor reserves that were harnessed to these enormous ghetto workshops in Lodz, Warsaw, Bialystok, and in the numerous labor camps. There were even significant interventions by these circles about ceasing for a certain time, or at least slowing the tempo of the physical extermination of the Jewish working labor pool, that resulted in conflicts and differences of opinion. When it came to deciding the fate of these labor ghettos, a backstage drama took place between the Reich Security Office (Himmler) and the Economic Office in the high command of the Wehrmacht. One must also bear in mind that some officials and Gestapo experts for Jewish matters were personally interested in maintaining the existence of the ghettos, both for material motives (bribes, gifts, confiscations) and because it helped them avoid the hated Eastern Front. [C]

There can be no doubt that such figures as Barash, Gens, and Rumkowski were informed about these differences of opinion between the economic circles in the Wehrmacht and the SS by local "good" Germans (mostly those who could be bribed) and the *Judenrat* heads based upon them, like a sure bet, their program of "saving the ghettos through work." [C]

In addition, the system of hypocritical deception, which the Nazis brought to perfection, was also able to draw into its net not a few *Judenrat* members. [C, rephrased here from A]

Thus, in the speech that Rumkowski delivered on January 17, 1942, already during the phase of deportations to Chełmno, he declared: "I have a firm hope on the basis of authoritative assertions that the fate of the expelled will not be as tragic as foreseen in general in the ghetto. They will not be behind wires and it will be their lot to engage in agriculture." With emphasis, he assured: "I guarantee with my head that not the least wrong will happen to the working person, and I say this not only in my name but on the basis of promises on the part of the authoritative factors."[7] [C]

Today we know that this work program of Rumkowski and those like him was a misleading illusion, that in the discussions between the political and military-economic factors of Nazi Germany it was not a question of stopping the murder of the Jews but of slowing its tempo to be able to make use of Jewish slave labor in the meantime. The military-economic leaders argued that the Jews could always be killed, even at the last moment, so long as Jews worked for the war machine for the time being. More realistic and wiser heads in the ghettos understood this. But in these "unprecedented times," those ghetto leaders, whose entire attitude toward the German governmental bodies was based on *shtadlones* [intercession] and bribery, could cling to the "work program" like a life raft. In any event, this illusion was shared by broad sectors of the Jewish working population in the ghettos, naturally under the influences of the *Judenräte* and their "work ideology." [C]

In connection with this stood also the second fundamental assumption of the *Judenrat* ideology, namely, that to save a part—the working population, those who seemed likely to survive, or from another standpoint those who were more valuable (the younger generation, intellectuals)—one could sacrifice the other part, the nonworking, the socially and culturally less valuable, in short, those who seemed less likely to survive. [C]

The most consistent advocate—to the point of cruelty—for this doctrine was the commander of the Vilna ghetto, Gens. This position found a dramatic formulation in the speech he delivered on October 27, 1942, at a meeting of the ghetto police, *Judenrat*, and leaders of the departments, after the *Aktion* in Oszmiana [near Vilna, today in Belarus], in which the Vilna ghetto police actively participated in the execution of four hundred Jews. [C]

Rumkowski, the head of the Lodz ghetto, was also captivated by this *idée fixe*, that by voluntarily handing over sacrificial victims he would save the rest of the ghetto from extermination. [C]

This was expressed dramatically during the frightful children-*Aktion* in September 1942 in Lodz, when Rumkowski's emissaries implored the hesitating mothers to give up their children because in that way "they were saving the ghetto." [C]

To complete the characterization of this doctrine, one must also add that this view of saving one portion of the Jews by handing over another portion to death was held not only by *Judenrat* leaders of the sort like Gens and Rumkowski but also certain circles and prominent individuals in Jewish society at that time (for example, Dr. Schiper in the Warsaw ghetto). [C]

From these characteristics of such figures as Rumkowski, Barash, or Gens, which we find both in contemporaneous sources and in later memoirs, it is evident that in these cases we are dealing not with morally depraved persons, wanton youths and degenerates, but with people of whom it also cannot be said that their actions were dictated by purely personal, egoistic motives. Regarding Barash, we know that he gave material support to the Bialystok underground movement and would participate in meetings with its representatives. Tenenbaum, one of the commanders of the Bialystok Ghetto Uprising, said of him: "Barash is an honest person, which is a large compliment for a chairman of a *Judenrat*."[8] [C]

Regarding Gens, the commander of the Vilna ghetto, Dworzecki writes: "He was a man filled with contrasts, with negative and positive aspects. Many people believed that the intent of all his actions was to save ever more Jews. . . . Jacob Gens personally conducted the expulsion of Jews from the ghetto; he would stand at the gate and direct the action. . . . On the other hand, the same Jacob Gens . . . helped with all his might to build the industrial workshops in the ghetto . . . often assisted all the cultural institutions . . . exerted himself to create ever more passes and workplaces for the ghetto to save, to the extent possible, Jewish scholars, writers, artists from death and hunger."[9] . . . [C]

This was how the *Judenrat* program appeared in its practical application. Naturally, this ideology was not the moving spirit in the actions of *all Judenräte*. In a certain number of ghettos, the *Judenrat* leaders were absolutely not ideologues but acted without any ideology, unwitting, fearful, and egoistic. In the activity of the *Judenräte*, much was dependent on the psycho-moral characteristics of the *Judenrat* members, whom the Nazis themselves would choose according to their executioner's taste and, above all, according to the prospective benefits they could bring to the Hitlerian plan for Jewish self-extermination. [C]

Introduction Notes:

1. Yeshaye Trunk, "Shtudye tsu der geshikhte fun yidn in 'varteland' in der tkufe fun umkum (1939–1944)" [A study of the history of the Jews in the Warthegau (region of Nazi Germany) in the period of extermination], *Bleter far geshikhte* II, nos. 1–4 (Warsaw, January–December 1949): 64–166 (141–44 quoted); this article is a slightly revised version of "Sotsyale antagonizmen in geto un di rol fun di yudenratn" [Social antagonisms in the ghetto and the role of the *Judenrat*], *Yidishe shriftn* 4, no. 6 (Warsaw, June 1949): 6–7.

2. Yeshaye Trunk, "Der fal rudolf kastner in likht fun der yudenratlisher ideologye" [The case of Rudolf Kastner in light of the *Judenrat* ideology], *Unzer tsayt* (New York, April–May 1956): 23–27.

3. Yeshaye Trunk, "Shtudye tsu . . ." (per note 1 above), in his *Shtudyes in yidisher geshikhte in poyln* [Studies in Jewish history in Poland] (Buenos Aires: Yidbukh, 1962), 171–289 (247–50 quoted).

Article Notes:

1. The Jewish underground movement in the Warsaw Ghetto could not forgive Czerniaków for not warning about the danger that was coming to the ghetto before his death.

2. Eyewitness account of Y. Samsonowicz.

3. Yisroel Tabaksblat, *Khurbn lodzsh: 6 yor natsi gehenem* [The destruction of Lodz: 6 years of Nazi Gehenna] (Buenos Aires: Tsentral-farband fun poyishe yidn in argentine, 1946), 149.

4. Archive of Jewish Historical Institute, Warsaw, eyewitness account number 923.

5. Only in the first deportation phase in the Wartheland, fall 1941, was the council unaware that the deportees were being sent to Chełmno (Ringelblum Archive, number 1118, about the council in Koło).

6. Haikah Grosman, *Anshe ha-Mahteret* [People of the underground] (Merhabit, Israel: Hotsa'at ha-Kibuts ha-artsi ha-shomer ha-tsa'ir, 1950), 163, 164.

7. [The translation of these quotations is taken from Isaiah Trunk, *Łódź Ghetto: A History*, Robert Moses Shapiro ed. and trans. (Bloomington: Indiana University Press, 2006), 319–20.]

8. Mordecai Tenenbaum-Tamaroff, *Dappim min ha-Delekah* [Pages from the fire] (Tel Aviv: Hakibbutz Hameuhad, 1948), 30.

9. M. Dvorzhetski, *Yerusholayim d'lite in kamf un umkum* [Jerusalem of Lithuania (Vilna) in struggle and extermination] (Paris: Yidishn natsyonaln arbeter-farband in amerike / Yidishn folksfarband in frankraykh, 1948), 306–7.

Part Two

ON THE JEWISH STREET

8

Yiddish Theater in the German and Slavic Ghettos during the Sixteenth Century

by Ignacy Schiper, 1927

IGNACY SCHIPER (see Selection 4 above) pioneered the study of early Yiddish theater in his three-volume *History of Jewish Theatrical Art and Drama from the Oldest Times to 1750*. It touches briefly on Jewish theater in antiquity and in Renaissance Italy and Spain but is devoted primarily to the theater of Yiddish-speaking Jews in Central and Eastern Europe. The first volume discusses theater practices in various times and places; the second and third volumes attempt to reconstruct the repertoire.

The work was pathbreaking but only partially successful. As Jacob Shatzky pointed out in a twenty-five-page critique, the field lacked useful preliminary studies, so Schiper needed to be "simultaneously the collector of material, the 'discoverer' of sources, the analyzer and the synthesizer." He generally praised the first volume but listed errors of research and interpretation in Schiper's reconstruction of the repertoire in the second and third volumes. A separate review by Max Weinreich advised that it would have been better if Schiper had published only the first volume.[1] Yet Shatzky declared it "a daring step for Dr. Schiper to leap without a compass . . . into a sea of untouched matters," and he concluded that Schiper had laid "a cornerstone for a modern scholarly approach" to Jewish theater.[2] In the absence of extant information, Schiper's method often consisted of inferring historical details about theater technique from the dialogue and stage directions found in the texts of Yiddish plays. Below are brief excerpts from Schiper's first volume.[3]

When we consider the paths on which the artistic aspirations of the German and Slavic Jews meandered during the sixteenth century until they reached the level of theater, a picture reveals itself before our eyes of entirely different lines and colors than the picture we saw in the Italian ghettos of the same time [in the preceding chapter].

Theater among the Italian Jews stood under the direct influence of the *court literature* and court society. Conversely, in Germany and in the Slavic countries we come across the characteristic phenomenon that the assimilation process does not run in the direction of the "upper classes" but indeed in the direction of the culture of the masses: here, Jews adopt forms of entertainment that are found among artisans, peasants, wandering students, and similar "little people." In Italy, dramatic works *by Jews* appear; in Germany and the Slavic countries in the same period, *Jewish* dramatic works arise. *There*, serious drama by Jewish authors and the art of Jewish court actors develop; *here*, a popular drama (in the broadest sense of the word) grows, mostly anonymously, and the art of acting does not surpass the level of sleight-of-hand.

The distinction also reveals itself in the field of language: The Jewish dramatists in Italy write their pieces in Italian or Spanish. Conversely, German and Slavic Jews create their folk theater pieces in the language of the Jewish masses, in *Yiddish*. There, a slavish imitation; here, if one may put it this way, "der veg tsu zikh" [the way to oneself; possibly a nod to the well-known novel of that name by Sholem Asch], with the help of German popular literature and theater.

In a word: *there*, artists and artificiality; *here*, naïve, primitive folk art. . . .

In the depressed Jewish German ghettos, over which always hung the danger of expulsion, collective *Fröhlichkeit* [merriment; gaiety] appeared only in exceptional cases. As in the Middle Ages, an occasion for merriment arose during family celebrations, especially during weddings, or at Purim- and Hanukkah-time. The same can also be said about merriment among Jews in Bohemia, from which they were driven several times during the sixteenth century. The Jews in Poland are no exception here, although Jewish life in Poland during the sixteenth century was much more peaceful than in the Western countries. . . .

The Art of Jewish "Fools" during the Sixteenth Century

The medieval *lets* [Hebrew: buffoon, joker] was transformed during the sixteenth century into a *nar* [German *Narr*; fool]: during the period of humanism, when the educated humanist came to the fore—the "proud author" around whom the dreams of "beautiful Jewish daughters" wove themselves—the medieval *lets*, who turned everything upside down, became a *nar* or a *marshelik* [jester at a Jewish wedding]. The "devil," the *lets* who appeared in the [Catholic] medieval mystery plays, became—on account of his weakness and powerlessness, a comic figure—and he remained a comic figure when he was appropriated by medieval secular merriment. In the very beginning, he was an evil spirit; he was called *herlequin* in the Romance countries, and he was portrayed as a "wild hunter" who drifted around in old woods and high mountains. The evil *herlequin* then became the *hellequin*, the comic *lets* in the religious plays. Ultimately, when he was appropriated by secular "merriment," he revealed himself to be "Arlecchino" [Harlequin], the name of a famous comic figure in the Italian folk comedy (commedia dell'arte). . . .

In Germany, during the Middle Ages, the evil spirit was called simply "devil," and in the time of humanism and Reformation, he acquired a satiric character and revealed himself as a *Narr*. The development process of the Jewish *lets* was closely connected with the development of the German "devil." Like the German "devil," the Jewish *lets* also revealed himself during the sixteenth century as a *nar*.

From the sixteenth century, we have sufficient rich material to know clearly the physiognomy of the Jewish *nar* and the role he played in Jewish social life.

The chief sources are the verse collections of Isaac [Eizik] Wallich and Menahem Oldendorf, which come from the sixteenth century and, on account of which, many interesting "numbers" were preserved from the repertoire of the Jewish fools. . . .

The Oldest Dramatic Works in Yiddish

The *narn-kunst* was the bridge that led to theater. Frequently, it happened that two or three *narn* [fools] gathered around themselves cheerful yeshiva students or synagogue choirboys and formed a group of "players," a "troupe," that for Purim or Hanukkah would produce serious synagogue plays, cheerful farces, or melodious interludes. At that time, such "troupes" were temporary, only for "playtime"; after the Purim carnival or after Hanukkah, they would disband. Such "troupes" would also include some musicians—so that we find among them all the elements of "merriment": the *nar*, who combined in himself the joker, dancer, magician, and piper; the *yeshiva student*, who brought youthful freshness and was the amateur actor; the *singer* from the synagogue, which had been carried away—as we have already shown [in a previous chapter]—by the stream of secular melodies; and also, finally, the *klezmer* [musician] who had succumbed to the temptations of the artistry of the Italian musicians. . . .

Performance Technique in the German and Slavic Ghettos during the Sixteenth Century

With the help of the texts of dramatic creations in Yiddish that come from the sixteenth century, it is possible to reconstruct to a certain extent the picture of how Jews "staged pieces" at that time, or in more modern terms, how Yiddish theater was performed at that time.

First of all, we are interested in the question: *who* performed, who were the "actors"?

Enough material is available for us to give a clear answer to that question, without needing to seek explanations or make use of analogies or suppositions. Among the Jewish "actors" of that time, we see in the German and Slavic ghettos three types of *narishe mentshn* [foolish people]: the *professional nar* or "joyful Jew," the yeshiva student, and the synagogue singer.

The professional fool is the "first of the actors": he is the director of the performance and at times also the author of the piece or at least the one who reworked the foreign drama that he would render more Jewish for the Purim repertoire. In the biblical comedies and synagogue dialogues, he plays the role of the *prologus* or *argumentator*—in the Purim farces and *inframezzos* [a musical piece between acts of a play] he appears as a messenger or choral director. . . .

When we consider, for example, the contrasting role of the cheerful yeshiva student in the Purim farce, we see that the messenger announces the entrance of the Purim players and then greets the audience with good wishes: "God give you a good Purim." Following this, he appears as one of the Purim king's suite and narrates the play. . . .

But the role of the messenger or *argumentator* does not end here.

As can be inferred from Yosef ben Benyamin's *Purim Inframesum*, he is also engaged in showing where the play should be staged, in arranging the players on the "stage," and giving them a sign when they should begin singing.

As shown by the text of the abovementioned Purim farce, it is also his task to characterize the players before they enter, to describe their appearance, announce the content of particular scenes and, if necessary, be the director of the dance. Thus, we encounter him *here*, as he gives a sign to the students that they should dance "with the goats"; we hear him *there*, as he announces the entrance of the Purim king, characterizing this person with a huge stomach as a *kishn-tsikhn* [cushion cover / pillowcase]. . . .

The second type of "actor" is mentioned by name in the same Purim farce: "We are worth our bread / The [yeshiva] students are here / Give us then wine, so rich / For we are so beautiful! / Short speeches and long breads!" And they were truly "worth their bread" and "so beautiful"—the *yeshiva students* who knew how to perform serious biblical comedies or exuberant Purim farces.

Regarding the third type of "actor," we arrive at a suitable image when we take into account the "process of secularization" of synagogue song, which we described exhaustively in one of the previous chapters—and supplement it with the picture that results from the *Purim-lid* of Yosef ben Benyamin. It is highly likely that Yosef ben Benyamin was himself a choral singer in a synagogue or even a *hazan*, who wrote a piece on the side in order to stage it with his choristers at Purim time during the feast with distinguished householders.

Appearances as a singer could also be made by professional fools or yeshiva students. In connection with the *narn*, we already know that among them there were also "joyful Jews" who excelled at singing and whistling, and, regarding the yeshiva students, it is well known from the Purim farce in Isaac Wallich's collection that they *sang* their roles according to the melody of a popular folksong, "Pumei, Pumei, ir Polen!" [ca. 1600, also called "Pumay" or "Pumai"]

The second question that we pose in considering the performance technique of that period is *the time* [of year] when the pieces were "staged."

A clear answer to this question is given by a few phrases in the texts of the farce and *inframesum* in Isaac Wallich's collection. In the farce, the messenger greets the audience: "Pumei, you dear companions / God give you a good Purim!" Regarding the *inframesum*, it is well-known that Yosef ben Benyamin "wrote it in honor of Purim."

In the same connection, it is also worth mentioning the introduction to the comedy "Shpil fun toyb yeklayn" [The play of Deaf Yeklayn; late sixteenth century], in which the custom of producing a "play" at Purim time is clearly shown: "It was customary then on every Purim / to put on a play about Deaf Yeklayn."

Besides Purim, "plays" were also produced at Hanukkah time. This is apparent from the dialogue by Zalman Runkel [d. 1562], who introduced a dispute between *Hanukkah* and other holidays. The dialogue is a *gelegnhayts-shafung* [a piece created for a specific occasion], and it was surely "staged" only at Hanukkah time, since only then would it be timely and make sense.

The texts of the dramatic creations in Yiddish that come from the sixteenth century can also clarify for us the question of *place*, where the pieces were performed.

In the Purim farce about the cheerful students, we find some phrases that certainly show the piece was performed in the house of a well-to-do Jew during a banquet. This becomes clear from the first few lines with which the messenger opens the play; he greets the "dear companions," namely, the members of the household who are sitting at the banquet, wishes them "a good Purim" and declares: "I enter with . . ." These phrases show that the players did not perform for an invited audience but, on the contrary, that they visited their spectators in their homes and performed the pieces there. In the entire farce, the atmosphere is formed from the situation in which the players encounter the residents. "Bring me ox meat!"—is a request by the messenger. Soon after, the student chorus asks the "dear gentlefolks" to bring [a variety of foods], in short: "Bring here the best foods / *that you have in the house.*"

In the house, the players occupied a corner, or they simply sat down at the table among the "dear gentlefolks" and performed the play. Many hosts, at Purim time or during Hanukkah, would erect a podium in their house so the players could succeed better with their play, appearing on a higher place. Such a type of podium was, apparently, meant by the words spoken by the choirmaster in the "*Purim-lid*" of Yosef ben Benyamin: "They step onto this 'plan'." . . .

It becomes clear that the "plan"[1] onto which our Purim players step is, according to the instructions of the choirmaster in the *Purim-lid* of Yosef ben Benyamin, a place raised above the spectators, a podium or simply some planks set on top of barrels or tables.

But there is more! The history of the "stage" for the *Fastnachtspiel* [German play performed on Shrove Tuesday, the day before the Fast of Lent] allows us to ascertain the time when the Jewish "plan" [stage] could first have appeared among the Purim players.

In the Purim farce of the cheerful students we see also that the play was staged, exactly like the older *Fastnachtspielen*, on the same floor level on which the spectators were located. We first encounter the "raising" of the performance place in the Purim *inframesum*, which is certainly several decades younger than the Purim farce.

The German *Fastnachtspieler* first indicate the "stage as a raised performance place" in 1550. The emergence of the "stage" is connected with the fact that, *around this time, the Fastnachtspieler stopped strolling from house to house* and would invite the spectators to a place under the open sky and perform their pieces there. To be well appreciated by the audience, they needed a raised place, and that led to the "stage." Since the mid-sixteenth century, the *Fastnachtspieler* performed on a "stage"—and also thereafter, when the performance took place in a tavern or in the "guild," namely, in the meeting hall of an artisan guild.

Just as with other customs and arrangements of the *Fastnachtspieler*, our Purim players also adopted the *Fastnachtspiel* stage and created their own "plan." But this could only have happened—as shown by the history of the *Fastnachtspiel* stage—not earlier than the second half of the sixteenth century.

Among the German *Fastnachtspieler*, the playhouse soon evolved from the "stage" (the first German playhouse was built by the *Fastnachtspieler* in Nuremberg in 1550). Among Jews, the development was much slower; the first Jewish playhouses, the "Purim theaters," appeared only at the end of the seventeenth and beginning of the eighteenth centuries. The chief cause of this delay in their development in the ghettos was that the Purim players did not stop going from house to house....

An important obstacle that made it impossible to build Jewish playhouses was also the temporary and mixed character of the player troupes. Among the Germans, for example, the *Fastnachtspieler* were almost entirely artisans—masters, journeymen, and apprentices; all belonged to a guild, and the player troupe was a sort of "dramatic section" of the guild. The guild became the financial and moral supporter of theater culture, and with its assistance the primitive stage could, with time, develop into the playhouse. It was altogether different in the ghettos. The players were a mixed element: professional *narn*, yeshiva students, synagogue singers, *hazanim*, and the like. In one troupe there could be players of various social classes, and that made it impossible to join theater culture and the Jewish guilds. Therefore, this important factor—which financed the playhouses among other peoples—was lacking.

Introduction Notes:

1. M. Vaynraykh, "Tsu der geshikhte fun der eltere ahashverush-shpil" [On the history of the older Ahasuerus-plays], *Filologishe shriftn fun yivo* II (1928): cols. 425–28 (427 cited).

2. Y. Shatski, "Di ershte geshikhte fun yidishn teater: tsu d"r y. shipers verk" [The first history of Jewish theater: On Dr. Y. Schiper's Work], *Filologishe shriftn fun yivo* II (1928): Cols. 215–64 (215, 262, 264 cited).

3. Yitzkhok Schiper, *Geshikhte fun yidisher teater-kunst un drame: fun di eltste tsaytn biz 1750* [History of Jewish theater and drama from the oldest times to 1750], vol. 1 (Warsaw: Kultur-lige, 1923), excerpts from chapters 4, 5, 6, and 9.

Article Notes:

1. The word "plan" is taken from German terminology. We encounter "plan" in Hans Sachs's drama titled "Der hürnen Seufrid," where we find a direction of stage technique such as: "Der herold drit auf den plan und schreit [The messenger steps onto the stage and shouts]." The word "plan" is used here as an indication of the raised stage. See Max Herrmann, *Forschungen zur deutschen Theatergeschichte des Mittelalters und der Renaissance* (Berlin: Weidmann, 1914), 41.

9

The Structure of the Jewish Guilds in Poland, Lithuania, and Belorussia in the Seventeenth and Eighteenth Centuries

by Mark Wischnitzer, 1928

MARK WISCHNITZER (1882–1955) was born in Rovno, Russian Volhynia (today Rivne, Ukraine), and received his doctorate in history from the University of Berlin in 1906. Like Schiper and others of his generation, his career was established in other languages before he turned to Yiddish in the 1920s. He began with historical works in Russian—as author of journal articles, as editor and author of articles in the *Evreyskaya Entsiklopedia* (Jewish Encyclopedia), and as editor and coauthor of a proposed multivolume history of Russian and Polish Jewry.

When he left the Soviet Union for Berlin in 1921, Wischnitzer repeated the same proficiency in German journals and as editor and coauthor of the *Encyclopaedia Judaica*. In Berlin, he also turned to Yiddish—as general editor of the Yiddish/Hebrew art journals *Milgroym/Rimonim*, of which his wife, Rachel Wischnitzer, was art director (see Selection 13), and as a contributor to Yiddish journals and the Yiddish encyclopedia. In Berlin, he became director of the Hilfsverein der Deutschen Juden, which aided Jews in leaving Nazi Germany. Settling ultimately in New York, he began to publish in English, while continuing to write in Yiddish, and he headed YIVO's Historical

Section between the death of Elias Tcherikower in 1943 and the arrival of Philip Friedman in 1948.

One of Wischnitzer's continuing interests was the history of Jewish artisans and craft guilds. His works on this topic followed the same course as his overall career, with articles in Russian, followed by German and then Yiddish, and finally a posthumous book in English.[1] The article below was the culmination of this work in Yiddish.[2] Its overt purpose is to recover the little-known history of Jewish artisans in early modern Eastern Europe. A tacit purpose is to provide arguments against the antisemitic accusation that Jews had always been an "unproductive" element, engaged solely in commerce and trade, by demonstrating that a significant number of Jews had been artisans, productively engaged in craftwork.

The economic history of the Jews in Poland, Lithuania, and Belorussia has, to the present day, been treated in an altogether stepmotherly manner. One of the problems in this important field, which requires fundamental investigation, is the history and structure of the Jewish guilds. . . .

The Polish, Lithuanian, and Belorussian, as well as Ukrainian Jews, occupied themselves, in contrast with the German Jews of the Middle Ages, not only with commerce and credit operations but, exactly like the Sicilian and Spanish Jews, who were in large measure—artisans.[1]

We find the first evidence of Jewish craft workers in Poland in the fifteenth century and in Lithuania somewhat earlier, in the fourteenth century.[2] Unfortunately, the sources from those centuries are so sparse that we cannot say how a portion of the immigrants from Western Europe took up craftwork—how they changed, so to speak, their occupation. It is unimaginable that Jewish artisans migrated in large numbers because, in the German city-states from which Jews were expelled, craftwork did not figure in their economic life, on account of the fierce policy of the local guilds: the guilds there were very strongly opposed to Jewish involvement in craftwork. The beginning of Jewish craftwork in Poland is, thus, still an obscure point in history. We know only that in the sixteenth century craftwork was already thoroughly widespread in Poland and Lithuania. In that century, one can already speak of a Jewish artisan class. Jewish artisans at that time worked not only for Jewish customers but also for non-Jewish consumers, chiefly for peasants on the land. They produced mass goods for the rural consumer. In agricultural areas, the urban artisan who provided his goods to the peasant masses became an important factor. However, the Jewish craft worker came into collision with the Christian artisan class, which was then already well organized in guilds created on the principles of Western European guilds. The Christian artisans soon felt the effects of competition on the part of the Jewish craft workers. Over time, this competition became so significant that stubborn and bitter fights began between the two hostile groups of urban artisans: the Christian guild and the unorganized Jewish artisans. We learn, incidentally, that furrier work was then a widespread craft among Jewish artisans in the Lemberg region and in Volyn, especially in Lutsk [today in Ukraine].

Precisely here in Lutsk, a fight ensued in the 1630s between the local furriers guild and the Jewish furriers, who would bring sheepskin coats to the markets in Klevan and Torchyn and sell them to the peasants for cattle. The grand duke of Lithuania, to whom Volyn then belonged, ruled that the Jews were permitted to continue to sell their work to the peasants but must compensate the guild with a set monetary contribution each year.[3]

Such attempts to oust the Jewish artisans from their positions were made in many other cities in Poland, Lithuania, and Belorussia. But all efforts by the guilds to halt the development of Jewish craftwork failed. Economic necessities drove the Jewish masses to craftwork, and the position of the Jewish artisans eventually became more secure. In the sixteenth century, during which Jewish craftwork became more deeply rooted in the economic life of the country, the Polish, Lithuanian, and Belorussian Jews were forced out of a whole range of occupations by other forces, societal elements much stronger than the guilds. The Polish Sejm [parliament] demanded from the crown in the fifteenth century that Jews not be leaseholders of taxes, mines, and royal estates and, in the sixteenth century, realized its demand. In Poland, the profession of farming out taxes on alcoholic beverages almost ceased among Jews. It should also be kept in mind that, since the end of the fifteenth century, a bitter fight had been waged between Christian and Jewish merchants. Although it was not possible for the Christian merchants to stop Jewish commerce, it is nevertheless likely that many Jewish merchants were forced to seek other occupations, especially after trading in grain became, by act of the Polish Sejm, a monopoly of the nobles.[4] These phenomena strengthened the growth of Jewish craftwork.

The economic reorganizations of Polish-Lithuanian Jews in the sixteenth century do not lend themselves to statistical research because we lack the necessary data, but the tens of records that deal with the fight of the guilds against Jewish artisans everywhere in Poland, Belorussia, and Lithuania[5] bear witness to the fact of constant growth of craftwork among the Jewish population.

The policy of the guilds opposed all unaffiliated artisans, including Jews, Armenians, Tatars, Orthodox Christians,[6] and others.

The unaffiliated artisan was considered a bungler, and such elements were persecuted by the guild with all possible means. The alternatives that stood before the unaffiliated artisan were either to join the guild or lose his living. For the Jewish artisan, joining a Christian guild was impossible, not only for economic and national reasons but also for religious reasons because the guild had its shrine, its altar, and its church. One must also remember that the guild was not only an economic organization but also a social union of people who had common religious and spiritual interests. This religious character locked the doors and gates of the guild to the Jewish artisan. The thought must therefore have occurred to Jewish artisans to organize a guild of their own to defend their common interests and achieve common goals. How important this act of solidarity was for the Jewish artisans is shown by the history of the struggle of the Grodno artisans against the local guild.[7]

The Jewish guilds in Poland, Belorussia, and Lithuania, which were created on the initiative of Jewish artisans, were a product of an organizational necessity of people who were closely bound by important, shared life interests. This was not an isolated case in the course of artisan history in general. Such groups of Jewish artisans were already found in the time of the Roman emperors and later during the Middle Ages in Sicily and in Spain.[8] In Poland, Lithuania, and Belorussia, however, a point arose that is worth mentioning. The Jewish guild in these countries crystallized in a fighting mood. Jewish artisans there were on the defensive, having to defend against attacks by the Christian guild. The necessity to protect their right to work drove the Jewish workers to organize themselves into separate corporations and guilds.

The question of the extent to which the organized Jewish community played a role in the process of founding guilds has not been clarified sufficiently to date. If we take into consideration the dependence of the guild on the community—we will return to this phenomenon—one needs to say that the community must have cooperated actively to a great extent in founding guilds. In each case, the community must have given its permission for the Jewish artisans to organize themselves into a guild,[9] as shown by a series of guild statutes. In this regard, the history of the Jewish guilds was similar to the history of guilds in general.

The well-known researcher of medieval German history, von Below, set forth the following thesis: "A guild is a compulsory union of artisans engaged in a specific type of craftwork in an urban community. The society must, however, be sanctioned by the highest power in the given urban community, i.e., by the municipal authorities."[10] This thesis is also very appropriate for the Jewish guild. The Christian guild needed the sanction of the municipal authorities, the Jewish guild—of the *kahal* [the leadership of the community]. Often, sanction was also required from the region under whose authority the *kahal* operated, as with all Jewish matters in general. This was the custom in the so-called royal cities. In the *czynszowy* [rental] cities and towns, the cities and towns owned by the nobles,[11] the guild needed to have, besides the sanction of the *kahal*, another sanction from the nobleman or his leaseholder. . . .

The guild called itself *hevre* [group; society], although we also find in the Jewish records the term *tsekh* or *tsekhe* (German *Zeche*) [guild]. The first guilds were established in the first half of the seventeenth century in the cities of Przemyśl, Kraków, and Lemberg.[12] In the eighteenth century, Jewish guilds were widespread, even in many small cities and towns. In larger communities, guilds existed for various types of craftwork, often four, five, six, or more guilds.

The principle of the guild was that all the artisans of a single craft in a given place of residence had to join the guild. If not, they were not permitted to work at their craft. In that respect, the statute of the Jewish guild did not differ from the general Christian guild. Jewish guilds would persecute Jewish artisans, nonmembers of the guild, just as strongly and pitilessly as Christian guilds did the unaffiliated artisans, even Christians. This was characteristic of medieval legislation.

A bachelor was not permitted to join the guild or undertake a craft independently. The guild was a society of married men, men with a household. This requirement was copied by the Jewish guilds from the general guilds. The underlying idea was purely economic. The man with a household, who had a wife and child, needed to have his rights protected by the guild to be able to exist. The unmarried man could very easily lower his prices since his needs were less than those of a family man. . . .

What purposes did the guild organization serve? First of all, the guild attempted to regulate the work opportunities and work conditions of the members. Competition among the guild members was not permitted to predominate, or at the very least was sharply limited. Each master had his permanent place in the market, and it was forbidden to steal customers. Each master had his regular clientele . . . , and the clientele was bequeathed from father to son, or son-in-law and grandson. In the *pinkes* [record book] of Keidan [today Kėdainiai, Lithuania], it says: "The son inherits the clientele from his father; if there is no son, a son-in-law or a grandson of a son or a daughter, if they are connected with the indicated guild. And if there is no heir, the guild inherits."

In the record books of the guilds, we find many regulations that deal with the problem of "trespassing" with regard to established clientele, a problem that preyed on the minds of the representatives of the non-Jewish guilds as well. However, economic life was stronger than all the fine regulations, and in the eighteenth century the Jewish artisan class grew enormously. According to the censuses of 1765 and later, it appears that artisans accounted for a quarter to a third of the Jewish population in Poland. Competition was frightful. In the *pinkes* of Keidan, we read how the artisans practically besieged the nobleman who came to town to order clothing. . . .

The income of the guild consisted of initiation and annual dues payments by the members, the payments by the workers and apprentices for the right to work, penalties for not upholding the regulations of the guild, and payments by those members with clientele monopoly privileges.

The expenses were not small. The leadership of the guild cost money. Orphans of artisans had to be supported and taught a trade. The fights and trials with the Christian guilds cost a lot of money. It was often necessary to buy from them to be able to work.

The history of medieval craftwork was filled with constant struggles between the city authorities and guilds. Sooner or later conflicts were certain to break out between the two important institutions of medieval city life. The city authorities were the agency that had given its sanction to founding the guild and had control over it. Over the years, conflicts arose between the controlling agency and the guild—conflicts that led to bitter disputes and bloody fights. The guilds were no longer satisfied with being independent but aspired to have their representatives in the city government. . . .

[The following two paragraphs come from the conclusion of Wischnitzer's 1922 booklet on the Jewish guilds, cited in note 2 above.]

After Poland was partitioned at the end of the eighteenth century, the old Jewish guild essentially lost its significance. Commercial life in Russia, Prussia, and Austria, i.e., in the countries that annexed Poland, was structured altogether differently. In particular, in Russia, which incorporated the largest portion of Polish Jews, Catherine II published an order (in 1775) making commercial employment unrestricted. The Jewish guilds lost their justification there. In the nineteenth century, societies—artisan unions—arose that assumed the former guilds' religious and charitable functions, but they acquired no economic power. Above all, these societies were governed by the spirit of unity, until the conflict between employers and employees penetrated even these patriarchal organizations (in the second half of the nineteenth century). The influence of new social conditions and new ideas resulted in Jewish journeymen and apprentices beginning to fight against the masters for their own economic interests.

The societies collapsed: the masters created an organization for themselves, and the workers—for themselves. With time, larger disputes arose, and strikes appeared. For that purpose, workers created "war chests" that became the germ of the Bundist organization. The last ten years of the nineteenth century were tumultuous in the Jewish provinces, and the conflict between employers and employees rose to the surface. But that is already a chapter of Jewish history of its own. . . .

Introduction Notes:

1. Mark Wischnitzer, *A History of Jewish Crafts and Guilds* (New York: Jonathan David, 1965), publications list on 314.

2. M. Vishnitser, "Di struktur fun yidishe tsekhn in poyln, lite un vaysruland inm 17-tn un 18-tn yorhundert," *Tsaytshrift* II–III (Minsk, 1928): 73–88 (abridged).

Article Notes:

1. See my article "Handverk" [Handicraft], in *Enzyklopädie des Judentums. Probeheft* (Berlin/Jerusalem: Eschkol, 1926), 56–57.

2. See Yitskhok Schiper, *Virtshaftsgeshikhte fun di yidn in poyln beysn mitlalter* [Economic history of the Jews in Poland during the Middle Ages] (Warsaw: Ch. Brzoza, 1926); and works by me: "Yevrei-remeslenniki i tsekhovaia organizacia ikh" [Jewish artisans and their guild organization], in *Istoria Yevreev v Rossii* [History of the Jews in Russia] (Moscow: Mir, 1914); *Yidishe balmelokhe tsekhn in poyln un lite* [Jewish craft guilds in Poland and Lithuania] (Berlin: Klal-farlag, 1922); "Der pinkes fun keydaner balmelokhe tsekh" [The minute-book of the Kėdainiai craft guild] *Bleter far yidisher demografye, statistik un ekonomik* 5 (Berlin, 1925): 72–77; and ibid., note 1 above.

3. *Russko-Evreĭskiĭ Arkhiv*, vol. 1 (1882), no. 179.

4. See my work, "A general overview of the political and social history of Jews in Poland and Lithuania," in *Istoria Evreev v Rossii* [The history of the Jews in Russia], vol. 11 [Russian] (Moscow: Izd-vo T-va "Mir," 1914), 43, 45ff.; also the work by Schiper in the same volume on the economic situation, 255, 267ff. [See Selection 43 below.]

5. *Regesty i Nadpisi; svod materialov dliā istoriī evreev v Rossīi* [Official records and inscriptions: a collection of materials for the history of Jews in Russia: 80–1800], vols. 1 and 2 (St. Petersburg, 1899).

6. In Lemberg, for example, it was difficult for Orthodox Ruthenians to join local guilds. See the interpretations in *Kwartalnik Historyczny* [Historical quarterly] XXXIX, no. 4 (Lwów, 1925): 626–27, where a review appears about a study by [Kazimierz] Chodynicki on religious relations in the guilds in Vilna in the sixteenth to eighteenth centuries. The reviewer speaks incidentally about relations in the Lemberg guilds.

7. See Y. Sosis, "Tsu der sotsyaler geshikhte fun yidn in vaysrusland" [On the social history of Jews in Belorussia], *Tsaytshrift* I (Minsk, 1926): 9–10.

8. See my article "Handwerk," in *Enzyklopädie des Judentums. Probeheft*, 56–57.

9. Thus, for example, in Posen, where the community issued a charter to the guild. See *Zeitschrift der Historischen Gesellschaft für die Provinz Posen* (Posen: n.p., 1895), 311. There were similar conditions in Kraków and Przemyśl. See Balaban, 317, 319; and Schor 64, 267.

10. Georg von Below, *Probleme der Wirtschaftsgeschichte* (Tübingen: Mohr, 1920), 274.

11. The jurisdiction and right of taxation were obtained by the nobles from the Polish Sejm in 1538/39. See Ezechiel Zivier, *Neuere Geschichte Polens*, vol. 1 (Gotha: Perthes, 1915), 416.

12. See the references in footnotes 1 and 2 above [among others from sections not included].

10

Two Communities in One City: The Jews of Lemberg from Medieval to Modern Times

by Meir Balaban, 1930

MEIR BALABAN (1877–1942) was born in Lemberg, Austrian Galicia (today Lviv, Ukraine), and received his doctorate in history from the University of Lemberg in 1906. He began lecturing in Jewish history at the University of Warsaw in 1928 and was promoted to assistant professor in 1935, becoming the only Jew in prewar Poland to hold a university position in Jewish history. His chief specialties were the histories of the Jews in specific towns and of Jewish communal organization.

In the early decades of his career, he worked almost exclusively in Polish or German. Like his colleague Moses Schorr, he was committed to Polish Jewish nationalism (as well as Zionism), but during World War I was appointed by the Austrian army to serve as "military rabbi" (without ordination) in Lublin. His student and biographer, Israel M. Biderman, recounts that in Lublin, Balaban encountered for the first time "Jewish intellectuals who used Yiddish freely, both as a language of daily communication and as a literary medium. He began to speak Yiddish and later wrote in the language as well."[1] Yet Balaban did not become an advocate for Yiddish-oriented Jewish nationalism; rather, like contemporary Zionists, he viewed Yiddish as an effective vehicle for reaching his desired audience.

In 1930, Balaban published a volume of his collected works in Yiddish, nearly all translated from other languages. In his preface, he noted (with some exaggeration) that in the previous thirty years, "the Yiddish reader has been given mostly compilations, odds and ends—and in such a watered-down form that little true scholarship remained." He resolved that, with this book, "I will draw the Yiddish reader into the circle of our past in Poland and interest him in the subject."[2]

One of the articles that Balaban composed originally in Yiddish for his 1930 volume appears below.[3] It is devoted to his home city of Lemberg. The article differs from his translated Polish and German works in using a shared vocabulary of Jewish terms that would only occur in writing for fellow Jews, which is common in Yiddish historical writing. Yet his manner of addressing the reader directly, as seen here, is not common. Using his own voice as the reader's personal guide was a persona he adopted in all languages, already present in his 1909 Polish history of the Lwów Jewish quarter ("Tear off the veil with me—reader. . . . Come with me through this street . . .")[4] and in his 1919 German history of Jewish Lublin ("And now let us begin our walking tour").[5]

Balaban continued to publish historical articles in Yiddish, particularly in the daily Yiddish press, from the 1920s until the Nazi invasion in 1939. Before his death from a heart attack in the Warsaw ghetto, he was director of the *Judenrat* archive and attempted to continue his prewar historical projects.

The Split

When I was still a child, I always wondered why my cousin was called a *shtotisher* [a city-person]. At first, I thought that was his name, and when I later became aware that his name was Landau, I did not understand the matter at all. In school I once heard from a friend that, in the "city," Boruch Schorr and his fine choir led the prayers, and some boys told me that they went on *Shabes* [Saturday, the Sabbath] to *the city* to hear that *khazn* [cantorial soloist]. Another time, someone at home told us that a relative of ours married a young woman who was very fine and respectable, but she had one fault: she was from the *city*. I understood that the word *city* meant some kind of terrible defect, an inferior state, and I resolved to investigate what sort of thing this was.

I did not have to wait long, because once on the very eve before *Shvues* [Shavuot, the Feast of Weeks], my *zeyde* [grandfather] said to me: "Meirshe, come, we are going into the city to the old *shul* [synagogue] because today is the *yortsayt* [death anniversary] of the martyrs, Reb Chaim and Reb Yeshoshue Reytses, who were burned in the marketplace about two hundred years ago." At this, I could not resist and bombarded my grandfather with so many questions that he did not know which to answer first: What does *city* mean; we already live in the city of Lemberg, so what does it mean to go into the city? Where is the old *shul*? Who is Boruch Schorr, and where does he lead the prayers with his choir, etc., etc.? My grandfather did not consider it worthwhile to answer the questions and said only this much: "Meirshe, my child, in Lemberg there are two *kehilot* [Jewish communities]: a *city* and a *suburb*; each of them has their own *shul*, with their own rabbi and own *khazn*. Just as we in the suburb have Rabbi Reb Hersh Ornshteyn, and *they* in the city have only a *magid* [lay preacher], in our *shul* the prayers are led by the famous *khazn* Reb Arn-Sholem, and they have some Boruch Schorr." "Yes," I replied. "*Zeyde*, you say, 'some Boruch Schorr,' and in school the children say that Arn-Sholem should burn in his grave for the sake of Boruch Schorr!" My zeyde became excited and for a moment was silent but suddenly responded, "Only idiots could say that—city fools!" And he gave such a sigh that I much regretted saying so "ugly" a thing.

We went into the city, through various streets, saw many fine Jewish shops, arrived in the "old *shul*," met Jews very similar to all other Jews, prayed the afternoon service together, and saw no difference between city and suburb. And yet, between the two *kehilot*, there prevailed a very large division, a chasm, which to the present day is still not filled in, a sort of contradistinction in all of life that could be felt at every turn. "What can you demand of her, that she should have sense, that she be from the city?"—our neighbor lady said to her maidservant. . . . There were once two *kehilot* in Lemberg, and although the division has not existed legally for a hundred years, it remained in daily life until almost the present day.

How Did Two *Kehilot* Arise and Which Was Older?

Eastern Galicia was once a duchy of its own, and its capital was at first Halych and later Lemberg. Russian dukes ruled here, and their castle stood on the present escarpment, where the mountain descends to Staryi Rynok [Old Market] Square, and where today stands the Temple [the Progressive Synagogue, destroyed by the Germans in 1942]. The name "Old Market" shows clearly that here was once the center of Russian Lemberg. From it also led the most important street—today, Zhukovsky Street—with its old Orthodox churches of St. Nicholas, St. Paraskeva, etc.

And where did the Jews live? Just where present-day Zhukovsky Street crosses Sinagogen Gasse (later, Bożnicza Street) ran the river, and a bridge connected both parts of the city. Jews lived from the other side of the river to the present-day river, where several mills churned, and to the Hintsplatz, where the hangman carried out his executions and the executed would hang on the gallows until the flesh was dried on their bones. And beyond Hintsplatz, far, far across swamps and rivers, was (and is until today) the oldest Jewish cemetery, which was already mentioned in the records in 1411 and where the Lemberg Jews and Karaites were buried until the great cholera of 1855. Only then did the city authorities close that cemetery and open the current new Yanov [today Yanivsky] cemetery.

Who were the Jews in the earliest Lemberg, where did they come from, how did they conduct themselves—these are questions about which all historical sources are silent, just as they say nothing about the city itself. The only certainty is that when the Polish king, Kasimir the Great, received the city as an inheritance (1340), Jews were there. In 1350, however, all of Lemberg burned so completely that the residents considered leaving the city and finding themselves another location. The king then ordered the felling of a large forest that covered the area of the present city, and in that new location erected the walls, which for approximately 400 years enclosed the city and protected it from the enemy in those dark times. . . . Into this new city moved all the Lemberg "nations," such as the Germans, Ruthenians, Armenians, Tatars, and each occupied their own quarter, but the Germans occupied the market and took over the city government. And Jews also entered the city and received their own quarter in the southeast, and here—at the very edge of the city, by the wall (today the corner of Boimuv and Sobieskiego streets), erected their synagogue. The larger portion of the *kehila* remained, however, outside the city and in this way created two separate *kehilot*: the holy community within the city and the holy community outside the city. Each had its own synagogues and study houses, rabbis, judges, cantorial singers, ritual slaughterers, etc., and only death united them, for they had only one common cemetery.

The City

Russian Jews lived in old Russian Lemberg, and German Jews arrived in the city after the great fire. We understand this from the privileges they requested and obtained from the Polish king and from their conduct as a whole. The Jewish quarter was comfortable from the beginning but with time was filled to the last spot. Jews bought up all the non-Jewish locations and laid out houses of stone and wood. In the center of the *kehila* they built the synagogue, a small structure for a *minyan* [prayer quorum] of twenty Jews, and opposite it the study house, slaughterhouse, steam bath, etc.

It was not, however, destined for the Jews to live in safety and security. Besides lawsuits with the city authorities over trade and craftwork, every few years a fire left half the city in misfortune. In 1521, all of Lemberg was destroyed by fire, and the city had hardly rebuilt itself when, in 1571, a new fire broke out in the Jewish quarter and reduced the houses to dust and ash. King Zygmunt August permitted the houses to be rebuilt, but only of brick and stone and not of wood. This order by the king, as well as a reorganization of the Jewish quarter, gave the quarter a new appearance. New houses were built and among them a new synagogue, larger and more beautiful than the old one. Rabbi Yitzhak ben Nachman [1500–1595] bought the location from the city authorities (today 27 Blacharska Street) and on it erected a synagogue and dwelling. The synagogue was built by the Italian master builder Paulo Romano from Tschamut [Switzerland] in the late Gothic style, and the detail, which can still be seen today in the very center of the vaulted roof—"Vayikra Hashem" [The Almighty said]—indicates that construction was completed in 1582.

This beautiful synagogue, which became known as the "Turei Zahav Synagogue," or the synagogue of the "Golden Rose," is today the third oldest in Poland,[1] and has a long and interesting history [it was destroyed in 1942 by the Germans]. In 1602 the Jesuits in Lemberg began to look for a place to build a church and a monastery, and, because the city authorities did not want to give them a place in the city, they informed the king that the place where the Jews built their synagogue belonged to the king and that the city authorities were not allowed to sell it to Rabbi Yitzhak; further, that Rabbi Yitzhak was not allowed to build a synagogue without permission from the pope. This little denunciation caught fire, and King Sigismund III appointed a commission to investigate the question. The matter lasted several years; many hearings were held, all costing a lot of money and ending very badly for the Jews. The final hearing awarded the place and the buildings to the Jesuits, and on February 28, 1606, with great fanfare they took over the synagogue and erected a cross on the peak of the roof. The Jews were devastated; the trustees of the *kehila* and especially the sons of the founder of the synagogue—Rabbi Mordecai and Rabbi Nahman bene Rabbi Yitzhak—moved heaven and earth to recover ownership of the synagogue. Most of all, Rose, the wife of Rabbi Nahman, a modest woman and a known beauty, lobbied on behalf of the community, and, thanks to all the intercessions [i.e., payments to the authorities], after three years, succeeded in having the synagogue returned. On the Sabbath after Purim, 1609, with great joy, the synagogue was renewed, and the city-*khazn* sang a Hebrew song specially written for the celebration by Rabbi Yitzhak Halevy, an older brother of the "Golden Rose." The self-sacrificing service of the "Golden Rose" to the synagogue remains in the memory of the Lemberg community to this day. Today, pious women light candles at her grave in the old cemetery.

The Suburb

At the edge of the Jewish quarter, there was a gate that was closed every evening. On the Sabbath, holidays, and non-Jewish festivals, the gate was locked from both sides, and no one could enter or leave. Inside, it was secure but unhappy; the tall houses and the narrow street with its still narrower alleys and dark courtyards threw a pall over anyone who entered. Here, sun and air were rare guests, and plagues in the quarter lasted for years. Twice a year the street was cleaned. No wonder that in the "Rehov ha-Yehudim" [Jews' Street] lay mountains of garbage that spread a frightful stench. People lived entirely differently in the suburb, outside the walls, in front of the Kraków Gate. . . . The Jewish population lived very close to the gate, and the large synagogue stood not far from the city wall—where the bazaar stands today on Krakówski Square.² In 1624, however, the synagogue and a portion of the Jewish houses burned down, and the city authorities allowed a new synagogue to be built only on condition that it be relocated away from the city walls. And so it was. In 1632, the *kehila* erected a new large synagogue in "the valley of the Posen Court." That is where it stands today, and the entire *kehila* quickly settled around it, so thoroughly that Jewish houses and Jewish streets surrounded the synagogue like children surrounding their mother.

Brothers in Misfortune and Suffering

On Shavuot 1648, the dreadful news arrived in Lemberg that, far away in the eastern regions of the Polish state, the Cossacks had rebelled against the government, joined with the Tatars, and were moving across cities and towns slaughtering Jews and burning their cities. The reports were increasingly frightful, and suddenly Jews with their wives and children appeared on foot and on wagons, telling stories that stood the hair on end. They were not allowed to enter the city because it was so crowded there, and the city authorities were afraid of a plague. But in the suburb, they were welcomed with open arms, clothed and fed, and taken into the homes. Yet the number of refugees grew daily, and soon flames from burning cities and towns could be seen. This was a sign that the enemy was already not far away. And the fires came constantly closer, and suddenly, on the neighboring mountains, Cossacks and Tatars appeared and began shooting at the suburb. It was Rosh Hashanah time. The population in the suburb saw that the situation was dire and moved their merchandise and valuables into the city, sent their wives and children to relatives and friends as much as possible, and the men themselves prepared to defend their homes and study houses. The synagogue was prepared like a fortress, and from the roof cannons were fired. However, the mayor of Lemberg, Martin Groswiener, saw that it was impossible to hold the suburb, and, not wanting the enemy to take the houses, synagogues, and churches, he admitted the entire population into the city and ordered the entire suburb set on fire and burned. With pain and fear, the Jews of the suburb looked on from the city walls at their misfortune and saw how the fire surrounded the roof of the synagogue. . . . [further paragraphs describe the ensuing siege by Chmielnicki and the payment of tribute by the Jews to save themselves]

During the Austrian Period and Today

The trustees from both *kehilot* were united, but conflict remained very strong in daily life. The city viewed the suburb people as having their bundle in hand, ready to flee into the city at the blink of an eye, while they—the city people—were sitting in peace and quiet in their homes and beautiful shops. And the homes and shops had already long not fit within the Jewish quarter but had occupied all the neighboring quarters (Russian; Serbian; Boimów, the foreign exchange district) and even most of the shops in the market. The Christian merchants tried by every means to drive the Jews back into the Jewish quarter (ghetto), tens of commissions came from Warsaw, and the situation led to blows and killings, but the Jews would not retreat from their places. It was finally the *Austrian government* that found the strength to drive the Jews out and in 1796 and 1800 made those quarters free of Jews. Where could the Jews go? There was no room in the Jewish quarter of the city, and so they moved into the *suburb*, which their fathers and grandfathers had left in earlier years. Here, space was sufficient, especially because Austria had removed the city walls and united the city with the suburb, and so the city Jews settled everywhere. . . . Jews understood business, and already by 1806 nearly all the houses in the lower broad street (nos. 1–20) were in Jewish hands. With time this street became the commercial center of the whole city, which attracted all the manufacturers, iron merchants, etc., and the "city" remained empty and lifeless.

Thus it was until 1867, when the constitution abolished the Jewish quarter and allowed Jews to live in the entire city. Wealthy Jews moved into Gentile quarters, and with time the boundary was erased between the Jewish and non-Jewish quarters and between the city and suburb.

The pious and poor segments of the population, however, remain in place to this day: they still live near the *city* or *suburb* synagogue, learn in the city or suburb study house, pose questions of Jewish law to Rabbi Leibele Broide in the suburb or to Rabbi Tzif in the city. They are ever-so-proud of "their" *khazn* and of their *shammes* [sexton] who summons them to the synagogue. And when—may it never occur—the cart goes by with a deceased Jew, they say with a sigh, "Blessed is the Almighty," and ask one another, "Was it a Jew from the city or the suburb who died?"

Introduction Notes:

1. Israel M. Biderman, *Mayer Balaban: Historian of Polish Jewry* (NewYork: Dr. I.M. Biderman Book Committee, 1976), 71.

2. Meir Balaban, *Yidn in poyln* [*Jews in Poland*] (Vilna: B. Kletskin, 1930), 6–7.

3. Meir Balaban, "Tsvey kehiles in eyn shtot (a kapitl fun der geshikhte fun lemberg)" [Two Jewish communities in one city (a chapter in the history of Lviv)], in *Yidn in Poyln* [Jews in Poland], 103–15 (abridged).

4. Majer Balaban, *Dzielnica Żydowska jej dzieje i zabytki* [The Jewish Quarter, its history and monuments] (Lwów: Nakładem Towarzystwa Miłośników Przeszłości Lwowa, 1909), 13.

5. Majer Balaban, *Die Judenstadt von Lublin* [The Jewish city of Lublin] (Berlin: Jüdischer Verlag, 1919), 85.

Article Notes:

1. The oldest two synagogues are to be found in Kraków: the Old Synagogue from the fourteenth century and the Remah Synagogue from 1557.

2. The bazaar was first erected in 1876.

11

The Young Historians Circle in Warsaw, 1923–1939

by Raphael Mahler, 1967

RAPHAEL MAHLER (see also Selection 3 above) and his colleague Emanuel Ringelblum founded the *Yunger historiker krayz* (Young Historians Circle) in Warsaw in 1923 under the guidance of their mentors, Ignacy Schiper and Meir Balaban. Thirty-five students of Jewish history (twenty-four men and eleven women) eventually participated, many remaining active well past their student years. The group ultimately became the Historians Circle of the Society for YIVO (Yiddish Scientific Institute) in Warsaw and published four collections of historical research from 1926 to 1938, all in Yiddish. They and their journal *Bleter far geshikhte* (Pages for history) were honored in postwar Poland when this name was continued in 1948 for the newly founded journal of the Jewish Historical Institute in Warsaw.

In 1965, Bela Mandelsberg (see Selection 16 below), a member of the Young Historians Circle killed during the Holocaust, was remembered in Israel with the publication of a volume of her collected Yiddish writings—in Hebrew translation. It was edited by her prewar teaching colleague, Nachman Blumental, and it included a memorial article about the Young Historians Circle by Mahler in Hebrew.[1] Two years later, in a volume of his own collected Yiddish writings, Mahler published a slightly revised version of the article in Yiddish,[2] which appears below.

The circle of young Jewish historians in Warsaw, a unique occurrence not only among Jews but in the scholarly world in general, was a result of various circumstances of its time. With the establishment of independent

Poland after the First World War, the number of Jewish students in the country, particularly in Warsaw, who chose history as the main subject of their studies grew constantly. From the professional standpoint, perspectives that had not existed in Poland before the war opened for such students: Jewish high schools that were founded by the tens across all of Poland were in need of professional teachers who received their education in universities. If, in the first years after the establishment of these schools, it was often the case that the subject of history would be taught by every teacher who had any connection to the subject, principally lawyers, the situation changed in the mid-1920s: the education ministry itself insisted on adherence to the law, that teachers of history, just like other subjects, should be credentialed graduates of universities in their field.

It is unnecessary to mention that, although the modest career of a high school teacher was the factor that made it possible for Jewish students at the universities to study history, this was not necessarily the sufficient motive for choosing this subject. The interest of the largest number of Jewish students in history arose from the social and national tendencies of that stormy period in Jewish life in Poland: revolutions and counter-revolutions in Eastern Europe and Central Europe, and the social ferment that was an enduring result; the national and political awakening of the Polish Jews and the great rise of the Zionist movement and of the Jewish worker's movement in its various parties; the struggle by Jews for their rights and for their economic existence in the face of discriminatory policies by the government; the increasing emigration to Palestine, which had just then been secured as a national home by the Balfour Declaration and by the British Mandate; and the powerful expansion of the Zionist youth pioneering movement—these were all factors that were liable to strengthen interest in social, economic, and national questions, not only in the present but in history.

Many Jewish students indeed started in the beginning to study general and political history in order to acquire the academic theory and research methods for Jewish history. The majority of them would choose Jewish themes for seminar papers as well as for master's studies and doctoral dissertations. One must mention in this regard the prominent historians of Warsaw University Marceli Handelsman (himself of Jewish descent), Wacław Tokarz, Jan Kochanowski, Henrik Mościcki, and the youngest of them, separately, Stanisław Arnold, as well as a series of their colleagues at the universities of Vilna, Kraków, and Lemberg, who without distinction of party affiliation (Professor Tokarz was an adherent of the nationalist, anti-Jewish Endek Party) very willingly accepted suggestions from their students about Jewish topics, and some even required such a specialization on their own initiative. This is also not surprising because, apart from two or three Jewish students in Warsaw who devoted themselves to ancient Jewish history, all the other Jewish students who chose Jewish topics did not depart from the framework of Jewish history in Poland. The Polish historians considered research on the Jewish past in Poland to be an integral part of Polish historiography in general. We see indeed that three of the Warsaw University historians mentioned, Tokarz, Mościcki, and Handelsman, incidentally all three former students of the well-known Professor Szymon Ashkenazi who was then still active in Warsaw (he died in 1935), just like their teachers, also published studies in the field of the history of the Jews in Poland.[1]

And yet, despite their interest in the history of Jews in Poland, they were not professionals in that field, and their Jewish students themselves needed to find their own path toward becoming acquainted with the history of their people. That was the situation in 1923 when the "Seminar for Jewish History" was founded at the Jewish Academic Home in Warsaw, the club of Jewish students on Nowy Świat Street that moved a few years later to its own spacious Jewish Academic Home on Praga Street. The initiator, organizer, and living spirit of the seminar was the young student from Sącz, Emanuel Ringelblum, today the world-famous hero and historian of the Warsaw ghetto. Ringelblum's exuberant initiative, his great stubbornness, his rare organizational talent, and above all his dedication with life and limb to the idea of elevating Jewish culture in general and Jewish scholarship in particular—we have these rare virtues of his to thank for the creation and existence of the first circle of young Jewish historians in Poland.

Ringelblum dwells on the principal tasks and goals of the seminar in his well-known article "Three Years of the Seminar for Jewish History," which he published in the first anthology of the circle, *Yunger historiker* [Young historian] (1926), as follows: "urging Jewish academic historians to select Jewish topics to read in the university seminars; acquainting the members of the circle with the bibliography of sources and historical literature about the history of Jews in Poland"; and the most important, "becoming acquainted with the specific methods and means one must use in Jewish research work."

The first members of the circle were Lipman Comber, Elazar Feldman, Hava-Jocheved Warszawska, and Bela Mandelsberg. In September 1924, the author of these lines, who had then settled in Warsaw as a teacher at the Askola School, joined Ringelblum in the leadership of the circle.

The patrons of the circle in the first years were Dr. Meir Balaban and Dr. Yitzhak Schiper.

Barely two years after the creation of the Young Historians Circle in Warsaw, in 1925, the Yiddish Scientific Institute, YIVO, was founded in Vilna, of which Ringelblum was one of the founders and among the first members of the Historical Section. Three years later, in 1928, the Institute for Judaic Studies opened in Warsaw,[2] which had the task of preparing teachers for Jewish high schools in the areas of Hebrew language and literature, Tanach [Hebrew Bible], and Jewish history. In the same year, Dr. Meir Balaban, docent at the same institute, was named docent of the chair for Jewish history at Warsaw University, the first and only chair for this discipline in Poland. On the face of it, all of these institutions fulfilled the tasks that the seminar at the Jewish Academic Home at first set for itself; stimulating the selection of topics in Jewish history would now be unnecessary, once the chair existed for Dr. Balaban, and his chair at the university and in the Judaic Institute also solved the question of giving direction to learning and research.

But indeed the fact was that the circle of young Jewish historians in Warsaw reached such a degree of success in the second decade of independent Poland, in the years 1928–1939, that the chief task of the circle was not alleviated with the rise of the scholarly and academic institutions for Jewish history, but became still more important for life: the more the number of Jewish students of Jewish history increased, along with the number of graduates in these studies, the greater the need for an organized circle to clarify problems of Jewish history from the standpoint of historical theory and research methods. It was indeed no accident that the discussions at the meetings of the circle, which took place regularly each month, were occupied with theoretical and methodological questions called forth by the reports that were read. After the founding of the Historical Section at YIVO in Vilna, in 1928, the seminar was officially incorporated into the section. After an interlude of a few years, around 1933, the circle was reorganized under the name "Historians Circle of the Society for YIVO in Warsaw."

The development of the Young Historians Circle is reflected in its anthologies that were published in the years 1926–1938. The first collection, which appeared in 1926 under the name *Yunger historiker*, was still a modest grouping of "first songs," as the editorship itself called it in the dedication to Simon Dubnow. The three members of the editorial board, Jacob Berman, Raphael Mahler, and Emanuel Ringelblum, published articles about theoretical and organizational questions of Jewish historical research. Besides these, the volume contained articles on historical topics by Jacob Berman, Hava Warszawska, Ester Tenenbaum, Bela Mandelsberg, L. Comber, Emanuel Ringelblum, and Pinchas Kon (from Vilna). The second volume of *Yunger historiker*, dedicated to Dr. Yitzhak Schiper on the twenty-fifth year of his historiographic work, appeared in 1928 with a scope of 150 pages. To allow space for larger studies, the number of participants was limited: R. Mahler, Bela Mandelsberg, Lipman Comber, Philip Friedman, and Pinchas Kon. The editor of the volume was R. Mahler.

The second volume established a format for the further anthologies, which also changed their name, as an expression of the development of the circle and its increasing ambitions: instead of *Yunger historiker*, the anthologies were now called *Bleter far geshikhte* [Pages for history], i.e., that the authors no longer considered themselves beginners. In the first volume of *Bleter*, which appeared in 1934, studies were published by R. Mahler, Elazar Feldman, D. Goldberg-Feldman, L. Comber, and Yeshaye [Isaiah] Trunk. The second and last volume of *Bleter far geshikhte* appeared in 1938 under the editorship of R. Mahler and contained larger works by M. Kremer, A. Eisenbach, Y. Trunk, M. Rosenblat, and R. Mahler.

In the foreword to the third volume, the number of members of the circle was stated as thirty. The young historians, the inspired volunteers in the field of scholarly research, were certainly worthy of having their names recorded in a memorial book of Jewish historiography in Poland. Most unfortunately, no list remains of the members of the circle, and we are able only to reconstruct it from memory. Here are the names of the members, whom we remember, who belonged to the circle over the years, some of them during all sixteen years of the circle's existence. We will list first the sadly smaller number of those who survived the great *khurbn*:

[Mahler then provides a paragraph of biographical information on each of the survivors: Aharon (Artur) Eisenbach, Helena Biderman, Jacob Berman, Dvorah Goldberg-Feldman, Raphael Gerber, Yeshaye Warshawski, Yeshaye (Isaiah) Trunk, Raphael Mahler, Aharon (Aaron) Sawicki, Elazar Feldman, Meir Kozhen, Joseph Kermish, and Meir Rosenblat.]

And here, to be distinguished from the living, is a list of members of the Young Historians Circle who were killed during the *khurbn* at the unclean hands of the German murderers, may their names be erased:

[Mahler then provides a paragraph of biographical information on each of the deceased: Israel Ostersetser, Falik Haffner, Hava-Jocheved

Warszawsha, Lote Wegmeister, Szymon Zajczyk, Ester Tenenbaum, Helena Czamarka (Mahler indicates that she died before the war), Natalia Lewinska (married name, Rotenstein), Bela Mandelsberg (married name, Szyldkraut), Celina Mendelson, Philip Friedman (Mahler indicates that he died after the war, in 1960), Shlomo Tsalel, Lipman Comber, Pinchas Kon, Esher Kotek, Mordechai and Ruzsza Koniecpolski, Aharon Koninski, Moshe Kremer, Arieh Rasin, Emanuel Ringelblum, Szmuel Szymkiewicz.]

May this list be an eternal light to the memory of the young historians who were killed in the very flowering of their young years together with the Jewish people in Poland, to the study of whose history they dedicated their best efforts and abilities with their entire youthful enthusiasm. With the murder of this elect group of individuals [*pliaed*], the foundation of the historiography of Polish Jews, which they had so monumentally prepared themselves to construct, was also destroyed. May those who spilled their innocent blood be cursed for all time!

Introduction Notes:

1. Rafa'el Mahler, "Hug HaHistoriyonim HaTza'irim B'Varshah," *Mehkarim le-toldot Yehude Lublin* [Studies on the history of Jews of Lublin], ed. Nachman Blumental (Tel Aviv: Hug mokire shemah shel B. Mandelsberg-Shildkraut, 1965), 29–38.

2. Rafoel Mahler, "Der krayz 'yunge historiker' in varshe," *Historiker un vegvayzer* [Historians and guides] (Tel Aviv: Yisroel-Bukh, 1967), 302–15.

Article Notes:

1. Ashkenazi, Mościcki, and Handelsman published their articles in the quarterly *Kwartalnik Poświęcony Badaniu Przeszlosci Żydów w Polsce, Rocsznik* I, zeszyt 1, 3 (Warsaw 1912). Already ten years earlier, Tokarz published his work in the quarterly *Kwartaknik Historiczny* 12 (1902).

2. Institut Nauk Judaistycznych.

12
Varied Were the Ways (of Jewish Resistance)
by Mark Dworzecki, 1946

MARK DWORZECKI (1908–1975, pronounced "Dvorzhetski"; see also Selections 33, 39, 42, and 48 below) reported that he was born either in Vilna (today Vilnius, Lithuania) or in Maytshet (today Moŭčadź, Belarus). He was a medical doctor before World War II, ultimately surviving the Vilna ghetto and several concentration camps, but losing his parents, wife, and two sisters. On escaping from a forced march in Germany in April 1945, he settled in Paris where he immediately began writing and lecturing and became president of the Survivors Union in France. His articles were published in Yiddish in the Labor Zionist press in Paris and New York and often reprinted in Hebrew in Tel Aviv. Many were advance chapters of his history of the Vilna ghetto, *Jerusalem of Lithuania in Struggle and Extermination* (Yiddish, Paris, 1948), which remains one of the basic texts on the ghetto.[1] In 1949, he settled in Israel, where he practiced medicine by day and wrote Holocaust history at night. The Hebrew translation of his history of the Vilna ghetto received the first Israel Prize in social science in 1952.[2]

One of Dworzecki's early articles—on the subject of unarmed resistance—presaged a major theme of his work and a new direction for Holocaust historiography. He observed that, in the early postwar setting, only the relatively rare instances of armed resistance by Jews were celebrated as heroic acts. Instead, he chose to emphasize the idea of "Amidah," of "standing up against" the Nazi occupier by all of the unarmed means, including passive, spiritual, economic, medical, sanitary, and cultural resistance, without which there would have been no survivors. Over time, his innovation received wide acceptance and ultimately redefined the study of Jewish resistance. The emergence of his ideas beyond Yiddish circles has traditionally been dated from his final work on the subject—his address on "The Day-To-Day Stand of the Jews" at the 1968 Yad Vashem conference on resistance, first published in 1971 (in Hebrew and English).[3] However, its origin lies in his prescient 1946 Yiddish essay that appears below.[4] His ideas were cited as early as 1949 by other Yiddish historians, and they set Yiddish research on the Holocaust ahead of work in other languages by at least a generation.

Wherever a Jew from the ghetto goes and comes, the question is put to him by his brother Jews:

Tell what you know, and what you heard, about Jewish resistance in the ghettos.

And with enchanted eyes, Jews listen to the stories of active Jewish fighting: and from line to line, from detail to detail, grows the whole epic of Jewish resistance in the ghettos, forests, and fronts—the epic that blinds with its tragic beauty—because we ourselves in the course of generations have lacked minimal consciousness of this hidden strength that lies dormant in the Jewish soul.

★ ★ ★

And when I hear, and when I myself speak, of those days and of those people who were engaged in active fighting, of whom only individuals remained alive and the majority were lost namelessly to eternity, and of the few who died fighting and became the synonym of all the unknown fighters of active Jewish resistance—

In those moments a question disturbs me:

—Do we not commit a great wrong against our murdered fathers and mothers, brothers, and wives, when we speak only of the active, armed fight in the ghettos—and we do not recount the other means of Jewish struggle?

And the question often disturbs me:

—Was armed resistance truly the one and only means of Jewish fighting in the ghettos, of Jewish resistance and struggle? And should we recount only this to children and to neighboring peoples?—

But there were also other ways of struggling—perhaps not as heroic—perhaps outmoded and naïve—and not effective—and not suitable—but they are still an expression of the Jewish will to fight.

★ ★ ★

And how many times—it seems to me:

From the vanished nights of catastrophe peer out at me so many silent eyes of thousands of comrades known to me in the ghettos, and of murdered tens of thousands unknown to me, and their quiet, pained complaint calls out to me:

We are those who fell without weapons in hand.

We are the millions—

None of our guides and leaders informed us or warned us that the day of destruction of millions was here!

And we never prepared ourselves for the defense of millions.

And no one taught us how to make weapons and what to do with weapons—

Only a few in our midst, and only thousands among the total of millions, had the good fortune to fall with weapons in hand—

But none of us had weapons in hand or had acquired knowledge of armed defense—

And thus did we go to death.

Do all of you survivors believe, and you yourself think—you who were in the ghetto—that we died without resistance and lived without struggle?

★ ★ ★

And so I see nights in the Vilna ghetto.

And I hear: soft taps in cellars and attics—Jews building hiding places, bunkers, underground ways and tunnels to the city outside, to sewers. And in the ghettos, there grew a Jewish underground city—the city of bunkers.

And here live unregistered Jews, preparing food, and wooden planks, and buckets of water—to be able to live there hidden for days, weeks, and months from the Germans and their intent to kill them—and here others also hid a book, and quietly wrote a poem or remembrance.

And in these bunkers, tens of thousands of Jews met their deaths, blown up by German dynamite, or suffocated by lack of air—or because the still cry of a child betrayed them and brought the steps of Nazi boots—

And only individuals among the bunker-Jews lived to see the glow of freedom—

And how then will Jewish history judge our bunker-brothers and bunker-fathers? Will it say this is how the Jews ran away from the fight; or, that this is how masses of Jews in those conditions of not being prepared and not being armed—in those conditions and despite those conditions—sought a way of struggling against the Nazi intent to destroy the unarmed?

★ ★ ★

In those days of hunger in the ghetto—of fifty grams of bread a day—

I see them, the abandoned children in the darkness of the last night watch; I see how their slender little bodies slip out from the ghetto through attics and holes to get a potato, a piece of bread, by begging from neighboring Christians—and to bring them into the ghetto—

I see the mothers, the lone mothers, who from the first day in the ghetto remained without their provider of food; I see in the gray mornings how they smuggle themselves out of the ghetto without passes, to barter a dress for something to eat from familiar Christian neighbors, and to bring it for their child—

(And I see how large numbers of them were caught and put in prison—from there to Ponar—and did not return again to their unsuspecting child)—

And thus I see all of the thousands of brother Jews who—returning from their work for the Germans—smuggle in through the ghetto gate a piece of forbidden bread, a little flour: in compresses around their body, in bandages around their feet, in hairdressings, in double lids of their carrying cases for tools—

(the bread and flour that were secretly exchanged for the price of a last garment, wife's wedding dress, wedding ring).

And thus I see how sacks of flour, and carrots, and beets were smuggled into the ghetto—through roofs, chimneys, holes in walls, attics, cellars, windows, and balconies, through coffins and through wagons of wood, through carts of garbage—

The doubt arises in my thoughts:

Is this what history will say: this is how the Jews in the time of their fateful murder risked their lives for bread and not for their honor?—

Or: This is how abandoned children, lone mothers, and defenseless masses who had never heard the name of resistance—unconsciously conducted economic resistance against the Nazi intent to destroy them through hunger?—

★ ★ ★

And thus I see the engineer Markus in the Vilna ghetto, with a helper prying tin from the roofs and making small inexpensive "furnaces," at the time when all the ghetto dwellers froze in thirty-degree frost without timber—

And in this way, he founded workshops in the ghetto and there were made planks for sleeping and wooden sandals for bare feet, and dishes for eating, and medical instruments and a saw and an ax—

And thus I see all of them in the ghetto who made washing compound from ash, and starch from potato skins—and helped to make endurable this unbearable life.

And few of them fell while fighting, and most of them were dragged to Ponar and murdered in the camps—

(And it seems to me that I hear their quiet request to the Jewish writer of history:

—On the day when you seal the book of Jewish resistance, ask yourself whether in our deeds there also lies resistance to the Germans' murderous intent.)

★ ★ ★

I see thus the Jewish doctors, nurses, and sanitary workers from the ghetto in the days of destruction, when the outbreak of the spotted typhus epidemic threatened, in the days when mountains of garbage, dung, and urine in the ghetto courtyards and the filth of dirty toilets threatened an outbreak of stomach typhus and a dysentery epidemic—

I see how medicines were collected from ruined houses, how outpatient urgent care was established, bathing and delousing stations—and the epidemics in the ghetto were interrupted—

And I see the old Dr. Fingerhut from Warsaw as he produces agents against pregnancy—at a time when pregnancy threatened death—

And I see Dr. Girshovicz from Vilna, as he produces vitamins in the ghetto, when the children were covered with abscesses from lack of vitamins—

And I see Dr. Lazar Finkelstein from Kovne, as he produces iodine in the ghetto when there arose in the ghetto the mysterious epidemic of "Struma"-sickness (enlarged thyroid) among 75 percent of the children—and I still hear the heated discussion—how many drops should one give to the children, when in a few days or so their murder awaits them—

And I hear the voice of the murdered doctors:

—It is nothing that we were murdered, but as long as we lived, we did not allow the German intent to kill us through epidemics to be realized.

(And perhaps the writer of history will record their action under the chapter: sanitary resistance of the Jews in the ghettos.[1] And perhaps he will say: it is madness to heal people for whom death waits.)

★ ★ ★

And thus I see the teachers in the ghetto, and the elementary schools and kindergartens that they erected, and their self-sacrifice in the studies and in finding a book for teaching and in organizing a children's holiday. I see a noble, unbounded love.

And I see thus the old teacher Moshe Olitski,[2] strolling among the children during their break from classes, and I hear his question to me:

—You see how the children are dancing? Do you rejoice? Do you love the children? I know: they will all be murdered—

And thus I see the writers, and they are writing works and memoirs so the time of barbarism will not be forgotten, and the poets write poems, and the artists paint pictures, and the performers put on Yiddish and Hebrew theater, and choirs sing Yiddish and Hebrew songs; and literary lectures and academic anniversaries—

And Z[elig] Kalmanovich, the man of pen and spirit, goes and complains to the ghetto Jews:

—"But no sadness!—but no sadness"—and little remained of the men of pen and spirit, of the teachers and their children—

(And perhaps the writer of Jewish history will say:

—It is madness to write poems, and put on theater, and teach children facing death—

And perhaps he will say:

—This is how the Jews produced cultural resistance against the German intent to break them spiritually before their murder—)

And thus I see them—

The rabbi who went to his death on the way to Ponar with a Torah scroll in hand, with songs of consolation [*Nahamu, nahamu*], and fell under the whip, finding consolation—

And the rabbi who went to the Estonian concentration camp with a Torah scroll wrapped around his body, and so worked while digging and carrying burdens, and daily awaited being caught at the gate with his concealed load—

(And perhaps the writer of history will say:

—"Unarmed they fell! . . ."

And perhaps he will record:

Thus they created moral resistance against the German intent to break the Jewish spirit, and thus in their own manner they struggled—)

* * *

And I hear those who say:

This is all merely an expression of a subconscious, primitive, fighting instinct for survival and of a feeling of self-preservation.

And I also hear the voice:

—The father of each conscious act of resistance is the subconscious instinct for life.

So, see and remember: the Nazis did not succeed in strangling the Jewish instinct for life in the ghettos. And the primitive individual fight for survival acquired the collective forms of organized popular struggle to outlive the enemy, to the point of conscious will to fight and die for the people's honor.

* * *

And when I hear about active armed fighting in the ghettos and forests, and about the underground emissaries from ghetto to ghetto—I see them all—the Zionist pioneer—the Bundist—the Betarist—the Communist, and a brightness streams forth from the thought:

The path of active fighting does not remain the inheritance of any movement but is the common inheritance of Israel in the ghettos. Might and readiness to fight slumbered in all strata of the Jewish people, but not all strata received the education to fight—and to do underground work—in time.

* * *

I see them and I recall the daily life of the simple Jew in the ghettos, and there is forged before my eyes an unbreakable chain of both the instinctive-individual and the collective-organized struggle of a nation in which the will for resistance lies deeply buried, but which at that time had not learned the doctrine of fighting and let itself be led astray by false illusions.

And I also know: the fight of the Jews in the ghettos ended with murder and with the victory of brutal strength, not because the ordinary Jew lacked courage and fighting spirit—but because the minimum conditions for Jewish victory were lacking.

So, should we tell our children and the neighboring peoples only about active Jewish resistance—or also about all the ways of Jewish struggle in the ghetto, in which the popular will for resistance is revealed—

Introduction Notes:

1. M. Dvorzhetski, *Yerusholayim d'lite in kamf un umkum* [Jerusalem of Lithuania (Vilna) in struggle and extermination] (Paris: Yidishn natsyonaln arbeter-farband in amerike / Yidishn folksfarband in frankraykh, 1948).

2. Meir Dworzecki, *Yerushalayim de-Lita bi-meri ube-sho'ah*, trans. by Ch. Sch. Ben-Avram (Tel Aviv: Hotsa'at Mifleget po'ale Eretz Yisra'el, 1951).

3. Mark Dworzecki, "The Day-To-Day Stand of the Jews," in *Jewish Resistance during the Holocaust: Proceedings of the Conference on Manifestations of Jewish Resistance, Jerusalem, April 7–11, 1968* (Jerusalem: Yad Vashem, 1971), 152–81.

4. Mark Dvorzhetski, "Farshidn zenen geven di vegn," *Unzer vort* (Paris, June 21, 1946) and *Idisher kemfer* (New York, June 28, 1946); Hebrew translation, "Darkhe ha-ma'avak ha-Yehudi ba-Geta'ot," in ed. Simon Rawidowicz, *Metsudah* V–VI (London, 1948): 519–23; condensed Hebrew version in Meir Dworzecki, *Ben ha-Betarim* (Tel Aviv: Kiryat Sefer, 1956), 51–56.

Article Notes:

1. [The topic of Dworzecki's first book, published the same year: *Kamf farn gezunt in geto-vilne* [The struggle for health in the Vilna ghetto] (Paris-Geneva: OSE farband, 1946). French: *Le ghetto de Vilna: rapport sanitaire* (Geneva: Union OSE, 1946).]

2. [Dworzecki's own first Hebrew teacher, in Vilna.]

13

The Wooden Synagogues in Poland before the Holocaust

by Rachel Wischnitzer, 1962

RACHEL WISCHNITZER (1885–1989) was born in Minsk, Belorussia (today Belarus), and became a prominent historian of Jewish art and architecture. She graduated as an architect from the École Spéciale d'Architecture in Paris in 1907 and received a master of fine arts degree from New York University in 1944. She and her husband, Mark Wischnitzer, published the pathbreaking, modernist Yiddish/Hebrew art journals *Milgroym/Rimonim* in Berlin from 1922 to 1924, to which she contributed regularly. Most of the 344 works in her bibliography appeared in German or English, with only occasional pieces in Yiddish.[1] She is unique among the historians selected for this volume in being unable to write in Yiddish but, wishing to communicate with a Yiddish-speaking audience, selected writings to be translated into Yiddish from German or English. Her publications in Yiddish include the entry on Jewish art in the Yiddish encyclopedia (1940) and a significant article on synagogue architecture in *YIVO bleter* (1947).

Many of Wischnitzer's later writings in Yiddish were book reviews published in *YIVO bleter*. The last and most comprehensive was her 1962 review of the Polish book *Wooden Synagogues* (1957), by the non-Jewish, wife-husband team of Polish architects, Maria and Kazimierz Piechotkowie.[2] It is noteworthy, first, for its compact exposition of the provenance of the book and its illustrations, the history of the renowned wooden synagogues, and the scope of related research by herself and others. But it is equally noteworthy in comparison to her review of the English-language edition of the same book that appeared two years later in *Jewish Social Studies*.[3] Typical of much Yiddish historical writing, especially after the Holocaust, the Yiddish review presumes a shared base of knowledge and concerns between author and reader. The English review is shorter, more sharply professorial, directed mostly at different points, and presumes no relationship with the reader, despite appearing in a Jewish publication. The Yiddish review is presented below.

According to what we know about the destruction caused by the Nazis in the archives and museums of Poland during the Second World War, it would be difficult to expect new scholarly studies in the field of synagogue architecture, simply for lack of research materials.

Already very early, the synagogues in Poland drew the attention of scholars and art lovers. At the end of the nineteenth century, the Kraków Commission for Art History began to publish works about synagogues. At the beginning of the twentieth century, Mokłowski and Gloger had already included synagogues in their histories of Polish folk art.[1] Both Jews and non-Jews expressed an interest in these structures, which made a definite impression on the Polish landscape. Alois Breyer, a young student at the architecture school in Vienna, knew indirectly from the painter Isidor Kaufmann about the synagogues in Poland and chose them as a theme for his dissertation. In 1910, he made a journey to Poland. He visited Kraków, Lwów, Piotrków, and a series of cities and towns where there were still wooden synagogues. His work was published in 1934 by Max Grunwald.[2] In 1947, G. Lukomski's book appeared, with a very unreliable text but with the virtue that it included reproductions the author had received from the Warsaw Polish Polytechnic. These reproductions were very welcome because it was thought that this collection of photographs in Warsaw had been lost. The present book brings the uplifting news that the majority of these photographs and drawings, made by Szymon Zajczyk, a victim of the Nazis, were miraculously hidden and are now once again in Warsaw. The authors of our book made use of this material.

Like Szymon Zajczyk, who was an architect and a historian of architecture [and a member of Ringelblum and Mahler's Young Historians Circle in Warsaw], our authors are architects who have devoted themselves to the study of art. Their book is the first in a project on synagogue architecture in Poland. It is richly illustrated with first-class reproductions that fill 143 pages. The synagogue in Grodno, for example, is represented by sixteen pictures. Of special interest is the drawing of the wooden vault in the synagogue in Przedbórz, which would simply delight Percival Goodman, one of our leading [American] synagogue architects, who reintroduced wood into synagogue architecture.

The authors begin their study with the problem of city planning, a difficult problem in Poland, about which several monographs have been published in the last few years. This chapter is illustrated with old maps of cities, in which they indicate the Jewish neighborhoods and where the synagogues appeared in the context of these neighborhoods. They indicate that only in Kuzmir [Kazimierz Dolny, Poland], near Kraków, and in Lemberg [today Lviv, Ukraine] were the Jewish neighborhoods true ghettos surrounded by a wall. Although Jews in other cities also lived in special neighborhoods, there was no known marked division between them and the other parts of the city. In addition—before it became very crowded in these neighborhoods—there was absolutely no difference in the width of the streets.

In the second chapter, they deal with the masonry synagogues of Central Europe and Poland. They base themselves on the works of [Alfred] Grotte, [Richard] Krautheimer, [Meir] Balaban, [Ignacy] Schiper, and [Moses] Schorr. The authors apparently did not see my article "Mutual Influences Between Eastern and Western Europe in Synagogue Architecture from the 12th to the 18th Century" (*YIVO bleter* XXIX (1947): 3–50), which also appeared in English in *YIVO Annual* II–III (1947/48): 25–68. The most important chapter is devoted to the problem of wooden synagogues in Poland, the actual theme of the book. The authors contend it is not the material—namely, wood, stone, brick—that determines the character of a building, but the purpose, or, as they call it, the "program" of the building. This is a fertile observation that put an end to the eternal discussion: what influenced what? Also important is the style of the period, which had a clear influence on the "program." Thus, for example, the unified, integrated style of the Renaissance replaced the medieval concept of the synagogue, and, thus, the influence of the mystical strivings of the Baroque period became visible when people experimented with effects of light in the enclosed *bima* [reader's platform]. Later, the Neoclassical style also influenced Jewish synagogue architecture, which became apparent in a soberer tone.

In the subsequent paragraphs, the authors deal with the relationship between synagogue architecture in Poland and local art. They contend that Jews were never as isolated as people sometimes assume. There were not only economic, but also cultural, relations between the Jewish and non-Jewish populations. Animosities were the result of class conflicts rather than national conflicts. The wooden synagogues, they argue, had their roots in a local tradition. Whoever the woodcarvers may have been—and some of them, we know, were Jews—they clearly show signs of Polish artistic work. This may be so or not, but a few examples of Polish wooden churches or secular architecture would substantially confirm this standpoint. Unfortunately, they do not provide such comparative examples. It is worthwhile to mention that the wooden churches in the Carpathian region, which W. R. Zaloziecky discusses,[3] show another type of structure, although here and there one finds similarities between them and the Jewish synagogues.

Although the authors are entirely objective in their evaluations, they have nevertheless slightly exaggerated the degree of influence in attempting to find local prototypes for Jewish synagogue architecture. This comes to the fore in their description of the synagogues in Gombin [Gąbin, Poland] (rebuilt 1893) and Szepes [Sierpc, Poland] with their double towers and round cupolas. They see in these art forms local influences. In truth, there are stonework influences that appeared in German synagogue architecture in the 1850s and from there spread to Poland.

The reproductions are arranged in alphabetical order. This has the virtue of making it unnecessary to number them in the text. In a separate section, there is a detailed description of the synagogues that are reproduced. In this way, the text is liberated from unrelated matters, and it is easier to find the desired item. Overall, the book is beautifully published. The spine is decorated with the two tablets of the covenant. An index would have added much to the book.

Introduction Notes:

1. Rachel Wischnitzer, *From Dura to Rembrandt: Studies in the History of Art* (Milwaukee–Vienna–Jerusalem: Aldrich; IRSA Verlag; Center for Jewish Art, 1990), 180–87 (which omits, however, nearly all her Yiddish book reviews, including the one presented here).

2. Rokhl Vishnitser, review of Maria i Kazimierz Piechotkowie, *Bóżnice drewniane* [Wooden synagogues] (Warsaw: Budownictwo i Architektura, 1957), *YIVO bleter* XLII (1952): 294–96.

3. Rachel Wischnitzer, review of Maria and Kazimierz Piechotka, *Wooden Synagogues* (Warsaw: Arkady, 1959), *Jewish Social Studies* 26 (October 1964): 252–53.

Article Notes:

1. [Kazimierz Mokłowski. *Sztuka Ludowa w Polsce* (Lwów: Altenberg, 1903); Zygmunt Gloger, *Budownictwo drzewne i wyroby z drzewa w dawnej Polsce* [Wooden architecture and wooden products in old Poland], vol. 1 (Warsaw: Lazarski, 1907).]

2. [Alois Breier, Max Eisler, and Max Grundwald, *Holzsynagogen in Polen* (Baden bai Wien: Grunwald, 1934).]

3. W. R. Zaloziecky, *Gothische und Barocke Holzkirchen in den Karpathenländern* (Vienna: Krystall-Verlag, 1926).

14

The Soup Kitchen and the Yiddish Theater in the Warsaw Ghetto

by Rachel Auerbach, 1977

RACHEL AUERBACH (1903–1976) was born in Lanowitz, Russian Volhynia (today Lanivtsi, Ukraine), and received her master's degree in psychology and philosophy from the University of Lwów in 1928. Before World War II, she worked as a journalist, writing in both Yiddish and Polish on psychology, education, and literature. In the Warsaw ghetto, at the request of Emanuel Ringelblum who directed many self-help activities, she organized a soup kitchen and then documented its activities for his Oyneg Shabes archive. In March 1943, she escaped from the ghetto and survived in hiding on the "Aryan" side.

Nearly all of Auerbach's writings during and after the war are in Yiddish and consist of reportage—engaged and expressive first-person accounts of people and events rather than "history." As she herself stated, "I write only on the basis of personal acquaintance, of personal encounters."[1] But starting with Ringelblum and the Oyneg Shabes project in the ghetto, she devoted her wartime and postwar careers to the service of history, and her coworkers were historians. In 1945, she established the oral history program at the Central Jewish Historical Commission in Poland under the leadership of Philip Friedman, for which she interviewed hundreds of survivors and trained others as interviewers. With the opening of Yad Vashem in Israel in 1953, she directed their oral history program for the remainder of her career, working closely with Nachman Blumental and Joseph Kermish.

Selections by Auerbach could be found for any section of this volume. She has long been known for her writings on Treblinka and on the Warsaw Ghetto Uprising. Most recently, the final volumes of her Yiddish memoirs about life in the Warsaw ghetto appeared in English, edited and translated by Samuel Kassow (the first volume in full, the second with related excerpts). Two additional selections from her second volume—on still further topics—are translated for the first time below.

The first is a portrait of her colleague in the soup kitchen, Chaim-Leib Kozlowski, who was active before the war in Agudas Yisroel (the world movement of Orthodox Jewry).[2] It is one of the rare instances in which religious Jewish life appears specifically in her writings or in non-Orthodox Yiddish historical writing in general. The second describes, as she would put it, the "final act" of Yiddish theater in the Warsaw ghetto and the surprising connection between the soup kitchen and the creation of theater in the ghetto.

Chaim-Leib Kozlowski, a Pious Colleague in the Soup Kitchen of the Warsaw Ghetto

Before the war, he was the editor of an Aguda [Orthodox Union] newspaper for youth. In the leadership of the soup kitchen, he represented the religious circles, raising issues about whether certain foods were kosher. It could be imagined that in his own setting he must, at least, belong to the liberal, progressive wing—to the sector that brought about a certain modernization of party life and perhaps indeed of lifestyle itself. Certainly, he had to be a scholar and a keeper of the commandments in all their minutiae. But at the same time, he was learned in secular Jewish communal life, better read in modern Yiddish literature than any of the dedicated "secular" cultural *apikorsim* [heretics, freethinkers].

In order not to draw attention on the street from passing German soldiers, he did not wear a beard. But he was also not clean-shaven. His cheeks were shadowed with a sort of prickly stubble of dark hair growth, which he would treat with a certain haphazardness, or with a dull razor. His ski hat, which most Jewish men wore during the occupation, he would not remove during meetings. Also, the overcoat, which almost always enveloped his thin, agile figure, had to be part of the hidden Jewish attire. The obvious "Jewish" nose dominated his narrow face, and a mischievous smile would sometimes radiate from his extraordinarily wise, bespectacled eyes.

Many times, I have recalled the spontaneous reciprocal closeness that developed between antagonistic, mutually isolated elements of the Jewish social fabric in connection with their collaboration in a joint assistance organization. Naturally, difference and prior estrangement created interest and attraction. Well known is the great friendship between the Left Poale-Zion [Socialist-Zionist] Dr. Emanuel Ringelblum and the young Rabbi Shimon Huberband, who, under Ringelblum's influence, matured into one of the most important chroniclers of the secret ghetto archive.

It would be a great exaggeration to compare my acquaintance with Chaim Leib Kozlowski to the deep closeness and understanding that existed between the radical Polish historian and the politically conservative religious leader. Nevertheless, in my extended encounters and conversations with the pious journalist, a paradoxical mutual interest and sympathy were expressed between two foreign worlds. His balancing on the boundary between two eras and fundamentally different forms of Jewish spirituality, his sharp wit, his passionate approach to the problems of the day, made him a more interesting conversational partner to me than any of the modern-educated colleagues from my own circle.

Walking along the corridors of the central kitchen at 5 Tłomackie Street, we would snatch a chat, exchange a joke. Kozlowski knew, apparently, not only traditional Hebrew but also modern Hebrew, because he would sign his name to a letter or report for the central organization without the vowels. I would, therefore—referring to this, for me, strange orthography—call him not Kozlowski but Kzlubski, and he would laugh heartily at that each time.

As a result, he would pay me back whenever he saw me, with a reference to my connection to Itzik Manger [the famous Yiddish writer with whom Auerbach lived for a while before the war], by beginning to hum the melody of "Gypsy, Play Me a Song, Green Leaves on the Fiddle," a Romanian-Gypsy folksong that Manger made over into Yiddish and popularized in Poland.

In the final period before the deportation, after January 1942, our two kitchens were converted into convalescent kitchens—his kosher and mine, not. As a result, we had common problems, borrowed food products from each other, intervened together about allocations, about budgets. We could not achieve much, but we tried.

★ ★ ★

As I have emphasized many times, the *frume* [religiously observant] Jews were swept away by the stream of destruction in a greater percentage than other classes of people. Kozlowski's wife, a young mother, was a teacher in a Bais Yaakov school [for Orthodox girls]. I happened to see them during the second or third week of the deportation. I no longer recall in what circumstances they parted from their sweet two-and-a-half-year-old child. Together with their parents, they had settled in a hiding place, and from there the child was taken along with the grandfather and grandmother. Mrs. Kozlowski was halfway out of her mind with sorrow and longing for her child. Unable to find any consolation for her, he brought her once, the poor thing, to me in the kitchen. They wandered around the ghetto like two shadows, and, as the third shadow, death strode after them. And when it was that death finally overtook them, I did not hear.

Intoxicated with pain, the young mother begged God to take her as quickly as possible, because "there" she would find her child.

Theater in the Ghetto

When the ghetto was instituted and the Jews were locked in among themselves, professional performing artists, to the extent possible, began returning to their craft.

As I have often written, the self-help activities of the house- and region-committees created a great demand for artistic forces, with whose participation entertainments were organized in order to extract more and more means from well-to-do circles for feeding those in need. Actors who already had something of a solo repertoire began turning out performances. Whoever lacked a solo repertoire began to seek reading material in which they could find items suited to recitation. The more popular stars of the Yiddish stage were showered with invitations, and they earned a profitable income. Besides recitation, others specialized in singing.

The dramatic artist par excellence Diana Blumenfeld [famed Yiddish actress and singer, 1903–1961] created a new genre in a song repertoire assembled from lyric-humorous and sentimental or comic-grotesque songs, which she interpreted in an original manner, achieving a colossal success with them. In addition, the "prima donna" of the youth theater, Dora Fakel [1941–1943; also Fakiel], began to appear on stage at the "Melody Palace" as a singer of folksongs. During the *Aktion* [round-up], Dora Fakel was seized in a Tebens-shop [factory of the Tebens German military uniform company], with which she later arrived at Poniatowa—and there, together with all the others, was killed on November 3, 1943.

★ ★ ★

Actual theater also existed in the ghetto. The attempt to stage a variety show in the "Scala" theater hall at first succeeded to a certain extent. After presenting one or two programs, however, the venture folded, and established prewar performers reappeared in the famous hall with their prewar repertoire. In general, the question of repertoire was very problematic. The occupation authority would not approve pieces with a serious subject matter. It was forbidden to perform "Tevye, the Milkman." So they began performing old pieces from a hundred years earlier in which, for a period of time, good dramatic actors appeared.

But the arrangement did not last long. This offering was not suited for this altar. In Warsaw, there was still a common element, which, for a while, made money from various forbidden businesses and was ready to come and see their own favorite stars who had to appear on stage with "a hop and a sing, with a dance and a spring," and indeed they quickly got what they wanted.

Regina Cukier [renowned operetta actress, 1899–1943] and other prewar favorites of this particular audience returned to the stage, and even those among them who had talent were prepared for every absurdity of the most pathetic operetta repertoire, so long as it would satisfy the audience's taste.

★ ★ ★

I was at "Scala" once or twice and also at the Polish performances of Turkow himself [famed Yiddish-Polish actor Jonas Turkow, 1898–1988] in the "Femina" theater and at the singing events of Diana Blumenfeld [his wife].

I recall the staging of *Shulamis*, which I saw in the summer of 1942, literally on the threshold of the expulsion catastrophe, already in the period of "pre-terror"—of the nighttime killings, which, among others, also reached a few people in the acting world. It is astonishing and a marvel that in this period there were still theater people in the ghetto at all who were able to prepare and present a new performance—a new conception of a Goldfaden spectacle!

As they already felt deep in their soul, this was their last chance, once more—for the last time in their lives—to absorb themselves in their beloved creative work, immerse themselves in another world, in an existence other than that in which they would soon play the last act of their personal finale.

Introduction Notes:

1 Rohkl Oyerbakh, *Baym letstn veg* [The final road] (Tel Aviv: Yisroel-bukh, 1977), 153.

2. "Khaym-Leyb Kozlovski—a frumer kolege in kikhn-tsek" in ibid., 42–48 (42–44 quoted); "Teatr in geto" in ibid., 134–41 (136–38 quoted).

Part Three

IN THE NON-JEWISH WORLD

15
Jewish-Christian Relations in Płock in the Sixteenth and Seventeenth Centuries
by Isaiah Trunk, 1938

ISAIAH TRUNK (see Selection 7 above, also 21 and 45 below) focused his research before World War II primarily on the histories of specific Jewish communities in Poland. The first was a brief history of the Jews in his home city of Kutno (1934), followed by a larger history of the Jews in the nearby city of Płock (1938, "Plotsk" in Yiddish). Płock was one of the oldest cities in Poland, at one time its capital, and it had one of the oldest Jewish communities, dating from at least the fourteenth century.

Trunk's history of Płock includes chapters on such topics as the Jewish court system, Jewish taxes, community organization, private life, and—presented below—Jews in the Christian setting.[1] It is notable in part for his coverage of active Jewish responses to anti-Jewish violence, which contradicts the traditional narrative of Jewish helplessness and victimhood.

Relations between Jews and the surrounding Christian environment were, in light of the sources, not the best. Approximately 15 percent of all official records relate to mutual attacks in acts of violence; there were years when the records had no other types of events to note.

At the same time, it must be emphasized that the role of the Jews in these events was, according to the sources, not only passive. Many records bear witness to the fact that the Jewish side was the aggressor. Out of 65 cases in which the Christian side was the aggressor, there were 20 (that is to say, 30 percent) in which the Jewish side was [also] the attacker.

That these cases were not simply about false accusations is shown by the court minutes, which confirm that the examining magistrate found such-and-such wounds on the Jew and on the Christian—and became convinced of the truth of the accusation. Even if we assume that the Jew was attacked and then wounded the attacker in self-defense (about which there is no evidence in the sources), we must say that Jews could well defend themselves. Also, during pogroms in the Jewish ghetto, certain individuals mounted some resistance (see below).

In light of these facts, we ought to correct somewhat our image of Polish Jews in past eras, which one is accustomed to imagining in accord with the statement in Proverbs [28:14], "Happy is the man who is always afraid." . . . [ellipsis in original]

Among the acts of violence against Jews, one ought to distinguish between collective and individual acts. Collective acts of violence (pogroms) occurred in Płock five times during the period under consideration: in 1534, 1570, 1579, 1590, and 1656. Therefore, we see that Jew-hatred and antisemitic acts begin to increase in the [1570s]. This is also confirmed by the continually increasing number of individual attacks in this period. Larger attacks also took place in the summer months of 1556, when, in connection with the trial in Sochaczew [in which four Jews were executed for allegedly desecrating the host], a wave of persecutions of Jews swept across Poland in general and in the province of Mazovia in particular [in which Płock was located], but no details about these attacks were preserved in the records.

There were also times that were somewhat peaceful, when the sources note only rare or almost no cases of mutual aggression. Thus, for example, the city and court records for the nine years 1603–12 record not one attack or anything similar. In general, mutual relations were more peaceful in the first half of the seventeenth century than in the sixteenth century.

The first known pogrom in the history of the Płock Jews took place in 1534. Its course was described in the sources in this manner:

On Passover night of the indicated year, a band of Płock students and journeymen with Benedykt, the son of Goldszmid, and mason Jan Jagerka in the lead, broke into the private homes in the Jewish quarter and also the synagogue, broke windows and doors, and committed a whole series of other crimes. The indictment against the attackers was entered in the city court on behalf of the Płock governor by the prosecutor, Marian Orlesza, and, at the same time he accused the Christian artisans of not coming to the aid of the Jews when they called out in the night (to which they were entitled according to the provisions of the general privileges: i.e., according to paragraph 35 of the Kalisz statute), but themselves took part in the attack; he demanded that the court punish the accused according to the royal statutes that had been issued against violators of Jewish rights.

The accused denied everything and tried to demonstrate their "alibi" (they claimed that at the time of the attack they were in the church confessing their sins).

The mayor, together with the city advisers, sentenced each of them to a *shvuah* [an oath administered by the judges], but the governor's prosecutor did not accept the judgment, demanding an appeal to the royal court, which the court allowed.[1] With regard to how the matter ended, we have not the least trace in our sources.

As we already mentioned, the sources also provide no exact details about the disturbances in 1556 in connection with the blood libel trial. That they were strong enough, particularly in Płock, is evidenced by the "Iron Letter" [letter of protection] from the king of July 3, in which he especially emphasizes this concern regarding the Płock Jews. Regarding the disturbances, it speaks in a general form, namely, that innocent people were put in prison and that Jewish property had been destroyed.

In 1570, community heads Jacob and Feliks Berman brought an accusation in the governor's court against the head of the cathedral school in Płock, whom they accused of inciting his students to commit a nighttime attack on the Jewish quarter: they broke into thirteen Jewish homes, broke windows and doors, and committed a whole group of other violent acts, wounding the Jews who put up resistance. . . .

After these events, the Płock Jews lobbied the king for a letter of protection. They received it on July 6, 1570; the king promised his protection and patronage and guaranteed the security of life and property and free trade.[2]

Nine years later a new attack took place in the Jewish quarter. We know about the course of events from the description of the court clerk, Jan Olszak, who gave the court the following explanation: At the request of the three community heads, Shlomo ben Efraim, Feliks the Small, and Jacob, he came to the Jewish quarter, and here in the houses of the trustee Shlomo, of Jacob, and Levek's widow saw traces of the attack, namely, shattered windowpanes, and torn-out doors and windows; these acts he blamed on the director of the parish school in Płock together with his colleagues.[3]

About 1590, the air of the city was again strongly charged with hatred of Jews. A year earlier unknown persons conducted an attack on the home of Abraham Hazan,[4] and in 1590 the largest pogrom against the Płock Jews in the period under discussion took place, in terms of the damage and crimes (apart from the destruction during the Swedish War in 1556–57).

According to the testimony of the community heads and court clerk, it took place in this manner: Friday night at about one o'clock in the Jewish quarter, a group of students, with Simon Bukart, Sulkowski, Uminski, and the son of the city recorder in the lead, broke in, and, smashing doors and windows in eighteen Jewish homes, committed acts of destruction and theft, as well as not respecting the synagogue, where they also smashed the door, and the bathhouse, where they tore out the shutters and shattered the windowpanes. . . .

We must, however, also mention an isolated fact that points to another attitude of the higher clergy of Płock toward the Jews. Thus, the bishop of Płock, Piotr, during the court proceedings in the episcopal court in Pułtusk on January 25, 1494, sentenced "Jacques" Stanisław Modzela of Łomża to prison for attacks and acts of violence he committed against Jewish merchants in Łomża; at which time, the court reporter, in his recital of the indictment, cited the bishop's decree about putting in prison "Jacqueses" who dare to attack Jews.[5] . . . [Returning to the main theme of attacks on Jews, several paragraphs discuss further attacks and the documents in which they were recorded.]

As one can therefore perceive from the abovementioned documents, coexistence between the Jewish and Christian populations was not, to put it mildly, the best. But the picture of mutual relations that we have attempted to sketch would be one-sided and false if we remained silent about the, truth be told, small number of facts that give evidence of the opposite—regarding peaceful coexistence and mutual trust.

Regarding peaceful coexistence of the Płock Jews with the Christian population, the records of the episcopal chapter of Płock from the first half of the sixteenth century preserve characteristic facts that point to very close social contacts between these two population groups: Jews spending time privately with Christians, drinking and amusing themselves at joint gatherings, using shared baths—which were, of course, much criticized in the Christian records.[6] Court records also frequently inform us about mutual trust and peaceful coexistence: we find Christians as representatives or patrons of the Jewish party[7] in arbitrations of disputes between Jews and townsfolk,[8] and the opposite—Jews who appear as authorized representatives for the Christian party[9]; Jews staying in Christian inns, drinking *hant-gelt* [earnest money; to seal a monetary transaction] with Christians,[10] employing Christian servants, and the opposite—Christian master artisans employing Jewish apprentices,[11] etc.

The church had grounds for disapproving of this close social contact—as shown by the relatively large number of trials of "Judaizing" Christians that took place in the episcopal court in the years 1539–51. Of course, the church intentionally exaggerated Jewish influence, rather than ascribing these trials to the spread of the Arian Heresy, which at that time found adherents among the Polish nobility and intelligentsia, and which was portrayed publicly as a Jewish heresy to discredit it.

So far, we have spoken only about the attitude toward the Jews on the part of the three classes: nobles, church, and townsfolk. But how did the mutual relations between Jews and the most numerous class—the peasants—appear?

The area of economic relations between the peasants and the Jews was, if we can judge by the sources, very narrow. Only in exceptional instances was the unpropertied and economically dependent peasant able to indulge in a loan from a Jewish moneylender. From the two surviving notices about loans made to peasants in the course of the entire fifteenth century, the first amounted to 40 złoty and the second to 50 złoty.[12] It appears that one of these peasants was not easily able to repay the debt because, as it was recounted in the notice, twice he did not appear in court and the third time declared that he could not bear the heavy monetary penalties and was better prepared to give the moneylender a portion of his property, to which the court agreed. In the course of the sixteenth century, loans to peasants were also a rare occurrence.

Jewish moneylenders, who accepted real property as collateral from their noble borrowers, became, by this means, the actual landlords of the peasants who lived there. Whether the Jewish landlord had the right of patrimonial jurisdiction over the peasants is highly doubtful. In the context of medieval social conditions, it is difficult to imagine the Jew in the role of a judge over his Christian peasants. Such a fact would stand in too stark opposition to the mentality of Christian medieval society and to the canon laws, which stated clearly that an "unbeliever" was not allowed to judge a Christian. The relatively frequent instances in the course of the fifteenth century when the Jewish moneylender appointed a Christian administrator, or sold the hypothecated collateral to one of the Christian clients,[13] were probably intended to eliminate the judicial difficulties that would arise from the fact that a Jew had obtained the right to land. . . .

Introduction Notes:

1.Yeshaye Trunk,"Di rekhtlekhe lage fun yidn in plotsk in 16tn un in der ershter helft 17tn y"h" [The legal status of the Jews in Płock in the 16th and in the first half of the 17th century], in his *Shtudyes in yidisher geshikhte in poyln* [Studies in Jewish history in Poland] (Buenos Aires:Yidbukh, 1963), 25–70 (52–70 quoted; abridged).

Article Notes:
1. *Akta miasta Płocka* [A.m.P.] 66, 99.
2. *Płockie gradzkie wieczyste* [P.g.w.] 51, 141.
3. P.g.w. 72, 102.
4. A.m.P. 47, 289.
5. *Monumenta medii aevi*, vol. XVIII, 62–63.
6. B. Ulanowski, *Acta Capituli Plocensis* XVI seculi.
7. P.g.w. 22, 43; A.m.P. 2; 43, 593; 52, 160°; 58, 932; 107, 593.
8. P.g.w. 42, 12°.
9. P.g.w. 7 [defective].
10. P.g.w. 18, 387°; A.m.P. 87, 211; 43, 279.
11. P.g.w. 42, 348; A.m.P. 79, 542; 9 [unpaginated] 1617.
12. Wyszogrodzka siem., wieczysta 3, 338, 341, 1479.
13. Wyszogrodzka siem., wieczysta 4, pars II, XX, 1480.

16
What Types of Taxes Did the Jews of Lublin Pay in the Former Independent Poland?
by Bela Mandelsberg, 1930

BELA MANDELSBERG (1901–1943) was born in Lublin, Poland, and received her master's degree in history from the University of Warsaw in 1928. She was one of the founding members of Ringelblum and Mahler's Young Historians Circle in Warsaw and published articles in their journal and other Yiddish venues before World War II. During the same period, she taught history at Jewish secondary schools in Lublin and gave public lectures on Jewish history in Yiddish. Mandelsberg endured the Lublin ghetto under Nazi occupation and was then murdered in Majdanek. Her husband, Meir Szyldkraut, survived in Siberia and eventually settled in Israel where he organized a circle of friends that published a volume of her writings in Hebrew translation, edited by her prewar teaching colleague Nachman Blumental (see Selections 28 and 49 below).[1] A scholarship fund was also established in her name that supported Holocaust studies by students at three Israeli universities.

Mandelberg's writings all relate to the history of the Jews in Lublin, toward which she was preparing a major work. Only her master's thesis and several related articles survive as indications of the proposed work. One of these is the article that appears below.[2] It is the only article in the memorial volume of her writings to be reprinted there in the original Yiddish rather than in Hebrew translation. It is unusual among works by Jewish historians of her time in dealing solely with the subject of taxes paid by Jews.

The tax system that applied to the Jews in old-time Poland and Lithuania rested on the same fundamental basis as in Western Europe. The point of departure for the tax system regarding the Jews in Western Europe was the belief that Jews were the property of the duke or king. If so, the duke or the king had the right to demand a reward from the Jews for the protection that he provided over his Jews. For this purpose, the rulers of Western Europe would receive payments from their Jewish population in kind or in money.

The Polish Jews were in the same situation. In return, however, the Jews were free from military service in times of war and from quartering soldiers. One of the most important sources of income for the state treasury in old-time independent Poland was the personal tax the Jews paid under the name of "Jewish head tax." This tax, like tariffs and gate taxes, was part of the regular state income. The other taxes were only temporary because they would be paid as one-time contributions.

The establishment of the "Jewish head tax" was explained by government circles thusly: that the Jews, as immigrants, a foreign element, took away part of the income sources of the local element; as a result, they were obliged to bear greater burdens regarding the state than the local population.

In 1549, King Zygmunt August ordered that a census be conducted of the Jews in the entire Polish state (together with Lithuania, which at that time belonged to Poland) to ascertain the number of Jews required to pay the "Jewish head tax." At first, this tax amounted to one złoty annually per man, woman, and child. In this connection, it must be remembered that the value of money then was much greater than today. An exception was made only for very poor Jews, who were freed from this tax.

The collection of the tax was associated with high administrative expenses, and so the Polish kings would grant a concession to rich Jews for collecting the "head tax" and would receive a set, one-time sum of money in advance.

The rate of the "Jewish head tax" rose constantly, which may be seen from the following comparison: in 1579, the total "Jewish head tax" amounted to 10,000 złoty, and in 1643 it amounted to 70,000 złoty—above all, in the seventeenth century, when the total expenses of the state grew sharply on account of the long and frightful wars with Russia, Sweden, Turkey, and the Cossack attacks, the rate of the "head tax" also grew two- and three-fold. In addition, the parliament levied various new ordinary and extraordinary taxes on the Jews. Thus, in 1643, King Władysław IV sent a universal [letter] to the heads of the Lublin community in which the king ordered them to join with the *kehilot* in Poznań, Kraków, Lemberg, and other Polish cities that had a large Jewish settlement and pay a one-time tax to the state treasury in the amount of 60,000 złoty. This sum was to be used to cover debts of the state. As the largest Jewish *kehilot* in Poland, the *kehilot* of Poznań, Kraków, and Lemberg received similar universals.

There are various opinions regarding the character and meaning of the indicated tax. Certain historians and political figures from those times maintain that the "Jewish head tax" was an insult to the Jewish community in Poland and Lithuania.

Butrymowicz [Matheus, 1745–1814], who was the author of a project to reform the Jews in Poland along new lines in the [eighteenth] century, supported this opinion and held that the tax was a disgrace for its creators and that he saw in it a tax on the Jewish religion.

The opposite view was held by Professor M. Schorr [Jewish historian, 1874–1941], who believed that the "Jewish head tax" in Poland did not have an insulting character like the "head tax" in Germany. It was only seen as an insult because Jews had to pay this tax in addition to others, as a special tax.

Irrespective of whether or not the tax was an insult, it is a fact that the establishment of this tax evoked passionate protests on the part of the Jews because, with it, the number of their overall taxes and burdens increased by still another. And, in addition, the Jews were burdened with various new municipal taxes at the same time.

Further, the Jews would pay the king and the royal officials from time to time with "gifts" for certain privileges. In general, in obtaining Jewish privileges a large role was played by—money.

And now, we will consider: which taxes did the Jews pay besides the "head tax"? In general, they can be divided into: ordinary and extraordinary. To the first category belong, in the course of the sixteenth, seventeenth, and eighteenth centuries: 1) "coronation tax"; 2) "boardinghouse tax"; 3) royal and municipal road tax (*szos królewski i szos miejski*); 4) *protowszcayzna* [a tax on the privilege of having a synagogue and cemetery]; 5) taxes on shops, merchandise, and craftwork; 6) taxes on having servants and journeymen. To the extraordinary taxes belong: 1) taxes on war expenses and 2) taxes "for the castle" (*na zamek*), which went into the private royal treasury.

Apart from the abovementioned were also the following taxes: 1) liquor excise tax (*czopowe*); 2) bridge toll (*mostowe*) and road toll (*drogowe*); 3) fair tax (*jarmarczne*); 4) butcher tax (*jateczne*); 5) customs duties and tolls (*cla i myta*).

The "boardinghouse" tax (*stancyjne czyli postój* [boardinghouse, i.e., stopover]) was imposed to support the royal court while traveling or during its stay in the city. The Lublin Jews paid this tax in the amount of 100 złoty per year in the course of the sixteenth and seventeenth centuries. The Polish population of the cities and towns also had the obligation to support drivers and horses for the officials while traveling and also to support them while spending time in the city on official matters. . . .

The royal road tax (*szos królewski*) was a tax on Jewish houses that were built on the king's ground.

Almost all the larger cities in Poland were built on ground that was the private property of the king and not of the nobility. These cities were called "royal," and they included Lublin. The rate of royal "road" tax that was paid by the Lublin Jews amounted to 4 złoty annually for each house that was located in the Jewish quarter. Conversely, for the houses located outside the Jewish quarter, the Jews paid a tax according to a certain agreement with the royal finance officials. In exceptional cases, two or three houses in the entire city were free of the tax. Only the Maharshal's Synagogue and the hospital of that time were free from this tax.

Along with the royal "road tax," there was also the so-called "city road tax" (*szos miejski*) which the Lublin Jews paid for the benefit of the Christian residents of "our castle." Simply put, for houses that were built on royal real property, the Lublin Jews paid a double tax: one a state tax, and the second a municipal tax. Incidentally, the second was not a regular tax but belongs to the group of extraordinary taxes.

Some Polish historians contend that the Jews in Poland generally did not pay the royal road tax. This opinion is not correct because the documents that pertain to the economic history of the Lublin Jews mention it many times. Until the second half of the seventeenth century, the Lublin Jews paid this tax. Only then, in the entire area of Lublin County, was it abolished and replaced with another tax called *hyberna* or "winter bread" (*hyberna, chleb zimowy*) [winter maintenance of the troops]. . . .

Taxes for Shops, Goods, and Craftwork

The Lublin Jews paid taxes for commerce equally with the non-Jewish merchants, chiefly for textile shops, butchers, and alcohol and liquor sales. Furthermore, they also paid the city government for the right to conduct business. In addition to all these, the Jewish textile merchants in Lublin also had to pay the city a special tax called *strygielt*. This was a tax on the bales of cloth. It has still not been determined precisely whether this tax was paid for each bale of merchandise or only for each ell of merchandise sold. In time, the Christian textile merchants were also burdened with this tax.

Taxes for Jewish craftwork were taken by the local artisan guilds, to which no Jews could belong because the guilds also played, among others, the role of religious bodies.

The city guilds forbade Jewish artisans from engaging in craftwork. So it was in principle. But because the prohibition could not be carried out in practice, the city guilds would give permission, supposedly as an exception, receiving in return regular systematic payment to the guild. The prohibition on engaging in craftwork, as well as the payment for permission, caused a sharp decline of Jewish craftwork in Lublin.

The framework of a newspaper article does not allow precise coverage of each type of tax separately. Therefore, we must limit ourselves here to describing the problem along general lines.

Regarding the extraordinary taxes, it is clear that the most difficult were those connected with expenditures for war. In particular, the seventeenth century was very difficult in this respect for the Lublin Jewish population because at that time Poland experienced a period of continual, frightful wars, of Cossack uprisings, as I mentioned briefly above.

The liquor excise tax (*czopowe*) was a tax the population paid to produce alcoholic drinks. The Jews of Lublin were engaged in this industry. In particular, from the time of the intensified struggle by the Jewish artisans with the guilds, they were pushed out of many economic positions and needed to move into new means of livelihood. At that time, they began in part to earn their living as estate managers and tavern keepers.

The bridge toll (*mostowe*) and road toll (*drogowe*) were paid by the Jews for traversing urban bridges and roads. In Lublin, this toll was also called *grobelny*, for traversing the *grobla* [embankment or causeway]. The Lublin Jews paid 5 grosz [5/100 of a złoty] for each wagon as *grobelny*, which amounted to approximately 300 złoty per year for the state treasury in the seventeenth century. This toll was paid along the rivers and on the roads that led to Turobin, Bełżyce, Kraśnik, and on the embankments of the Luboml region (today [before World War II] Lubomelszczyzna) [today Liuboml, Ukraine].

The fair tax was paid by the butcher shop owners in the form of tallow or money.

Regarding taxes, the Lublin Jews paid the same rate as the Christians. This situation was established in Lublin by King Zygmunt August on the basis of a special privilege for the Lublin Jews. But, already in a succeeding century, i.e., in the eighteenth century, the auditors/inspectors (*lustratorzy*) of Lublin County transmitted the question of the taxes for Jewish merchants to the general Sejm in order to revise the indicated royal privilege. This took place at the specific request of the Lublin Christian citizens, who pushed for an increase in taxes on Jews to reduce competition in commerce.

It must also be mentioned here that the Lublin Jews were obligated to carry out various city works, chiefly repairing the city fortifications (*fortyfikacje miejskie*). With time, the indicated duty was converted into a monetary payment.

The Lublin Jews paid special taxes for the Catholic clergy: 1) for the right to make use of synagogues and the cemetery and 2) a yearly tax on Jewish houses. The question arises, how did it happen that Jews were required to pay the Catholic clergy? The reason derives from the premise that the Catholic Church suffered a material loss on account of the places occupied by Jews and not by Christians who would have brought in income for the church. The tax was thus intended to compensate for this grievance.

If we also added the taxes paid by the Jews to the Jewish *kehila*, as the autonomous organization of the Jewish community, it would form a clear picture of the very considerable financial burden that the Lublin Jews carried during the period of the former independent Poland.

Introduction Notes:

1. Bela Mandelsberg-Shildkroyt, *Mehkarim le-toldot Yehude Lublin* [Studies on the history of Jews of Lublin], ed. Nachman Blumental (Tel Aviv: Hug mokire shemah shel B. Mandelsberg-Shildkroyt, 1965).

2. Bela Mandelsberg, "Vos far a shtayern hoben getsolt di lubliner yuden in amoligen umobhengigen poyln," *Lubliner togblat* 20, January 23, 1930, and 26, January 30, 1930 (slightly abridged); reprinted in ibid., 161–68 (in Yiddish only).

17
Jewish Home Industry in Old-Time Poland
by Emanuel Ringelblum, 1935

EMANUEL RINGELBLUM (1900–1944) was born in Buczacz, Austrian Galicia (today Buchach, Ukraine), and received his doctorate in history from the University of Warsaw in 1927. He is best remembered as the organizer of the secret Oyneg Shabes project in the Warsaw ghetto, the comprehensive and heroic effort to document the Jewish experience of Nazi rule—today known as the Ringelblum Archive and housed at the Jewish Historical Institute in Warsaw, also renamed in his honor.

Before the Holocaust, Ringelblum was an advocate for Jewish historical writing in Yiddish (the language in which his own *Notes from the Warsaw Ghetto* would be written). Like his colleague Raphael Mahler, who became his partner in the Young Historians Circle in Warsaw, he was committed to a Marxist approach to historical writing, but he differed from Mahler in only occasionally emphasizing class conflict in Jewish society. Many of his works provide arguments for Jewish rights in the Poland of his day, based on Jewish contributions in the past, and cover such topics as Jews in old-time Warsaw, Jewish doctors, Jews in the Kościuszko uprising of 1794, and Jews in guilds and manufacturing.

Ringelblum was also active in the group of free loan societies that assisted poor Jews in Poland during the worldwide depression of the 1930s. From 1930 to 1938, he edited their journal, *Folks-hilf* (Popular help). The organization was dedicated to finding means to "productivize" Polish Jewry, which led to another form of purposeful writing—intended to offer historical remedies to current problems. An example is the following article on the Jewish home industry in textile work during the seventeenth and eighteenth centuries.[1]

One of the most important issues that exist today on the agenda of our community life is, without doubt, the problem of strengthening the economic positions of our Jewish population in Poland. In connection with this, people often mention the necessity of finding new ways of earning a living, which some contemplate finding in home industry.

To the present time, the past of the Jews in Poland has still not been adequately studied. We know very little about how Jews lived in former times. And from what they drew their sustenance we also know little. But one thing is certain: that the Jews played an immensely important role in the craftwork of the time. They also occupied an outstanding place in home industry.

The oldest information about Jewish home industry is preserved in an antisemitic work by the professor at Kraków University, Sebastian Miczyński, *The Mirror of the Polish Crown* (printed for the first time in 1618). In this work, which contains an abundance of information about the economic life of the Jews in the largest Polish cities, such as Lublin, Lemberg, and particularly Kraków, we read the following about the participation of Jewish women in home industry: "The Jewish women take away from modest (Christian) girls and widows their livelihood because they make: lace, silk or linen threads, buttons, bows, silk-work, gold embroidery and all other types of embroidery, even the silks of the regalia and the pearl crowns on the monstrances (religious implements) . . ." [ellipsis in original], and the greatest antisemite in seventeenth-century Poland complained that "if Christian women make something, they have nowhere to sell it."

The pious professor cannot bear that Jewish women are working for Polish noblewomen, so he concocts a libel against them, that they are thieves: "The Jewish women who are summoned by the powerful noblewomen to embroider or set something with pearls swallow the very best pearls or precious stones and set the worst." Miczyński goes on further to say how the Jewish women embroiderers retrieve the swallowed pearls, but here I must refrain from saying . . . [ellipsis in original]

The above-cited quotation from Miczyński's book is invaluable. We deduce many things from it. First, we see that Jewish women and girls dedicated themselves very strongly to embroidery and to what we mean by the word "home industry" in general. Because, if not, Miczyński would not have found it necessary to write about it in his book, which was addressed to the Polish Sejm [parliament] deputies.

Second, we can deduce from the quotation that the Jewish women were good workers, that their workmanship approached perfection, that not only Polish noblewomen, who had a great love for dressing well, but even the church, which after all fought the Jew very ardently, willingly or unwillingly had to accept the work of Jewish women. As we see, our grandmothers, who did not graduate from any vocational schools, occupied the first rank in embroidery, gold embroidery, etc. The Christian women could not withstand the competition from the Jewish women.

One hundred eighty years later, at the end of the eighteenth century, a new picture of Jewish home industry reveals itself before our eyes in the province of Greater Poland [west-central Poland]. During the partition of Poland, this province (in the region of Poznań) was taken over by the Germans, and at that time various entrepreneurs appeared who began developing the new German province. Among the entrepreneurs who sought their fortunes, a rich Jew, Veitel Heine Ephraim [1702–1775], particularly distinguished himself. In Germany, he had a large factory that manufactured lace. In this factory, Jewish and Christian workers made lace.

When this part of Greater Poland, later called the Nets-District (after the river Nets—in Polish: Noteć), ended up in Prussian hands, he moved there. In these regions, especially in the cities of Wieleń, Czarnków, Koronowo, etc., Jewish girls and women had long been occupied with making lace. Now, Veitel Ephraim applied to the Prussian government and proposed that he would train the Jewish women to make better lace, that he was ready to invest all that was needed, but that he had one condition: that they could not sell their handiwork to anyone but him. Ephraim began to implement his proposal and hired approximately 1,500 Jewish women. The lace from his workers was very good. Everything would have gone according to plan if not for the dense heads of the Prussian bureaucrats. At that time a series of expulsions began from the provinces newly acquired by the Prussians. Nonproductive elements were expelled, and among them even . . . [ellipsis in original] 106 Jewish women workers from the city of Czarnków. Ephraim pleaded for mercy from the government and warned that the Jewish women who were expelled from Germany to Poland would train Polish Jewish women in the new methods of making lace.

At that time, lace-making was the most important branch of livelihood for some towns: in the city of Schneidemühl, out of 188 Jewish residents, 130 were lacemakers; in Wieleń—200 out of 473; in Łobżenica—150 out of 283, etc.

In short, one could confidently assert that in Greater Poland, the majority of Jewish women were employed in home industry.

But in the part of Poland that still remained free for approximately twenty-three years (until 1795, when Poland ceased to exist), Jewish women also occupied a place in home industry.

For this information about the participation of Jewish women in home industry, we are indebted to interesting economic changes that took place then in Poland. At that time, the Polish nobles, rich Christian urban bourgeoisie, and, in part, also Jews were engaged in building large-scale industry, specifically manufacturing. Lively work was taking place at that time to make Poland independent of outside markets, so attempts were made to develop a textile, leather, and metal industry. The rise of industry was intended not only to enrich the country but also to create a workplace for the masses of idlers, vagabonds, and beggars who went roaming and searching throughout Poland.

The Polish statesmen of the time also sought to draw the Jewish population into industry to make them productive. As a result, when development proceeded in the industries in which Jews, particularly Jewish women, occupied important positions in the form of home industry, these home industries were indeed utilized strongly as the starting point for a higher economic level for manufacturing.

Thus, for example, we read that in the much-famed calico [more likely, percale] factory in Niemirów, whose products were sought throughout the world, Jewish women were employed who spun cotton thread and even made the forms from brass. When the king visited Niemirów, he could not help but praise the factory. In various brochures and even one antisemitic work, this factory was mentioned, and, at the same time, emphasis was made that among the 300 women workers there were also Jewish women.

It is subject to doubt whether the Jewish women who worked in the Niemirów factory were previously engaged in making cotton thread at home, but they had certainly been employed in a similar branch of production, such as, for example, spinning wool and the like.

That this was indeed the case is demonstrated for us by a second very interesting fact about Jewish home industry, in Horodnica, near Grodno [today in Belarus]. There, in the 1770s, the Lithuanian finance minister Antoni Tyzenhauz [1733–1785] founded an entire manufacturing center. This undertaking, large for its time, then employed approximately 3,000 workers. It is known that for his textile factories and weaving workshops Jewish women, together with Christian women, spun wool and flax threads at home from wool and flax *przędza* [yarn].

It may be assumed with almost complete certainty that there was no large textile factory in Poland in which Jewish women did not participate, whether as workers in a factory or, as in Horodnica, at home.

I believe that the examples brought forth will certainly be sufficient for one to assert with the completest certainty that the old-time Polish Jews and Jewish women also earned their living to a certain degree from home industry.

It would be interesting to determine whether the Jews also retained these positions in home industry later, and, if this did not occur, what the reasons were that led to its decline. This determination would teach us much.

Introduction Notes:

1. Emanuel Ringelblum, "Di yidishe hoyz-industrye inem altn poyln," likely published in *Folks-hilf* (issue 5 of 1935, per Jacob Shatzky's Ringelblum bibliography in the 1953 reprint edition, but not in the version posted at Historical Jewish Press: https://www.nli.org.il/en/newspapers); reprinted in Emanuel Ringelblum, *Kapitlen geshikhte fun amolikn yidishn lebn in poyln* [Historical chapters from former Jewish life in Poland], ed. Yankev Shatski (Buenos Aires: Tsentral farband fun poylishe yidn in argentine, 1953), 126–30.

18
The "New Settlements" in 1808: How Belorussian Jews Responded to the First Order to Settle in Agricultural Colonies in Russian Ukraine

by Simon Dubnow, 1932

SIMON DUBNOW (see Selection 1 above) contended with the lack of an official Jewish archive—and the resulting impediment to writing Jewish history—with his well-known appeal in 1891 for the Jewish public in Russia and Poland to collect and send him Jewish historical documents. The originals and copies of Jewish communal records, as well as private papers, obtained by Dubnow over the course of his career form the core of his collected papers, held today by YIVO at the Center for Jewish History in New York.

Although Dubnow turned to scholarly writing in Yiddish too late to compose his major works in Yiddish, he supported the journals published by YIVO with contributions of shorter works, often relating to historical documents in his collection. The following is a typical example in which he sketches a document's historical context, quotes at length from the document (of which a photographic copy was "tipped in" on the facing page, in the best practice of the time), and then summarizes its significance. The article also serves as an example of one of the recurring topics of Yiddish historical work—the many plans, some realized and others not, to reform and "productivize" Russian Jews by resettling them in underpopulated agricultural regions such as eastern Ukraine, Crimea, and ultimately Birobidzhan.[1]

This was a time of hope mixed with great anxiety and misfortune. First, Tsar Alexander I issued the "Statute for Jews" of December 1804—"a mixture of freedoms and restrictions"—on the one hand, a strong desire to grant Jews equality; to divert them from odious occupations, from tavern-keeping and *arenda* [estate-management of villages], attract them to agriculture, craft-work, and industry, and educate their children in general schools; but, on the other hand, to begin forcibly expelling Jewish residents from the villages and impoverishing tens of thousands of families who had lived from *arendas* for hundreds of years under the Polish regime. According to the custom of the time, economic reforms were made through edicts, through strict decrees, and, before they could arrive at new sources of income—agricultural colonies or factories—Jews were deprived of their old occupations. Thousands of families, expelled from the villages, wandered in the poverty-stricken cities, and the Jewish communities could help them only with paltry donations.

The expulsion from the villages began in Belorussia in January 1808. Still earlier, in 1806, when they were already awaiting this misfortune, groups of village Jews in the Mohilev and Vitebsk districts turned to the governors with requests to be transported to the agricultural colonies in New Russia [Ukraine]. Families from the Tcherikov area [today Cherykaw, Belarus] under the leadership of Nachum Finkelstein and fifty-three families from the Mstislav area [Dubnow's birthplace, today in Belarus] under the leadership of a certain Shafrantsik, for two years beat a path to the doors of Russian officials in the district capitals and the ministers themselves in St. Petersburg, but the government had not yet allotted any plots of land for the colonies, or prepared a roof for them over their heads, and postponed the migration to which they had driven everyone. Finally, the first groups moved out of their places in the summer of 1808. The Mstislav group, consisting of 271 souls, left after *Shvues* [Shavuot, the Feast of Weeks]. What took place in the old communities on the departure of the migrants, and what they themselves felt, leaving for a faraway land (at that time, the journey from Belorussia to the Kherson or Ekaterinoslav districts by horse and by boats on the Dnieper lasted a couple of months), one can see from a living document: a sort of minutes in the *pinkes hakohol* [community record book] of Mstislav, of which the old original is in my possession.

Several weeks after the colonists from the Mstislav area departed, the following brief account was recorded in the *pinkes* (page 68) in memory "for coming generations":[1]

"So that your generations will know and be able to tell the coming generation, and children who will be born will tell their children about the mercy that the creator, blessed be his name, showed to his people the Children of Israel in the present time, we decided that the matter should be inscribed with a pen of a scribe in the *pinkes hakohol*. May one remember the favors of the almighty and praise him for his goodness and mercy shown to our brothers the Children of Israel, as he promised in his holy Torah:'And even when (they should be in a hostile country), I will not scorn them and not reject them,' and so on.

"Several years already passed—and scarcity much intensified *bavoyneseynu horamim* [because of our many sins], and the gates of livelihood are locked. The income does not cover the expenses and the indispensable needs (of the *kehila*). A great many of our brothers the Children of Israel became impoverished, and even the well-to-do can no longer carry the heavy expenses of helping those suffering in need, who multiply and grow because of our many sins. It becomes literally black before the eyes [as if to faint] when one looks at their poverty and their troubles: little children begging for bread (and there is none).

"But now God took pity on his people and created a cure for the plague. He caused, so that we might find grace and favor and mercy with our lord, the tsar, the powerful and merciful Alexander Pavlovich, may his glory be increased, his officials and advisors. He issued an order two years ago that it should be announced to the Jewish masses: whoever wants to uproot himself from his home and settle in new cities (places), which are called *novi shilenyes* (new settlements), it is permitted for him to do so. There, he will be given his own parcel of land,[2] namely, for each male person fifteen measures, called *desyatins* [a land measure equal to 1.095 hectares; 2.7 acres], and will also be given from the treasury of the tsar, may his glory be increased, money for expenses to build houses, buy plowing equipment, oxen and all that they (farmers) need. In addition, for several years (approximately ten years)[3] after they occupy the land, they will be free from all taxes according to the law of the tsar, may his glory be increased. Further, until they are finally settled, each person will be given provision for necessities of food. After several years, they (the colonists) will begin gradually to pay each year, according to the grace of the tsar, may his glory be increased, until everything taken now has been repaid to his treasury.

"From our *kehila* and the surrounding places, on the 24th of Sivan in the year indicated below, one hundred fifty-five (155) male persons, large and small, and one hundred sixteen (116) female persons, in total, males and females, two hundred seventy-one (271). May they be productive and multiply, and may God bless them. The leaders of the community and the wealthy men of our *kehila* helped them with various things. On the first occasion, two years ago, when the authorized representative traveled there (to New Russia [the new territories in Ukraine]) to get parcels of land to settle, the community gave him approximately two hundred rubles for expenses. In addition, last winter, they were given fifty rubles for expenses (of the journey) to Mogilev to carry out the matter and conclude it successfully. On the day of their departure, the abovementioned Sunday, they were given the horse and wagon and other expenses that were necessary for such a journey, one hundred fifty rubles from the community treasury, one hundred rubles from the burial society, thirty rubles from the funeral society, in addition to donations from individuals, property owners, which amounted altogether to ———[4] as well as bread provisions (food for the journey). . . ." [followed by the scribe's signature, the date—17 Menahem Av, TaKSaH (1808)—and a list of Torah scrolls and other holy books that he gave the travelers on behalf of the community for use in their new home]

This document reflects the entire economic condition and the mood of the Jewish masses in Belarus at the beginning of the nineteenth century. They awaited both harsh decrees and salvation from the "merciful king" Alexander I. The decrees were realized: Jews were driven without mercy from the villages. But the salvation did not arrive. The colonists hoped they would be brought to the "New Settlements" and that they would be sustained and fed "until they are finally settled" in the new locations. But it turned out altogether differently. After a difficult journey, which lasted several months, the migrants arrived at the steppes of the Kherson Governorate, where they were allotted parcels of land without houses, without even tents or booths. They had to build and, at the same time, wander about in the field, plowing soil that had never before been plowed, suffering from hunger, cold, and epidemics; they lacked wood and water; they had no mills to grind grain. Many died, others fled to the cities, and only those who remained built the first colonies: Sde Menucha [today Kalininskoye], Bobrovyy Kut, and others.[5]

Difficult were the birth pangs, the labor pains of the new village-settlement in Southern Russia, and weak was the newborn child. And here remains one of the largest issues in Jewish history: rebuilding economic life on new foundations. If not for the dead bureaucratic system and the inertia of the Jewish masses, this event would have created a revolution in our economic history.

Introduction Notes:

1. Sh. Dubnov, "Di 'novi-shilenyes' in yor 1808: vi hobn zikh vaysrusishe yidn opgerufn oyf der ershter psure vegn erdarbet-kolonyes in dorem-rusland," *Ekonomishe shriftn fun yivo* II (1932): 33–34.

Article Notes:

1. I translate it here from Hebrew into Yiddish, keeping as close as possible to the original. A facsimile follows.

2. The original reads: "HN"Y of land." The abbreviation could mean "Hazakat nekhosim," a right of possession of one's own parcel of land.

3. The words in parentheses were written between the lines.

4. Here a blank space was left, where the total should have been indicated.

5. See V. N. Nikitin, *Evrei Zemledeltsy* [Jewish Farmers], chap. 1 (St. Petersburg, 1887); Sh. Dubnov, "Historical Announcements" [Russian], *Voskhod* 8 (1893): 24–28; idem., *Die neueste Geschichte des Jüdischen Volkes* (Berlin: Jüdischer Verlag 1920–1923), §50; S. IA. Borovoĭ, *Yevreiskaya zemledelcheskaya kolonizatziya v staroi Rossii* [Jewish agricultural colonization in old Russia], chap. 7 (Moscow, 1928); Y. Leshtsinski in the YIVO *Ekonomishe shriftn* I (1928): 31.

19

Jewish Cantonists—Young Boys Recruited for Military Service in Tsarist Russia, 1828–1956

by Saul Ginsburg, 1933

SAUL GINSBURG (1866–1940, see also Selections 30 and 44 below) was born in Minsk, Belorussia (today Belarus), and graduated from the law faculty of St. Petersburg University in 1892. Of the nearly three hundred articles listed in his bibliography, the first third appeared almost entirely in Russian until the early 1920s, while the remaining two-thirds were written in Yiddish. He and his colleague Pesach Marek first became known for their pathbreaking project of collecting and publishing Yiddish folksongs, completed in 1901. Two years later, Ginsburg became cofounder and coeditor of the first daily Yiddish newspaper in Russia, *Der fraynd* (The friend). Refusing to adapt to Soviet Communism, he left Russia in 1930 and eventually settled in the United States, where he continued to write. His collected Yiddish works appeared in five volumes from 1937 to 1946.

Ginsburg was a transitional figure in the development of Yiddish historical writing. Unlike the later generations of university-trained historians, he and the older Jewish historians in Eastern Europe were self-taught in history. Many, like himself, were trained as lawyers, and they intended to take a first step toward countering Jewish legal disabilities and official antisemitism in Russia by documenting them.[1] And yet this focus on the negative events of Jewish history was contrary to the newly evolving ethos of Yiddish historiography, which emphasized the generally positive, internal aspects of Jewish history.

With a career deeply engaged in both the Russian and Yiddish periods of Jewish historical writing, Ginsburg became a historian of two moods—as did his one-time colleague in St. Petersburg, Elias Tcherikower. Ginsburg and Tcherikower were the only pre-Holocaust Yiddish historians to embrace equally the lachrymose (as Salo Baron later famously called it) and anti-lachrymose conceptions of Jewish history.

For Ginsburg, the untold tragedy of Russian Jewish history was the ordeal of the cantonists, the young Jewish boys "recruited" into the tsar's army between 1828 and 1856. He commenced his work on the topic in 1924 with a pair of articles in *Di tsukunft* (The future) in New York, which he developed further in the Minsk *Tsaytshrift* (Periodical) in 1928, then revised and expanded in twelve installments in the New York *Forverts* (Forward) from 1933 to 1934 and finally presented as a comprehensive work of ten chapters in his collected Yiddish writings in 1937. The following are excerpts from the introduction and sixth chapter of the completed work.[2]

Introduction

In the long history of suffering of the Russian Jews, the time of Tsar Nicholas I occupies a special place because of its extraordinary cruelty. This was a time when the severest oppressions, evil decrees, and persecutions spread unceasingly over the Russian Jews and turned their lives into a chapter of pain and misfortune. And, among the countless sufferings that were destined for the Jews in Nicholas's time, without a doubt the most frightful was the suffering of our cantonists, the little Jewish recruits who were torn from their parents (in the years 1827–1856), sent away to the farthest Russian areas, and tormented in the cruelest manner so that they would accept the Russian Orthodox faith.

Everyone has heard or has read something about the frightful fate of the old-time Jewish cantonists. One must say, however, that their history of martyrdom is to this day still little known. A few compilatory treatments, historical notices, several memoirs of former cantonists, and a few literary accounts on this theme—that is almost all that our literature possesses so far about this. We know only individual, partial, mostly accidental episodes, but we do not yet have a detailed conception of the tormented course of the little Jewish martyrs' lives. And this is entirely understandable: until the most recent time, we were lacking the most important material, which could give us a clear, complete picture of the whole cantonist tragedy with all its fearful details. We were lacking the official materials that were lying hidden in the Russian governmental archives, and no one had access to them.

Being already long interested in the history of the little cantonists, I collected everything about them that I could find in the Hebrew, Yiddish, and Russian literature. I would also search out old, retired soldiers from Nicholas's time who had the bitter fate to be taken as recruits in their childhood years; I would inquire and take notes about their experiences of the misfortunes they once endured. But I felt the material that I assembled by this means was not sufficient. And so, I did not yet consider it possible to write about it. I had to put it aside for later in case I succeeded at some time in locating the most important—meaning, official—material, and recently after a long time my hope was fulfilled.

I received access to the Russian state archives, and among the thousands and thousands of various documents that I studied there, I came across an entire pack of papers that have a direct connection to the history of the Jewish cantonists: still unpublished imperial orders, ordinances, reports and instructions from ministers and from the Synod (the bishops and other high officials of the Russian Orthodox faith), letters and statistical materials, messages from missionaries and priests, reports from various military, civilian, and clerical officials, etc.—an entire hoard of new, extraordinarily important and interesting materials about the cantonist drama that are still unknown to both the larger Jewish public and our historians. Studying these innumerable old, time-yellowed documents, I would often tremble with fear. . . .

The frightful suffering of the unfortunate children demands its *tikun* [redress]; it should remain permanently in the memory of the people. The history of suffering of the Jewish cantonists must finally be written. . . .

Moral Compulsion to Convert

After the long, very difficult, and painful journey, chiefly on foot, in which children would die from cold, hunger, and sickness, our little recruits from the faraway Jewish regions would finally arrive at the canton. Already the first welcome must have thrown the Jewish children into fear. In almost every battalion, lower-ranking officers would be sent several miles ahead to meet the newly arriving Jewish cantonists, and they attempted to persuade them that they should immediately convert, or else they would have the greatest troubles. Most often, on the journey, the transport officer had already taken from the boys all the things that were connected to the Jewish religion; and if not, it was done immediately on their arrival. "The first day, as we were brought into the Arkhangelsk Battalion," recounted former cantonist I. Itskovitch, "they took from us our *sidurim* [prayer books], *arbe kanfes* [fringed ritual undergarments], and *tefillin* [prayer boxes]; what was done with them, whether they were put down somewhere, or destroyed, I do not know."[1] The same was reported by another recruit, from Irkutsk. And when a boy hid his little *arbe kanfes*, and then it was discovered, he was cruelly whipped.[2] On arriving, the children were sternly warned against speaking any Yiddish among themselves or praying "*zhid*-like." "If someone noticed that we conducted a conversation with one another in Yiddish, we were beaten for it," recounted former cantonist M. Spiegel.[3]

When a new party of Jewish boys would arrive, the officer in charge would inform them in the clearest manner what was expected here. "The commander of our battalion, Diakonov," wrote a cantonist from Arkhangelsk, "said at once on receiving our party that so long as he would live, not one of his battalion would leave a Jew."[4] In 1857, a group of converted Jewish soldiers in Odessa declared that they were baptized by force in the Kiev area cantons. At the official hearing, they related how they were greeted: as soon as they were brought there, they were distributed among various companies. The commander of the first company, Captain Borodin, immediately asked: which of you wants to be baptized? All remained silent, so he ordered the sergeant, Antipov, to hand them over to the junior officers, who should force them to convert. In the fifth company, the commander, Shelepovski, posed the new arrivals the same question and, not receiving from them the answer he wanted, ordered the junior officers to take the necessary measures for them to be baptized. In the other companies it was still worse. "Right after coming to the company," complained another soldier, "we were led into the workhouse and rods were brought there. The sergeant ordered us all to undress and asked: who wants to be baptized? Only four replied that they were willing, and the others remained silent; the sergeant beat several of them and ordered the junior officers to see to it that all would convert by the next day."[5] Such treatment was given to the Jewish boys not only in Kiev but everywhere. . . .

The worst, however, was that everywhere, wherever the Jewish cantonist might turn, he always heard the demand: "Convert!"—and no one was content with mere words. The "mildness," the "calm, peaceful, teachings" that the instructions from the Synod recommended the priests should use in turning the Jewish children to the Russian Orthodox faith [discussed by Ginsburg in a previous chapter and reproduced in an appendix] applied only on paper, but in reality they played no role at all. The entire missionary work in the cantons was based on coercion. To get Jewish boys to convert, a double form of coercion would continually be brought to bear against them: moral and physical.

The moral, or psychological, coercion had the purpose of creating among the little Jewish children such a mood as would make them feel ever more alone, helpless, and forlorn. The intent of this was to weaken their will and their ability to resist. For this goal, an entire series of methods was used to attempt to separate the cantonist from any Jewish environment, sever him from everything that had a connection to Jewishness, so that he would forget his family, his former home, and the faith in which he was educated. This system of psychological coercion that prevailed in the cantons, and was conducted so methodically, was reflected clearly in the official reports, descriptions, and information from the priests and military officials that are extant in the government archives. . . .

Among the Jewish boys who were kept in the Siberian cantons (in Irkutsk, Tomsk, Tobolsk, Omsk, Krasnoyarsk, and in other cities), there was one group that was in somewhat more agreeable circumstances for a while, in comparison with their comrades who were brought here from the faraway Jewish cities. As our readers recall [from a previous chapter], the sons of the Jews who were themselves, or their parents, exiled to Siberia were considered by a special law to be cantonists. According to the general order that applied to sons of soldiers, they were raised in the homes of their parents, and only when they became fourteen years old were they taken into the battalion (while the other Jewish boys could be taken at twelve years old). And when the Siberian boys arrived in the cantons, their situation was much easier because they had here, in the same city or somewhere not far, their parents or relatives whom they could see from time to time.

The missionaries were very discontent with both these conditions. The Irkutsk bishop, Nil, wrote in his report to the Synod of September 21, 1844, that he "used all possible means to turn the Jewish cantonists to the Russian Orthodox faith; consequently, in the Irkutsk half-battalion, there remained only four unbaptized cantonists. And these, too, could surely be convinced if not for the influence of their local relatives who hinder this." In a letter to Bishop Georgy, the commander of the Tobolsk half-battalion, Major Abramov, explained the incomplete success of the baptismal work in his canton, saying, "The parents of the cantonists meet secretly with the children and, in accordance with their deep-rooted fanaticism, the parents prevent them from converting, they strengthen the children in their Jewish superstitions." In January 1845, the Irkutsk bishop, Nil, posed a suggestion to the chief prosecutor of the Synod, Count Protasov, that he had received from the priest of the Irkutsk half-battalion: "The Jewish cantonists should be permitted to meet with their relatives only in the presence of someone among those cantonists who are already baptized"—which would make it possible to control their conversations.

Reporting (on November 12, 1943) to Count Protasov that in Tobolsk thirty-two cantonists had already been baptized, the local bishop, Vladimir, further wrote: "As it appears, the others were also ready to assume the Christian faith, if the Tobolsk Jews were not preventing them and making them stiff-necked. I hope, however, that time and the frequent religious teaching will, with the help of the Holy Spirit, sooner or later also convert them into children of the Russian Orthodox Church." Nevertheless, the bishop did not, however, want to rely entirely on the "holy spirit." He found it necessary to suggest at the same time: "Those thirteen Jewish cantonists whose parents live in Tobolsk should be transferred to the Omsk half-battalion, and in their place, thirteen Jewish cantonists who have no parents in Tobolsk should be brought from there.

The constant complaints and messages from the priests and commanders about the "harmful" influence of the Jewish parents were eventually effective. On April 15, 1845, Nicholas I ordered: "The children of the Jews who arrive in the cantons are allowed to meet with their parents and relatives only in the canton itself and only in the presence of a teacher or officer." The imperial order was directed against the Jewish cantonists who came from Siberia, and he intended to tear them, like all the others, away from their households. . . .

Dissatisfaction was also expressed by the missionaries about the fact that the sons of exiled Jews were taken to the Siberian cantons only when they became fourteen years old. The priests did not cease complaining that, regarding Jewish children, such an arrangement was harmful and hindered the missionary work: since the Jewish children remain at home until the age of fourteen, they receive there a solid religious education, they become proficient in the laws and become attached to the Jewish faith; and when they are thereafter taken into the military units, it is difficult to persuade them to be baptized. The priest from the Irkutsk half-battalion complained in his report to the bishop: "Having the children with them to the age of fourteen, the parents fill them with superstitions and hateful ideas about Christianity, so that thereafter they have no trust or interest in all the teachings and beliefs of the Christian religion. To overcome this, the Jewish children must be taken to the cantons as soon as they turn seven years old." The Irkutsk bishop, Nil, was greatly interested in the question and corresponded about it with the governor-general of eastern Siberia. He too believed that the Jewish children should not be left so long with their parents and that they should be taken to the military units not later than turning eight years old. The Irkutsk bishop posed the matter to the chief prosecutor on January 12, 1845, emphasizing its great importance. Their pious efforts had success. On April 15, 1845, an imperial decree was issued: "From now on, all sons of the Jews in Siberia who, according to the law are considered cantonists, shall be taken to the cantons not later than becoming eight years old, and this shall apply to those sons who are already older than eight and live with their parents or relatives."

The children would be separated from their parents not only physically. The cantonists, who had been torn from their households and thrown into the faraway Russian regions, received word about home from time to time. Nearly all our cantonists knew how to read and write in Yiddish. A message from their faraway home was the only joy that was possible for the unfortunate children. And what a consolation it was for the parents, from whom their little son had been taken by force, to receive word from him that he was alive and not baptized! Naturally, in their letters, parents would remind their children to keep their Jewish faith. The missionaries were highly dissatisfied that the Jewish cantonists were corresponding with their parents. They constantly pointed out that this had a "harmful" effect on the children, and they would thereby disturb them. "The Jewish cantonists are being strengthened in their faith by the letters that they receive from their parents," complained the bishop of Arkhangelsk, Georgy, in his report to the Synod of October 24, 1844. In addition, the Pskov bishop, Nafanail, emphasized in his report to the synodal chief prosecutor, Count Protasov (of December 5, 1844), that "the parents and relatives reprove and constantly request in their letters to the cantonists that they should remain loyal to the Jewish faith."

And if the parents did not even touch on any religious subject in their letters, the missionaries held that, in general, correspondence between Jewish cantonists and their parents was harmful. They continually demanded that this single, weak thread that still united the children with their home also be severed. The bishop of Saratov, Yakov, complained in his letter of December 19, 1844, to Count Protasov: "The cantonists of the Saratov battalion write to their parents, they also receive letters from them, and all in Yiddish. The unconditional demand should be made of them that they write in Russian and let the parents know that they should also send Russian letters to them." Demanding a hundred years ago that Jewish fathers and sons should send each other letters only in Russian actually meant: forbidding them to write to each other; and this was indeed the intent of the tormentors. From the same bishop's message to Protasov we learn, incidentally, about a fine rule that prevailed in many battalions: when a letter would come from the parents in the name of a Jewish cantonist who had already been convinced to convert, the letter was returned with a short notation on the envelope saying that such a cantonist is no longer here; "because (so he explained to the bishop) in being baptized, the Jewish cantonist was given another name and another family." It is easy to imagine what parents experienced and how many tears they poured out when they received the returned letter with such a notation about their child. But this little concerned the pious souls. . . .

All these means of psychological coercion that we have mentioned were intended to tear the cantonist away from Jewishness, to distance him from Jews, and erase in his memory all experiences about his former home. They had, so to speak, a *negative* effect. As we will see later [in a subsequent chapter on inducements to conversion], positive means of spiritual coercion would be applied simultaneously in an attempt to draw the Jewish children closer to the Christian faith.

Introduction Notes:

1. See, e.g., Maxim Vinaver, "When Lawyers Studied History," in Lucy S. Dawidowicz, ed., *The Golden Tradition: Jewish Life and Thought in Eastern Europe* (New York: Schocken Books, 1967), 242–48.

2. Shoyl Ginzburg, "Di tsayt ven m'flegt in rusland avekraysn kleyne idishe ingelakh fun zeyere tates un mames" [The time in Russia when they used to tear small Jewish boys away from their fathers and mothers], *Forverts*, New York, December 10, 1933, sec. 2, p. 3; first portion reprinted as introduction to "Yidishe kantonistn" in Shoyl Ginzburg, *Historishe verk*, vol. 3: "Yidishe layden in tsarishen rusland" [Jewish suffering in tsarist Russia] (New York: Shoyl Ginzburg 70-yohriger yubiley komitet, 1937), 3–6 (quoted here), and Ch.VI, 72–84 (abridged).

Article Notes:

1. I. Itskovitch, "Reminiscences of a Cantonist from Arkhangelsk" [Russian], *Evreiskaia Starina* V (1912): 57.

2. S. Beilin, "Some Stories about Cantonists" [Russian], *Evreiskaia Starina* II (1909): 116.

3. M. Spiegel, "From the Notes of a Cantonist" [Russian], *Evreiskaia Starina* IV (1911): 254; *Voskhod* VII (1884): 25.

4. Itskovitch, 59.

5. Archive of the Ministry of War. Department for Military Areas; judicial matters, no. 10/117.

20
Antisemitism and Pogroms in Ukraine, 1917–1918: On the History of Ukrainian-Jewish Relations
by Elias Tcherikower, 1923

ELIAS TCHERIKOWER (1881–1943) was born in Poltava, Russian Ukraine (today in Ukraine), and briefly attended university in St. Petersburg in 1905 until his arrest at an illegal social democratic meeting. Until World War I, he was active as a writer on Jewish historical topics for Russian-language Jewish journals and the Russian Jewish encyclopedia. In New York at the start of World War I, he was influenced by his townsman and childhood friend, the pioneering Yiddish philologist Ber Borochov, to turn from writing in Russian to Yiddish. He declared, "From then on, I have written in Yiddish. It is unnecessary to explain what it means for a writer when he finds his language."[1]

Late in 1918, he settled in Kiev, where the short-lived Ukrainian republic promised Jewish national autonomy but became, during the Bolshevik suppression of Ukrainian independence, the site of the mass murder of Jews. With other scholars, he undertook a wide-ranging project to document the killings, and he wrote two volumes on the pogroms in Ukraine. The introduction to his first volume appears below.[2] His work is pathbreaking in the development of Jewish historical writing because it presents the context and proximate causes of the violence without the customary resort to a litany of inevitable Jewish suffering (in contrast to Dubnow's preface in the same book).

Tcherikower was the founding head of YIVO's Historical Section from 1925 until his sudden death in 1943, serving as both the editor and coauthor of several volumes of historical works in Yiddish. Like Ginsburg, he alternated between pessimistic and optimistic approaches to Jewish history. Among the latter were his interests in Jewish socialism, French-Jewish history, and the history of the Jewish labor movement in the United States. In his writings on Jewish historiography, he was the first to distinguish between schools of Jewish historical writing on the basis of language, finding in Yiddish historiography an emphasis on economic, social, and cultural topics.[3]

Paradoxically, his pogrom studies, which focused principally on causes and events, and less on Jewish experience, left him unprepared to apply his own observations about the potential of modern Yiddish historiography to the experience of Nazism. His best-known Yiddish essay, "Jewish Martyrology and Jewish Historiography" (1941),[4] laments the inadequacy of modern, objective historical methods to document overwhelming catastrophe—a task that would soon be undertaken by the next generation of Yiddish historians whose works appear at the end of each section of this volume.

In spring 1919, when a new wave of "Petliura" pogroms spread across Ukraine [named for Ukrainian leader Symon Petliura], a witness to the fearful events in Izyaslav, in Volhynia, jotted down in the *pinkes* [record book] at home the following words:

> Two hundred and seventy years ago in the same Volhynian town of Izyaslav, Reb Nosn[1] sat and kept a *pinkes* of those fearful days, the days of Bogdan Chmielnicki and the massacres of 1648–1649, and recorded the entire misfortunes and calamities that our people endured. Could he have imagined then in his mind that so many generations later, after about

two hundred and seventy years, after entire periods of progress and scientific advancement, of lofty social ideas, after periods of amazing inventions and discoveries, that sitting in the same town the writer of these lines, who bears the same name as he, the author of *Yeven Metzulah*, and who is, as is known in our family, a grandson of the fifth generation—would with a bloodied heart also keep the *pinkes* of the fearful calamities that the grandsons of Chmielnicki brought upon our people?

Such words were written by a witness from our time, a great-grandson of the author of the famous historical chronicle, seeking the historical thread of the Jewish persecutions in Ukraine that stretched from Chmielnicki's years through the Haydamaks [in whose uprisings Jews were killed in the seventeenth and eighteenth centuries] to our time. And in truth, a writer of history is literally astounded at how the picture of Jewish suffering in the seventeenth and eighteenth centuries resembles that which took place before our eyes in recent years in Ukraine. In the storm of revolution, the blood of the Ukrainian peasant blazed with old spirits and feelings. From the moldy ashes in which historical Ukraine lies covered, traditions were revived from Cossack times, from the *Zaporozhian Sich* [semiautonomous Cossack state], and from wildly free and merciless Haydamaks. "Let the steppes burn! The time has come to exchange the peasant's fur coat for the nobleman's caftan"—with that cry the peasant Haydamaks went to join the uprising led by Zaliznyak, in the eighteenth century, at the time of the Koliivshchyna [revolt against Polish rule]. This was in essence a social revolution—and *in fact* the rebels, the peasants, set off across Ukraine "with their knives in their bootlegs to put an end to the Jews," as recorded in the poem *Haidamaki* [1841] by the genius of Ukraine, Taras Shevchenko. The Ukrainian folk epic of that time also told how "the cursed Jews were crucified with sabers."

As in the prior years, precisely now, too: the civil war and national struggle that engulfed the entire region awakened elemental peasant uprisings, partisan movements headed by *atamans* and *bamkes*, a primitive rural anarchism—and it also awakened wild national passions and a blind, burning hatred of Jews. The resistance movement of the peasants almost everywhere in Ukraine was transformed into a pogrom *toykhekhe* [the biblical list of divine punishments of the Jews], which occupied one of the first places in the history of the Jewish people's misfortunes. According to the historical sources, during the ten years of Chmielnicki's persecutions, as many as a *quarter million* Jews were killed and as many as seven hundred communities destroyed. In the period of the later Haydamak pogroms, in the eighteenth century, fifty to sixty thousand Jews were killed. The time has not yet come to give an exact accounting of the number murdered in the *latest* pogroms in Ukraine. But, according to the information available, it is possible to say with certainty that this is not less than in the time of Chmielnicki and is much greater than in the time of the Uman slaughter. The historical chronicles, the little bit that remains as a remembrance of those years, give an account of frightful dramatic moments that the Ukrainian Jews survived in fire and slaughter. But whoever is familiar with the documents from *our* pogrom period would be convinced that our period is perhaps richer in such frightful experiences. And just as in former times, the pogrom drama unfolded in the same framework—principally on the right-bank region of the Dnieper, where the cradle of the former Jewish slaughters was located, in the area between the two main rivers of Ukraine—between the Dnieper and the Dniester.

In Ukraine, the one-time Cossack and Haydamak revolts are already long forgotten. Many years ago, the country lost its independence and was incorporated into the whole of the Russian Empire and was transformed into a group of small southern Russian governorates. But whenever a *mass* pogrom movement against Jews broke out in Russia, it occurred in "Southern Russia," i.e., exactly on the territory of Ukraine. As long as Russia was ruled by the tsarist regime, which leveled everything, the whole country lay in a "stony faint," as the Russian writer Herzen once wrote—no one noticed this constancy in pogrom outbreaks in Ukraine. But in 1917, when the revolution awakened the country, all the bands were torn from it and the *differentiation* of the Russian Empire and the singling out of its national areas (Ukraine among them) began, and this phenomenon became clear and noticeable. Jews had large settlements in Lithuania, Belarus, partly also in Latvia and some points in central Russia (the war "refugees")—but mass murders of Jews invariably took place just in Ukraine. This fact was an instructive historical marvel.

At the start of the 1880s came the first eruption of mass pogroms in Russia, which lasted nearly three years. The first pogrom was in Yelisavetgrad [today Kropyvnytskyi, Ukraine] (on April 15, 1881). The movement thereafter encompassed the Kherson, Kiev, Ekaterinoslav, Chernigov, Volyn, Poltava, and Podolia governorates—altogether 150 points. And all the points, with small exceptions, belong to the Ukrainian governorates; but in the Kiev Governorate itself, forty-eight cities and towns suffered. Following a pause of twenty-three years, in October 1905, mass pogroms again took place, which this time took on a much broader and more frightful character. In the course of four or five days, 690 places of Jewish settlement were destroyed. Looking at the geographic spread of the movement, we see the same phenomenon—the chief territory of the pogroms was again Ukraine: but in the Chernigov Governorate itself there were 329; in Kherson, 82; in Poltava, 52; Ekaterinoslav and Kiev, 41; in Podolia, 37; and in the Bessarabia Governorate, which is adjacent to Ukraine, 71 pogroms. In comparison with this, the number of pogroms in other governorates was insignificant, and in Lithuania and Poland, where the Jewish settlement is larger than in Ukraine, there were almost no pogroms at all. In the riots of the 1880s, the peasants took no outstanding part, the chief role being played by the urban rabble, who were incited by antisemitic agitation and led by the hand of the police; this urban rabble of the southern governorates was often not purely Ukrainian—it consisted of *declasirte elementn* [those reduced to lower status], new arrivals from the interior Russian regions, and Russified local petit bourgeoisie. In the October pogroms of 1905, however, the local peasant—the old resident of Ukraine—was already going together with the urban mob, and in places even ahead of it. The extent of the peasant participation in the October events is seen in the fact that, out of 690 pogroms, 626 took place in villages and market towns. Easily and without great effort, the hand of the Russian police incited the peasant, the city resident, and the rabble against the Jews, precisely in the governorates of Ukraine; in other regions where Jews lived, they were not able to accomplish this to such an extent.

The Ukrainian national movement, as a mass movement, was still slumbering in those years, but a social movement of the Ukrainian village was already in full force. The participation of the popular element in the first Russian Revolution, in general, can actually be dated from the mass uprising of the peasants in the spring of 1902 in the Poltava and Kharkov governorates, namely, in Ukraine. The revolutionary movement was exceptionally strong in "southern Russia." The Ukrainian village demonstrated a strong, impulsive revolutionary power. In its social-political convulsions, the echo was felt of the old-time violent "*Zaporozhian Sich*" and of the free Cossack society that have now been resurrected from the dead.

In the first period of the revolutionary movement, in the years 1902–1907, the peasant movement was not stained with Jewish blood. Pogroms were characteristic of the *reaction* and the police regime. But in the revolution of 1917 and later, the impulsive revolt shook the Ukrainian village to its very depths, and in the atmosphere of the explosive civil war, mass persecutions and murders of Jews suddenly broke out.

The Russian revolt violently captured the peasant from Ukraine not only because there still lived in him the memories of former Zaporozhian Cossack freedom from the sixteenth to eighteenth centuries, although this doubtless also unconsciously played a large part, but principally—because of the influence of the frightful socio-economic conditions in which the peasant from Ukraine lived until recent years. In no region of Russia were there such large and rich feudal manors of the nobility as in the Ukrainian landed-estate "economies" and "possessions"—on the one hand, and on the other—nowhere was there such a shortage of land among the peasants, who often had no measure of land at all, as here. The contrast was too sharp. According to the figures in the agricultural census of 1916, in the Ukrainian governorates, *one-fifth* of the entire farmed land area belonged to the nobles, while in all of Russia in general only one-tenth belonged to them; on average, each noble agricultural estate in Ukraine measured 112 *desyatins* [1.095 acres or 2.7 hectares per *desyatin*]. The result was that the rich Ukrainian governorates, which fed Russia and, in part, Europe, produced a surplus of peasant population and a mighty percentage of migrants (*pereselents*). The Ukrainian peasant was forced to leave his country and go in search of free land in distant places—in Siberia, in Middle Asia, partly in the Don region, in northern Kavkaz. According to the figures in the "Statistical Data about Agriculture in European Russia," one-fourth of the entire Russian migration to the Asian provinces for the twenty years from 1885 to 1904 came from three Ukrainian governorates—Poltava, Chernigov, and Kharkov, which in this way lost almost 5 of each 1,000 persons from the village population, while the loss in general for Russia amounted to only 1.4 per 1,000 persons. A smaller migration, although also a very significant one, occurred from the right [western] bank of the Dnieper. The revolution satisfied this sharp hunger for land. But soon after began the large, terrible hunger for goods.

Researchers of Ukrainian life point out another important phenomenon that undoubtedly played a role as a force in the great outrages of recent years—the strong cultural backwardness of the Ukrainian peasant. The statistics show that the Ukrainian governorates counted many more illiterates than the general population in Russia.[2] According to figures from the population census of 1897, the average percentage of those who could read and write among the population of Russia in general was 23.3; in a few Great Russian governorates it even reached 36.1, while in the Ukrainian governorates the percentage was not greater than 16.4 (Chernigov Governorate), and it fell to 10.5 (Podolia) and 9.4 (Volyn) and in a few places still lower—to 6.3 (Ovruch district).

Also characteristic is that the last two governorates, the most backward, belong to the *right bank* of the Dniester. The backwardness of the Ukrainian population, as Ukrainian researchers have pointed out with complete accuracy, is in the largest measure the result of the years-long tsarist policy, the policy of national repression, which did not allow the local population any schools in their mother tongue. Until February 1905, even translation of the *gospel* into Ukrainian was strictly forbidden! It was the village, which had not yielded to the influence of Russification, that suffered more than anyone from this policy.

Were the persecutions of the Ukrainian village against Jews influenced chiefly by the historical moment—the "memory of blood" about the times of Chmielnicki and [Cossack general Maxim] Krivonos, of Gonta and the slaughter at Uman, or did the causes lie exclusively in the socio-economic conditions of present-day Ukraine, and above all in the burning hatred borne by the village toward the city, where the chief role in commerce was played by the Jews? To answer the question with complete certainty, one must have a certain perspective, distance oneself more from our epoch of revolutionary violence and political entanglements. Yet this violence still continues, the period has still not closed its circle, and we ourselves are still participants in the chaos that came upon the world. We stand too close to the flow of events. In such a situation, strict and exact definitions are not possible. To the extent, however, that one can judge according to the great number of facts that have now been collected, economic motives played a large role in the psychology of the peasant in his active hatred toward Jews. Life, human necessities, and lifestyle became primitive, altogether as in times long past, almost like a thousand years before. The war and the revolution created such a demand for goods—mainly in the village—as we seldom find in history. Salt, kerosene, sugar, manufactured goods, nails and, in the beginning, also small change, elementary things necessary to life, became rarities. The small amount of goods that the city and town possessed were in the hands of the old traders and storekeepers from Ukraine—the Jews. In time of war and anarchy, commerce acquired the character of speculation. The war and revolution undermined all previous foundations of social morality and awakened the beast within people. It began to seem as if everything was permitted. All these causes together led to the hunt by peasants in the city for manufactured goods or salt to become, in fact, foremost a hunt for

Jewish wares and Jewish property—and suddenly and everywhere a hunt for the Jewish soul and Jewish blood. These feelings were sharpened in the peasant mind by the propaganda of the primitive civil war, on the one hand, and by the propaganda of national chauvinism, on the other.

The hateful relations between village and city in fact acquired the character of a national struggle for the reason that the cities in Ukraine were, in a certain measure, non-Ukrainian, that the urban bourgeoisie was mostly Jewish or Russian. "History did not give us a bourgeoisie," writes the well-known Ukrainian writer and political leader V. Vinnichenko in his history of the revolution in Ukraine. "The ruling classes in Ukraine—were not Ukrainian." "To this day no bourgeoisie exists in Ukraine that considers itself Ukrainian"—so also wrote the deputation of the central Rada [parliament] in its memorandum to the Provisional Government in May 1917. In this premise, there is some exaggeration because it does not take into account the strong *village* bourgeoisie, which the Ukrainian peasantry also comprised: the middle *khliborobs* [farmers], who organized themselves into the "Ukrainian Democratic Farmers Party" and in April–May 1918 took such an active part in creating the "Hetman Ukrainian State" together with rich nobles of the "All-Ukrainian Union of Landowners," and also those purely Ukrainian *kurkuls* [pejorative term for rich peasants], against whom the agitators of the civil war wanted to incite the poor and middle peasants in recent years. But, regarding the city and town, Vinnichenko's theory was correct. In commercial life, especially in small- and middle-sized trade, where the buyer, the peasant, and the seller, the Jewish city-dweller, meet each other face to face—the Jews were prevalent. The cities and especially the market towns in Ukraine were mostly in Jewish hands, particularly in those governorates that lie on the right bank of the Dnieper. The figures of the popular census of 1897 show—and the proportions are also valid for recent years—that in these governorates—Kiev, Podolia, Volyn, partly Kherson, the average percentage of Jews in the governorate, including also the villages—was 12 to 13. But in the cities, the Jewish population reached: in Kiev and Kherson governorates, 31 percent; in Podolia, 41; and in Volyn, 51. In certain cities and market towns, the percentage was significantly greater. There are locations where Jews constituted as much as 90–95 percent, and it approaches even 100 percent of the entire population. It is important to point out the percentage of Jews in those locations that experienced the frightful pogroms and slaughters. Thus, for example, in the Volyn governorate: in Gritsev [Hrytsiv], where one of the first pogroms took place, in September 1917, the Jews constituted 98 percent; in Kamen-Kashirskiy, where [Stanisław] Bułak-Bałachowicz conducted a slaughter in fall 1920, Jews constituted 99 percent; in Zhitomir [Zhytomyr], Jews constituted 47 percent. In the Kiev Governorate: in Berdichev [Berdychiv], 78 percent Jews; in Radomyshl, which experienced an entire group of pogroms, 69 percent; in Uman, 58 percent; in Fastov [Fastiv], where the Denikin forces conducted a well-known slaughter, 52 percent; in Ignatova, a shtetl that was almost completely erased from the world, 84 percent; in Tetiev [Tetiiv], which is known for its slaughter in March 1920, 95 percent Jews. In the Podolia Governorate: in Proskurov [Khmelnytskyi], 49 percent Jews; in Bershad, 85 percent; in Trostianets, 55 percent; in Felshtin [Hvardiiske/Gvardeyskoye], 95 percent; those are all locations that experienced frightful pogroms and some (like Trostianets and Felshtin), mass slaughters. Such a large place was occupied in the city by the Jewish population.

On the other hand, the village in Ukraine felt very strong and occupied the most important place in the economic system of the country. Ukraine is the true peasant-region in Europe. According to the newest population census of the years 1920–1921, in the twelve present Ukrainian governorates, there are as many as 26 million residents, of whom more than 21 million live in the villages.[3] But if we exclude from the accounting the four largest cities—Odessa, Kiev, Kharkov, and Ekaterinoslav, which themselves have almost 1,300,000 residents, and also the part of the Donetsk coal region that has now become considered Ukraine, the peasant character of the region will be still clearer. Precisely here, in the "peasant state," is where the great revolt, that initially went under the banner of star-studded "Bolshevism," ran wild. And when the Ukrainian village would not recognize the communist policy and imposed authority of the Soviet government in Moscow and entered into a stubborn, armed conflict, through its *povstantses* [rebels] and "partisans," against the Soviet government, assailed with its entire fury, above all, the Jewish city and town where the Jews played the chief role. Jews constituted not only a significant, but also very active, element of the city and, more than other parts of the population, were drawn into political and revolutionary life and also occupied an important place in the Communist Party and in the Soviet apparatus. Jewish Communists would often occupy the most distinguished posts and energetically carry out the "Muscovite" policy. Here, like everywhere, the Soviet government conducted its program mercilessly and, with the greatest momentum, pushed the region into civil war, especially in the village, and at the same time ignored the complicated mutual national relations that existed in Ukraine and the unavoidable outbreaks of pogroms. This policy of blowing fire into a gunpowder depot gave the opponents of the Soviet Union the impulse to spill rivers of innocent Jewish blood.

These were the social circumstances in Ukraine at the moment of the revolution. The four-year war had already prepared all the elements for the outbreak of anarchy in the country and in the village in particular; it also created the moral decline that made possible the mass crimes of recent years. The revolution, which came as an answer to the war, was not capable of stopping these processes of ruin and anarchy and filling the abysses. On the contrary, it strengthened and exposed these processes still more. The war instructed millions of people in the techniques of handling weapons and pathologically militarized the psychological surroundings. People entered into an environment of "intimate relation with cannons" and weapons, which proved to be so dangerous. During the World War, two fronts fatefully befell Ukraine—the Southwestern and Romanian. And when the World War ended, a more dangerous *internal* war broke out, a fraternal struggle, a war in every settlement, on every street, a stubborn and merciless civil war. The ideology of war, the art of war, of military methods, the morality of the fronts, of attacks, of *velfishe griber* [voracious pits or graves], and of states of siege had—as before—a mighty influence in life, even though the World War had already long ended. The war and revolution gave the Ukrainian populace more weapons in hand than all other regions. The Ukrainian peasant, his sons—the soldier, the deserter, the partisan—brought with them to the village, from the external and internal fronts, a tremendous quantity of weapons that would be buried for a while in the ground. And consequently, in Ukraine all the civil clashes and almost all the pogrom riots bore an armed and, usually, bloody character.

There was one additional force that played a prominent role as an element of the pogrom-psychology, which is—the great spread of *adventurism* that was generally characteristic of recent years in shaky Europe and which in Ukraine assumed a very broad, almost pathological form. Historic Ukraine had already become well acquainted with this phenomenon in the sixteenth and seventeenth centuries. Adventurism was in fact the father of the Cossack state. The Cossacks of the *Zaporozhian Sich*, headed by their *atamans*, would engage with people of other faiths—Tatars and Turks—in the mitzvah [commandment] of war for the sake of victory by the cross over the half-moon. But the true impetus for these wars was the pursuit of fast riches and booty: the robberies would bring in a wealth of possessions. This nature of the old-time Cossack state was also pointed out by the Ukrainian historians.[4] Such adventurism was already widespread across all of Europe from the time of the Crusades and in essence had the same motives. In present-day Ukraine, the Cossack adventurism of the seventeenth century was resurrected with a new strength; groups of *condottieri* [mercenaries] from the revolution appeared, fanatics from modern Crusades. And the object of the Crusades became—the Jewish shtetl.

As a result of all these causes, Ukraine was transformed into a place of provoked, armed, bloody conflicts, of unceasing political upheaval and changes of government. The number of governments that changed by the moment in Ukraine has no precedent in history. Thus, from the February revolution until 1921, Kiev experienced fourteen to fifteen political upheavals, almost all by force of arms. Uman, for example, experienced as many as twenty-five. In many small locations, the number was still greater. On that shaky ship, in the atmosphere of uncontrollable anarchy, the mass crimes of the pogroms became possible.

Introduction Notes:

1. E. Tsherikover, "Ber Borokhov—vi ikh ken im" [As I know him], *Literarishe bleter* 4, no. 52 (Warsaw, December 30, 1927): 1024.

2. E. Tsherikover, *Antisemitizm un pogromen in ukrayine 1917–1918: tsu der geshikhte fun ukrayinish-yidishe batsyungen* [On the history of Ukrainian-Jewish relations] (Berlin: Mizrekh-yidishn historisn arkhiv, 1923).

3. E. Tsherikover, "Yidishe historyografye," *Algemeyne entsiklopedye*, vol. Yidn I (Paris: Association Simon Dubnow, 1939), 284–302.

4. E. Tsherikover, "Yidishe martirologye un yidishe historyografye," *YIVO bleter* XVII, no. 2 (March–April 1941): 97–112; "Jewish Martyrology and Jewish Historiography," *YIVO Annual* I (1946): 9–23.

Article Notes:

1. Nathan Hanover, the author of the historic chronicle *Yeven Metzulah* ["Deep Mire" (Psalms 69:3)] about Chmielnicki's persecutions. [In English, see *The Abyss of Despair (Yeven Metzulah): The Famous 17th Century Chronicle Depicting Jewish Life in Russia and Poland during the Chmielnicki Massacres of 1648–1649*, trans. Abraham J. Mesch (New York: Bloch, 1950).]

2. See, for example, the collection *Ukrainskiĭ Vopros* [Ukrainian question], 3rd ed. (Moscow: Zadruga, 1917), 154. The collection was published by the Ukrainian leaders at the time of the war in Russian.

3. See the article by Khristian Rakovsky, "Soviet Ukraine in 1921" [Russian], *Izvestia*, January 6, 1922, on the results of the popular census.

4. See N. Vasylenko, *Ocherki po istorii Zapadnoĭ Rusi i Ukrainy* [Essays on the History of Western Rus and Ukraine] (Kiev: N.IA. Ogloblin, 1916).

21

On the Causes of Jewish Defenselessness against the Nazis and the Strength of Jewish Resistance

by Isaiah Trunk, 1953

ISAIAH TRUNK (see also Selections 7 and 15 above) was prompted by the tenth anniversary of the Warsaw Ghetto Uprising, in the spring of 1953, to write two articles on the subject of Jewish resistance. Both addressed the question of why armed Jewish resistance had come so late—after nearly all the Jews had been murdered—and was therefore so weak.

The first article reported the conclusions of his own research, listing the many impediments to Jewish resistance.[1] The thinking was original and the writing intemperate, barely concealing his emotional response. The second was dispassionate but limited to a discussion of views already published by others. Trunk selected the second article for inclusion in his 1962 volume of collected writings, presumably because of its more "professional" tone.[2] Trunk's first article, however, excels in its early and original analysis of the subject. It is presented below.

The problem of the extermination of European Jewry at Hitler's hands, which constitutes a radical turning point in our 2,000-year history, has two sides: an external, seen from the German Nazi side, and an internal, Jewish side. . . . [Trunk then devotes a few paragraphs to German motivations and actions.]

The second aspect of the problem, the interior-Jewish side, can be formulated in the questions: What sort of factors made it possible for the Nazis to succeed in leading the Jewish population to such a condition that it would passively and defenselessly follow German orders regarding "emigration" and "resettlement," knowing from prior examples from other places—and feeling clearly—that it meant extermination? And secondly, why did Jewish resistance, where it found a way to break through to the surface, come so late and therefore so weak?

The Causes of Jewish Defenselessness

We must be satisfied here with enumerating some of the principal points:

1. The extermination plan for European Jewry was prepared by the Nazis with the entire precision and specificity that was characteristic of the Germans. The Nazi murder of the Jews was not the result of a spontaneous outbreak of Jew-hatred that was transformed into pogroms, theft, and murder of the defenseless Jewish population—as was often the case in Jewish history—but was a calculated plan, developed with the participation of the most respected statesmen, top military personnel, and scholars—specialists in mass murder. For the first time in history, the Jewish people stood face-to-face with such an enemy.

    The strategy of the Nazis' extermination plan consisted of isolating, surrounding, exhausting, and surprising the Jews so that, after a long period of "preparation" through starvation, terror, and demoralization, they would passively let happen to them what the Germans demanded of them.
2. The ghettos, with their indescribable living and sanitary conditions: in their provisioning, which was below the level of starvation, they had the goal—besides isolating and surrounding the Jews—of driving them to physical and psychological dehumanization. The permanent starvation and indescribable want that prevailed in the ghettos transformed the Jews into shadows of a person; they weakened and dulled the normal life urges and psychological reactions among the Jewish masses.
3. The Nazis employed against their victims a system of cynical and refined deception to induce in the minds of the unfortunate victims

a disorientation so complete they would be unaware—to the last minute, already standing in front of the gas chamber—that the final goal was murder.
4. Mass murder, which the Nazis employed against the Jewish population, stood in such clear contradiction to the ethical worldview of even the simplest Jew that it was impossible for him to believe that a civilized state in the heart of Europe would apply the system of physical annihilation to a peaceful, innocent population. No one wanted to believe in this frightful secret, despite all the warning sounds that traveled from ghetto to ghetto.
5. The Nazis ruled the ghettos according to the old proven formula of "divide and rule," through a deceptive system of all types of certificates and identity cards, whose possessors were temporarily singled out to remain alive, which succeeded in creating a confusion of minds and division of hearts in the ghetto.

In nearly all the ghettos the Jews were divided according to their material situation and according to their position in the Nazi law of (temporary) right to life: in nearly every ghetto there were small groups of privileged people (to which belonged the members of the *Judenrat*, the Jewish ghetto police and their families, skilled workers, specialists) who received from the Nazi executioner the "mercy" of struggling longer for their physical survival. On account of the horrible ghetto conditions, where one person's temporary salvation could come *only* at the expense of others, this bitter struggle for bare life assumed tragic-dramatic forms.

The Nazis deliberately tried to sharpen the antagonisms and social conflicts in the ghettos. This was one of the means of morally disarming the ghetto population, weakening the feeling of national solidarity in order to deal with divided, quarreling, mutually hostile groups.
6. The Nazi plan also consisted of making the victim assist in his own destruction to spare the executioner extra effort and exertion. In this diabolical plan of self-extermination, an appropriate role was established for the *Judenräte* [plural of *Judenrat*, Jewish Council] and the Jewish police, who, with few exceptions, transformed themselves into expositors of German authority in the ghetto.

Already in the first phase, when the total extermination plan for the Jewish population had not yet been put in motion, the *Judenräte*, with good or bad intentions, cooperated with the German authority in confiscating Jewish property, assembling files of able-bodied workers and dispatching them to forced labor.

They were also the disseminators of various harmful rescue illusions, such as, that in return for good work for the German authority, Jews would remain alive, and they thereby weakened and paralyzed the resistance force of the ghetto masses and combated the thought of passive and active resistance.

As a rule, in the period of deportation *Aktionen* [round-ups], the *Judenräte* cooperated with the deportation commissions and extermination commands. Some acted in accordance with the false proposition that, to save—as it seemed to them—even a portion of the Jews, the most valuable, one must agree to deliver into German hands the others, the less valuable; others did so for the sake of simply egoistic reasons, to save themselves, their families, and relatives. In a large number of ghettos, the Jewish police were recruited from wholly or partly underworld figures who used the period of disorder and lack of rights to "make a living." Within their ranks the majority became informers, Gestapo agents; they were the executioners' deputies and cooperated with them in all their crimes, searches, hunts for people, executions, transporting the victims to the death camps, etc. Almost everywhere, the Jewish police transformed themselves into a direct instrument of destruction, facilitating and assisting the Germans in carrying out their bloody task.

The Heroism of Uprising

The points mentioned above attempt to characterize the physical and psychological situation of the ghetto Jew that enabled the passive, unresisting path to death.

Against that background, however, shine the acts of heroism of the ghetto fighters and of the not-at-all rare instances of individual and collective revolts in the ghettos, by partisans, and even in the death camps, about which only bits of information reached us (given that all their participants and witnesses were killed immediately or later).

Regarding the very concept of resistance—it has been used in broader or narrower interpretations. In the first case, i.e., in passive resistance, which the ghetto Jews conducted against the Hitlerian plan of physical and psychological dehumanization, we are dealing with a permanent process of resistance. The ghetto Jew applied every means in order to live longer than the Nazi plan anticipated. He struggled against hunger, the isolation of the ghetto, created a ghetto economy literally from nothing, refused to allow the image of God to be torn from him. Within the crowded ghetto walls, in the most inhuman living conditions, the ghetto Jew created a network of cultural institutions, such as schools, yeshivas, clubs, and concert and theater halls, to preserve the spiritual and humane in this valley of tears that the Germans wanted to turn into a human jungle. The ghetto Jew established social, cultural, and sanitary institutions that continually, daily, resisted and countered the Nazi blitz strategy in the war with the Jewish people. This passive resistance, which also had its martyrs and saints, found its expression in cultural, religious, economic, sanitary, and even political struggle (the underground press and secret radio receivers).

In its narrow interpretation, in the sense of active, armed resistance, this resistance came too late and therefore could not have the scope that it might have had if it had broken out when the majority of Eastern European Jews were still alive.

We have already mentioned above a number of influences in this direction. Here, we will dwell on a series of other points that characterize the subjective and objective situation of Jewish resistance.

1. The Jews in the ghettos felt as if they were in a hermetically encircled, besieged fortress. Aware of their own weak forces and knowing the hostile attitude of the Christian surroundings, they saw no possibility of rescue in even the most fortunate case, in which they would succeed in escaping by force from the ghetto walls. On the contrary, the ghetto walls gave an illusion of closely confined security with regard to the hostile environment. If, however, there was no chance of rescue in fighting, the most important impulse for going to battle was lacking. Dying purely for the sake of honor is a matter for select individuals and not for the masses.

2. Connected with the hostile attitude of the external world is the tragic shortage of weapons. (Until January 1943, the Warsaw ghetto had ten old pistols.) The few pieces of weaponry that were bought and smuggled in from the so-called "Aryan side" did not make it possible to fight on a wide scale. The productive abilities of the ghetto in this area were, for understandable reasons, very limited.

3. The fear of collective responsibility, a system that was imposed by the Germans in all the occupied countries with the utmost cruelty—weighed upon the leaders of the resistance movement like a mountain. They were afraid that, with each premature and improperly prepared act, they were hastening the final extermination of the entire ghetto community, for whose fate they felt responsible.
4. The terrible instability of the ghetto situation, when one day was not similar to another, when disorienting and disconcerting German orders would, in a short span of time, rain down onto the heads of the ghetto residents and make impossible any plan of action for a long period of time and undo and render obsolete previously adopted decisions, as was the case in Bialystok and Częstochowa.
5. To correctly evaluate the problem of resistance, we must compare the behavior of other peoples in similar (and often incomparably better) situations. From that comparison, it will be seen that the civil population, for example, in Poland, France, and other occupied countries, also rarely ever mounted active opposition during deportations, mass arrests, and executions.
6. Escaping to join the partisans in the Eastern European regions provided limited possibilities for rescue on account of the confined nature of the region, but primarily on account of the antisemitism that was widespread in the partisan ranks themselves.

It is therefore a demonstration of great moral strength and heroism that, despite all of this, thousands of young and even older Jewish people sought and found that difficult and dangerous path toward fighting and, with their blood, inscribed heroic chapters in the history of the Jewish people's fight against its bloodiest enemy—Nazism.

Introduction Notes:

1. Sh. Trunk, "Yidisher umkum un vidershtand (tsu der kharacteristik fun unzer khurbn)" [Jewish extermination and resistance (on the characteristics of our destruction)], *Lebns-fragn* 24 (Tel Aviv, April 1953): 3–4.

2. Sh. Trunk, "Di problem vidershtand in undzer khurbn-literatur" [The problem of resistance in our *khurbn*-literature], *Di tsukunft* (New York, May–June 1953): 253–57; reprinted in Yeshaye Trunk, *Shtudyes in yidisher geshikhte in poyln* [Studies in Jewish history in Poland] (Buenos Aires: Yidbukh, 1963), 298–307.

Part Four

YIDDISH LITERATURE

22
The *Brantshpigl* (*Burning Mirror*), 1596—The Encyclopedia of the Jewish Woman in the Seventeenth Century

by Maks Erik, 1926

MAKS ERIK (Zalmen Merkin, 1898–1937), Yiddish literary historian and critic, was born in Sosnowiec, Poland. During the 1920s, he specialized in Yiddish literature from the period before the end of the eighteenth century, particularly the *muser-sforim* (morality books) of the early seventeenth century. An example is the following article on the *Brantshpigl*,[1] which became part of his major work, *History of Yiddish Literature: From Earliest Times to the Haskalah Period* (Yiddish, Vilna, 1928). The article begins, as shown, with a numbered list.

Erik settled in the Soviet Union in 1929, where he was appointed director of the department of Yiddish literature at the Jewish academic institute in Minsk and, thereafter, Kiev. To conform with official Soviet disapproval of the study of Old Yiddish literature in the 1930s (as a retreat from revolutionary scholarship), he changed his focus to the Haskalah period. Nevertheless, he was arrested in 1936 during Stalin's Great Purge and died the following year in a camp in Siberia.

1. *Muser-sforim* [ethics books of Jewish literature]—these are a half-religious literature; their purpose is religious, their tendency—clerical, but the material with which they operate, the object of their strictures, is the everyday, real, stubborn secular life. In the cracks of the multibranched religious lifestyle appear the words of *muser*; it hopes to discipline life, but it fails to notice the internal turn of events, adapts too slowly and conservatively, and the void remains invariably threatening, the crack—invariably dangerous. As a result, the tremendous significance of the *muser-sforim* for cultural history: not only do they give a great many details about the internal Jewish life of former times; not only can the experienced eye, on the basis of the *muser-sforim*, imagine a static, frozen "old-time" life of earlier generations—they also give character to the dynamic, to developments in the mental and spiritual life of our folk masses. And more important in this regard are precisely the Yiddish *muser-sforim*; the Hebrew ones are more abstract, more theoretical, more removed from life—the Yiddish ones by contrast are generally based on concrete details, real and everyday issues, are more intimate, necessarily also less dogmatically devout. They are good natured, inexpensive, readable—in a word, earthier. But linguistically the Yiddish *muser-sforim* also have great value: for understandable reasons, their language is very folksy, immeasurably more natural than the artificial "literary language" of our novels from the same time.

   The high period of the Yiddish *muser-sforim* is the sixteenth and seventeenth centuries—more so the seventeenth than the sixteenth. It is the classical period of the Old Yiddish *muser-sefer*, not only because in this period the great *muser* encyclopedias were created—the *Brantshpigl* and the *Lev Tov* [Good Heart]; but also for the quantitative measure of *muser-sforim* production; and for the diversity of this literature: countless small, cheap *muser-sforim* for the poor woman, and simultaneously, large, heavy volumes; *muser-sforim* solely for women, *muser-sforim* solely for men, and eventually for both sexes; *muser-sforim* that covered only a few issues. For example, the *mitzvot* [commandments] pertaining specifically to women (bread, laws of ritual purity, kindling of Sabbath lights), and *muser-sforim* that are genuine encyclopedias, that encompass almost every question and concern of a Jewish woman from former times. The present article is devoted to this type of "encyclopedia"—the *Brantshpigl*, which governed the Jewish woman during the entire seventeenth century.

2. The author of the *Brantshpigl* is Rabbi Moshe Henoch's (i.e., son of Henoch) Yerushalmi Altshuler of Prague. In the list of Prague Jews from 1546 there is a Henoch "*from the old shul*," of whose children the first is Moshe—no doubt the later author of the *Brantshpigl*, Moshe Henoch Altshuler. . . .

3. The *Brantshpigl* is an original work; no [earlier] Hebrew work existed. . . . I doubt also whether a later Hebrew translation was published, as it was written specifically for women; even *mitzvot* and laws that touched upon the man no less than the woman were covered exclusively from the standpoint of the woman. . . .

The first printed edition of the *Brantshpigl* that has come down to us appeared in Basel in 1602; the second in Prague—in 1610; the third Hannover—1626, then Frankfurt-Main—1676 and 1706, etc. . . .

4. The copy that I am using is from the Prague edition of 1610, which was published while the author was still alive, in the city of his birth. . . .

5. The *Brantshpigl* quickly became popular; it was published in a series of editions that educated generations of Jewish women—among them Glikl of Hameln—and it inspired a series of imitations. . . .

It is easy to single out the positive virtues of the *Brantshpigl*, which can be expressed under the following five headings: First, the *Brantshpigl* was an original work written for the woman, only for her; it abbreviates chapters for the man that have little value [for her], and speaks expansively about the truly female matters, the problems of female modesty, of sexual life in the broadest sense of the word, of sexual hygiene, of menstruation—of raising children, of housekeeping. It is characteristic that it breaks off its advice about raising boys with the moment they go away to *cheder* [religious school]—as they are then leaving the authority of the woman, *and the* Brantshpigl *is a woman's book*. Second, in any event, the *Brantshpigl* was written originally in Yiddish, without an accompanying Hebrew text. Third, the *Brantshpigl* is a book that is *hostile to the world, but not foreign to it, and it is distinguished by its practical spirit*. Contrary to certain other *muser-sforim*, in the *Brantshpigl*, the general ethical principle is only a springboard, a point of departure, for detailed, concrete examination of life and advice for living. The author was a sort of respectable man of the people; he was far from the estrangement from the world of rabbinic hairsplitting. He was trusted by the Prague *kehila* [community], and his book is not an ordinary religious book, but a book of religious policy that tries to convert the usual iron truths into the small change of everyday worries and concerns. He has a sharp eye for everything that goes on around him; he knows his audience; between him and his public, there is no barrier; he often relies on old persons and on customs of old women; he puts directly into the woman's mouth the words with which, in various cases, she should turn to her husband, to strangers, acquaintances. He loves the detail, and every little insignificance seems to him important and distinguished; thus, he writes in absolute seriousness a chapter about how one should sit in an outhouse. He knows the power of love; he takes the opportunity to recount the story of the *hulda u-bor* [the marten (rodent) and the pit]; he also knows about sexual perversities, and he criticizes lesbian love. In great seriousness, he prepares a chapter (38) that "states, when she lies, how she should lie neatly in bed." He has his system of education and separates the education of the boy from the education of the woman. From this, one can clearly discern the fourth heading: the *encyclopedic nature* of the *Brantshpigl*. It is a handbook that includes almost every instance of the ordinary life of the Jewish woman of the time, that tells: how to please the groom, and to comfort injustices, what to do if the husband plays cards, and how to entertain guests; how to be at the table and how to conduct oneself in synagogue; how to treat the maidservant, and how to salt meat. This brings to mind the fifth virtue of the *Brantshpigl*—its beautiful construction, which first gives the general principle with appropriate quotations and examples, while not losing sight of the general principle and setting up a practical, concrete section of equal standing—with which it is clear to us that the *Brantshpigl* is *the central, classical Yiddish morality book*.

But this must be said: the *Brantshpigl* is a morality book for the rich, well-off Jewish woman; only she, only her needs and interests does the author have in mind. External signs already betray this: it is a large, thick, and exceptionally expensive book. But, in addition, the picture of the Jewish home that arises in the mind after acquainting oneself with the book breathes with the air of wealth and secure living; one eats a lot and is sated; one has servants—for whose sake—a chapter on how to succeed with servants; one dresses in wealth—on account of which frequent warnings against luxury; the author demands that girls be dressed cleanly and beautifully from childhood on so they will know later how to please the husband. The woman who is chastised and corrected here is not the quiet woman of the people who is worn out by life and troubles, whose mood expresses the prayerful petitions of the poor. On the contrary, it is mainly an *eyshes-khayl* [traditional "woman of valor"], a woman who is energetic, talkative, has a ready reply for everything, gets involved everywhere, a woman who still wants to live (the author complains, for example, that girls cannot dance because the older, married women take up the dances and push them aside)—a woman who is empty, yet presumptuous.

6. First, therefore, comes the general ethical principle, then citations intended to support it, extracts from the canon, from the experiences of great men, from logic and life experience. In this way, the following six groups of authorities and sources appear in the book: the first group are the *khakhomim* [sages] and their explications of the Tanach [Hebrew Bible], their teachings; the second are the *khokhmey hakabole* [sages of the Kabbalah], whom the author accords particular respect—he quotes them but in a general form, and his sources in this group are chiefly the *Zohar* and *Sefer Hasidim*; the third group are the *khokhmey hamuser* [sages of the ethical teachings], and here one finds both the Hebrew *muser-sforim*, primarily *Hovot ha-Levavot* [Duties of the Hearts], and the Yiddish ethical literature, which the author is adept at citing; the fourth are the *khokhmey hafilisofim*, and by this one means the Jewish scholars of the Sephardic-Arabian period or general ethical works, such as *Ben ha-Melech veha-Nazir* [The Prince and the Sage]; . . . With this is connected the fifth group of sources, the *mayse-bikhlekh* [story booklets] in Hebrew and Yiddish that the author knows exceptionally well; . . . Incidentally, Moyshe Henoch nowhere inveighs against reading from stories and novels . . . but criticizes sharply the poems that speak about the beauty of women and of love. The sixth source, the most important, from which he draws the most, so to speak, is life—experience, observation. . . .

Thus, we are dealing with a man of the people, a man who lives among the people; a man with knowledge, yet not too greatly educated; a man of piety, yet with a sense for the needs of everyday life; a naïve, tendentious writer, yet a good observer. Only such a person could have created the handbook for a respectable, well-to-do Jewish woman in the seventeenth century.

7. The purposes of the book are spelled out altogether chaotically in the two [separate Hebrew and Yiddish] introductions and the first three introductory chapters. The book is called *Brantshpigl* because it is a mirror in which the person can notice how soiled his soul is and attempt to purify it; it is called *Brantshpigl* because it is not a bad mirror that shows everything small, but rather a mirror that shows everything engorged, and people will consider that each misdeed is not small, and also that each mitzvah is not small. The book is an original work in Yiddish, for four reasons: first, because it is written for women, and for men who are like women and do not understand Hebrew books with their hairsplitting arguments; true, there are many fine Yiddish *muser-sforim*, but they do not tell about the benefits of the next world or the suffering of Gehenna, about which the great figures of the Kabbalah teach and write; and if one reads the book seriously and conducts oneself according to its instructions, the author will also write about secrets of the world to come for his readers, to the extent that he knows them. Second, women are also very important, inasmuch as they raise the children to learn Torah and take them to the rebbe, etc. Third, one must begin with a small thing and then enlarge it; the author begins that way in Yiddish, and other old, learned people should do the same for men in Hebrew. Fourth, the author takes into account that it will gain him more customers (one can understand it both in an educated way and according to its plain meaning). . . .

But in the introductions, the Hebrew and the Yiddish, and the first chapters, as well as throughout the entire book, the chief motif of the *Brantshpigl* resounds: the times are bad and corrupt, today is worse than yesterday, and tomorrow will be worse. The only hope that remains is for a sign of the messiah. Mores decline: the women mix with the men on the street and at meals, whether they are friends or not, and yell and speak with each other and are not ashamed, and one can yell at them, but it does not bother them at all, and young women put on beautiful clothes, silver, gold and pearls, like girls in olden times, they look the men in the face and dance, and because of them the girls cannot dance, and they bring small children with them and teach them such things from childhood on, and it does not bother them that there are also outsiders present; and they are constantly boasting about their deeds, and when someone reproaches them, they say the reverse; and they do not give way to men, even when they are old and gray; and involve themselves in the men's conversation and say no, as if the men were telling lies, and shame them; and they even undertake to answer questions of Jewish law; everything that was, in olden times, a disgrace has today become an ordinary, normal event . . . [ellipsis in original]

This complaint runs through the entire book, the fear for Jewish family life, which is losing its former modesty, whose framework becomes looser, freer, from day to day. To restore the fractured mores—this is the purpose of the book; this is the slogan that bids the author to "light a fire." At whose expense should this repair take place, on whom should this new burden lie most of all, who should suffer most from the pressure? Clearly, it is the woman, whose life is a reflection of her husband's favor, of his deeds. The author looks down from above at the woman—he does not conceal it at all. He often speaks humorously—resigned to the inherent inferiority of women. He does not fight, for example, against the impulsive speech of the woman; it is clear to him that this would be hopeless; the woman must employ, as it is, the talkativeness that was given to her. Thus, he writes an entire chapter in which he deals with the question of how speaking can also be made useful. Elsewhere, he writes that he prepared this book because, if he had preached orally, it would have resulted in his being surrounded by conflict, and he does not want to quarrel, particularly with women. It is not fitting, and it also has no purpose; and Moyshe Henoch mentions the story of Alexander the Great and the Amazon women who convinced the great king that it would not pay for him to fight them; if he won, a victory over women would be no victory at all, and if he were defeated, there could be no greater disgrace . . . [ellipsis in original]

In light of the larger purpose of life, which consists of striving for the world to come, the entire life of the woman should serve her husband: a boy should not be dressed in fine clothing; on the contrary for a girl, so she will know later how to charm her husband. If her husband seeks pleasure outside the home, the woman is obligated to try to furnish it at home. For the sake of peace in the home, the author's strict adherence to the commandments often becomes milder; he recommends to the woman that, if her husband loves cards, she should take up playing with him herself at home so he will not leave home; if he likes another woman, she should try herself to satisfy and attract his desire—she should foresee and anticipate all his wishes and direct them to the good. Words of advice, half-foolish, half-wise, always naïve, are not lacking in the *Brantshpigl* . . . [ellipsis in original]

Introduction Notes:

1. Maks Erik, "Bletlekh tsu der geshikhte fun der eltster yidisher literatur un kultur: I. Der brantshpigl—di entsiklopedye fun der yidisher froy in der XVII yorhundert" [Pages on the history of the oldest Yiddish literature and culture: I. The *Brantshpigl*—the encyclopedia of the Jewish woman in the seventeenth century], *Tsaytshrift* I (Minsk, 1926): 173–77 (abridged).

23
On the Sources of the *Mayse-bukh* (Book of Stories), 1602
by Israel Zinberg, 1926

ISRAEL ZINBERG (1873–1939, see also Selection 31 below), literary historian, especially of Yiddish literature, was born in Lagowica, Russian Volhynia (today in Poland). He studied chemical engineering at the Polytechnic Institute in Karlsruhe (now in Germany) and received his doctorate in Basel, Switzerland in 1898, which led to his permanent employment as a chemist at a steel mill in St. Petersburg. His magnum opus is his nine-volume *History of Literature among the Jews*, which he commenced in Russian but rewrote and continued in Yiddish until his death (Yiddish, 1929–37; Hebrew, 1959; English, 1972–78). It would become the single most all-encompassing and sustained work of Yiddish historical scholarship.

Zinberg did not embrace the Bolshevik revolution and continued to publish his works in all the major Yiddish journals abroad (as well as his *History*, which was published in Vilna, then part of anti-Soviet Poland). He was arrested for subversion late in 1938 and soon died of illness in the Soviet Far East.

The following essay—a corrective to Ignacy Schiper's review of a work by Maks Erik on the classic *Mayse-bukh* (collection of Jewish folk stories)—was noteworthy both for its content (which emphasizes the Jewish origins of the stories) and as an example of the worldwide "conversation" conducted by Yiddish scholars during the pre-Holocaust period.[1] Above all, it serves to fortify the creation narrative of a culturally independent Jewish nation in the Diaspora. When it appeared in the leading Yiddish literary journal *Literarishe bleter* (Literary pages), it was the front-page story.

After a great delay, I received the issue of *Literarishe bleter* in which Dr. Y. Schiper's interesting article on Maks Erik's book was published. Dr. Y. Schiper also touches there the issue "about the origin of the *Mayse-bukh*." In it, he displays great expertise, makes successful suppositions, and yet comes to a not entirely correct conclusion. This occurs, in my opinion, because in his article Dr. Schiper commits a methodological error that is also felt, unfortunately, in places in his very distinguished work on Jewish theater. Dr. Y. Schiper emphasizes with great insight the strong influence of the external cultural environment on the Jews in the Middle Ages while they created their "Old Yiddish" literature and theater. But he forgets, unfortunately, at times that he is dealing with an entirely original community, with its own lifestyle, with a very old culture that matured over thousands of years.

According to Dr. Y. Schiper's schema, Old Yiddish verse is divided into two periods: the first, which includes the last three centuries of the Middle Ages, and which is "permeated with a courtly culture that developed in the knightly palaces"—this is the period of the Jewish troubadours and "galliards" [dancers], when chiefly versed romance and folksong prevailed; and the second period (from the sixteenth to the mid-seventeenth century)—where Old Yiddish literature adapts itself internally "to the emotions of the bourgeoisie, as well as the mood of the peasants who had just immigrated from the towns" and first began to assimilate with the urban population which "now adopts the leading role in literature in place of the earlier knightly class."

From this standpoint, Dr. Schiper also considers the question of the origin of the *Mayse-bukh*. Dr. Schiper emphasizes that "the roots of the *Mayse-bukh* are in the medieval *Spielmann* [wandering bard] era," because he supposedly found a few stories there that deal with biblical material, for example, the story from the Scroll of Esther and the like, which originally circulated in the form of rhymed poems in the manner of the *Spielmann* poetry, and only later was this "original *Spielmann* source," under the influence of "bourgeois emotion," transformed into prose stories, to which later was added the legend-cycle that arose around the person of Rabbi Yehuda Hasid. "The development history of the *Mayse-bukh*," concludes Dr. Schiper, "lasted more than two and a half centuries, from the end of the Middle Ages to the middle of the eighteenth century."

Dr. Schiper is, however, somewhat mistaken. It lasted significantly longer; it is also much more complicated than Dr. Schiper indicates. I agree completely with Dr. Schiper when he emphasizes so strongly the great significance for the development of Yiddish literature of the rising bourgeoisie, the city-person, who became an important social factor toward the end of the Middle Ages, and this gave him the impetus to strive also for cultural and political power and to assume the leadership role in place of the earlier courtly class. But here the process is more complicated than Dr. Schiper indicates in his article: unfortunately, I cannot dwell on this. This issue is too important to be handled in passing.[1] But one must remember, above all, that the Jew was indeed the typical city-person in medieval Germany. The *first* city-person, one could say. The Jews of the Rhine provinces—in the depths of the Middle Ages—laid the first foundation stones of urban settlement in Germany. It is enough to mention the well-known "privilege" that Bishop Rudiger Speyer granted the Jews of his parish in 1084: "Whereas," declared the clerical prince, "I want to make a city from my town, I have invited the Jews." and further emphasized the bishop: "I find that I will increase the honor of our city a thousandfold when I will invite Jews into its gates."

The Jews, however, were not only the city-people, but also the world-merchants, the large traders, and *yodai derohim* (guide-Jews), who would trade with the entire world; and not only the Italian and Sephardic Jews, but also German Jews from the Rhine cities, like Regensburg, for example, would travel across the Slavic East toward Asia Minor and from there, from the rich Muslim countries, bring not only expensive fabrics, spices, and diamonds but also written and oral cultural treasures. And still much earlier than the "era of the bourgeois emotion" in German literature, when, as Dr. Schiper emphasizes, the "newly emergent anecdote-writer and novelist" appeared—the European Jews assumed with great skill the particular literary style that was very beloved in the states of India and among the Arabs: entertaining, amusing, and indeed at the same time also instructing and edifying: and all this with the help of light anecdotes and short stories. Every cultural historian indeed knows very well how important and significant the middleman role of the Jews was in the field of European folklore. Themselves an Eastern people, acquainted with the Arabian and Greek sources, who received many oriental-Indian legends, fables, and stories, the Jews in the Middle Ages were the connecting link and middlemen between the Eastern and Western worlds. Perhaps more than all others, they led the European West to become acquainted with many oriental motifs, with the treasures of the Indian and Persian-Greek legends and legendary world. In that dark period, when the cultural treasures of former generations lay buried and forgotten, the Jews[2] were among "the very few watchmen who loyally guarded the riches of legends, fables, and romances from the classical East"; and thanks to these watchmen, a significant portion of the riches, in a roundabout way through Arabia and Spain, later penetrated Christian-European literature.

Dr. Schiper mentions, in passing, *Das Buch der Beispiele der alten Weisen* [*Ben ha-Melech veha-Nazir*] (*Kalila wa-Dimna*) and remarks at the same time that, under this title, "a Yiddish reworking of the famous Indian fable treasury *Panchatantra*, which penetrated Europe in the period of the Crusades, was preserved." And indeed this book *Kalila va-Dimna*,[3] the most noteworthy treasure of Indian world-wisdom, which had such a mighty influence on all of European folklore—reached Christian European peoples exclusively through Jewish hands.[4]

The Jews in the Middle Ages did not, however, only translate foreign books of stories and fables but also wrote their own. Already in the eleventh century, much, much earlier than the period of "bourgeois emotion" in German literature, a baptized Jew, Moshe ha-Sefardi (his Christian name was Peter Alfonsi), prepared a collection in Latin of thirty-three tales and stories, *Disciplina clericalis*. "Whoever wants to study the course over which the oriental tales migrated to Europe," asserts such an experienced expert as Moshe Steinschneider, "must take into account Alfonsi's *Disciplina* as one of the most important milestones that marks this course." And all cultural historians indeed emphasize the great influence that Alfonsi's work had on the development of the European novella.[5]

Yet Jews did not write storybooks only for non-Jews,[6] but also for themselves. I am not speaking about such works as Zabara's *Sefer Shaashuim* [The Book of Delight, c. 1200], where a fantastic coil of clever tales, fables, parables, and sayings unwinds for the amazed reader. This book is already in *maqāma* style, i.e., in rhymed prose with poems in their midst. But plain storybooks, written in simple prose, were also already present among Jews in the depths of the Middle Ages. And indeed, through these books, one can see how the fruits of folk wisdom and the flowers of folk dreams and aspirations gradually change their form, enriching themselves with new elements, and then also serve as a new source for further folk creativity.

Already in the first half of the eleventh century, the famous Rabbi Rabbeinu Nissim [in Spain] prepared a collection of stories from the Quran in Arabic, and this collection was indeed soon reworked into Hebrew in two versions (first printed in 1519). Dr. Schiper points out that the oldest prose treatment of biblical themes in the cycle of stories of the *Mayse-bukh* is the story about King Solomon that is in a manuscript from Parma (written in 1511). But indeed already in the depths of the Middle Ages, among Jews there were special collections of "Parables of King Solomon." And one of them was even printed (in *Bet ha-Midrash* IV). The story in the Parma manuscript, Dr. Schiper emphasizes, was written in the "naïve folksy style of the *Mayse-bukh*." But many stories in the old *Sefer Hasidim* in the very same folksy style were already preserved, not in the long-famous version that was printed in Bologna, Basel, Kraków, and Slavuta, but indeed also in the Parma manuscript, which was first printed thirty-five years ago. It is sufficient to mention the extraordinarily beautiful story about the scholar with the shepherd, who was such a terrible ignoramus that he did not know a single prayer and would pray each morning to God in his naïve manner: "Master of the Universe! As is known to you, if you had cattle and gave them to me to guard, although I guard for everyone for pay, for you I would guard for free—so strong is my love for you!"[7]

There is now no further doubt at all that, still earlier than the Yiddish *Mayse-bukh*, storybooks of the same naïve folksy nature existed in *Hebrew* manuscripts. A few of them were even published in recent times, for example, the collection that Israël Lévi printed in the French *Revue* in the 1890s.[8] I have no doubt at all that this collection, published by Lévi, was composed in Germany and in the Hebrew language. From the collector, one even senses "Germanisms," or more correctly—Yiddishisms. And if one wants to research the sources of the Yiddish *Mayse-bukh*, one must indeed, above all, compare the collected material with all the Hebrew sources; one must also even take into account such a book as *Shalshelet Kabbalah* (The Chain of Tradition) by Gedaliah ibn Yahya that was published at the same time, according to Steinschneider's hypothesis, as the first publication of the Yiddish collection of 302 stories under the name *Mayse-bukh*. Already from ibn Yahya's work itself (not speaking of *Shevat Yehuda* [Scepter of Judah by Solomon ibn Verga, 1550] and many other collections), Dr. Schiper would be able to convince himself that in the sixteenth century the person of

Rabbi Yehuda Hasid was not the only one around whom a cycle of "legends" was erected—in the Middle Ages, many other great rabbinic figures, like Rashi, Rabbi Yehuda Halevy, Abraham ibn Ezra, the Rambam, Rabbi Eliezer of Worms, etc., had already become beloved heroes of the popular imagination, which surrounded them with a golden thread of the most marvelous legends. These legends went from mouth to mouth and, with love, were also written down.

Only as one makes this comparison does the source of folk creation reveal itself, and one sees manifest how, in the same surroundings, the identical motif, the identical story, was gradually transformed, became covered with new details, while other details disappeared. Reading, for example, in the *Mayse-bukh*, the story about Yosef Mokir Shabbat [Joseph who treasures the Sabbath], one must compare it not only with the version in *Masekhta Shabbat* [tractate of the Talmud on the Sabbath] but also with Rabbeinu Nissim's collection. In story no. 222 (according to the Wilmersdorf edition), a legend from the Talmud (Sanhedrin 104) and a story from Rabbeinu Nissim's collection[9] were intertwined as secondary episodes. Intertwined in another story from the *Mayse-bukh* (no. 144) is a story from *Mishlei: Shlomo ha-Meleh* [the biblical book of Proverbs, attributed to King Solomon]. Especially interesting is one of the most beautiful stories that the *Mayse-bukh* contains—the story with the saintly Rabbi Hanina. The story is very complicated, full of fantasy. The hero of the story has to deal with an enchanted frog, with talking animals and fowl, even with a fish that speaks like a person, followed by pitchers with *Gehenna*-water and Heaven-water and still many other novelties. Many details were without doubt taken from European folklore—but remade altogether Jewishly. However, this beautiful story is also in the Hebrew collection that Lévi published (there, the saintly rabbi is called Yohanan), but in another version. Many details were told entirely differently there than in the *Mayse-bukh*. The same also repeats itself with the story about the Jewish Pope. In the twelfth century (1130–38), in the course of eight years, Anacletus II, who was descended from Jews, sat on the papal throne. At the same time, he was a lover of the Jewish people, on account of which his enemies called him: Jewish pope (*Judaeo pontifex*). This made such an impression on the Jewish environment that an entire legend was created about a Jewish child who was stolen as a child from his parents and converted. The child had the abilities of a genius, with time attained a prominent position, occupied the position of bishop, and was later chosen as pope. Ultimately he returned to his Jewish faith and died as an observant

Jew. This story appeared in the *Mayse-bukh* (no. 87, Wilmersdorf edition). But it is also in various versions in Hebrew sources.[10]

It is clear: no one can deny that the Old Yiddish secular literature drew very much from the Old German and was, for a long time, under its strong influence; yet one should also not forget the second very important factor: the influence not only of the external environment but also the internal. This is especially necessary for such a collective anthology as the *Mayse-bukh*. With an overly sharp *mekhitse* [synagogue screen between men and women], some "Yiddish" researchers are already separating the Old Yiddish literature from the Hebrew literature.

Introduction Notes:

1. Yisroel Tsinberg, "Vegn di mekoyrem funm 'mayse-bukh,'" *Literarishe bleter* 3, no. 131 (Warsaw, November 5, 1926): 725–27; reprinted in Y. Tsinberg, *Kultur-historishe shtudyes* (New York: Morris S. Sklarsky, 1949), 306–13.

Article Notes:

1. I speak about this fully in my *Literatur-geshikhte* [History of literature].

2. [The word "Jews" is deduced here from the context: the first printing in *Literarishe bleter* is defective, reading *dalet-yod-yod-[broken nun]* at the end of a line (an anagram of *yod-yod-dalet-resh, Yidn*/Jews); in the second printing the word appears as *dalet-resh-yod-yod* (*dray*/three), an obvious mis-correction.]

3. Incidentally, Dr. Schiper is slightly mistaken: *Kalila wa-Dimna* and *Panchatantra* are not one and the same. The *Panchatantra*—this is purely a clumsy, crippled transformation of the *Kalila wa-Dimna*. The Brahmins, the bitter enemies of Budda's adherents, avenged themselves on the spiritual child of their opponents, and the former "lawbook" and guide for kings and princes was transformed into a simple book of fables.

4. A baptized Jew, John of Capua, made use of the Hebrew translation for his Latin translation, and this Latin text was the source of the Spanish, Dutch, Italian, and English translations. . . .

5. See, e.g., G. Dapping, *Les Juifs dans le moyen age* [The Jews of the Middle Ages] (Brussels, 1844), 98–99.

6. A portion of Alfonsi's work was already translated in the Middle Ages into Hebrew under the name *Sefer Henoch* (1516).

7. *Sefer Hasidim* (Berlin: Mekitzei Nirdamim, 1891), nos. 5–6.

8. Israël Lévi, "Un recueil de contes juifs inédits" [A collection of unpublished Jewish tales], *La Revue des études juives* (1903): 205–13; Ad. Neubaer, *Catalogue of the Hebrew manuscripts in the Bodleian Library* I (Oxford: Clarendon Press, 1886), 520–22.

9. *Hibur Yafe Meha Yeshua* [An elegant composition about deliverance].

10. See, e.g., *Bet HaMidrash* V, 148–52; ibid. VI, 9–137.

24
Three Hundred Years of the *Tsene-rene* (Bible Stories for Women), 1616
by Jacob Shatzky, 1928

JACOB SHATZKY (see also Selections 6 above, 46 below) created, in the immediate shadow of the Holocaust, a personal memorial to the destroyed world that was and would remain his principal subject—in the form of a collected volume of his previous writings on Jewish history in Poland. In the introduction, he recalls, "The Jewish historian in Poland was the ammunition supplier for the rows of Jewish fighting masses. The arguments and evidence that a historian excavated in dusty and dark archival cellars . . . were used in the fight for rights in the forum of the Polish Sejm [parliament], in the speeches of political and national leaders, in the passionate polemic in the press." Turning to the present, he laments, "Of the lively, energetic, and dynamic chapters of Jewish history in Poland, only silent printed pages remain." And he concludes, "A few of those pages I have collected here. In the shadows of generations, one can consider the past. This book is a memorial to that past and a spark of faith in the future."[1]

Of the articles in this collected volume, only one is devoted to a literary topic—the *Tsene-rene*—among the most popular of all books published in Yiddish.[2] It is an example of a historian's treatment of a literary work, differing from the other selections in this section on Yiddish literature (by literary historians) in its greater emphasis on reception than on influences. The book's title, *Tsene-rene* (Come and see) comes from the Song of Songs 3:11.

Three hundred years ago in the city of Prague, a Jew by the name of Yankev ben Yitskhok [Jacob, son of Isaac] was buried. This Jew had been a wandering *magid* [preacher] who traveled across cities and countries giving heartfelt sermons and probably selling Yiddish religious books for women and girls. He was not, however, an ordinary "itinerant bookseller" who distributed someone else's works or sold works by others. He himself wrote a series of books, both in Hebrew and in Yiddish, and preferred to deal with his own works than those by others.

This Yankev ben Yitskhok was the author of the most beloved and popular book that existed in Old Yiddish literature. The name of the book was *Tsene-rene* [a compressed form of the Hebrew phrase, *Tsene u-rene* (Come and see)]. Yankev ben Yitskhok was a Polish Jew. He signed himself: Yankev ben Yitskhok Ashkenazi. . . . He was an extraordinary preacher. His adaptations of *midrashim* and *agadot* [biblical exegesis and legends], which were interspersed into his *Tsene-rene*, demonstrate that he used them in his sermons. In his travels across the world, he probably came to rest in Prague, where he died in 1628. . . .

For more than three hundred years, *Tsene-rene* has marched across cities and towns, villages and settlements, in all the places where there was or still is a Yiddish-speaking community. The success of *Tsene-rene* is one of the greatest achieved by any composition in Old Yiddish literature. Even the *Mayse-bukh* [see Selection 23 above] is left in its shadow. It is sufficient to say that since the first edition of *Tsene-rene* was published in Lublin in 1616, to date 126 editions of this beloved, popular book are known. The book was also published in many countries. In Germany, Bohemia, Russia, Poland, Galicia—everywhere it was reprinted, and reprinted to this day.

This work was even translated into Latin. In 1661, a Christian by the name of Yohannes Schubert published a portion of the *Tsene-rene* in Latin. In 1846, a French translation appeared. There is also an unfinished German edition of the *Tsene-rene*.

What is the cause of the popularity of the *Tsene-rene*? It is above all the character of the book. *Tsene-rene* is not simply a translation of the *Chumash* [Pentateuch], a dry rendering into Yiddish of a Hebrew text. In the Old Yiddish literature, there are such mechanical, literal translations of the Hebrew Bible, which are very reminiscent of the translations used by our teachers in religious school. . . .

Tsene-rene is a heartfelt, poetic recounting of the *Chumash*. It is a rendition in poetry. The work is interspersed with Rashi [the leading medieval

Jewish commentator, 1040–1105], the *Aggadah* [extra-legal portion of ancient rabbinical literature], and various commentators. Here are blended morality and fantasy, ethics and flexibility. The preacherly tone in the *Tsene-rene* is well employed, with feeling, with proportion, with taste.

The language of *Tsene-rene* is soft and rhythmic, expressed in the heartfelt wording, the melodious phrase, that is so affecting in its intimacy, folksiness, clarity, and simplicity.

A few examples will help to show the beauty of *Tsene-rene*. In Parshas Bereishis [the first chapter of the book of Genesis], there is just such an interpretation of the verse: "God said, let there be light and there was light" [1:3]:

> The Holy One created two lights. One light is the sun and the other light is the moon. They illumine the world, and the Holy One created another light for the righteous for when the messiah will come. That light is very great, but the world was not worthy of such a great light. Therefore, the Holy One hid the light for the righteous [in the world to come]. . . .
>
> Or such a fantastic version of Parshas Vayehi [the last chapter of the book of Genesis]: Jacob said to Joseph. If you want to ask me why am I burdening you that you should carry me to the land of Canaan to bury me there and not in the land of Egypt? I buried your mother in the field, on the way, where she died, and I did not take her to the cave of our other ancestors, even though she died quite close to the city of Bethlehem and I did not take her there. Certainly, you resent me for this. However, you should know that the Holy One told me to do this, that I should bury her on the way. When Israel will leave Jerusalem for the exile of Nebuzaradon, Israel will pass on that road. Rachel will pray for Israel from her grave and the Holy One will accept her prayer.[1]

Such a tone and style must have appealed to the heart and spirit of the Jewish woman, for whom the book is actually intended.

"*Tsene u-rene b'nos tsien*"—Come and see, you daughters of Zion! To the daughters of Zion spoke the author, although "*b'ney tsien*" [sons of Zion] also delighted in the book, and the elementary teacher also made use of it.

The success of *Tsene-rene* kept many Jewish publishers and writers busy. In the years 1676–1679, two Yiddish translations of the Tanach [Hebrew Bible] were published; one by Joseph Witzenhausen and the second by

Jekuthiel ben Isaac Blitz. In their introductions, both attacked the *Tsene-rene*. But neither had any success. Witzenhausen's translation appeared altogether two times; Blitz's—only once. These Yiddish versions of the Tanach were too dry, too pedantic, to please the "women and girls." The ignoramus did not want to have dry teachings, but simple sincerity. In the period of the Mendelssohnian Haskalah [the Jewish Enlightenment], Mendelssohn's translation of the Pentateuch [into German] was promoted as a means of suppressing the *Tsene-rene*.

"*Tsene u-Rene–style*"—is what Mendelssohn ironically called the mixed Hebrew and Aramaic style of the Polish rabbis.

The *maskilim* [adherents of the Haskalah] in Austria brought about a prohibition on reading the *Tsene-rene*. Joseph II, the Austrian emperor, was even on the side of the *maskilim*. A report at the end of the eighteenth century held that many Jewish books were harmful, but most of all—the *Tsene-rene*, because "it spreads superstitions."

In truth, this was a decree for the sake of Mendelssohn's translation, which had not had any success. In the same decree, which forbade the use of the *Tsene-rene*, teachers and ordinary Jews were recommended to use *Etz Hayyim*, i.e., Mendelssohn's translation of the *Chumash*.

Even the official support for Mendelssohn's *Chumash* did not help. The *Tsene-rene* was popular and beloved in Germany, just as much as in Poland and Galicia. Even when Yiddish began to disappear more and more as the "spoken language" of German Jews, the *Tsene-rene* was still well-read with fervor.

Even in that period when the "daughters of Zion" poured out tears over Goethe's *The Sorrows of Young Werther*, mothers were given a falsified *Tsene-rene*.

In what lay the falsification? Mendelssohn's *Chumash* was simply taken and reprinted with a title page saying, *Tsene-rene*, so that people would think it was the true, beloved Yiddish-*Chumash*, but printed in "German with Hebrew letters." Such an edition appeared in Basel (Switzerland) in 1822, exquisitely printed and published. In 1861, a publisher in Fürth (Bavaria) published a book for Jewish women written in German but printed with Hebrew letters, and he named the book *Tsene-rene*. . . . In this way, attempts were made to combat and eradicate the book. There was seldom success with decrees from rulers and *maskilim*, so it was attempted by devious means, by smuggling Mendelssohn's German language under a Yiddish title page from this popular book.

But the *Tsene-rene* defeated them all because there, where it disappeared, no similar book could take its place. Why was this the case? Because *Tsene-rene* is, above all, a work of art. "The simplicity and modesty of style," says a Yiddish literary historian (Zinberg), "the characteristic rhythm and harmoniousness of tone of a deeply believing soul—give this book a specific charm. The book dominated the spirit of the Jewish woman, becoming her guide and teacher."

And besides this, the language of the book is important. This is the best Yiddish in the Old Yiddish literature: juicy, pure in nuances, folksy and simple. Yankev ben Yitskhok Ashkenazi has rightly earned the name, "the Luther of the middle period of the Yiddish language," with which he was crowned by the literary historian Maks Erik.

Tsene-rene is a product of Polish Jewry. The book was created in the period of economic flowering of Polish Jewry, when no one could have dreamed that the end of the golden era was so near. The acts of Chmielnicki in 1648 devastated Jewish life in Ukraine and in other parts of Poland. The mind could not have conceived of this tragedy. The heart sought a source of consolation. *Tsene-rene* became, next to the Psalms, the most beloved book of the Jewish woman because it satisfied her emotional needs.

On the ruins of the economic reality, the heart and spirit calmed themselves with the gentle, soft, heartfelt words of the Yiddish Chumash.

In this lies the great secret of the success of the *Tsene-rene*.

Introduction Notes:

1. Yankev Shatski, *In shotn fun over* [In the shadow of the past] (Buenos Aires: Tsentralfarband fun poylishe yidn in argentine, 1947), 7–8.

2. Yankev Shatski, "Dray hundert yor 'tsene-rene,'" *Literarishe bleter* 5, no. 31 (Warsaw, August 3, 1928): 597–99; reprinted in ibid., 69–76 (abridged).

Article Notes:

1. [English translations from the *Tsene-rene* are quoted from Morris M. Faierstein, ed., *Ze-enah u-Re'enah: A Critical Translation into English* (Berlin: W. de Gruyter, 2017).]

25
The Tales of Rabbi Nachman of Bratslav (1815): Hasidism and Yiddish Literary Creativity
by Shmuel Niger, 1932

SHMUEL NIGER (Shmuel Charney, 1883–1955), Yiddish literary critic and historian, was born in Dukora, Belorussia (today Belarus). Early in his career, he turned from writing in Russian and Hebrew almost exclusively to Yiddish, ultimately producing more than 4,000 articles (and several books) on Yiddish authors and their works. In 1913 he became editor of the pathbreaking literary journal *Di yudishe velt* (The Jewish world) and the first collective work of Yiddish linguistic scholarship, *Der pinkes* (The record book), both published in Vilna. The latter included his best-known historical work, "Yiddish Literature and the Female Reader" (which does not lend itself to being excerpted or condensed for translation). In 1919, Niger settled in New York, where he became the leading American Yiddish literary critic.

The piece that follows comes from a larger work on the tales of Rabbi Nachman of Bratslav and their influence on the development of Yiddish writing. Niger presents an alternative theory of the development of new Yiddish literature, tracing its origins to Hasidic storytelling rather than primarily to the literature of the Haskalah (as suggested by Meir Wiener in Selection 26 below). He first treated this subject in 1921,[1] and he published the monograph translated below in 1932, reiterating his main points in the Yiddish encyclopedia in 1942.[2] His thesis was disputed by the well-known

Yiddish literary critic Elihu Shulman,[3] and Niger responded with a rebuttal that quoted supporting statements from the works of Chaim Zhitlowsky, Y. L. Peretz, Ber Borochov, Zalman Reisen, Max Weinreich, Israel Zinberg, and Weiner himself.[4]

Niger's monograph is a bridge, both in chronology and evolution, between the secular appreciation of Hasidic storytelling begun by Peretz and the theoretical analysis of Hasidism pioneered by Martin Buber. The following are the first two chapters (out of ten) from Niger's 1932 monograph, in which he presents his main argument, before turning to Rabbi Nachman and his tales in the later chapters.[5] The author's style includes the frequent use of ellipses (. . .). All that appear here are original to his writing.

Nachman of Bratslav—a rebbe, Hasidic rabbi, venerated to this day by the Hasidim of Bratslav, a religious leader in whose every word students have sought holy intentions, secret knowledge, and secrets of the law—how is it that he should take up such a "simple" thing as stories? How could it be that he happened to create materials we can accept as purely artistic—that he happens to have left works that draw the older religious literature and the new purely secular Yiddish word closer to each other? How was this possible? Yet there are no two greater opposites than that Hasidic world, which brought forth Rabbi Nachman, and the literary art that became possible thanks to the bitterest enemies of Hasidism, the *maskilim* [adherents of the Haskalah]. How is it possible to unify two such contrasting elements as Hasidism and literature? What is the origin of the stories that are, from one side, holy to the Hasidim of Bratslav and, from the other side, also of great value in our modern, present-day eyes?

To answer the question, one must clarify the connection that existed between a) Hasidism and Yiddish, b) Hasidism and artistry, and c) Hasidism and the source of Rabbi Nachman's stories. Only then can one appropriately evaluate their value.[1]

Hasidism and Yiddish

Hasidism refreshed, awakened, and in a wonderful manner enriched the religious feeling of the Jewish masses and the religious thought of their leaders. Yet Hasidism is more than a religious movement. It was a new way of life and a new style. It introduced a fresh enthusiasm in the collective creativity of the masses and a mighty boldness in the often-unconscious artistry of individuals.

Before anything else, we will dwell upon the effect this new force in Jewish life had on our folk language.

It made the language richer and more refined, elevated it, and opened for it (and perhaps also for all of Yiddish literary creativity) new, deep sources.

Hebrew and the literature in Hebrew were also shaken by Hasidism, and irrigated, fertilized, and imbued with new strength. (Incidentally, the period of Hasidism, as far as I know, has still not been studied from this standpoint.) I am speaking here about Yiddish. In the soil of the Yiddish language, the Hasidic movement left deep traces, sowed countless fresh seeds. It affected Yiddish, first, psychologically, and secondly, linguistically.

The psychological accomplishment consists in making Yiddish more respected, honored, elevated. Thanks to Hasidism, ordinary Jews became more powerful in their own estimation; as a result, the language of ordinary Jews also received greater respect. The scholar was demoted, the literature of the scholars lost the strength it had held over all important matters, and the shameful stain of being a language "for women and ignoramuses" was partially removed from Yiddish. The ignoramus himself no longer considered himself to be such a plebeian. Hasidism gave him the possibility and hope of elevating himself to a higher level. It said to him (in the name of the BeShT [Israel ben Eliezer Ba'al Shem Tov, 1698–1760]) that being able to study is not everything. Thus, it said to him from the BeShT's mouth, one may be a great scholar and yet: "He may study Torah continuously, pray and afflict himself. In truth, however, his effort is all for naught, because he lacks attachment (*deveikut*) to the Creator, blessed be He, as well as the perfect faith that is required for constant attachment unto Him, blessed be He. He is unaware of the essential form of worship,"[2] etc. He, the BeShT himself, had the merit to be a leader among Jews not because he "stuffed his belly with *Gemara* [the explanatory, concluding portion of the Talmud] and *poskim* [rabbinic commentators]," but because he prayed with great intention—and praying with intention, reciting a chapter of Psalms with the heart, this every proper Jew can do. Hasidism taught him (in the name of the BeShT) that with every word one can be united with God, and "it must not be just a word of Torah or prayer, it can be a word that one utters in speaking with a person in the market" . . . and one can be elevated by this to the level of a *tsadik* [a saintly figure] . . . The BeShT taught no brilliant ideas. He held before himself an ordinary *siddur* [prayerbook]. He begins there with *Ma tovu* [Gen. 24:5; "How goodly"] and finishes at the end with Psalms.

"It can be that a person will become a great *tsadik*, even if he had not learned much," Rabbi Nachman of Bratslav also declared . . . and if the person, he said, "even declined to the lowest level, heaven forbid, he can still unite himself with God and return himself to Him, because He is everywhere (*Melo kol ha'aretz k'vodo* [The whole world is full of his glory])" . . .

There is no longer any barrier standing between the scholar and the "ordinary" sinful Jew; in any event, the language of the scholars could no longer rail so strongly against "lowly" Yiddish, particularly once Yiddish (and here we cross over to the purely linguistic influence of Hasidism) began indeed to become ever nobler and finer.

Thanks to the closeness and the combining of the great individuals, the rebbes, with the ordinary multitude; thanks to Hasidism being an original synthesis of spiritual aristocratism and love of the people, a confluence of individualism and mass ecstasy—the language of the people became, almost like Hebrew, an organ of higher spiritual life.

The Yiddish language was enriched with new, nobler words, with new, more aristocratic expressions. The Hasidic rebbes, unlike the *misnagdic* rabbis [the Orthodox opponents of Hasidism], spoke no Hebrew, but only common Yiddish, and their Yiddish was of a loftier sort because they allowed themselves to speak with the people about the greatest and most wonderful matters. There was no longer such a sharp difference between scholarly language and coachman language, between the Yiddish of urban Jews and the coarse language of villagers. All, including the coarsened tradesmen, and the tenant farmers, were seated at the rebbe's table, heard the rebbe's teaching, memorized and repeated—and often also made use of such new, wonderful words [all from Hebrew] as *madreyge* [level], *nitses* [spark], *remez* [sign], *hafle-vofele* [wonderful], *pile-ploim* [marvels], *dveykes* [ecstatic communion with God], *hislayves* [fervor], *hisoyreres* [spiritual awakening], *hispayles* [enthusiasm, ardor], *tikn* [improvement, repair] . . .

The rebbe's language was not the dry language of the *misnagdim*. His ideas came from the heart, his scenes were created from a waking fantasia, his thoughts were visions, his words shone, burned, they often reached the roots, the naked roots of the world—and the rebbe could no longer, in Hebrew or in Yiddish, make use of the ordinary expressions, the half-congealed quotations from scripture. He needed a livelier, richer, juicier, and more scenic language. He sought to explain to the people and to himself new, intimate, sharp religious experiences, he immersed himself in fresh spiritual springs—and he had to have a fresh, a refreshed language.... So, in their oral teachings, the Hasidic rebbes interspersed new words, often from Hebrew words they themselves coined, and, conversely, in writing (Hebrew) they often used Yiddish expressions. In certain cases, they wrote entirely in Yiddish—and wrote about lofty and difficult matters. Unlike the Kabbalists of earlier times, they also did not hesitate to speak or write in Yiddish in a manner that was deliberately common and understandable by everyone...

They were not ashamed even to pray in Yiddish—and for this reason: for them, it was seldom the customary prayer, the established wording of the prayerbook. They complained that *Rachmana liba bai* ["The Merciful One desires our heart"; Mishnah Menachot 13:10]—God wants our heart, and our heart cannot speak with a foreign mouth, according to a previously prepared text. They put more store in worship than in learning, and they longed for lively, fresh, engaged prayers.

It was said of the BeShT that when he prayed once in a village in a barn, the barrels of grain that surrounded him trembled with fervor and danced together with him... And Hillel Zeitlin [writer, philosopher, 1871–1942] related about his own great-grandfather, a relative of the rebbe of Lyady: It was after Yom Kippur, the Hasid of Lyady said to the other Hasidim: "Today's prayers do not suit me. In our praying today I have not seen the divine light... We have not prayed today with devotion." "So," asked the Hasidim, "then what should one do?" "If you will follow me," he answered, "let us do this: let us observe Yom Kippur again. Perhaps the second Yom Kippur will be more successful. Who says that one should repent only on the tenth day of Tishrei? Why should one not also repent on the eleventh of Tishrei?" And the congregation followed him—for "Hasidim are not dry *misnagdim* who are constantly consulting the calendar and code of Jewish law."

Hasidim, old-time Hasidim, sought the divine *light*, not the *letter* of the prayer. As a result, they often prayed in their own words; they prayed from the heart, not from the prayer book, and the language of their heart was Yiddish.

Marvelous religious songs were created, hymns in Yiddish, not women's petitionary prayers, which existed earlier, but indeed true prayers—such as the "Kaddish" or the "Duda" of Rabbi Levi-Yitzhak of Berdichev.

The Hasidic rebbes themselves used Yiddish for their prayers, and they also told the Hasidim to do the same.[3] They knew, not only felt, the importance of Yiddish. And not only the first, but also the later Hasidic rebbes knew this.

When Leon Mandelstam [writer and *maskil*, 1819–1889] suggested to Rabbi Mendele of Lubavitch that he should agree to a German translation of the prayerbook, Rabbi Mendele answered him in a letter that it was not right to force the Jewish people to use a language in which they understood nothing and that they should use their own language, Yiddish, which they had already spoken for several hundred years.[4]

And the rebbe of Lyady, Rabbi Dov Baer [1733–1827], who composed a booklet in Yiddish with the name *Pokeah 'Ivrim* [Open (my) Eyes, 1832], writes in the introduction: ". . . and, incidentally, this is useful even for the scholar, because it is said in Yiddish. Therefore, it awakens the heart of the person to carry out what he says."

In general, in the period of Hasidism, Yiddish ceased to be only an "everyday" or "women's" and "ignoramus's" language. It became a language that was also suited to exalted matters, for holy secrets, deep intentions.

It did not, in truth, take, nor would it take, the place of Hebrew. In the popular religious consciousness, Hebrew was and remained a sacred language, the language of holiness, the only language in which truly holy, truly important religious books ought to be written.

Nevertheless, Yiddish was elevated to a higher level—morally and purely linguistically. No longer were people ashamed, as I mentioned previously, to insert bits of Yiddish into Hebrew-Aramaic religious books and articles; the Hebrew itself of the Hasidim became strongly Yiddish-ized. A process began in Hebrew that is very similar to that which occurred in medieval Latin, which was strongly influenced by the surrounding folk dialects.

And not only did many Hebrew words enter the spoken Yiddish language; a converse process took place: Yiddish enriched Hebrew. Many new words and meanings of words that arose in the atmosphere of the spoken language were adopted from the Hasidic—and only the Hasidic—Hebrew. The rhythm of Hebrew itself became softer, suppler, livelier under the influence of the enriched, refined, Hasidic-influenced Yiddish . . .

The influence, importance, and value of Yiddish increased. And with it rose the ability of our folk language to become an instrument of new, nobler, and deeper creations—the ability that had then already begun to be realized . . .

Hasidism and Artistry

Thanks to the Hasidic movement, Yiddish became a better literary instrument. But still more importantly, new melodies—and new players—were added to it.

As always, in times of great popular agitation, in times of spiritual unrest and religious ecstasies—the eyes of people were also thirsting to see visions: wonders became ordinary matters, ordinary matters became wonderful ("The greatest miracle is nature itself")—and among both individuals and the people fantasy ran wild, this deepest source of artistic creation . . . The religious movement itself, which the BeShT brought with him, was therefore also the beginning of an artistic awakening. But not this alone. There appeared great leaders, secretive personalities—and the people's power of imagination had someone around whom to weave the golden thread of his history of marvels; new motifs and new heroes were added to what the Kabbalists previously gave us. No longer could one be satisfied with Joseph della Reyna, with the Holy Ari, with Rabbi Hayyim Vital, with the Maharal of Prague; a new source of fantasizing and creating opened: Rabbi Israel Baal Shem Tov and his great students.

Rabbi Israel Ba'al Shem Tov considered himself the creator of Hasidism: he was also its creation. And whoever wants to write the history of Hasidic folklore must begin with the BeShT's history—not with the fantastic stories that were created about him, but perhaps indeed with his life story, which itself is known to us more from Hasidic legends than from historical documents, and one can say that the very image of the BeShT is in large measure an artistic image, a product of Hasidic folk creation. It is not even known when the BeShT was born. Only a few facts of his life are historically reliable. The miracles and wonders that are told of the BeShT and the later Hasidic rebbes are, in most cases, not truth but poetry. In the beginning, they were, like all folk creations, oral teachings, folklore. Later they were written down, published, and now we are justified in embracing them as monuments of our written literary art.

They are full of fantasies, of marvels, of symbols: they are not realistic, but then is realism the only form of art? Are the Indian, ancient Jewish, and Greek mythology, which are so out of the ordinary and so far from reality, then not a product of artistic creation? What then are works of art? Worlds that are liberated and purified of their coincidences; realities that are restored to their source. But not this alone. Art is also a dream come true, a vision clothed in flesh and blood . . . and these are the legends about the BeShT; they and all the other Hasidic stories of miraculous deeds and marvelous histories: poetic creations . . .

And although this is poetry (of a higher or lower sort—but still poetry), we regard it differently and set it higher than the majority of religious books that remain our inheritance from the rabbinic world. We regard it as something that has in itself a spark of art, not as a piece of old goods. And it does not matter that the Hasidic rebbes and their deeds appeared, at first glance, to be further from us than the rabbis with their religious books. It is not important that the Hasidic saintly figures were always enemies of secular culture, while the *misnagdic* rabbis of the same period had individuals among them who favored just exactly secular scholarship—such as the Vilna Goan or the Polish Torah authority Rabbi Yehuda Leib Margolies. This does not change the situation. In the main, rabbinic culture left us only Torah and its exposition and interpretation, and we no longer have the taste for this; we leave it for the yeshivas, for the Jewish theological seminaries, for Jewish cultural history.

The opposite is true of the largest portion of the Hasidic creations. We are able to make use of these themselves. We listen gladly to Hasidic melodies at concerts and sing them heartily at our little celebrations. The same is true of the best Hasidic tales. To this day, they still nourish our fantasy. They fertilize (and will still fertilize) our new literature. And this is, of course, not because we believe in the miracles and wonders that were recounted about the saintly men, but on the contrary, because we no longer believe. Religious marvels are marvelous facts for believers; for nonbelievers, they are marvelous works of art.

The stories from the Hebrew Bible and from Indian or Greek mythology are for us also no longer facts. Nevertheless (or indeed as a result) we delight in them. We feel in them poetic symbolism, expressiveness, the art of storytelling. And we now also look this way at the Hasidic marvel stories, and we consider them one of the most beautiful rings in the developing chain of our literature. We look at them from an artistic and literary-historical standpoint. (We know that they come mostly from the people, but collective poetry is also poetry.) Collective poetry, like every true poet, uses the tools of selection and augmentation. And the people did just this in the period of Hasidism. Figures were singled out who awakened the people's curiosity; the popular soul could not rest on the fact of their distinctiveness—and raised them to the level of its idea, its vision. The people beautified, perfected those who kindled in them a thirst for beauty and perfection . . . In the reality there was but a hint, a start; the congregation of Hasidim came and, with its creative fantasy, made from the hint a bit of perfection; from the start—conjured a middle and an end . . . For example, the BeShT was suddenly revealed. At first, he was a common Jew, and suddenly he became a miracle worker, a holy man. A light appeared in the darkness. And so the legend wove the thread further and recounted that the BeShT's birth, not only his revelation, took place in a marvelous manner and that if he had wanted to, he could have brought the messiah . . . The old yearning was awakened for those who know the secret of redemption, the eternal yearning for a leader and redeemer. The desire to see holy souls was kindled again. And so the people—with the help of its power of imagination—saw. A thirst burned in them for miracles: (in the popular fantasy) miracles took place . . . And I truly do not know who created whom: the rebbe the Hasidim, or conversely, the Hasidim the rebbe—inasmuch as the great leadership itself was to a certain extent a child of myth and outgrowth of the people's brilliant creative force . . . One thing is certain: together with the enrichment, the invigoration of religious feeling in the period of Hasidism, an extraordinary rebirth took place in the world of Jewish literature. Jewish artistry awakened, and creative fantasy ran wild.

Introduction Notes:

1. Sh. Niger, "R' nakhman bratslaver un zayne 'mayses'" [Rabbi Nachman of Bratslav and his 'stories'], *Di tsukunft* (New York, October 1921): 602–6 (November 1921): 657–63.

2. Sh. Niger, "Yidishe literatur fun mitn 18-tn y"h biz mitn 19-tn y"h" [Yiddish literature from the mid-18th century to mid-19th century], *Algemeyne entsiklopedye*, vol. Yidn 3 (New York: Dubnov-fond un tsiko, 1942): cols. 65–70.

3. Elihu Shulman, *Di algemeyne entsiklopedye, opteyl: Yidn, band 3: a kritik un opshatsung* [The general encyclopedia, vol. Yidn 3: A critique and evaluation] (New York: Undzer epokhe, 1942), 7.

4. Sh. Niger, "Vegn dem onheyb fun der nayer yidisher literatur" [On the beginnings of the new Yiddish literature], *Jewish Book Annual (5705/1944–45)* 3 (1944): 37–49 (Hebrew numbering).

5. Sh. Niger, "R' nakhman braslaver un zayne sipurey-mayses" [Rabbi Nachman of Bratslav and his tales] introduction to Yona Spivak (Jonah Speavack), *R' nahman braslaver in geshtalt fun zayn "Mayse mit di zibn betlers"* [Rabbi Nachman of Bratslav in the image of his "Story with Seven Beggars"] (Warsaw: B. Kletskin, 1932), I–LXXXI (I–XII quoted); reprinted in Sh. Niger, *Bleter geshikhte fun der yidisher literatur* (New York: Sh. niger bukh komitet baym alveltlekhn yidishn kultur-kongres, 1959), 111–88 (111–20 quoted).

Article Notes:

1. The historical, biographical and other factual data in this work are taken (when no specific source is noted) from *Shivchei ha-Ran* [biography of Rabbi Nachman of Bratslav]; *Sipure mayses, vunder mayses fun rabi nakhmen braslever* [Wonder tales of Rabbi Nachman of Bratslav]; S. A. Horodetsky's *Hahasidut vehahasidim* [Hasidism and Hasidim, Berlin, 1923]; Abraham Kahana's *Sefer ha-Hasidut* [Book of Hasidism, Warsaw, 1922]; S. Dubnow's *Geshikhte fun khasidizm* [History of Hasidism, Vilna, 1930]; Hillel Zeitlin's *Rabi Nahman mi-Braslav: hayav ve-torato* [. . . His life and teachings, Warsaw, 1910] and *Hasidut*; S. H. Setzer's *Vundermayses fun R' Nakhman Braslaver* [New York, 1929].

2. [English translation quoted from Jacob Immanuel Schochet, trans. and ed., *Tzava'at ha-Rivash: The Testament of Rabbi Israel Baal Shem Tov* (New York: Kehot, 1998), 60. The Yiddish version of this text quoted by Niger was credited by him to Sh. Ts. Zetser's translation, *Di tsavoe fun Besh"t* (The testament of the Besht).]

3. Among the *misnagdic* rabbinic giants, there were later also some who loved to translate the prayers and to pray in Yiddish. For example, Joel Entin relates about the Magid of Horodne who lived in Minsk (at the end of the nineteenth century) that "in order to comment on the praying himself, in order for the praying to be truly deeply felt, he would immediately translate each word himself into Yiddish" (*Di naye varhayt*, New York, October 1, 1925). But these were exceptions.

4. See Avraham Shmuel Heilman, *Beys rebe*, vol. 3 (Berdichev, 1902), 17–18.

26
On the History of Yiddish Literature in the Nineteenth Century: Haskalah Period
by Meir Wiener, 1940

MEIR WIENER (1893–1941), Yiddish and German prose writer and literary historian and critic, was born in Kraków, Austrian Galicia (today in Poland). He settled in the Soviet Union in 1926, where he was appointed director of the literature and folklore section at the Institute of Jewish Proletarian Culture in Kiev and, later, head of the Department of Yiddish Language and Literature at the Moscow State Pedagogical Institute.

Much of Wiener's work focused on Yiddish literature of the Haskalah period, notably his collection of articles *On the History of Yiddish Literature in the Nineteenth Century* (Kiev, 1940), of which the following essay is the introduction (signed, "Moscow, January 1939").[1] It treats the Yiddish literature of the Haskalah as the bridge between old and modern Yiddish literature (but see also the article by Shmuel Niger, Selection 25 above). Wiener volunteered to fight in the Soviet army during World War II and was killed in action.

Like all Soviet Jewish scholars of his time, Wiener was able to work and publish only by avoiding political hazards. One strategy was to focus on the Haskalah period rather than the modern period, but the difficulty in studying any aspect of Yiddish culture is illustrated by his convoluted statement at the end of his second paragraph. On the one hand, Yiddish was the official language of Soviet Jewry, and Yiddish culture was a permitted field of study. On the other hand, nationhood was forbidden to Soviet Jews, and Yiddish studies were acceptable only if they disavowed Western-style Yiddish nationalism. Wiener therefore attempts the impossible task of identifying Yiddish solely with the "folk masses" (by ignoring the vertical integration of Yiddish culture) and opposition to Yiddish with "nationalists and all manner of Zionists and reactionaries" (by ignoring Yiddish-oriented Diaspora nationalism, the Zionist use of Yiddish for organizing and publicity in the Diaspora, and the use of Yiddish by right-leaning religious and secular movements).

It is widely believed that the *new* Yiddish literature of the nineteenth century began with Mendele [S.Y. Abramovitsh (1835–1917)].[1] Suddenly, one beautiful morning in the 1860s, Mendele and his work descended from heaven. About the earlier period of *new* Yiddish literature, even in circles of literary experts, vague concepts hold sway, such as there being some sort of "prehistory"—of an accidental sort, such as unconnected attempts and fragmentary matters—that had slight importance on its own and was chiefly suited to investigations and speculation by philologists and literary "archaeologists."

The lack of interest in the older works of the *new* Yiddish literature, the contemptuous appraisal of these works, echoes at times . . . the old ideas of the implacable "Hebraists" about the plebeian "maidservant," as they considered the Yiddish language and its significance and value in comparison with the "mistress"—the Hebrew language and literature. Apparently, disrespect of the language and creativity of the folk masses still prevails—as it did formerly in accusations of supposed "illicitness"—among nationalists and all manner of Zionists and reactionaries.

Because, in truth, the story of Yiddish literature of the nineteenth century *up to* the 1860s is not at all like the superficial, ignorant, or ill-intentioned "experts" present it or wish to convince others about it. Yiddish literature of these six-seven decades deserves to be considered not only with attention and seriousness but also with love.

In his article "The History of Yiddish Literature,"[2] Shulman reproaches the *maskilim* [adherents of the Haskalah] for not having written in Yiddish.

"And for entire decades (he means from the end of the eighteenth century to the 1860s—*M.W.*) not a single healthy word has been heard from it (meaning Yiddish—*M.W.*)." He was simply ignorant of the literature of this period.

The *Old Yiddish* literature from the fifteenth century to the end of the eighteenth century can boast *a great number of books overall* and a richness of topics and genres. In this Old Yiddish literature, there are: biblical and secular epics, original and translated knightly romances and other prose fiction, poetic creativity in various genres, characteristic folklore plays, a great quantity of stories and legends, novels, religious and moralizing (*muser*) works, historical works, chronicles, memoirs, and a great many translations and treatments of the most varied literatures.

The *new* Yiddish literature, namely, the secular Yiddish literature in the new Yiddish language of the East European countries, started at the end of the eighteenth and beginning of the nineteenth centuries, and its *first* period ended in the 1860s, just on Mendele's arrival in Yiddish literature. Up to the 1860s was the period of the *typical* "pure" Haskalah [the Jewish Enlightenment], the early Haskalah, and indeed in this *first* period the language and literature were readied for the appearance of the classical writers, Mendele, Sholem Aleichem, and Peretz.

The literature of these six-seven decades is, with regard to "quantity"— the number of books—very unimpressive. Regarding genres, the literature is one-sided. Most works are from the dramatic genre (comedies and dramas), folksy stories, not much literary prose, still less (literary) verse, which is more or less almost exclusively folkloric. With time, research will discover other such works here of greater or lesser value, which are known to us so far only by name or are entirely unknown. This will not bring to literary history any great changes in the "quantity" of the literature of the period.

If so, can one indeed perhaps conclude that even the term "literature" is an exaggeration for these hundred or so books? Can one indeed perhaps contend that this term is justified only conditionally, and only if one takes into account the historical perspective, the historical connection of these tens of books with the Old Yiddish literature on the one hand and with the rich development of literature that has come since the 1860s on the other hand?

No! These works deserve the term "literature" not for the sake of their "before" and "after," and not only because they prepared the way for the classical development literarily and historically, but *for their own sake, for the sake of their own value.*

The literature of the period is not just prehistory and nothing more. It has an independent value. The question arises: In what lies its conceptual and artistic value? In what way is it *original and independent*? Up to that time, the spiritual culture of the Jews in the East European countries came to expression mainly in Hebrew. If so, a further question arises: Is there a difference between the Yiddish and Hebrew fine literature of the time? What significance and value does the Yiddish literature of the time have in comparison with the Hebrew literature?

So long as we do not answer these questions, we lack the correct measure and perspective in studying the Yiddish literature of the period. One must not forget that the Hebrew literature of those several decades had hundreds and perhaps thousands of works. Yiddish literature existed at that time only in Galicia, Ukraine, Poland, and Lithuania—Hebrew literature also in Germany, Italy, Holland, Turkey, and many other countries. *Geographically*, the range of its creation and influence was incomparably broader.

The Hebrew literature was a literature of and for the intelligentsia. . . . The new *Yiddish* literature was then still in its swaddling clothes, thin and primitive, written by toiling, educated, democratic, oppressed, and backward folk masses. Often, these works have a naïve, almost *lubokish* character [referring to the popular style of illustration in Russian children's books].

Hebrew Haskalah literature had to withstand many attacks, but it nevertheless had more possibilities for being printed. At times it received a certain moral and material support from influential enlightened bourgeois circles. Yiddish literature was attacked and denigrated even by enlightened, educated people themselves, even by many representatives of the Hebrew Haskalah themselves. And no one supported it—because the masses, to whom it was addressed, were themselves helpless in the material and cultural sense.

Printing a Yiddish book was almost impossible. It took endless effort and struggle. There had to be miracles for a Yiddish book to appear in print at that time, and still more miracles for it to be preserved to the present day because the Hasidim and all sorts of obscurantists were determined that no trace should remain to see the light of day.

What independent significance could such literature have, what original value?

And yet these slender booklets had everything—both independent significance and originality. Not only in itself but indeed also in comparison with the immeasurably larger, multifaceted Hebrew literature that was much richer in traditions. Still more: in the matter of *originality*, one can say that the *fine Yiddish literature of that time* surpassed the Hebrew literature of that time.

Despite the numerical richness, the colorfulness, and the influence of the ancient and classical medieval Hebrew literature and other literatures, the Hebrew belles-lettres of the time—and for a good amount of time earlier—was poor in content. From the entire eighteenth century to the 1850s, one can name only rare works that truly have an *artistic* value, for example: in the eighteenth century, the dramatic poem "Migdal Oz" [The Tower of Victory] and in part the dramatic play *La-Yesharim Tehilla* [Glory to the Upright] by the talented poet Moshe-Hayyim Luzzatto, and in the first half of the nineteenth century, the satires of Joseph Perl and Isaac Erter and a few elegiac poems by Avraham Dov Lebensohn. These are artistic oases in the broad steppes of the Hebrew *melitzah* [elaborate pseudo-biblical style] of the period. To the names listed, some could no doubt be added, but not many. . . .

The remaining, relatively rich in number, Hebrew belles-lettres from the eighteenth to the second half of the nineteenth century consists chiefly of epigonic imitations, artistic amusements, content-poor rhetoric, and doubtful convictions; in short: of *melitzah* in the well-known sense, where one arranged, whittled, fussed over the word, but without living content. Certainly, one can find a striving for beauty, a longing for a finer life, a yearning for lofty ideas and noble feelings—but the striving, longing, and yearning were only realized here in rare instances. Ordinarily, it seldom extended beyond the limits of dilettantish, artistic amusement. The difficult, eventful life of the Jewish people in this century and a half—and this is, by the way, the time of enlightenment—found almost no *living*, *direct*, realistic echo in the Hebrew belles-lettres of the time. It had, with rare exceptions, no living connection with the people, no true influence on the people, and in some cases was even estranged from the folk masses.

It is understandable that the people were indifferent to this literature—both to the phrases about love for the Hebrew language and to the embittered, reactionary ideas of Samuel David Luzzatto, as well as to the mainly superficial and shallow verses of Naphtali Hirz Wessely and to the beautiful *melitzah* of Meir Halevy Letteris, and to the entire inflated, self-styled classic and pseudo-romantic genre in general.

When one comes from this congealed atmosphere to the simple booklets of the Yiddish literature of the time, one inhales fresh, living air, the air of folk life. Here is the freshness of a beginning, somewhat like the act of creation, when one breaks old canons and draws a line under the past and begins anew. Yiddish literature was then mostly naïve and primitive, but its freshness and liveliness compensated for it.

Whoever wants to be informed about the true, intimate, everyday life of the Jewish people at that time must turn to these Yiddish "booklets." From the Hebrew *sforim* [learned or holy books] of the time, he will gain little knowledge; from the Yiddish, he will perceive with all his senses the taste of life, the appearance, the mood of the folk masses in those years.

Of course, the Yiddish literature of the time also did not descend from heaven. In its entire "primitiveness" it is connected with traditions of the older *Yiddish* and still more of the new *Hebrew* literature, with influences of Western European literature and Russian literature. It could not possibly be otherwise. No innovations in literature, even its independence and originality, arise from within itself, without various influences from the past and present. Chiefly, however, the novelty arose from the influences of the life of the present. And innovation in literature is indeed dependent on how much the literature is open and sensitive to the influences of the present, of the current life of the people. And this is indeed the most important difference between the Yiddish and Hebrew belles-lettres of the time.

The belles-lettres of the *Jewish* Enlightenment in the Yiddish language was focused directly on the life of the people, on the everyday social needs of the time, in the manner they were then understood. The character of this artistic Yiddish literature lay in the character of the life of the Jewish folk masses of the time, in their tragic circumstances, in their creativity. This literature was one of suffering, of struggle. It loved the people, and the people loved it. If the books could not be printed, the people disseminated the poems—by heart, orally, in the theater piece—by manuscript, in the tens, in the hundreds.

Here, in these folksy booklets—just as in the folk stories and folksongs, but in a more concrete, more realistic manner—one can take the pulse of the people directly, reveal the undisguised character of the people, the nature of its spiritual life, of its lifestyle, of its ideals and its striving for justice, freedom and light. And this is the characteristic originality of these beautiful popular creations. . . .

The language in which the people spoke is a powerful concentration of life, as the form of the people's living movement, as its creation, as the expression of its culture. The language itself, as such, already contains a great measure of the people's life. Without it, one cannot succeed if one wants to feel the pulse and the taste of this life and embody it in artistic scenes.

The value of the Yiddish literature of the first half of the nineteenth century lies not only in its historical tendencies, in having artistically embodied the social strivings of the people, but also in having *for the first time* powerfully and artistically preserved this life itself, with its "everyday" hardships and suffering, with its human joy, with its creativity and striving.

The value of such a type of early, incipient literature cannot only be assessed with "purely artistic" measures, according to the principles of official poetry, according to the degree of success of the artistic methods applied. Its value is higher. In such work, where the fullness of life is still little restrained in the canons, and where the writer can draw chiefly from life—there is something that, from this strength, creates, changes, and develops the artistic laws and measures.

[Israel] Aksenfeld's *Shterntikhl* [The headband, 1861] and his comedies, [Shlomo] Ettinger's *Serkele* [the name of the protagonist, ca. 1839], and the folkloric stories (not to mention poetry) of that time belong to the type of creation whose value is *less* connected with the language itself and its expressiveness than ordinary prose and dramatic works. For example: in translation, they indeed lose more of their *objective* value than prose and dramaturgy *of a more highly developed artistic type*. The significance of the language itself here is *objectively* greater. Here, the language itself has a greater share in the artistic "substance" of the work, so to speak. In this category such naïve, in part "naturally grown," works are similar to poetry that loses a piece of its soul in being retold in prose or translation. The language—the linguistic untilled ground that is full of fertile juice and unrestrained life, of thoughts and feelings collected over generations—is preserved artistically here *for the first time*. With this, as the literary plow touches the primeval linguistic terrain, it arouses a great, accumulated creative strength. Such a form of first-time preservation is already in itself a significant accomplishment, although in such cases it was more difficult at that time than usual to ascertain the dividing line in literature between the creativity of the people and the individual accomplishments of the author.

The Yiddish literature of the nineteenth century received many and varied influences, including very valuable influences from the Hebrew literature of the time—especially concerning knowledge and culture in general and the Weltanschauung of the Enlightenment in particular, which, at that time in the Jewish environment was formulated in the Hebrew language.

But impulses for *artistic* creation in realistic prose and drama—stimulations for creating scenes of actual, everyday life, living figures, and living feelings—Yiddish literature, at least until the 1860s, received very little from Hebrew literature because they were almost nonexistent there. The influence of the Hebrew prose of the time (Mapu's *Ayit Tzavua* [1858]) almost led astray such a great talent as Mendele—then at the beginning of his creative work (*Ha-Avot veha-Banim* [The Fathers and the Sons, 1868]), until he drew upon and clung to the lowly traditions of the Old Yiddish literature.

And just exactly this lowly Yiddish language, the "labored" Yiddish booklets and Yiddish folksongs, stories, etc., gave to the old, rich and erudite Hebrew literature many *living* artistic impulses and stimulation—not only regarding scenes and types, but also regarding the cultivation of the new Hebrew language of the new Hebrew prose style, which based itself on [Joseph] Perl's, [Isaac Baer] Levinsohn's, [Judah Leib] Gordon's style and most of all on Mendele's style, and this means—on the influence of the Yiddish language and literature.

In the Yiddish literature of the first half of the nineteenth century, for the first time in hundreds of years, the people began to talk about themselves and their life, not in abstract statements and chroniclers' reports, not in stories with an admixture of fantasy, but in living, authentic, original literary scenes.

Various European influences affected such a work as Ettinger's *Serkele*, especially the dramaturgy of the Enlightenment. But already the fact in itself that, with his Enlightenment tendencies, he introduced into Yiddish literature an ordinary, lively everyday style was at that time (c. 1825) a great accomplishment. To do so, and to such a degree as was done by Ettinger, was far from being a self-evident and widespread practice in the European and Russian dramaturgy of the time. At the same time, it must be remembered that this style was *set down in such abundance and liveliness here for the first time*. In such instances, the writer can get lost in the abundance of observations, so that the material dominates him. Ettinger, however, dominates the abundance arising from this newly established style admirably and fashions it artistically.

Hebrew literature from the eighteenth to the first half of the nineteenth century has nothing to compare with such a realistic work as Ettinger's *Serkele*, neither in the quantity of life preserved in writing nor in mastery of the form. This comedy, which was written about 115 years ago, is, to this day, in the artistic sense, perhaps even the best in Yiddish literature—not to mention Hebrew literature, which had no dramaturgy.

And furthermore: Aksenfeld's work receives and captures a mighty part of the active, intimate life of his time. And about which artistic-narrative work in the Hebrew literature of the time could this be said, apart from Perl's *Megale Temirin* [Revealer of Secrets, 1819]? Certainly: in the works of Mapu, Gordon, Smolenskin, there is incomparably more culture, more erudition; their works are indeed immeasurably more intellectual, multicolored, and therefore in a number of details immeasurably richer. But the works of such a writer as Aksenfeld possess more vitality, more living juices. Compared to the vigorous, powerful, if indeed a bit primitive Aksenfeld, even the richly endowed Smolenskin still looks anemic. Aksenfeld's novel *Dos shterntikhl* has the genuine charm of natural growth, of immediacy. Here, the ideas of the Haskalah—the striving for enlightenment—receive folksy, popular outlines, the abstract "heavenly daughters" are embodied in their earthly figures. About which older Hebrew prose writer of artistic literature until the 1850s–1860s can this be said? The Yiddish folkloric and half-folkloric satiric poems opposing Hasidism and rebbes, the poems about recruiting [for the tsar's army], the love songs, etc.—what can be compared with them in the Hebrew literature of the time until Gordon?

These older works of the new Yiddish literature were based on real life, on the needs and strivings of the folk masses. These books have a history, a historical connection from generation to generation; here, there is a development, a tradition, from phase to phase: [Isaac Abraham] Euchel, [Yankev-Mortkhe] Volfzohn, [Menahem-Mendl] Lefin, the anonymous author of *Di genarte velt* [The deceived world, 1816], Aksenfeld, Ettinger, Levinsohn, [Abraham Ber] Gottlober, [Isaac Mayer] Dik, [Isaac Joel] Linetzky, [Abraham] Goldfaden, Mendele, etc., etc. And we can ascertain the same in the path from the old folklore poem to the half-literary, half-folkloric folksong. This literature knew what it wanted. This is called *literature* in the original sense of the word.

No sources, from either historical scholarship or belles-lettres (in Hebrew and other languages), can replace the promise of this literature for grasping the true nature and perceiving clearly the intimate, daily life of the people, of the masses in that time, their actual nature, their feelings, their social ideas, their thoughts, dealings, hopes, strivings, and the creativity of their commonplace, ordinary day. The literature of that time is not only a characteristic cross section of the history of Yiddish literature but one that has an original and self-evident significance of its own. It is not only an important collection of historical documents, an interesting chapter of

Jewish culture, of Jewish history in general but also a collection of memorials to the creativity of the people in one of the most difficult, gloomy periods in its history.

Introduction Notes:

1. Meir Viner, "Forvert tsu der ershter oyflage" [Forword to the first edition], in his *Tsu der geshikhte fun der yidisher literatur in 19-tn yorhundert* [On the history of Yiddish literature in the nineteenth century]; first published, Kiev, 1940) (New York: Yidisher kultur farband, 1945), vol. 1, 9–22 (quoted here; abridged).

Article Notes:

1. It is worthwhile to mention a curiosity: the researcher of Old Yiddish literature Elazar Shulman wrote in the introduction to his book *Sefat Yehudit-Ashkenazit ve-sifrutah* (Riga: A. Levin, 1912/13, p. 6) that from the end of the eighteenth century to 1860s Yiddish literature almost ceased to exist . . .

2. In Sholem-aleykhem, ed., *Yudishe folks-bibliothek* 2, section 3 (Kiev: Y. Sheftil, 1888), 121.

27
Four Unknown Yiddish Plays from the Mid-Nineteenth Century
by Max Weinreich, 1930

MAX WEINREICH (1894–1969), Yiddish linguist, literary historian, and sociologist, was born in Kuldīga, Russian Courland (today in Latvia). He received his doctorate in linguistics in 1923 at the University of Marburg with a dissertation in German on the history of the Yiddish language and dialects. He was one of the founders of YIVO (Yiddish Scientific Institute) in 1925 and became its principal leader both in Vilna and again in New York after 1940. Weinreich's major work is his four-volume *History of the Yiddish Language* (Yiddish, 1973; English, 2008). Throughout his career, he wrote and spoke on scholarly topics as well as public issues affecting Jews, first as a minority nationality in Europe, then as a fast-assimilating immigrant group in America, in both instances proposing measures to strengthen Jewish identity.

The following article, one of his many historical studies of older Yiddish texts, appeared in a volume on Yiddish theater edited for YIVO by Jacob Shatzky.[1] It is a detailed treatment of selected texts of the general type discussed by Meir Wiener (in Selection 26 above). The reference in the opening paragraph to "Z. Reisen's lexicon" is to the well-known *Lexicon of Yiddish Literature, Press, and Philology* by Zalmen Reisen, published in Yiddish in Vilna, 1926–29.[2]

In the YIVO archives, there is a booklet of a few hundred pages, written by hand, that was sent by the collectors circle of the Y. L. Peretz Association in Częstochowa [Poland] in 1928. The Częstochowa Friends became aware of it from a notice in Z. Reisen's lexicon (vol. 1, col. 738) that the literary estate of the writer Wolf Demant (1830–1897) from Brody [today in Ukraine] remained with his son Simon, a pharmacist. This Simon Demant's pharmacy, in Chortkiv [today in Ukraine], was taken over by a Christian owner after his death. The Friends went to inquire of him whether anything remained of S. Demant's papers. They were fortunate. They received the indicated booklet (the written area is approximately 16 x 10 cm), which was well bound, and in addition to this a notebook with Yiddish poems and a memorandum, written in Polish, with a project for reforming the Jewish schools. These materials, which indeed originated with Wolf Demant, were sent off to the YIVO archives.

I am deliberately relating all the details so precisely to show that with a bit of effort it is still possible today to rescue many things that are related to our past, and often important things. The package that arrived from Częstochowa puts a new light for us on the history of Yiddish drama in the nineteenth century. In the bound booklet were four plays, which were absolutely unknown until now. Considering the small number of Yiddish plays that have come to us from before Goldfaden's time [Abraham Goldfaden (1840–1908), the recognized founder of modern Yiddish theater], four new pieces at once contribute a tremendous amount of elucidation.

Admittedly, the result is a bit unexpected: Wolf Demant himself had only an indirect connection to the pieces. He copied them over in his own hand, and that is all. On the last page of the booklet, we find a postscript: "Recopied in Brody in the month of August of the year 1863 by Wolf Demant, teacher in the German Israelite secondary and girls school."

It is well known that recopying one's own or another's work was a beloved occupation among the *maskilim* [adherents of the Haskalah, Jewish Enlightenment].[1] The *maskilim* felt themselves isolated among the broader mass of Jews, their possibilities for propaganda very limited, yet wanting to make an impression. They were cut off from the old-fashioned societies with their feasts and institutional leaders; the form of present-day community life with associations, committees, etc., did not yet exist. Therefore, they had a lot of time, and they wrote.[2]

The four pieces under consideration by us are:

1. "*Mondrish* [aka Buffoon] / or / character sketch of merchants in Iași [Romania] in the year 1858 / farce in three acts / by / Yeshaye Gutman [Shaye-Meyer Finkelshteyn, 1806–1870]," 41 pages.
2. "*Der kolboynik* [The know-it-all] / or / the switched bride and groom / farce in 5 acts / by / Yeshaye Gutman," 77 pages.
3. "*Di dray shvesterkinder* [The three cousins] / comedy in three acts / by / Yeshaye Gutman," 39 pages.
4. "*Der ziveg* [The match; Betrothal] / or / what is meant to be / is what comes true / comedy in 5 acts / by / H. Sh. R. N. [Hersh Reitman / Hirsh Raytmen, 1808–1866]," 46 pages plus 2½ pages of notes. . . .

The social environment that was depicted in the four pieces is not foreign to us; we know it from many Haskalah works, but, on the other hand, there is still much here that is unique, independent, that helps us to see the Yiddish Haskalah literature in a new light.

Setting aside the question of the artistic execution—we will soon return to this—we find in all four pieces excellent portrayals of actual life.

We have before us the Jewish environment in the twilight between old and new, reflected in Brody itself or in places illuminated by the light of Brody.

In the nineteenth century, several times we come up against the fact that, unexpectedly, smaller places play a large role in Jewish spiritual development. In Galicia—Brody, not Lemberg [Lviv] and not Kraków; in Congress Poland—Zamość, not Warsaw and Lublin; in Lithuania a bit later—Zhager [Žagarė], not Kovne [Kaunas]. The only exception was perhaps Vilna [Vilnius].

More Yiddish writers came from Zamość, but in terms of the general spiritual environment, Brody was probably not behind Zamość. It is sufficient to mention such names of Brody residents as Yitshak Erter, the author of *Ha-Tsofe levet Yisrael* [Watchman at the house of Israel, 1864], and Yehoshua Heschel Schorr, the editor of *He-Halutz* [The Pioneer, 1852–99].

Nevertheless, regarding Brody, it is not difficult to establish the cause of its central role. The city blossomed economically, and when an economic decline began (c. 1880), it quickly declined culturally as well. The period of prosperity derived from an entirely special situation.[3] As soon as Brody became part of Austria after the First Partition of Poland [1772], Joseph II favored it with his mercy. The privileges consisted in transforming Brody and its surrounding area into a free commercial city; this means that all types of merchandise could be imported here and exported from here, to and from abroad, without border tariffs. This greatly elevated the commercial and general economic significance of the city. It became a center that was closely connected with the Leipzig fairs, and in the opposite direction, its connections extended to the southeast as far as the Black Sea. As a result of the commercial influence, representatives of Brody commercial firms also went on the road, and some continued to live in the newly occupied areas.

In addition, this was an almost purely *Jewish* city. When Joseph II was here in 1774, he is said to have remarked: "Now I understand why I am called King of Jerusalem" (one of the titles of the Austrian emperors). In the 1850s, the statistics indicate 26,000 residents in the city, of whom 22,000 were Jews.

Brody was renowned in the Jewish world, not only as a geographical location but as an idea, almost a symbol. The Brody Haskalah influenced not only the nearby province of Galicia, but it "colonized" the entire territory up to the Black Sea. If Odessa became a center of the Haskalah, when Gehenna burned ten miles from it, this was in large measure thanks to the immigrants from Brody. Bezalel Stern, the director of the first school for Jewish children in Odessa, came from Brody; in 1840 a special "Brody School" was built in Odessa (just as in Vilna, a "Berlin School"). In Lemberg and even in Vienna, Brody natives took an important place in Jewish society. In this way, the light of the Brody Haskalah shone far into the distance. . . .

We already understand why, among the *maskilim* in Brody, the highest position was held by the bookkeeper and, stemming from him, the merchant, and not the student (like Redlich in *Serkele* [by Shlomo Ettinger, 1839]), and not the writer (like Gutman in *Kleyne mentshele* [The Little Man by Mendele Moykher Sforim, 1864], not the teacher (like the Litvak in *Dos poylishe yingl* [The Polish Lad by Isaac Joel Linetzky, 1869]). The Brody Haskalah was more practical, economical, and firmly established. This is also reflected in our four pieces. [Weinreich then quotes a page of dialogue from *Mondrish*.]

Flink [the name means "quick" or "agile"], the pioneer of Brody ways in Iași, stands like a living being before our eyes. He is a fine man, and Shmulik the Pole and his family are fine people, and Esther the chambermaid is a fine person; all of them come from Brody. All the others who surround them are common, ordinary people. Rabbi Chaim's entire business depends on Flink, from Brody.

A second Flink, but in a smaller format, is Yosele Frantsoyz [The French] of "The Three Cousins." How he got ahead is not hard to see. A few years earlier, he still wore a long *kapote* [religious frock coat], like Simkhele, the rabbi's son, and was spiritually similar to him in general. But Yosele is a more active character who broke free of the fetters and "made himself independent" during the time when Simkhele only played with the idea of eventually emancipating himself. Now, Yosele's home is the place of refuge for a whole group of young people who feel forlorn in the traditional setting, so forlorn that, if not for this home with its broken-down benches, they would not even have a place to shave in private.[4]

Our Haskalah writer is not satisfied, however, with casting charcoal black against snow white. He knows that a false Haskalah also exists. Royze from the *Shvesterkinder* looks like a younger sister of Yetkhe in *Laykhtzin un fremelay* [Frivolity and piety by Aaron Wolfssohn, 1796].

Flink and Yosele are Finkelshteyn's positive types. And what is noteworthy is that they also emerge as living beings, especially the first—not mannequins like the Markuses in *Laykhtzin un fremelay* or in *Serkele*.[5] This attests to the writer's talent.

But it is understandable that the negative type, the *dramatis personae* from the old world, appears before us full of life—both the *kantorshtshik* [about a banker, exchange broker] and his client Fonye in Iași (*Mondrish*) and Itsikl and Rivke-Feyge (*Shvesterkinder*), as well as the old Dovid in *Kolboynik*. They are indeed easier to characterize.

In *Ziveg* we have a new and an old world in one family: Shimen, the old-fashioned Jew, and his brother, the doctor; the Haskalah already caused a rip in the closed Jewish community. But there was no rupture between each other. The doctor is the more educated one, in any event smarter, in any event more inclined to be conciliatory, because he knows that in the end he will still be right. And it turns out otherwise.

The depiction of the poor in the *Ziveg* is extraordinarily successful. At almost the same time, we already have two treatments in Yiddish literature of the same environment: in Dik's *Der hazn* [The cantor] (Vilna, 1874, pp. 19–24) and in *Fishke der krumer* [Fishke the Lame by Mendele Moyker Sforim, 1869]. Something of a romantic curiosity drew the bourgeois writer to the life of the beggar: they stand out from the crowd; their doings often border on the criminal, but among them there is more temperament, more assurance, more color.

A novelty is the enlightened rabbi in the *Shvesterkinder*. Have you heard of a rabbi who believes in [romantic] love? Have you ever heard of a rabbi waving away the fact that someone shaves or goes around with his head uncovered? Finkelshteyn's rabbi did not disapprove of a groom, saying instead: a beard one can let grow; a yarmulke costs only a penny. A similar figure appears only as Mendele's rabbi in the *Kleyne mentshele*. It is a conscious opposing of rabbi and rebbe, where the rabbi already has the scent of the German Reform rabbinate.

Der kolboynik should appeal to a very particular interest. The piece portrays Jewish Hungary, a corner that has not found any reflection in Yiddish literature, if one does not count [Moritz Gottlieb] Saphir's *Der falsher Kashtan* [The impostor posing as Kashtan].[6] And in the nineteenth century, this Jewish Hungary experienced a development of a unique sort: from strictest Jewishness through German civilization to 120 percent Magyar assimilation. Here, in Finkelshteyn, we have the first two stages: the Hasidic rebbe type of Jewishness and the German Haskalah. But this was already sufficiently new, particularly because the world he depicts is so out of the ordinary; I can recall no other depiction of the life of Jewish students in the literature of that time. The light-effects in the piece are so cleverly done that the group of students stands out well against the background of the old-fashioned Jewish community in Budapest. And as a result, one sees that the author does not lie somewhere in a back alley and look up at the students as if at celestial beings.[7] It appears that he knew their life at first hand.

In this, Finkelshteyn is a distinct innovator.

Another aspect that looks new is the relaxed attitude of his heroes to questions of morality. We are accustomed to thinking that the *maskil* Markus must be an exemplar for all Israel, like a pomegranate stuffed with virtues [referring to the supposed 613 seeds in a pomegranate, symbolizing the 613 commandments of the Torah], above criticism; from this comes the lifelessness of the *maskilic* characters in all known works of this time. As a result, Shloymele in Reitman's *Ziveg* is also such a wooden figure. Finkelshteyn goes another way. His Flink is alone with the woman of the house (with the philosophical remark: "I am just a human being!"), and Klugman [meaning "clever"] does everything that is forbidden, no better than his own father, Rabbi Osher, and Khaim the *kantorshtshik*. But Flink and Klugman have the virtue of being *maskilim* and clever youths as well, and it appears as if Finkelshteyn would say to us: there is no absolute measure of morality; youth, cleverness, and education compensate for many things.

Along with what is new—which we emphasize with amazement—as a step from the stock character to the individuality of the writer and of the hero—in our pieces, we nevertheless attest at every turn to the influence of known familiar materials, ideas, and motifs, and if we have discovered in several details differences in comparison with earlier Yiddish theater pieces, we must, however, note many more analogies.

The canvas for all conflicts in our pieces is family relations: yes *shidekh* [match], no *shidekh*, good *shidekh*, bad *shidekh*—the treatment turns on this. And in any event we have the *maskilic* conclusions: marriage without love leads to misfortune; do not chase after lineage; do not chase after the dowry; virtue is rewarded. . . .

Now we need to consider the issue of the attitude of both our authors toward the linguistic instrument, to Yiddish. On the basis of all that we see, there can be no suggestion of a hostility to Yiddish in the circle of the Finkelshteyns, Reitmans, and Demants. On the contrary, there was a bond with Yiddish. Yiddish was their natural, colloquial language to the extent it related to daily matters. Their modest literary activity was also reflected in Yiddish (for which a *maskil* with their knowledge of German could have used High German, as we already saw in Ettinger's failures).

On the other hand, they were not conscious that Yiddish was something of a social force that came to play a role. *Studying* [or teaching] Yiddish is not worthwhile—everyone already knows it in any case. Agitating for Yiddish was not necessary because everyone spoke it in any case, and if not it made no difference, so long as there was a Yiddish heart. Demanding rights for Yiddish did not arise in their time, when Polish had hardly any rights in Galicia and Ukrainian no rights at all. The natural language of *education*, of enlightenment, of bread, was German. Yiddish was a matter for the heart, of sentiment and affect, and it played a greater role among sentimental, humorous, affable people than among sober intellectuals. . . .

At that time in Galicia, German was the only language of the administration, courts, and books, without doubt. As a result, we notice more than once in the pieces that, when the characters begin to speak about more abstract matters, they switch to German. In addition, the language of love, or more correctly, of flirting, was German (let us recall what Peretz wrote thirty years later about the poverty of Yiddish in the field of love terminology!). On the other hand, however, wherever we find a person of feeling, a buddy among the characters, he speaks Yiddish even if he is a student, as if that were possible. We have a wonderful scene in *Kolboynik* where Klugman *demands* that one should speak Yiddish and relates that there is an agreement to that effect among the Jewish students in Budapest. . . .

In recent years, we have already had many occasions to refute the ill-conceived idea that the *maskilim*, even including the Yiddish writers, hated the Yiddish language. Our four Brody pieces lead us to revise still further that one-sided view. [Such *maskilic* opponents of Yiddish as] David Friedländer [1750–1834] and Tuvia Feder [1760–1817] must not obscure our view of Ettinger, Reitman, and Finkelshteyn.

So far, we have ascertained in our pieces the elements of the fight against obscurantism and in favor of enlightenment. But they arose from an artistic impulse no less than from a direct desire to fight. We must, therefore, also attempt to analyze the works from the artistic side. . . . [followed by several paragraphs discussing artistic virtues and weaknesses in the pieces].

Regarding Finkelshteyn, we can be sure of an additional factor: he was frequently on the road for the sake of his business dealings and, without any doubt, saw non-Jewish theater.

In *Mondrish*, another fundamental element of dramatic energy among Jews reveals itself, the *Purim-shpil* [Purim play]. One can debate how great a part the *Purim-shpil* played in the development of our modern theater,[8] but the existence of that part no one denies. In *Mondrish*, where the traditional *Purim-shpil* is presented in a modern staging, we see an organic union of old and new in Yiddish theater production. And when we also take into account that the players in *Mondrish* were indeed none other than wandering Brody singers, we have before us all the material from which Goldfaden, in the same Iași twenty years later, established the structure of the new Yiddish theater.

Introduction Notes:

1. Maks Vaynraykh, "Fir umbakante teatershtik fun mitn 19tn yorhundert" [Four unknown plays from the mid-nineteenth century], *Arkhiv fun der geshikhte fun yidishn teater un drame* [Archive of the history of Yiddish theater and drama] (Vilna–New York: YIVO, 1930), 175–203 (175–77, 194–203 quoted here; abridged).

2. Z. Reyzen, *Leksikon fun der yidisher literatur, prese un filologye*, 4 vols. (Vilna: B. Kletskin, 1926–29).

Article Notes:

1. See, i.e., my introduction to *Ale ksovim fun shloyme etinger* [All the writings of Solomon Ettinger] (Vilna: B. Kletskin, 1925), XXVII and XLVI.

2. Feivel Shapiro, collector for YIVO in Brody, wrote me in a letter of January 14, 1930: "Demant's son, Dr. Demant in Brody, recounted that his father would write for entire nights."

3. See the book by S. Barącz, *Wolne miasto handlowe Brody* [Free-trade city of Brody] (Lwów, 1865). See also the article "Brody" in *Evreĭskaia ėntsīklopediiā* (St. Petersburg, 1906–13) and in the *Encyclopaedia Judaica*, vol. IV (Berlin, 1929), 1091–96.

4. See *Di dray shvesterkinder*, I, 7.

5. The name *Markus* for the hero, the *maskil*, became so ingrained that neither Dovid Zahik in his later *Di roze tsvishn derner* [The rose among thorns] (Piotrków, 1884) nor Sholem Aleichem in *Yaknehoz* (Kiev, 1894) could find a better name.

6. See Z. Reyzen, *Fun Mendelson biz Mendele*, vol. I (Warsaw: Kultur-Lige, 1923), 71–77.

7. Like, for example, the abovementioned Dovid Zahik.

8. See, for example, the article by Dr. A. Mukdoni in *Goldfaden-bukh* (New York, 1925), 7.

28
Yiddish Literature under Nazi Occupation
by Nachman Blumental, 1946

NACHMAN BLUMENTAL (1902–1983;[1] see also Selections 35 and 49 below) was born in Borszczów, Austrian Podolia (today Borshchiv, Ukraine), and received his master's degree in Polish literature from the University of Warsaw in 1928. Before World War II, he wrote frequently on Yiddish culture and literature, especially folklore, and was a *zamler* (collector) of Yiddish folklore for YIVO (Yiddish Scientific Institute) in Vilna. He survived the Nazi occupation in the Soviet Union, but his wife and son were killed by the Germans. On returning to liberated Poland, he immediately joined the Central Jewish Historical Commission (CJHC) directed by Philip Friedman and, on Friedman's departure, succeeded him as director from 1946 to 1949. He then settled in Israel, where he was a researcher at Beit Lohamei HaGeta'ot / Ghetto Fighters' House and, from 1953, at Yad Vashem. He wrote several books and hundreds of articles in Yiddish and served as editor or coeditor of a dozen documentary collections and *yizkor* books published in Yiddish or Hebrew. He is best known for the special project on which he worked from 1945 until its publication in 1981—his collection of expressions used by Jews during the Holocaust, *Verter un vertlekh* (Words and sayings; see review in Selection 49).

Before World War II, Blumental was a teacher in a Polish Jewish secondary school in Lublin in which the use of Yiddish was forbidden as a risk to the school's accreditation. He nevertheless delivered clandestine lectures on Yiddish literature for which he was dismissed but ultimately reinstated under pressure from the local Yiddish press. After the war, at the CJHC in Poland, he returned to his favored subject of Yiddish culture but focused on a new time period. He wrote often about wartime Yiddish literature and also supported the postwar publishing of writings on the Nazi era by contributing forewords to at least twenty books by other authors, as well as occasional book reviews.

Below are excerpts from four works by Blumental about Yiddish literature during the Nazi period. The first comes from the published version of the paper he delivered on September 19, 1945, at the CJHC's Second Academic Conference in Lodz, titled "Introduction to the History of Literary Creativity in Yiddish at the Time of the German Occupation." This is followed by brief excerpts from Blumental's writings about three works by others relating to the Lodz ghetto.

The Characteristics of Yiddish Literature under German Occupation[1]

It is known that during this time not only people who considered writing their profession, but also very ordinary people, would write. There arose a sort of *epidemic* of writing—there were writers who were indeed acquainted with the rules of orthography, but also people who were half or entirely illiterate. Naturally, these last improvised! All classes wrote: old, young, large, small—thus, for example, an unknown reviewer writes about a manufacturer in Lodz by the name of Zilberstein, an older Jew, a member of the Ger group of Hasidim, who would stay up at night, to the great amazement of his wife and children, and write poems in Yiddish. In the beginning, he would write without concern for form, but gradually he also acquainted himself with the problems of rhyme and rhythm and aspired to a literary expression of his experiences. Doing so, he did not forget God . . . or rebbe. Such facts can be enumerated in the thousands. People wrote—thoroughly interesting literature by master baker Jacob Hiller; and very interesting experiences by shoemaker Czechowicz and metalworker Fogelman (poems and memoirs). One can say that everyone wrote if they had the physical possibility of doing so, creating literature, honest, human literature. . . .

This literature reached the audience, like long ago, in the spoken language: salons were created where the newest creations were read aloud even by "great" writers in Lodz, Warsaw (in public places as well as in private homes); poetic-artistic performances were organized (i.e., by house committees). This was for the intellectuals; for the ordinary public there was the troubadour—the folksinger—or as he was called in the Lodz ghetto, street singer.... People circled around such a poet in the street—he stood on top of a crate, or a cask, and recited—and the audience shed rivers of tears when he sang a lament or split their sides with laughter when he joked about the ghetto leaders.... The martyred Lodz poet S. Shayevitsh [Simkhe-Bunim Shayevitsh / Szajewicz, 1907–1944] wrote about this fact in a letter on February 10, 1942: "As I once already told you, there is no solution but to imitate the old-time troubadours, minnesingers, and our Jewish Brody Singers, bringing forth one's own poems, becoming preachers who go to the people with their sermons."

But the same troubadour, just as in the Middle Ages, has another function: he is not only an art singer—he also fulfills a social function. His task is to inform, alert the audience, convey the latest news—a sort of living newspaper.

After each new ordinance by the authorities, after each disgraceful act by the *Judenrat*, after each important event—there emerged a poem, a parody, a scene, a joke, a saying. The street reacted quickly and sharply and—mercilessly! Yiddish literature hovered between these two extremes—chiefly the popular literature—during the ghetto period. From one side, aspiring to memorialize the most frightful act of violence in the world, transmitting the inhuman to eternity; from the other side, seizing the everyday, the passing event, often even the humorous in the great global struggle between good and evil....

The literature is chiefly oral—and poetry is easier to memorize and to recite—therefore the preponderance of poetry: works that in our evaluation—according to their nature—are prose, come to be written in verse....

What were the chief characteristics of this literature? Here I will only outline rather than discuss the subject.

1. First of all, to our great amazement, it is conspicuous that the feeling or thought of despair occurs in so few poems. The poems were written by a dying people in the most frightful conditions—but nevertheless, they frequently and very clearly sounded the hopeful motif: right will prevail!

2. A second point: in events that took place, the poet saw above all the savage, barbaric, inhuman people who had fallen to the lowest level of bestiality. The literature was directed against them: a literature that summoned to struggle, to vengeance. On the contrary, we find almost no apologetics, no defensiveness. The Jews are suffering because they are Jews, but no one dwells on the concept of "Jew."
3. Motif: there are complaints to God for allowing it; "*eicha*" poems [how poems], from the poem "How could it be? Why do you not speak out against the non-Jew?" [new versions of an anonymous poem from the 1919 Ukrainian pogroms, beginning with "How"—the first word, and hence the name in Hebrew of the book of Lamentations].... We also do not find the motif of fighting with God in the folk literature.
4. An innovation in Yiddish literature is the motif of fighting with the enemy, the call to resist. Excelling in this regard were the Young Vilna group (Shmerke Kaczerginski, Leyb Rosental, Hirsh Glik), from which emerged partisan songs, etc.
5. There is a very widespread motif that I would call, "my home"-motif: "I once had a home," or "I want to be home again."
6. Another motif, which occurs in nearly every introduction to works of poetry or prose, is a complaint about the lack of appropriate words to describe what has happened. (This complaint is made not only in Yiddish literature and not only by ordinary writers but even experienced writers.)

Introduction to the Lodz ghetto poetry of murdered poet S. Shayevitsh (1946)[2]

From the garbage of the ghetto, people unexpectedly brought the Central Jewish Historical Commission old pieces of paper, and among them a long Yiddish poem—with the signature S. Shayevitsh. Thus, the Yiddish writers did not forget, so to speak, their mission in the most frightful conditions of the ghetto! A poem, a "large poem," as the author himself called it, and more correctly: the poem "Lekh-lekho" [Go Forth] together with a second poem by Shayevitsh, "Friling tashab" [Spring 1942]—the most powerful poetic creations in Yiddish that we have had occasion to read in the past few years. . . .

How did the Yiddish writers live in the ghetto? We find an answer to this in the letter from Shayevitsh to Shmuel Roznshteyn [1895–1944; editor of the official ghetto newspaper]. One trembles to read it. The gentle, delicate Shayevitsh was a sort of janitor in a storehouse for precious goods. He was attacked—even physically, to the point of bleeding, by the assembled hungry mob. And in that difficult work from sunrise to late in the evening, Shayevitsh together with his wife and five-year-old girl nearly died from starvation, and he asked Roznshteyn, who played the role of a magnate in the ghetto, for another position, in a quiet place: in the [civil] court or in the religious court. The description of his life in the ghetto is already an interesting historical document. But in the letter we find something more: we find Shayevitsh—the poet. There are not many writings in Yiddish literature like this, about the process of poetic creation, as in Shayevitsh's letter. He felt in himself the power to create and the urge to create, but because of his difficult work could not devote himself to what governed his entire soul, his entire essence. He actually felt as if his heroes demanded that he bring them into the world. That this is not just a turn of phrase is felt in each of his lines. Invoking the names of his parents, who were not long deceased and who seek salvation from him, gives the work a deep, intimately openhearted tone.

But in the letter one also sees the mark of the time. Shayevitsh hurried with his poem because he was afraid he would not live to see it completed. And here emerges Shayevitsh's genius. With his poet's strength, he sensed, already in September 1941, what many "great" Jewish political and community leaders were utterly unable to understand, even in later times. And his poet's premonition did not deceive him. He departed on a transport from Lodz, but when and to where, no one knows. . . .

All that was experienced in the ghetto finds its echo in the poems: the suffering and pain of each day, hunger, want, fear for the coming day, and pride in spite of the enemies; despair and woe on account of innocent murder—and certainty that vengeance would eventually come. And the thought bothered the poet constantly: why did God bestow a death sentence—and he could give no answer to the question. And in the matter of God—we have here a rich range of experiences, from submissiveness to open revolt; from hope and faith in the Master of the Universe to total resignation: "For when a person is slain, one also slays his God."

On the stories of the Lodz Ghetto by surviving author Isaiah Spiegel (1953)[3]

What sort of book in Yiddish could draw the Yiddish-reading public in America itself and in the world at large closer to understanding the frightful process that brought about the murder of European Jewry than Shpigl's stories? And who among us would not wish to know how our brothers and sisters lived and how they were murdered in the German Nazi Gehenna?!

When we say that in Shpigl's stories we have the *history* of the Lodz ghetto we must emphasize equally that this history was written not by a historian but a writer, an artist. Nevertheless, this history is no less correct and "true" than the writings of a true historian, if not more . . . [ellipsis in original] It is true that Shpigl did not operate with "historical" material, he cited no sources, he brought no documentary evidence, he summoned no witnesses; he also made use of no dates, no numbers, no statistics, and nevertheless his book is more convincing than a scholarly treatment that possesses all of those but does not have the unmediated evidentiary power of a story by Shpigl. . . .

A number of serious scholarly works were preserved from the Warsaw ghetto that deal with starvation. In those works the signs of starvation in the human body were analyzed precisely. Shpigl gives us a literary-artistic treatment, an effective illustration of the scholarly studies—an illustration that is no less convincing than the scholarly works but is much more approachable, understandable, and clearer for the general readership. Thus, for example, you have the appearance of a "ghetto person" in general. "His thin, flat body was consumed by starvation. When he would walk down the narrow street on a sunny day, not even a living human shadow was cast behind him. Something of a sparse/scattered shadowy spot slunk after his collapsing body and trembled like the shadow of a bird floating past" (p. 93). A macabre paradox: the "ghetto-person" even had no shadow! . . .

Yeshaye Shpigl did not miss any important event of Lodz ghetto life. He remembers the first, small oppressions, he mentions the burning of the synagogues that took place already in November 1939, he does not forget the smallest German order, such as surrendering the house pets, the prohibition on playing the works of German composers, etc. He turns to more important events: expelling the Jews from the better streets and forcing them to settle in Jewish streets around "Baluter Ring" [Bałucki Rynek, a plaza in the Jewish quarter], and then the creation of the ghetto and the first transports that were indeed sent from the ghetto to work outside the ghetto, and the gradual transition to transports to murder; later, the transports of the Western European Jews who arrived in Lodz, etc.—and the inner life of the ghetto—hunger, the nourishment of the Jews: the noonday meals, the "plots," the special ghetto foods, the living conditions, ghetto illnesses, ghetto funerals, etc.

The poet looks at everyone—although he "lived" alone in this Gehenna—with his good-natured eye; he sees not only the bad that comes from the enemy, from the Germans, but he also sees the beautiful, the good among the victims.

Foreword to a novel about ghetto life by surviving author Rachmil Bryks (1969)[4]

I will dare to say in the foreword to the new book, *The Paper Crown* by Rachmil Bryks [Yerakhmiel Briks, 1902–1974], what I wrote previously in a review of another of his books: that the author is not merely a storyteller who seeks themes and strives to treat them according to certain accepted norms.

From the start, his theme is a specific one: the inner life of the Lodz ghetto, which can be considered, to a certain degree, a symbol of all the ghettos in Eastern Europe during the Hitler period. This is already the author's fourth book—in a series—on this theme. And in reading it we feel that *the author lives with the ghetto; he is still entirely there*. From the manner of writing and from what we know of his private life, it is inconceivable that he would ever leave *his theme*. That is a great virtue from both the historical and artistic standpoint.

Although we already have more or less precise monographs on the general history of the Jews in Lodz at that time, we lacked a precise depiction of their everyday and internal Jewish life: about what the Jews said to each other, about what they thought, how they felt, their psychology, their folklore, what they believed, how they looked, what sort of clothes they wore; how the police and other officials were dressed, what sort of hats and what sort of epaulets, what sort of insignia, what sort of ribbons, what sort of shoes. What sort of meals they ate, in what sort of places they lived, how they obtained their meager bit of food, how they passed the day, their language, etc. All of these are depicted for us by Bryks in his characteristic and lively manner: he gives us a museum. . . .

Bryks writes with the language spoken by the Jews in the Lodz ghetto: with new words and new sayings and with songs that were sung as a reaction to each new event; and if the author says something of his own, it is so suited to the public at large that it is difficult to distinguish whether they are his own words and expressions or whether he adopted them from the people; for example: "If one does not pay the stomach, the eyes go on strike, the head goes on strike." Or: "Man and wife, a walking store." They walk along the street bedecked with things to sell. It is entirely possible that this is the author's property—a question that is not yet able to be resolved. . . .

The story "The Paper Crown" belongs to the category—as it was once called—"pages of life," and, in that, its significance for the historical research of that period is incalculable: this is history in an artistic form.

Introduction Notes:

1. The year of Blumental's birth is stated correctly here (contrary to the *New Lexicon of Yiddish Writers*, the obituary published by Yad Vashem, and my previous book on the Yiddish historians), for which I am grateful to his son, Miron Blumental.

Article Notes:

1. Nakhman Blumental, "Der yidisher literatur unter der daytsher okupatsye," *Yidishe kultur* 8, no. 1 (New York, 1946): 6–11; revised and expanded version reprinted as the first two chapters of his *Shmuesn vegn der yidisher literatur unter der daytsher okupatsye* [Chats on Yiddish literature under German occupation] (Buenos Aires: Tsentral-farband fun poylishe yidn in argentine, 1966), 19–38 (excerpts).

2. Nakhman Blumental, introduction to S. Shayevitsh, *Lekh-Lekho* [Go forth] (Lodz: Centralna Żydowska Komisja Historyczna, 1946), 7–16 (excerpt).

3. Nakhman Blumental, "A literarishe geshikhte fun lodzsher geto" (review of Yeshaye Shpigl, *Likht funem upgrunt* [Light from the abyss] (New York: CYCO, 1952), in *Di goldene keyt* 17 (Jerusalem, 1953): 244–49 (excerpt).

4. Nakhman Blumental, foreword to Rachmil Briks, *Di papirene kroyn* [The paper crown] (New York: Yerahmi'el briks bukh-komitet, 1969), 5–7 (excerpt).

Part Five

PRESS, POST, COMMUNICATIONS

29
Life and Language as Reflected by Yiddish Testimony in the Responsa Literature from the Beginning of the Fifteenth to the End of the Seventeenth Century
by Zalman Rubashov, 1929

ZALMAN RUBASHOV (Zalman Shazar, 1889–1974) was born in Mir, Belorussia (today Belarus), and studied Jewish history with Simon Dubnow in St. Petersburg from 1907 to 1910, later attending the universities of Freiburg, Strasbourg, and Berlin. Uniquely, among the authors selected for this volume, he did not pursue a career as a scholar. Rather, his writings—on Jewish history, biblical criticism, and Jewish literature, as well as original prose and verse—accompanied a lifelong career in Zionist politics as a founder of the *Mapai* (Labor) Party, editor of *Davar* (the party's daily Hebrew newspaper), member of the Israeli Knesset, minister of education, and third president of Israel from 1963 to 1973.

As Rubashov explains, he was prompted by Dubnow to "assemble a collection of materials on the history of the Jews in Poland during the seventeenth century," based in part on the responsa literature (the *shayles-utshuves*, rabbinic "questions-and-answers" to issues of Jewish law). The resulting work was published in 1929 in the first volume of YIVO's *Historishe shriftn* and has continued to be cited, both in the Yiddish original and his Hebrew translation of 1971. The main portion of the article consists of 268 verbatim quotes of witness testimonies in Yiddish—often the only records of incidents from daily life and of the spoken language of the period—drawn from the published records of twenty-three rabbinic decisors, each with a brief preface by Rubashov. In addition to explaining his goals and methods for collecting the historical materials found in Jewish court documents, his general introduction—which appears below—offers a brief history of the genre of responsa literature and its differing evolutions in Western and Eastern Europe.[1]

Jewish historiography has long known the treasures of historical and ethnographic materials that are hidden in the old folios of rabbinic responsa. Without having any intention of writing the chronicle of their generation or preserving the traces of their historical situation and lifestyle, the authors of the responsa literature unexpectedly became the faithful collaborators of later historical research. The rabbinical court did not limit itself to the framework of religious life but decided all the related matters of Jewish law, whether in legal details or generalization, regarding either business or family matters, and regarding community life or spiritual and moral matters. And to the great rabbi or yeshiva head whose name was world famous, one turned from near and far for still another judgment in each difficult case. And if all the minutes of the courts had been preserved, we would have today a sure guide to the dim caverns of our past. No one, however, preserved the minutes of the rabbinical trials.

All that remains are the judgments, in which significant rabbinical authorities demonstrate scholarly brilliance and legal innovation. Gradually, the storyline of the actual case that invoked the dispute and demanded adjudication—mired in a sea of fine argument and erudition—was inserted into the brief question, and emphasis was laid on the long, ingenious, scholarly answer. And this answer, written by the eminent rabbi with the great name, rescued for later historical research the actual everyday case that often sheds a bright light on dim areas of scholarly, political, social, and intimate spiritual life. This entire historical material—which is scattered throughout the rich responsa literature and represents a far-flung legislative scholarly correspondence between rabbinic authorities, spread over all the countries of the Jewish dispersion and across centuries—has not to this day been collected, is little studied, and is not even enumerated anywhere precisely. But none of the most serious historians has failed to benefit from these treasures of source material, and from Leopold Zunz to today every faithful researcher has sought in them bricks for his scholarly edifice.

Just as unexpectedly, the authors of the responsa folios also became the faithful guardians of the Jewish vernacular language of their time.

To clarify the true course of events that are at issue in a doubtful case, as is customary in legal proceedings, witnesses would be heard. On that testimony often rested the fate of fortunes and the happiness of families, at times matters of universal importance in religious observance—for example, questions about *yayin-nesech* [whether certain wine is kosher] or *hatarat agunot* [the freeing of married women with missing husbands]. As a result, the authors often based their judgment on a word from the witness. For this purpose, it was especially important to have the *precise text* of what the witness said—indeed, exactly as he said it, not translated and not stylized. In this way, the testimony became a juridical act that most often took place in the presence of the court, given under oath, and precisely, word by word, recorded in the minutes by the court reporter, usually with an indication of the time and place. These testimonies in Yiddish were then incorporated into the Hebrew question or response and conveyed in that way through the centuries on the reliable back of the rabbinical law. When one compares a question that was dealt with in various treatises by rabbis who were located far from one another, both in place and in time, one is amazed at the pedantic precision with which the exact texts of the original testimony were preserved in all places. Often, the transcription varies—the reporter spelled the spoken or written word as it was accepted in his region and in his time—but the word itself and the complete sentence remain the same everywhere.

When one looks closer at these Yiddish testimonies that are spread across the responsa literature, one also notices a certain course of development in the tradition and in the fate of this type of document.

At the start, in the fifteenth century, the home of these testimonies was the old Jewish *kehilot* [communities] in Germany. The *kehilot* were small, the issues local, and the rabbinic jurisdiction absolute, in the beginning. Rabbi Jacob Moelin [1365–1427], Rabbi Israel Isserlin [1390–1460] and

Mahariv Weil [early fifteenth century], Maharam Mintz [fifteenth century], and Rabbi Israel Bruna [1400–1480] cite, usually in parentheses, a sentence or two that a witness said *"b'loshn ashkenaz"* [in the language of Ashkenaz; i.e., Germany], when it is important to them to cite the words of the witness precisely for the matter at hand. These Yiddish sentences are usually very short, without context, and also usually without the name of the witness, where he lived, and when he said it. It became different in the sixteenth century when the center of gravity of the responsa literature shifted to Poland. In Kraków, in Lemberg, in Lublin, and even in the small *kehilot* of the provinces, there were giants of the Torah, leading heads of yeshivas, who were esteemed in distant lands and to whom people sent questions from all over the world. The juridical function of the *beth-din* [rabbinical court] was already much evolved and developed and was based on firm rules and traditions. Already in the responses from the Maharshal [Rabbi Shlomo Luria, 1510–1573], we find the form of the witness document that would remain traditional thereafter: he began with the name of the witness and his father's name, and after that came all that the witness said, word for word, recorded by the court reporter, as well as the day and the month and the time of year, the name of the city, and usually also the names of the judges before whom the testimony was given. At the time of the "last *Geonim*"—Rabbi Joseph Katz [ben Mordecai Gerson Ha-Kohen of Kraków, 1510–1591] (author of *She'erit Yosef*), Rabbi Meir Katz [Ha-Kohen, c. 1579–1642] (father of the "Shach" [Rabbi Shabtai Ha-Kohen]), the Maharam of Lublin [Rabbi Meir ben Gedalia, 1558–1616], Rabbi Joel Sirkis [1561–1640] (author of *Bayit Chadash*), and Rabbi Yehoshua Katz [Falk, 1555–1614] (author of *Pnei Yehoshua*), during which the responsa literature grew enormously—the number of these testimonies increased. Often an entire line of testimony in a matter, appended to the question, would be circulated in the appropriate order among the rabbis and yeshiva heads from whom a judgment was requested. And in the second half of the seventeenth century, after the Chmielnicki years, when Polish rabbis traveled all over the world and settled abroad in faraway *kehilot*, they spread with them the network of the responsa literature, and the testimonies in Yiddish began to flow from every country and region in which Jews lived and spoke Yiddish in every dialect and manner of speaking.

The more that scholarly study of Old Yiddish literature develops, the clearer it becomes that for the study of the *everyday* Yiddish language, as it truly lived in the mouths of the Jewish masses and not in literature, these rabbinic testimonies were not only the most reliable but also perhaps truly the *only* source. Most works of Old Yiddish that have reached us tend toward literariness. The lexicographic literature and the collections of traditionally taught biblical terms in Yiddish, as well as a large portion of the Tanach [Hebrew Bible] translations, were tied to Hebraic sources and are filled with expressions and forms of expression that were never used in daily life. Conversely, the romances and storybooks matured, in a very large measure, together with the German language and with the style of German. . . .

It was not for nothing that Ber Borochov, already in the first years of his philological research, . . . set forth the rule: "If we want to acquire a conception of the everyday Yiddish language of that time, the dominant literature will give us no information and we must depend on the sole documents that remain from that time (by and large the testimonies in the trials in the responsa literature)."[1] To some degree, realizing Borochov's intention is the purpose of our work. . . .

This work also has its own bit of history. Shortly before the World War, at the request of my rebbe, Prof. Sh. Dubnow, I undertook the project of the Jewish Historical-Ethnographic Society in St. Petersburg to assemble a collection of materials on the history of the Jews in Poland in the seventeenth century on the basis of the responsa literature and the homiletical and ethical writings. After the outbreak of the war, the connection between the society and me was broken. But I continued the work, and the treasures of the Jewish community library in Berlin, where I spent the war years, to a significant degree afforded me the possibility of carrying out the work. According to my plan, the work would be divided into separate chapters on economic history, relations between Jews and their neighbors, inner life of the community, everything that has a connection to the Council of the Lands, family life, culture and education, divorce, and customs. At that time, I undertook the testimonies in *Yiddish* only to the extent that they had historical value. I quickly noticed, however, that the historically "worthless" Yiddish testimonies, which would thus not be in the book, also have significant linguistic-historical and bibliographic importance. And I began to transcribe them as well, thereby breaching the earlier plan for the work. Later, it became clear to me that the framework of the book was not at all suitable for this Yiddish collection. To make use of their value for linguistic history, all of the testimonies in Yiddish needed to be gathered together, without regard for their content. To these should also be added the testimonies from non-Polish responsa writings, and at the same time, they should not be limited to the seventeenth century alone but should, as far as possible, also include the Yiddish testimonies from the older responsa literature. But for various reasons I had to delay my work. In the meantime, it happened that I visited cities with large Jewish libraries, and it became possible for me to augment the collection—until the collection grew and, from the publishing standpoint, became too large. Printing the full text of all the testimonies verbatim, as they were transcribed by me, would have required a book of its own; but this would have meant putting off the work still further. In addition, not everything in the testimonies is of equal value, except to a limited number of research specialists. Therefore, I had to choose a middle course for the time being. I transcribed all the passages from testimonies that were known to me up to the end of the seventeenth century, without regard to place or content, and used the excerpts that characterize the style and the language of the document and convey its *historical* content. . . .

At a glance it might seem that the collection of these Yiddish testimonies belongs exclusively to the field of Yiddish linguistic research and is more suited to a philological collection. But the interest that the *language* of the documents holds for the Yiddish linguist does not diminish the value that the *content* of the documents holds for the Jewish cultural historian and the student of Jewish history in general.

The historical researcher will find assembled here new material regarding the old dispute about the everyday language of Jews, both in Germany (in the fifteenth century) and in Poland (in the sixteenth century). He will find important information about the complicated Jewish money- and pawn-businesses in the late Middle Ages, about the difficult fate of the Jewish traveling merchant, about the earliest beginnings of Jewish craftwork, about the course of Jewish migration, and about the fate of those who emigrated abroad, about the neglected situation of the village Jew and about the Jewish traveler on foot and on horseback on faraway roads, about the attitudes of the Jews toward their non-Jewish neighbors and of the non-Jews to Jews. There are also materials here—at times full descriptions, at times traces—of purely historical events, such as wars, massacres, pogroms, libels, and expulsions, in part well known, in part not yet made use of. The student of the Jewish way of life will find in them a wealth of particulars and important details—of the tangled family relationships and moral questions, community issues and general matters, customs and clothing, and the like.

A historical *treatment* of the material cannot yet be undertaken. For that, it would first be necessary to publish the *entire* remaining historical material from the rabbinic literature or at least the responsa literature, from which the *Yiddish* testimonies that are printed here are a small and incidental fragment.

It is worthwhile to mention that the Sephardic rabbis also often tended to include in their responsa writings the speech of the witnesses in the language in which they were spoken—namely, in *Spaniolish* [Ladino] or *Arabic*. . . . For the history of Sephardic Jewry and the Jews in the East in general, entire treasures of historical material still lie locked away in the testimonies, almost completely untouched. . . .

I do not imagine that the collection is complete. Up to the present day, as noted, there is no complete list of the entire responsa literature, and, further, some of the books are so rare today that they cannot be found even in the richest libraries. Not all that is extant did I know how to seek, and not all that I sought did I succeed in finding. It is especially unfortunate that I did not always find the *first* edition of each book and often had to make use of a second, sometimes a third, edition. Sufficient room still remains for the researcher to broaden and enlarge the collection. . . . [followed by transcriptions of the Yiddish testimonies]

Introduction Notes:

1. Z. Rubashov, "Yidishe gviyes-eydes in di shayles-utshuves fun onheyb XV bizn sof XVII yorhundert," *Historishe shriftn fun yivo* I (1929): cols. 115–96 (115–24 quoted; slightly abridged). Reprinted in Hebrew, Zalman Shazar, "Gviot-edut be-lashon yidish be-sheelot u-tshuvot mi-thilat ha-meah ha-hamesh-esre ad sof ha-meah ha-shva-esre," in *Orei dorot, mekharim ve-he-'arot le-toldot yisrael ba-dorot ha-ahronim* (Jerusalem: Mosad Bialik, 1971), 239–319.

Article Notes:

1. B. Borokhov, "A gerus fun far dray hundert yor" [A greeting from three hundred years ago], *Der pinkes* (Vilna: B. A. Kletskin, 1913), 354.

30

The Jewish Postal Service in Tsarist Russia during the Early Nineteenth Century

by Saul Ginsburg, 1932

SAUL GINSBURG (see Selections 19 above and 44 below) alternates between two themes in his studies of Russian Jewish history: frightful persecution, accompanied by forced conformance (as in his articles on the cantonists, pogroms, and Jewish converts), and an energetic Jewish creativity, resilience, and self-reliance (as seen in his articles on the Yiddish press, Haskalah, Jewish magnates and scholars, Jewish bandits, Yiddish folksongs, and Jews who helped to defend Russia against Napoleon).

The latter category includes the article presented below on the phenomenon, virtually unknown in writings by other historians, of the private Jewish postal service that operated in the Jewish Pale of Settlement in tsarist Russia in the early nineteenth century, which had particular importance during the Napoleonic Wars.[1] For the work of a scholar not originally trained as a historian (as was typical of his generation), the article nevertheless demonstrates Ginsburg's historical method, in which he presents (after an opening anecdote) the broader non-Jewish context, the immediate Jewish context, and then his specific topic, usually based on archival sources—to which he gained access after the Russian Revolution.

When one speaks among us Jews about someone's lack of punctuality, one usually jokes about the "Jewish post." There are many sayings and anecdotes about how the Jewish post was always late or making various mistakes. It was said, for example, that a certain merchant once made an appointment with the postman—the wagon driver—to come "Sunday-Monday" to pick up an urgent letter. But the postman came for the letter on Monday, a week later. And when the merchant reproached him, the wagon driver gave him clearly to understand: "You said 'Sunday-Monday.' So, you meant Tuesday-Wednesday. Which meant I should come on Thursday. But that is almost *erev Shabes* [Friday night, Sabbath eve], so I arrived today." In another story, the wagon driver arrived unexpectedly a full week past the agreed-upon time, busy and preoccupied, stumbled over the threshold, and collapsed. Raising himself up, he exclaimed: "This is what comes from hurrying!"

There are other jokes and stories on the same theme. Listening to them it would seem the "Jewish post" that existed years ago in Russia did truly excel in lateness. But such an opinion of it would be false and not agree with reality. In truth, the old-time Jewish post ran faster and more accurately than the government post of the same time, and it often served the interests of the residents much better than the state post office.

For the organization of a postal service to satisfy the needs of the population properly, and especially the business circles, a whole group of certain conditions is necessary. Here we will mention only a few of the most important: 1) the country must have a sufficient number of post offices to make it possible for everyone, wherever they may live, to send and receive letters easily; 2) the cost of postage must be cheap, and paying for it—as well as sending and receiving letters in general—must not be encumbered with unnecessary formalities, difficulties, or loss of time; and 3) everyone who sends a letter must be secure in knowing that it will be sent promptly, as quickly as possible, and that before it is received by the intended recipient no one will have read it.

These chief conditions, on which a normal postal service depends, were always lacking in Russia. The number of post offices here was always very small. At the end of the nineteenth century, for example, all of Russia had only 4,781 post offices, while England had 20,400; Germany 33,220; and the United States 71,260. In connection with this, one must also consider Russia's immense area in comparison with other countries and the distance from one Russian village to another. In 1897 even a central governorate like Moscow had an average of one post office for every 116 villages, and in the governorate closest to Moscow, Tver, just one post office for all 276 villages. For every 10,000 residents, England then had 5 post offices; Germany 6; The United States 10; Switzerland 11; and Russia only seven-tenths of a post office for the same number of residents. In Russia, there were such far-flung places that the mail was delivered only once a year. It is a well-known fact that the report of the death of Tsar Alexander III arrived in some faraway places only a year later.

In addition to the exceptionally unsatisfactory number of post offices, for a long time in Russia there was another circumstance that impeded postal connections. In all civilized countries, it was understood many years before that the government should not be afraid of financing the post, that well-ordered and inexpensive postal relations are extremely important for the development of commercial life. The Russian government, on the contrary, insisted for a very long time that the post ought to create revenue; not only that it must not be financed, but that it must produce more revenue. As a result, the tariff for sending letters was very expensive for a long time. It depended on the distance the letter was to go. Russia once had as many as 700 different postal tariffs. Only in 1839 was a certain simplification put in place that set just 52 tariffs, corresponding to the number of governorates then possessed by Russia. Each governorate had its own tariff, and to send a letter to another governorate incurred a further cost; if the letter traversed several governorates, they would exact another price. And if the letter was addressed abroad, the cost was again different. The postal tariff was not only very expensive, but paying it was also associated with difficulties. Unified postmarks were introduced in Russia only many years later. There were also no mailboxes. When someone wanted to send a letter, he had to bring it into the post office. The official would weigh the letter and set how much one had to pay for it according to the distance and weight. The Russian factories at that time made only coarse, very heavy sorts of paper (thin, so-called "postal paper" began to be manufactured in Russia much later), and this increased still more the postal expenses that were already so very great. One could not send letters every day—there were only set days for this, and the same was true for receiving letters.

Because the post offices were very few in number, to send a letter from a rural area, and even from small towns, one needed to travel a long distance each time to a larger city and plan ahead not to miss the "post day," or else one needed to stay in the city and wait until the post was again accepting letters. And when someone had finally given his letter to the post, often after much effort and loss of time, he could not know even approximately when it would be received by the person to whose name it was addressed. Letters would sit for a while until someone sent them out, and the post generally worked slowly, without hurrying. The roads in Russia were very poor (construction on the highway between St. Petersburg and Warsaw, for example, was begun only in 1840), and this was a great impediment to regular postal relations. Not only would the post be frightfully late, but no one could be sure it would reach the person to whom it was addressed. The old-time postmaster in Gogol's famous comedy *The Inspector*, who loved to peruse the letters that people entrusted to him, was not an exception. The postal officials unceremoniously opened each letter that caught their eye, and when the content seemed interesting, they would keep the letter, enjoying it themselves and giving it to their friends and acquaintances to read. The Russian police of the time were very serious about inspecting postal communications. If you acquaint yourself with the archival documents of the "Third Section" [the secret police], you see clearly that its agents would very often seize everything they considered suspicious and that many investigations and trials were conducted by the police on the basis of such intercepted letters.

For the reasons we have briefly outlined, the Russian government post lagged behind the demands of life for a long time. It was not able to satisfy the needs of commercial relations, which had begun to grow and develop. This was especially noticeable in the western region and the areas near the border with Prussia and Austria (Lithuania, Belorussia, Volyn, etc.), where commerce lay entirely in Jewish hands. The Jewish merchants, many of whom had commercial relations abroad, could not manage with the backward, poorly organized government post. They needed a postal apparatus that would be more ramified, located closer to the populace, and that would work faster and cheaper. This led to the same result we observe in the period of the Middle Ages in Western Europe: because the government did not create any regular postal connections, it was done by each organization itself that was especially interested—the artisan guilds and the universities. . . .

At the end of the eighteenth and beginning of the nineteenth centuries, Russia was in some respects still not entirely removed from the Middle Ages. It is therefore no surprise that the local Jews created a separate post of their own. Besides the merchant class, this was also needed by the *kehilot* [Jewish communal institutions] of various cities that had many common interests and often needed to write to one another and, in addition, by the leading rabbis, to whom people everywhere would turn for rabbinic decisions. Especially interested in the possibility of faster and more secure postal connections were the so-called "deputies of the Jewish people" who were chosen under government order in the time of Alexander I by the *kehilot* and would stay in St. Petersburg during the years 1803 to 1825. Their task was to provide the government the information and clarifications used for developing various laws and orders relating to the Jews. The deputies would send writings and requests to the ministers and government offices, and they tried to effect ameliorations for the Jews. Understandably, their work demanded they be in constant contact with the Jewish *kehilot*. The deputies received from them all the necessary sums of money and information, and they would report to the *kehilot* about everything that was planned in St. Petersburg about the Jews and what must be done to avert this or that decree or achieve a certain improvement in the Jewish situation. For both parties it was very important for the communication to arrive as quickly as possible, and, furthermore, the letters could often not be trusted to the ordinary post on account of their content.

Word of the specifically Jewish post already reaches us from the very beginning of the nineteenth century. It was organized to be very practical and expedient. It had its own routes, which connected various regions and very often reduced the usual travel distance between them. The tens of Jewish taverns served as post offices. The letters would be transported by the wagon drivers, and in extraordinary cases, where special speed was needed—by special persons. The government post would use the ordinary broad country road. The Jewish post would, besides that, also use secondary pathways, and in this manner the distance between various points would be greatly reduced. In spring and fall, when the rains made the roads impassable, the Jewish post would creep along, where the non-Jewish post was unable to move from the spot.

There were no formalities or difficulties to be dealt with. Before me lies an entire collection of early letters that were sent through the Jewish post from various Jewish cities and towns. It is simply amazing how everything was done in those years. Envelopes were as yet unknown; sealing wax was not available everywhere, so it was seldom used to seal a letter. Usually, one would just fold them and, on the outer blank page, write to where and for whom the letter was intended. For example [in Hebrew]: "To the well-known, eminent Mr. Yakov Katzenelson in Bobruisk"; or, "To my learned friend, Mr. Yitshak Moshe Baksht in Berdichev"—inscriptions taken from old letters in my possession. The exact address was seldom used, but this did not impede the letter from coming precisely to whom it was intended. Stating explicitly the street and house was altogether unnecessary because the Jewish "postman" in Bobruisk did not need to be told where Yakov Katzenelson lived, and the one in Berdichev knew for himself the address of Yitshak Moshe Baksht. Often, a letter was marked: "S"T" with a certain number. This meant that the letter had not been paid for, and on receiving it the addressee should pay *Skhar-tirkhe* ("compensation for the trouble") in the amount of so many kopeks. Almost always, a letter was marked: "BHDR"G"; unabbreviated, this means, *B'herem d'rabenu Gershom* [under the prohibition of Rabbi Gershom]—a reference to the precept established by the famous Rabbi Gershom of Mainz more than 900 years ago that one must not read another's letter. As a Talmudic expert, Rabbi Gershom was esteemed so highly that he received the title: "Light of the Diaspora." And this reference to the decision of the famous rabbi was sufficient in those times for outsiders not to glance at the letter on the way.

Because the Jewish post was organized very practically and simply, it was able to function very precisely and quickly. In every instance, it worked much faster than the other communications of the time. We have a most interesting example of how the Jewish post would overtake them. The matter is related to the very start of Napoleon I's war with Russia, in 1812. As is known, the French military began to cross the river Nieman (Memel) and enter Russia near the village of Panemon [today Aukštoji Panemunė, Lithuania]—on the 11th of June [Old Style], nine o'clock in the evening. The nearest commander of the Russian corps, General Baggovut, received the first news of it on June 12 at noon, and he immediately sent a report by special courier to the chief commander of the Russian army in Vilna [Vilnius]. A report about Napoleon's crossing the Nieman was also sent to Vilna to the Russian interior minister by the Kovno [Kaunas] police chief, Bistrom. The interior minister received Bistrom's message during the night of June 12 to 13. But Baggovut's report to the chief commander in the same city of Vilna only arrived much later—on the morning of June 13. As the Russian military historian N. Polikarpov indicated, this was explained by the fact that the Kovno police chief used the *Jewish post*, which very quickly dispatched his report to Vilna and overtook the courier whom General Baggovut also sent with the same information.[1]

Overall, the Jewish post was very useful to the Russian government during the war with Napoleon in 1812. As is known, the Jews in Lithuania and Prussia displayed much loyalty to Russia. Jews were still not taken to be soldiers at that time in Russia; as a result, they were able to assist the Russian army chiefly by collecting and sending information about French military units, their movements, plans, etc. In this regard, the Russian military leadership owed much to the Jewish population, and indeed strongly involved in this was the Jewish post, which would quickly supply the necessary information. During the first period of the war, which took place in Lithuania and Belorussia, the secret reports of the Russian commanders were full of information and messages from Jews, who were often noted in them by name. Similarly, these were often noted simply as "Jewish information." For example, in General Ignatov's secret report to Duke Bagration of July 18, 1812, we read: "According to Jewish information that arrived from Shklov [today Škloŭ, Belarus], all hostile forces are assembled between Shklov and Bikhov [today Bychaŭ, Belarus], no French are farther away than Shklov, and under Marshal Davout's command there are 120,000 men." Such anonymous "Jewish information," without personal names—mostly indicates those items of news that would arrive from *kehila* institutions and were sent by way of the Jewish post. Y. Sanglen, who was the commander of the Russian military police in 1812, writes in his memoirs about the contacts he had with the *kehila* institutions at that time, and he bears witness to the speed with which the Jewish post worked. Thus, for example, Jews were the first to inform him in Vilna about the pending arrival of Napoleon's delegate Narbonne; they were also the first to send [Sanglen] Napoleon's proclamation to the army.[2] We are informed not only by Russian military figures about the important role that the Jewish post played in 1812. The same is also stated, for example, by the French officer Auguste de Sayve, who participated in the Franco-Russian War. "The Jewish post, this secret contact," he writes in his memoirs, "was loyally devoted to Russia, and it demonstrated an extraordinary activity."[3]

It may well be that in the course of Alexander I's reign the government was tolerant and did not persecute the Jewish post because they remembered the help they received from it during the war with France. It changed in the time of Tsar Nicholas I. The attitude of the government toward the Jewish post became hostile and permeated with suspicion: first, it reduced the income from the government post; and second, seeing that Jews would mostly not trust their letters to the ordinary post, it must mean that they indeed had something to hide from the government! At the end of 1827, Nicholas issued an order to be strictly observed that Jews should use the government post and not make use of any other connections. In Shklov, where Jews had significant commercial relations abroad, investigations were undertaken into letters that were sent from there without using the ordinary means. But the investigations, which were also conducted in other cities, discovered nothing. It was difficult to combat a secret postal organization that satisfied a certain demand of life. With time, still another ground arose that greatly increased suspicion against the Jewish post: The Polish nobles in the western regions would joke about it, giving it the name "Pantofle-Post," but nevertheless they would also often use it to send and receive letters. As a result, the government began to look especially askance at it after the Polish uprising of 1831. They suspected that the nobles corresponded in this secret manner with the Polish revolutionaries and emigrants who took refuge abroad. In the government archives of that time, we find a series of secret investigations into Poles who sent their correspondence by way of Jews.[4]

In November 1837, Nicholas I received word that in the Volyn Governorate the secret post was especially highly developed, and he ordered the strictest measures against it. The "Third Section" inquired of the local police director, Colonel Bek, who replied that in Volyn "there is a secret Jewish post in every city that works extraordinarily fast, so that the Jews find out before the respectable public about all the news from St. Petersburg and what is going on in the ministerial offices." According to his report, letters were sent secretly by Jews both within the country and to recipients abroad through the areas in Volyn that were near the border. The chief of the "Third Section," Count Benckendorff, consulted with the post minister, Duke Golitsyn. The latter replied that, in his opinion, the border customhouses and the police should be sure to conduct the fight against Jewish postal relations; further, the more the Jews would be forced to use the government post, the more the police would be able to control the content of the Jewish letters. The finance minister issued an order to the customhouses in the Volyn Governorate to combat letter smuggling; in addition, the entire matter was conveyed to the Kiev governor-general so that he would take care of it.

They were not satisfied with this. Benckendorff and Golitsyn agreed on this sort of ingenious idea: in November 1837, Golitsyn ordered that *all* Jewish letters that arrived or were sent from the post in Zhitomir [today Zhytomyr, Ukraine] were to be forwarded to the post in Radzivilov [today Radyvyliv, Ukraine] and from there, together with the local Jewish letters, be transported to the St. Petersburg post. Here, they would all be translated into Russian and sent to the post minister, Golitsyn. The two government figures hoped by their action to discover a mass of hidden Jewish "secrets," but in this they deceived themselves. The order was in effect for fifteen months, and for the entire time, in all the Jewish letters that were sent from Zhitomir and Radzivilov to St. Petersburg for inspection, nothing suspicious was discovered. As Golitsyn himself wrote on April 5, 1839, to

Benckendorff, the matter only "caused a great delay in the post. For example, Berdichev is located only 47 versts [1 verst = 1.1 km] from Zhitomir; but Jewish letters arrive from Zhitomir in Berdichev not sooner than *twenty-five* days later. This," the post minister pointed out, "led to a situation in which the Jews almost completely ceased writing to each other through the government post." As a result, Benckendorff and Golitsyn jointly decided in April 1839 to repeal their ill-conceived order. The police had no greater luck: as the Kiev governor-general Bibikov reported, in the Druzhkopol [today Zhuravnyky, Ukraine] customhouse, among a transport of leather that was bound for Galicia, a sack with sixteen Jewish and three Polish letters was discovered, but the letters had no suspicious content. . . .

In 1877, the interior minister, in accordance with a request of the Vilna governor-general Albedinsky, decided to send to the Perm Governorate two Vilna Jews (Avrom Tiomim and Shmuel Shapiro) who were suspected of conducting the secret Jewish post in Vilna. It was possible that the two Jews would carry letters on occasion, but the suspicion against them was unjustified because no secret Jewish post organization then still existed. As we saw, it arose at a time when the government post was still not able to satisfy the needs of the population. The more the government post developed, however, the less the Jewish commercial class needed their own postal organization; it became unnecessary and died a natural death. . . .

Introduction Notes:

1. Shoyl Ginzburg, "Iden hoben gehat an eygene post in amoligen rusland" [Jews had their own post in old-time Russia], *Forverts* (New York, May 29, 1932), sec. 2, p. 1; reprinted as "Di amolige idishe post" in Shoyl Ginzburg, *Historishe verk*, vol. 1: Yidishe layden in tsarishen rusland [Jewish suffering in tsarist Russia] (New York: Shoyl Ginzburg 70-yohriger yubiley komitet, 1937), 215–28 (quoted here; slightly abridged).

Article Notes:

1. N. Polikarpov, "Ocherki Otechestvennoĭ Voĭny" [Essays on the Patriotic War], *Novaiā Zhizn'* [A new life] X (1911): 159–66.

2. "Zapiski Ia. I. de-Sanglena" [Notes of Y. I. de-Sanglen], *Russkaiā Starina* [Russian antiquity] III (1883): 543.

3. Auguste de Sayve, *Souvenirs de Pologne et scènes militaires de la campagne 1812*, 2nd ed. (Paris: P. Dufart, 1834), 250.

4. Archive of the headquarters of the police corps, no. 26. Archive of the "Third Section," 1st Expedition, 1837, no. 221; 3rd Expedition, 1877, no. 227.

31

The First Yiddish Newspaper in the Russian Empire, *Kol mevaser*, and Its Time, 1862–72

by Israel Zinberg, 1913

ISRAEL ZINBERG (see Selection 23 above) preceded his comprehensive work on the history of Jewish literature with individual studies of episodes in the history of Jewish writing and publishing. Commencing in 1900, these appeared in the leading Russian-language Jewish journals and the Russian Jewish encyclopedia. Although many addressed topics on Yiddish literature and the Yiddish press, they lacked a suitable venue for publication in Yiddish. In 1912, with the founding of the highly regarded Yiddish journal *Di yudishe velt* (The Jewish world), of which he was also an editor, Zinberg gained the ability to publish his literary-historical research in Yiddish. This journal, which was founded in St. Petersburg (and relocated to Vilna in 1913), published new works by leading contemporary Yiddish-language authors of scholarly writing (including Ginsburg, Niger, Weinreich, and Zinberg) and literature (including Mendele, Perets, Sholem Aleichem, Sholem Asch, and Dovid Bergelson).

Zinberg's first and most substantial article in *Di yudishe velt*—serialized in the first four issues of the new journal—was a study of the first Yiddish newspaper in the Russian Empire, *Kol mevaser* (Voice of the herald, or Messenger of good tidings), established in Odessa in 1862. Presented below are excerpts that describe the context and events that led to the creation of *Kol mevaser* and its immediate success.[1]

Zinberg uses the article to provide ammunition from the 1860s for the language debate of his own time. In the period between the Russian revolutions of 1905 and 1917, the role, if any, that Yiddish should play in Jewish education was the most contentious issue before the Society for the Promotion of Enlightenment Among the Jews, the umbrella organization of Jews in the Russian Empire. The immediate context of his article is that the society had traditionally promoted Russification over Jewish nationalism in the schools it supported. The internal conflicts of the society mirrored the struggle in Russian society between supporters of autocracy and democratization.

Following near-fistfights over the language issue at the meetings of 1905 and 1906 (at which Zinberg was a delegate), the society decided, at first tentatively, in April 1911 that Yiddish "has a place both as a language of instruction and as a subject for study." During the period when this article by Zinberg was serialized (from January to April 1913), preparations were being made for the election of delegates to the society's December 1913 meeting, at which it resolved unequivocally that Yiddish would be the principal language of instruction in the Jewish schools supported by the society.

Quietly and unnoticed, last year the Yiddish press in Russia passed the second jubilee of its existence. October 11 marked fifty years since Aleksander Zederbaum in Odessa published the first issue of the weekly *Kol mevaser* as a "Jewish German supplement" to *Ha-Melitz* [The Advocate, a pioneering Hebrew newspaper]. This date signifies an entire epoch not only in the developmental history of the Yiddish press but also of Yiddish language and literature.

The Yiddish language was a stepchild among the Jewish intelligentsia of the Haskalah period, a stepchild that was regarded with hatred and disrespect. A noteworthy page in the history of Yiddish culture is occupied by this attitude of the Jewish intelligentsia toward the daily language of their own people, but, to get more quickly to my chief point, I will not dwell overly on that detail.[1] I will only mention that their haughty disrespect and powerful hatred of *Zhargon* [Yiddish] was inherited from the Berlin Haskalah. Among the first Jewish "enlighteners" in Prussia, the so-called "students of Mendelssohn," Yiddish—in which they saw nothing more than a corrupted and impure German—became the symbol of the darkness of exile, of the servile life. And the more they aspired to European culture, to a new, free life, the stronger their wish to banish Yiddish, which they inherited from the isolated and hated ghetto, and to turn to the language of their cultural environment. In the eyes of the Jewish members of the Enlightenment, the ghetto language became a sort of yellow badge that their grandfathers wore in the Middle Ages. It is therefore no surprise that we encounter hatred of Yiddish among nearly all the best progressive representatives of the German Jews from the time of Mendelssohn to Graetz and Steinschneider.

Along with Enlightenment ideas, our Russian *maskilim* [adherents of the Haskalah, the Jewish Enlightenment] also adopted from the German *maskilim* their hatred and disrespect for Yiddish. For the German *maskilim*, the matter was entirely plain and simple: the corrupted German should be exchanged for pure literary German, the language of the homeland. But among the Russian and Polish *maskilim*, the language question was a bit more tangled: German was not after all the national language in Warsaw, nor in Vilna or Berdichev. But this did not matter at all to our *maskilim*, who were, fundamentally, no less detached from real life than their opponents, the "obscurantists," the Orthodox. In any case, they contended that the odious Yiddish, which made us the object of jokes and laughter among the peoples of the world, must exit the stage and be replaced by a respectable language: it made no difference whether by German, or perhaps Russian or Polish. . . .

But life is much stronger than all types of doctrines and theoretical ingenuities. Although the *maskilim* in Russia, from Tuvia Feder and Yitzhak Ber Levinzon to Gordon and Smolenskin, waged war against "the language of the servants"—many of these *maskilim* literati themselves, against their will, nevertheless aided the development of the Yiddish language and its literature. Each of the *maskilim*, who did not want to block out reality and sincerely tried to benefit their people, eventually needed to rely on the help of the folk language in their struggle for enlightenment and improvement. More than anything, they were forced to do so by Hasidism, against which the *maskilim* conducted the bitterest fight. Hasidism, as a genuine folk movement, from the beginning on, used the language of the masses as the best means of agitation and struggle. As a result, one of the *maskilim* of that generation, Aleksander Zederbaum, recounted with great regret: "For a while, Hasidism began to use this means to spread among the people fanatical writings, miracles, and holy men, one lie greater than another. The printers made an entire speculation from it, printing as many as 80,000 copies of such rags on blotting paper, and the masses bought it cheaply like warm fruit cake. . ."[2] [ellipsis in original]

This folk literature created a large reading public, especially among women; and in order to fight against the influence of the Hasidic "fantastic writings," the *maskilim* had no other choice than to apply their own weapon, which the Hasidim had used—the folk language, plain *Zhargon*.

"In many cities of our country," recounts a writer [Joachim Tarnopol] from that period,[3] such as, for example, Vilna, Odessa, Mohilev, Berdichev, etc., that have whole groups of educated Jews, in these enlightened circles there exists a different type of literary undertaking: people pass the time in reading aloud stories, dramatic scenes, entire brochures with poetry or prose, in plain Polish Jewish *Zhargon*. And these booklets, which are read before the whole assembled audience, ridicule in a very pointed manner many foolish customs, obsolete superstitions, and false Hasidic "views."

Most interesting, however, is that this *maskilic* Yiddish literature remained a mostly handwritten literature. Printing their works in ordinary Yiddish, publicly emerging as an author of Yiddish books—the *maskilim* of the time could not bring themselves to do. . . .

It is altogether no wonder that the majority of the writers about whom Tarnopol wrote did not publish their Yiddish works, even when they were certain these works would have great success. Yitzhak Ber Levinzon's *Hefker-velt* [The world of chaos] was a great success with the public, but it was distributed only in manuscript and as a result was published fifty years later [in 1878]. Dr. [Shlomo] Ettinger's theater piece *Serkele* [the name of the protagonist, ca. 1839] was also not published in the author's lifetime, and, only after his death, an unknown person secretly, without permission from his heirs, published Ettinger's works in Prussia—not from the genuine original, but from a copy filled with mistakes. . . .

It is therefore no surprise that, during the early 1860s, on account of the great changes that were then taking place in Russia, a specifically Jewish press was created in Russia, which first published newspapers in Hebrew (*Ha-Melitz*, *Ha-Karmel* [Mount Carmel], *Ha-Tsefirah* [The Morning/Dawn]) and in Russian (*Razsvet* [Dawn], *Sion* [Zion]), but not in ordinary Yiddish.

The first ten years of Alexander II's reign saw a complete revolution, not only in Russian but also in Jewish life in Russia. The great reforms that were introduced at that time in Russia, particularly the freeing of the peasants, which led to a true revolution in the economic life of the country, the railroad network that began to develop in Russia in the 1860s—all of these brought forth enormous changes in both the economic and spiritual life of the Jewish Pale of Settlement. In these uninvited circumstances, the Jew could no longer lead his former isolated life. Many old life-springs suddenly ran dry, and in their place brand-new ones were created; the Jew sensed how much he was bound by various economic threads to the Christian environment, and his interest in knowing what was happening in the outer world began to grow ever greater. In the Jew of the Pale, all these circumstances increased still more the desire to read a newspaper—a desire that was first awakened in him by the great Crimean War [1853–56]. Soon after the war, when it was still difficult to obtain permission for a Jewish newspaper in Russia, the Hebrew *Ha-Magid* [The Preacher], which was published in the Prussian town of Lyck near the Russian border, enjoyed a certain popularity among Russian Jews. In 1858, Joseph [Osip] Rabinovich [1817–1869] and Joachim Tarnopol sent a request for permission to publish a weekly Jewish newspaper in Odessa in Russian: *Razsvet*. Although their request was strongly supported by the famous [Nikolai] Pirogov, who was then the educational curator of the Odessa district, Rabinovich and Tarnopol were not at first permitted to publish a newspaper in Russian but in "Hebrew or in the Jewish German language used by the Russian Jews."

But Rabinovich and Tarnopol wanted nothing less than a Russian newspaper through which they could converse with Russian society; as a result, they had no intention of using the permission they received.[4] It was therefore handed over for use by another of the Odessa literati—Aleksander Zederbaum.

This man, with whom the history of the Yiddish-Hebrew press in Russia is so closely connected, was a remarkable phenomenon: a man with scarcely any education, half-middleman, half-*shtadlan* of the old-fashioned sort [intercessor/lobbyist with the government on behalf of the Jews], and a great boaster as well. And this little-cultured and not especially sympathetic communal leader was endowed with an iron, indefatigable energy, and in him burned a constant, fervent spark of love and devotion to the Jewish people and their interests. . . .

There are many legends about how Zederbaum would beat a path to the door of *nachalstvo* [the authorities] with his *khodatzystves* [intercessions]. People even recounted how, by accident, he became a person with strong connections to the authorities: he once saved the life of a Christian girl who nearly drowned, and by chance the girl was the daughter of an eminent official. As the story goes, inasmuch as Rabinovich and Tarnopol had no desire to use the permission to publish a newspaper in Hebrew or Yiddish, Zederbaum requested that this permission be transferred to him. The late Elazar Shulman [1837–1904] recounted, in the name of Zederbaum himself, that at first Zederbaum was a bit ashamed to publish a newspaper in ordinary Yiddish, so he indeed requested that he be permitted to publish a newspaper in Hebrew and in German with Yiddish letters.[5] With the influence of Pirogov, Zederbaum received this permission, and on September 29, 1860, the first issue of *Ha-Melitz* appeared—"a central organ for Jewish matters in the Hebrew and German language."

For the first two years, *Ha-Melitz* did indeed appear in both languages, i.e., between the Hebrew articles, German ones in Yiddish letters also appeared from time to time.[6] The practical Zederbaum soon realized, however, that the German articles on the page were truly a wasted effort; no one needed them, and no one read them. Zederbaum then arrived at the idea of putting aside his embarrassment and, in place of German articles, tried publishing a supplement to *Ha-Melitz* in ordinary Yiddish. With the forty-second issue of *Ha-Melitz* in 1862, Zederbaum published a large notice on four full pages in Yiddish, in which he announced the news that he intended, together with *Ha-Melitz*, to publish a separate newspaper, *Kol mevaser*, "in ordinary Yiddish so that the ordinary public and even women would know what takes place in the world."

But Zederbaum considered it necessary to justify himself at once to the opponents of Yiddish. "We know very well that present-day supporters of the Enlightenment shout that people should be broken of the habit of speaking Yiddish and be made accustomed to speaking the language of the country; perhaps they are not entirely correct, because in the country where one lives, one should understand the language; but in exactly what language should one speak with the ordinary public for them to learn what is necessary for each person, if they understand absolutely nothing but Yiddish."

On October 11, 1862, the first issue of *Kol mevaser* appeared, as a supplement to *Ha-Melitz* in . . . a truly folksy language, simple, ordinary, as a man speaks to his neighbor, that any uncultured woman could understand. Several years later, Zederbaum recounted how difficult it was for him to achieve in the beginning:

"The most difficult problem," Zederbaum wrote in 1870, "is that *Zhargon* itself consists of several *Zhargonish* dialects that conflict with each other and are almost unintelligible to each other: Lithuania, Volyn, Ukraine,

Podolia, Poland, New-Russia, and Bessarabia each have another pronunciation, another construction, some other words and expressions taken from the peoples under whom they live—try writing a newspaper today that will be accepted by everyone! In addition, *Zhargon* has, after all, no grammar and no orthography; the speculators in pulp fiction have corrupted the language and the people's taste; and, further, every writer creates a new form of spelling from scratch; and to bring all of this under one system was more difficult than running a European newspaper."

The "one system" under which Zederbaum for the first time "brought" his newspaper was the Volyn pronunciation, and the way each word was pronounced there is how it was also spelled in *Kol mevaser*. Each issue of *Kol mevaser* would carry foreign and domestic news as well as correspondence from the Jewish Pale of Settlement. From time to time there would also appear political reports and biographies of great figures, but more often—popular scholarly articles about Jewish history, pedagogy, and education, and especially about natural science, which then, in the 1860s, was very much in fashion. Weakest, in the earlier period, was the section for fine literature: nearly all the poems and stories that were printed there (mostly translations from German) had no literary value. In content, *Kol mevaser* was generally similar to its older brother, *Ha-Melitz*, during the earlier period. But, nevertheless, from the first issues on, something was noticeable in *Kol mevaser* that was not noticeable at all in the Hebrew newspapers: that is the spirit of true folksiness, the closeness and connection with the broad social classes of the people. . . .

Every reader, and more often—every female reader, came with her advice about what should be written in her newspaper. A prosperous housewife found it necessary for *Kol mevaser* to print still more articles about things that would be of interest to housewives and indeed took occasion to address the question of how to conduct oneself while baking *challah* [the Sabbath bread] for the *challah* to turn out well.

Zederbaum, with his practical view, soon observed that he was proceeding in the right direction, even though some *maskilim* took great offense at his publishing a newspaper in Yiddish. Already a few months later, Zederbaum indicated how popular and beloved his newspaper was among the broad social classes of the people. . . .

"Only now," declared Zederbaum, "do we see according to the subscribers that the public is satisfied with us. We ourselves are also convinced, and others have told us, how ordinary people and boors, old folks and women, sit in the marketplace or Friday evening at home, or wagon drivers, ignoramuses, artisans in taverns, people who have no other language they can read or understand, and they read *Kol mevaser* with such hunger and rapt attention, enjoying everything they read."[7]

Interest in *Kol mevaser* increased still more when, in place of translated, largely talentless and childish stories, original sketches, scenes, and stories of Jewish life began to appear. In *Kol mevaser* at the end of 1864, the first work by Mendele Moykher Sforim [S.Y. Abramovitsh (1835–1917)], *Dos kleyne mentshele* [The Little Man], began to appear and was enthusiastically received by the reading public. A great impression was made by the famous work of Yitzkhok Yoel Linetzky [1839–1915], *Dos poylishe yingl* [The Polish Lad, 1867].[8] The folksy language and gentle good-natured humor made the work extraordinarily beloved and popular among the public, and the young Linetsky suddenly became widely known. . . .

To acquaint the reader with the attitude of *Kol mevaser* to the *Zhargon*-question, we must first pause to mention an original figure who is entirely unknown to the present public. This is Yehoshua Lifshitz from Berdichev. He was a person with a certain European education; naturally, from the Ashkenazi tradition; in the German style, as was the custom among the *maskilim* of his generation. Like many other *maskilic* literati, Lifshitz also wrote popular articles about natural science in the 1860s. But in one respect Lifshitz was an exception among the majority of his *maskilic* colleagues: this is in regard to *Zhargon*. And most remarkable is that Lifshitz did not approach the *Zhargon* question with just purely practical calculations; he considered the folk language not only a comfortable and useful means of spreading enlightenment—he saw in it also significant national-cultural value. Not altogether clearly, watered down with *maskilic* phrases of the time, Lifshitz nevertheless dared already at that time to take a stand for the idea that *Zhargon*, so hated by the *maskilim*, was the basis on which Jews could and should construct their own national literature.[9] . . .

As soon as *Kol mevaser* began to appear, Lifshitz used the opportunity to express strongly and clearly his opinion about the *Zhargon*-question in a long article, "*Di fir klasn*" [The four types].[10] Without doubt, this article has significant historical value, and for the present-day reader it will be a bit surprising that, as we will show, many of the complaints and arguments that the fighters for the Yiddish language use today were already very clearly set forth by this old, long-deceased Lifshitz.

First of all, Lifshitz considers the Jewish folk language not at all a *zhargon* but an "entirely separate language"—"our mother tongue." . . . He complains: "Everyone says it is corrupted. I must admit that I absolutely cannot understand for what reason people could say that a language in which so many thousands of people, an entire nation, live and go about their business is corrupted. 'Corrupted' is properly said of something that was better and became worse. But how does it follow that other languages were better from the very start? Were they given, then, as if at Sinai? They arose, just like our language, from various other languages, but why are they not called corrupted?" . . .

The Society for the Promotion of Enlightenment Among the Jews [founded in 1863 to support modernization of the Jews in tsarist Russia] turned to Zederbaum with the request that in *Kol mevaser* he should increasingly "purify it of *Zhargon*" and in that way gradually "convert it into a simple German language." . . . However, the practical Zederbaum thanked them for the advice and politely gave the St. Petersburg society to understand that the matter was not at all as simple as it appeared. "This is," Zederbaum replied, "a great mistake . . . a language that is used by nearly two million Jews in Russia, apart from the nearby countries . . . [ellipses in original] such a language, no matter how corrupted it may be, people could not be persuaded to abandon even in a hundred years." . . .

This constant emphasizing of the importance of Yiddish aroused still more *maskilim* against *Kol mevaser*. It should also be remembered that, by the end of the 1860s in certain circles of the Jewish intelligentsia, the purely assimilationist tendency had become especially strong. They, this intelligentsia, were already agitating not only for the Russian language but indeed for complete Russification, for becoming "Russians of the Mosaic faith."

"It is known by all," declared the society in its report for the year 1866, "and no one doubts the solid historical truth that Jews are obligated to merge with the population of the country where they live and differ externally only in their faith."[11] . . .

[In subsequent paragraphs, Zinberg relates that *maskilim* opposed to Yiddish then complained to the government that the permission given to publish a Jewish newspaper only allowed *Ha-Melitz* to be "half Hebrew and half Jewish German," not Yiddish—and that reinforcing the use of Yiddish would frustrate the government's goal of Russifying the Jews.]

Zederbaum left at once for St. Petersburg, and, as he himself recounted, hastened to convince the "higher officials and intelligentsia" that he,

Zederbaum himself, also knew "how vitally necessary it was for the country and for the Jews themselves that they become accustomed to speaking the language of the country"—that he himself was also an opponent of Yiddish—but he was no longer convinced "that any means other than Yiddish itself would be able to discredit itself and show Jews how it harmed them at every step," and indeed, that he was supposedly publishing *Kol mevaser* for that purpose alone. And along the way, Zederbaum pointed out the error of his opponents who wanted to ban *Kol mevaser*. Zederbaum considered those who held that view to be "witless" because they assume, he said, "by the fact of how quickly they adopted Russian as a mother tongue, that one could also teach a new language to an entire nation, that one only needed to use some stricter measures, and Yiddish would be suppressed if no newspapers in it were allowed to appear."

It was not difficult for Zederbaum to show that such measures could only cause harm. In the end, the energetic Zederbaum accomplished perhaps still more than he expected. First, the authorities at the interior ministry permitted—"exceptionally," as Zederbaum recounted—*Kol mevaser* to appear as an independent newspaper entirely separate from *Ha-Melitz*; and second, he was also permitted to publish a Jewish newspaper in Russian under the name *Posrednik* [Middleman/Intermediary].

In this way, in 1869, issue number 29 of *Kol mevaser* appeared, no longer as "a supplement to *Ha-Melitz* in the Jewish German language" but as an independent "Jewish people's newspaper in their everyday language." . . .

Introduction Notes:

1. Y. Tsinberg, "Der 'kol mevaser' un zayn tsayt," *Di yudishe velt* 2 (Vilna), no. 1 (January 1913): 89–98; no. 2 (February 1913): 83–90; no. 3 (March 1913): 72–80; no. 4 (April 1913): 74–81 (quoted; greatly abridged); all four installments reprinted, without footnotes, in Y. Tsinberg, *Kultur-historishe shtudyes* (New York: Morris S. Sklarsky, 1949), 159–89.

Article Notes:

1. For further details, see S. L. Tsinberg, "Zhargonnaya Literatura i ee Chitateli" [Yiddish literature and its readers], *Knizhki "Voskhoda"* ["Dawn" Booklets, St. Petersburg] no. 3 (March 1903): 45–71; no. 4 (April 1903): 35–55.

2. *Kol mevaser* 22 (1869): 147.

3. Joachim (Hayyim) Tarnopol, in his work: *Opyt sovremennoi i Osmotritel'noi reformy v oblasti iudaizma v Rossii: razmyshleniia o Vnytrennem i vneshnem byte russkikh evreev* [The

experience of modern and prudent reform in the field of Judaism in Russia: Reflections on the internal and external life of Russian Jews] (Odessa: L. Nitche, 1868), 86–87.

4. Later, Rabinovich and Tarnopol were able to obtain permission for a Russian newspaper.

5. See E. Shulman, "Etlekhe verter iber di zhargon-literatur" [A few words about Yiddish literature], *Der yud* [The Jew] 18 (Kraków, May 3, 1900): 15–16.

6. The author of the articles was the contributor to *Ha-Melitz*, Dr. Aharon Goldenblum [Zederbaum's son-in-law], who died recently in St. Petersburg.

7. *Kol mevaser* 1, no. 24.

8. The first chapters were printed under the title "A Polish Lad." Linetzky signed himself with a pseudonym: Eli Katzin Ha-Tzahakali.

9. It is worthwhile to note the following characteristic detail: Lifschitz had a certain dislike of the new Hebrew literature of that time; he also used rather sharp language against it in the introduction to his Yiddish–Russian dictionary.

10. *Kol mevaser* 1, no. 21.

11. Prilozhenye K *Gakarmeliu* [Appendix to *Ha-Karmel*] 2 (Vilna, 1868).

32

The Attitude toward Yiddish of the Russian Authorities in Vilna during the 1860s: On the History of Jewish Bookselling in Vilna

by Pinchas Kon, 1929

PINCHAS KON (?–1941) arrived in 1919 in Vilna (today Vilnius, Lithuania), where he graduated from the law faculty of the university—which is all that appears to be known of his early years. By occupation, he was a lawyer, and he became prominent as a leader of the Vilna Jewish community. During the Nazi occupation of Vilna, he was forced to serve as a member of the first *Judenrat* and, with other members, was soon murdered by the Nazis. His life and career have yet to receive appropriate attention.

By avocation, Kon was a student of Vilna's Jewish history, and he would search the municipal archives for relevant documents. In contrast to other Yiddish historians, he became almost exclusively a "documentary historian" whose many articles present the information to be gleaned from each newly discovered official record (and in contrast to Dubnow, his documents come almost entirely from official sources rather than private parties). His writings were broadly welcomed by the Yiddish historical enterprise, with its notable lack of official Jewish archives. Although his scope of endeavor was modest, his articles were published as widely in Yiddish journals as those of any Yiddish historian and were often cited by others.

Many of Kon's topics were single-fact discoveries, such as the birthdate of a notable Jew or the founding date of a Jewish institution or building. Others uncovered the many (often unsuccessful) attempts to obtain government permission to open a Jewish school, printing house, or other business. In each, he would sketch the historical context of the document, quote relevant portions, and explain the larger consequences. Such is the case with the article below, which uncovers—in a request to open a Jewish bookstore in Vilna in 1865—the tsarist government's language policy of the time regarding the Jews.[1]

The beginning of the nineteenth century is a period of ascent in the history of the Yiddish book. The Yiddish book—or more correctly, Yiddish *booklet*—which was already a mass-produced article, was now receiving a more widespread distribution. The appearance of Isaac Meir Dik [well-known novelist, 1807–1893] gave rise, certainly, to a continually growing circle of Yiddish readers. The Yiddish booklet gained new, wide-ranging masses of readers. The editions of Yiddish books in Vilna, for example, far exceeded the similar editions in all other languages of Vilna. This increase in consumption naturally called for a greater volume of business for Yiddish book sales.

In Vilna, the center of Jewish book production, there were a few young *maskilim* [adherents of the Haskalah, the Jewish Enlightenment] who wanted to open new bookstores, seeing in Yiddish bookselling a source of income. One of them was a certain Rafael ben Feivish Falk.

At that time, obtaining permission for such a business in Vilna was not an easy matter. After the Polish Uprising in 1863, the drive for Russification here intensified, and permission to open a bookstore had to be obtained from the governor, who in such cases would conduct an entire *shayle-utshuve* [rabbinic "question-and-answer" court proceeding].

The abovementioned Falk submitted his request in mid-1865. The governor, who did not want to decide for himself such a "difficult" matter as giving permission for a Jew to conduct a business in books and booklets, applied to the director of the Vilna Educational Region, I. Kornilov, to inquire whether there was any obstacle on his part.

This application gave the director the opportunity for an extended response, in which he discussed thoroughly the Jewish cultural problem and particularly the government's attitude toward the development of literature in the Yiddish language. For us, his conclusions are of special historical interest. Kornilov wrote:

> At the present time, the intent of the government regarding the Jewish population of the western region is that, with the help of enlightenment, the former separateness of this population will be weakened, and they will be drawn closer to the Russian people. For this purpose, Russian elementary schools are being created for Jews in the cities and towns, the Russian language is being introduced in all Jewish educational institutions, means are being adopted to distribute Russian books among the Jews, and a few Jewish holy books are being translated into Russian. It is therefore very much to be hoped that the language used by the Jews as their vernacular, and in the books designated for the Jews, should gradually be replaced by the Russian language. It is nevertheless well known that many Jews, stubborn fanatics, act in a clandestine or indirect manner against the abovementioned measures by the government, which aspire to Russify their fellow Jews.
>
> This resistance expresses itself in part in their attempt to strengthen the dominance of *Zhargon*. It may be observed that recently a great many different brochures and announcements written in *Zhargon* have appeared. It has also been observed that *Zhargon* becomes filled with ever more German words, probably under the secret influence of the Jewish German propaganda that is striving not to Russify, but for the—for us, dangerous—Germanization of the Jewish masses.
>
> The opening of new storehouses for Jewish books will, contrary to the intent of the government, lead to the spread of *Zhargon* and weaken the influence of Russian education among Jews. Two Jews have now expressed their request to open a Jewish bookstore in Vilna: the indicated Raphael Falk and Shmuel Feigenson,[1] who sent me a separate memorandum. There is no doubt that if their request is satisfied, other Jews will copy their example and then the efforts of the government to spread Russian education among the Jews will be made very difficult. Apart from this, if there was no

need for new Jewish bookstores until now, such a need is now much less, when, on account of the [recent] permission, Jewish artisans received the right to settle in the interior governorates. Their number will therefore decrease in the region, and, necessarily, the number of users of Jewish books will also decrease. Incidentally, I believe that requests of this sort, like the Jew Falk's and from other Jews, need not be considered because there is absolutely no special need to open new Jewish bookstores, not in Vilna, nor in the other cities and towns of the governorates in the northwest region.[2]

Naturally, after such a reply from Kornilov, the request from the interested party to open a new Jewish bookstore in Vilna failed.

But the curator was not satisfied with forwarding his reply only to the governor who inquired of him about the matter. On December 11, 1865, he also sent a copy of the indicated reply "to the esteemed" governor-general of Vilna. This office was then held by the successor to the famous "[Mikhail] Muraviev the Hangman," General [Konstantin Petrovich] von Kaufmann, who ruled five governorates: Vilna, Grodno, Minsk, Vitebsk, and Mohilev.

Kornilov's opinion was not the opinion of an individual. It also found favor with the governor-general. In the margin of Kornilov's note, von Kaufmann wrote with a pencil: "The opinion of Kornilov is entirely correct. If the Jews understand their own interests, they will assist in spreading among themselves knowledge of the Russian language and not *Zhargon*. The editors of *Vilensky Vestnik* [Vilna Journal] should be informed of this in order to prepare an article about the Jewish Question." Kornilov's "educational" letter was indeed forwarded for use by the indicated editors. On the letter is a further notation: "Returned from the editors. April 27, 1866."

This is what the Russian authorities thought of Jews and Yiddish sixty-three years ago. Has much changed in this regard? . . . [ellipsis in original]

Introduction Notes:

1. Pinkhas Kon, "Di batsyung tsu yidish fun di rusishe makhthober in vilne in di zekhtsiker yorn: A bletl tsu der geshikhte fun yidishn bukhhandl in lite (loyt arkhiv-materyaln" [The attitude toward Yiddish of the Russian authorities in Vilna in the sixties: A page on the history of Jewish bookselling in Lithuania (according to archival materials)], *Literarishe bleter* 6, no. 2 (Warsaw, January 11, 1929): 24–25 (unabridged).

Article Notes:

1. Shmuel Feivish Feigenson [Faygenzon, 1837–1932] is today one of the survivors of the old generation in Vilna. Later, he joined the Romm printing house where in the course of sixty years he was a director. He also wrote under the pseudonym ShP"N Ha-Sofor. See Z. Reisin's article, "90-yoriker yubiley fun a talmid-Khokhm," in *Literarishe bleter* 46 (November 18, 1927): 895–96. [See also, "Talmudic Printer Dead in Vilna at Age of 95," *The Jewish Herald* (Providence, R.I.), April 15, 1932, first unnumbered page after p. 5.]

2. Archives of the Vilna Governor-General, 1863: 253/39–40, on the subject of book storehouses and stores.

33

Ghettos and Concentration Camps Seeking Contacts: A Chapter of Jewish Resistance

by Mark Dworzecki, 1949

MARK DWORZECKI (see Selection 12 above, also 39, 42, and 48 below) studied and publicized Jewish unarmed resistance to the Nazis in all its forms. Most such resistance occurred within the walls of the ghettos and camps. Support for this resistance came from attempts to communicate across German-occupied territories by people who risked their lives to smuggle messages, money, weapons, and calls to revolt along a network of secret routes from one sealed ghetto to another.

In 1949, Dworzecki wrote about the *shlikhim* (emissaries), nearly all women, who traversed the routes between the larger ghettos in Poland and Lithuania, including Warsaw, Bialystock, Vilna, and Grodno. The introduction to this 1949 article appears below.[1] The remainder of that article describes the heroic actions of the emissaries on the basis of his own observations in the Vilna ghetto—which is not included here, as it has become less authoritative in the face of more detailed later studies.

Dworzecki's evolution from lay to professional historian is seen in the second excerpt below, taken from his history of the German camps in Estonia, for which he received his doctorate at the Sorbonne in 1967 (see review in Selection 48).[2] This later work is based on interviews of 174 eyewitnesses—26 conducted by Dworzecki himself—and dozens of published accounts by survivors. The chapter titled "Secret Contacts Between the Camps" appears below. He explains that, because he had experienced the camps himself, he "used the utmost caution to recount the events, not according to his own recollection, but on the basis of as many eyewitness accounts as possible."[3] It is an example of the Yiddish historians' many efforts to use Jewish sources for Holocaust research.

Ghettos and Concentration Camps Seeking Contacts

When we speak about the uprising in the Warsaw ghetto, and when we sanctify the memories of the resistance fighters, we are sanctifying at the same time the memories of all the resistance fighters in the ghettos and all those who fell in the ghetto revolts and partisan fights.

Research on the Jewish *khurbn* and struggle also ought to recover a little-noted and still less studied chapter: how contacts were formed between ghetto and ghetto at a time when the ghettos were isolated islands in the Nazi ocean. Moving around outside the walls of the ghetto was linked with death. Jews had absolutely no right to travel by train or automobile, and in general they had no right to appear anywhere outside the ghetto without a German convoy transporting them to their work. No Jew who was caught anywhere outside the ghetto ever returned alive.

The mission of being emissaries was taken on spontaneously, and on their own initiative, by members of the pioneering Zionist youth movements. They were suited to this because, for a long time before the German invasion, they had already conducted many activities of an underground nature and, among themselves, had trained young secret emissaries, secret liaisons, with the fervor of self-sacrifice.

Sending word, finding out what was happening in all the ghettos, making known the mass transports to death, warning against false illusions regarding German intentions about resettling Jews, conveying news of what was taking place in all the ghettos, issuing calls to action and resistance—these were the tasks for which the pioneering youth sent emissaries from ghetto to ghetto. The ghettos were isolated from one another. The Jews felt doubly unfortunate, not knowing what was happening around and within Jewish life. Various fantastic rumors would suddenly arise and disappear. Often, pessimistic news pervaded the ghetto: there are no longer any Jews in Poland, Lithuania, and Ukraine—and by accident we are the only island of living Jews. And at other times, optimistic, celebratory, truly messianic rumors would circulate: only among us in the ghetto; only among us are there transports to death; but elsewhere the Jews are living just as before, without executions, without deportations, without attacks; and they are only waiting to be exchanged for German prisoners of war to be freed from the Nazi yoke.

But deep in their hearts the Jews in the Nazi ghettos knew that the Jewish fate was the same in each place under the Hitler regime and that what happened in Vilna, without any doubt, also awaited other ghettos and that whatever took place far away in a secluded small-town ghetto also awaited Warsaw and Bialystok.

In dangerous missions from ghetto to ghetto, young pioneering Zionist men and women revealed themselves through sacred boldness and with a strength of boundless loyalty. Many of them, unknown until the war, sensed in themselves an inner call to engage in service to the Jewish underground and to dedicate their lives to the honor of the Jewish people.

Every thought of resistance still circulated like a dream waiting to be awakened. And the pioneering dreamers traveled from ghetto to ghetto; stole across borders on foot and on wagons; secretly sneaked aboard trains occupied by the Gestapo; entered the ghettos on days of expulsions, carried messages of warning, and summoned Jews to fight. . . .

Secret Contacts between Camps in Estonia

Simultaneously with the last deportation from the Vilna ghetto to the Estonian camps, every letter-writing contact was severed between these Jews and the remaining Jews of the ghetto who had been transported to the Kailis and HKP Blocs [labor camps in Vilna, outside the ghetto]. . . . The inmates of one camp were now completely isolated from the other camps. No one knew where the other camps in Estonia were located, or how many there were, and where the people close to them had been sent. With great effort, the inmates began to seek contacts between the camps. In particular, they received help from the Dutch workers who would convey news from camp to camp. Inmates also began writing "letters" on boards, barracks walls, and sacks of cement that would be sent from camp to camp. [Dworzecki then provides the following compilation of eyewitness accounts, organized by camp name, alphabetically in Yiddish.]

Goldfilz [also called Goldfeld]: While the author of these lines worked there in the sawmill, he began writing letters, Hebrew and Yiddish, on the boards that were sent to other camps. On the boards, he also noted the names of Goldfilz inmates. A short time later, parts of walls came back from Klooga with names and news of the Klooga inmates on them.[1]

Vaivara: The typhus sufferers who were brought from various camps to Vaivara would tell the Jewish medical personnel there about the events in their camps. And because of them, the news would also spread among other people in Vaivara.[2] The central food warehouse for all the camps was located in Vaivara. From time to time, trucks would come there to transport products. From the trucks, the Vaivara inmates calculated that in Estonia there were fourteen camps connected with Vaivara.[3]

Jewe: The Dutch drivers who would transport the typhus sufferers from Jewe to Vaivara became the links between the inmates of both camps.[4]

Lagedi: The watchmen who accompanied the transport from Lagedi "A" to Stutthof [concentration camp near Danzig] returned to Lagedi "B." From them, H. Kruk [Herman Kruk; diarist of the Vilna ghetto, 1897–1944] learned about the fate of the 2,000 deportees.[5] From them, he also learned that eighty Jews from Klooga were transported to a new camp—Lankila.[6] When the so-called "doghouses" were sent from Klooga for the prisoners in Lagedi (who spent day and night under the open sky), more news from the Klooga inmates was found on the walls of the huts.[7]

Narva: News about the inmates in Narva came to Shavel as early as October 30, 1943. The news was brought by Estonian women who came to Shavel with a German military transport.[8] Word also came to Narva from the Vilna partisans in the woods. In Narva, Sheftel [Aryeh Sheftel, 1905–1980; future Israeli politician] met with a friend in the United Partisan Organization who escaped to the Neroche Forest. He [Sheftel] received an order to return to Vilna on a partisan mission to the HKP Bloc. During a German *Aktion* [round-up] there, he was captured and deported to Estonia.[9]

Sonda: A common bathhouse served the inmates of Sonda and Kiviõli. There, in the bathhouse, the inmates from Kiviõli would get news about life in Camp Sonda.[10]

Soski: The camp was not far from Kuremaa. The head Jewish inmate from Soski, together with his assistants, would come to Kuremaa from time to time to deal with technical matters. In this way, news was also conveyed from Soski.[11]

Ereda: The camp was isolated from all other camps. But it was known that not far from it was Goldfilz. Baruch Goldstein [1922–1987] decided to make contact with Goldfilz. He was on the way to deliver soup to the inmates who were working along the way. When he reached Camp Goldfilz he accidentally met the author of these lines, who was working on the "*shtreke*" [?, literally "stretch"]. I introduced him to Zvi Cepelewicz.[12] In this way, ties were established between the underground in Ereda and the underground in Goldfilz.

Kuremaa: The inmates of Kuremaa would carry news to the inmates from Soski during the visits of the head Jewish inmates. There was an instance when an Estonian woman fainted while the author of these lines was visiting the pharmacy at Kuremaa. He rendered assistance on the spot, and in return she delivered a letter from him to Camp Klooga.[13]

Kiviõli: In May 1944, a transport of boards arrived in Kiviõli from Klooga with more names of Klooga inmates on them.[14] On the bags of scrap lumber (often also inside the bags) there would be notes in Yiddish from various camps.[15] The desire to be in contact, to be informed and to inform others, was so strong that even those deported to their deaths did not lose the will to make their fate known. In this way, the people deported to their deaths in Kiviõli and Ereda, among them Dr. Wolkowicz and the head inmate Israel Cepelewicz, wrote in blood on the trucks that they were being killed.[16]

Klooga: The "board-letters" that would come from Goldfilz to Kiviõli have already been mentioned. During the evacuation of Camps Kiviõli, Ereda, and others (July–August 1944), the evacuees wrote inscriptions on the cement sacks that were left in the camps. The sacks were later sent to Klooga. In this way, people there learned about the evacuation from the camps.[17] The secret contacts of Klooga with the other camps were very intense. In the first month of the existence of Klooga, people there already knew what was taking place in the camps.[18] The Klooga inmates would often write notes on the barracks walls that were fabricated in Klooga and sent to the camps. Such messages were also shipped to faraway camps like Riga and Kaiserwald. After the liberation, people learned that the messages had reached those places.[19] Messages to Stutthof from Kiviõli and Lagedi deportees reached Klooga by means of the SS men who accompanied the transports. These messages helped to reassure the Klooga inmates and convince them that people were not deported to their deaths but, instead, plausibly to work.[20] And perhaps, in this very conveyance of reassuring news, lay a Nazi joke about "bringing and reassuring"? During the mass slaughter in Klooga, when they began to lead the first groups into the forest, a boy, Max, broke away and ran to the camp, announcing that those brought to the forest had been shot.[21]

A witness to the strong desire for events in the camps to become known to the residents of the ghetto as well is the story of Moshe ben Baruch Shabtel, who escaped from the Estonian transport destined for "special handling" that went through Shavel. He told about the frightful life in Camps Vaivara, Jewe, and Ereda.[22]

A witness to the instinctive desire for coming generations to be informed is also found in the diaries of the camps: some of them were buried in Lagedi, in the presence of witnesses, and were later unearthed by one of those who survived.[23]

Introduction Notes:

1. M. Dvorzhetski, "Getos un kontsentratsye-lagern zukhn kontaktn: A kapitl fun yidishn vidershtand," *Kiem* 2, no. 4 (Paris, April 1949): 899–904 (899–900 quoted).

2. M. Dvorzhetski, *Vayse nekht un shvartse teg (yidn-lagern in estonye)* [White nights and black days (Jewish camps in Estonia)] (Tel Aviv: Y. L. Perets, 1970), 274–79 (complete chapter).

3. Ibid., 28, 30.

Article Notes:

1. Meir Dworzecki (oral recording, Hebrew, Tel Aviv, 1965), 66; Israel Segal (oral recording, Hebrew, Tel Aviv, 1965), 3.

2. Haya Tarshis (questionnaire, Yiddish, Tel Aviv, 1966), 3; Henrik Lilienheim (oral recording, Polish, Tel Aviv, 1969), 6.

3. Tarshis, 3; Henrik Lilienheim (oral recording, Polish, Tel Aviv, 1969), 6.

4. Baruch Goldstein (oral recording, Hebrew, Tel Aviv, 1966), 8ff.; Yitzhak Koyfman (Polish, Tel Aviv, 1961), 36ff.

5. And here are some excerpts from Kruk's diary, August 29, 1944: "The watchman who accompanied (from Stutthof) recounted that in Lagedi there were 2,000 Jews from Estonian camps, among them—Mark. From there, they traveled by ship to Danzig." *Moreshet* 2 (1964): 77 (*Moreshet* indicates in note 13 that for the name "Mark" he meant "Mark Dworzecki").

6. Ibid., 58.

7. Isak Niemenczyk, "Megiles estland: zikhroynes fun a kovner yid, vos iz farshlept gevorn keyn estland" [Scroll of Estonia: Memoirs of a Jew from Kovno who was dragged to Estonia], *Landsberger tsaytung* [survivor newspaper in the Landsberg D.P. Camp in Germany] (1946): 4.

8. Eliezer Yerushalmi, *Pinkas Shavli* (Jerusalem: Mosad Bialik/Yad Vashem, 1958), 298; entry for October 23, 1943.

9. Aryeh Sheftel (oral recording, Hebrew, Tel Aviv, 1965), 11.

10. Additional testimonies from inmates.

11. Goldstein, 8ff.; Koyfman, 36ff.; Dworzecki, 66ff.

12. Dworzecki, 66.
13. Ibid.
14. Nisan Anolik (speech in Russian, Riga, 1946), 3; this is how he learned about his father in Klooga.
15. Tarshis, 5.
16. [Additional testimonies from inmates.]
17. Tarshis, 6.
18. Segal, 8.
19. Hillel Seidel (oral recording, Hebrew, Beit Lohamei HaGeta'ot / Ghetto Fighters' House, 1969), 5.
20. Abraham Obiedzinski (oral recording, Yiddish, Tel Aviv, 1965), 6.
21. Ibid.; Seidel, 15.
22. Yerushalmi, 354–58; entry of February [18], 1944.
23. Anolik; the diaries and notes of H. Kruk were discovered thanks to the accident that, of those watching while the manuscript was buried, his brother Nisan Anolik (Ankuli) survived. [Other sources indicate that, of the surviving brothers Nisan and Benjamin Anolik, it was Nisan who both observed and retrieved the buried manuscript.]

34
Unknown Letters by Zelig Kalmanovich in the Vilna Ghetto to Isaac Giterman in the Warsaw Ghetto

by Joseph Kermish, 1983

JOSEPH KERMISH (Jósef Kermisz, 1907–2005) was born in Złotniki, Austrian Galicia (today Zolotnyky, Ukraine), and received his doctorate in Polish history from the University of Warsaw in 1937. Before World War II, he worked as a "public historian," usually for the Warsaw Jewish community, writing entirely in Polish. He survived the Nazi invasion in the Soviet zone of occupied Poland and, after the war, became the founding director of the archives of the Central Jewish Historical Commission in Poland. On arriving in Israel, he was briefly founding archivist at Beit Lohamei HaGeta'ot / Ghetto Fighters House and, after 1953, founding director of the archives at Yad Vashem.

Kermish devoted his postwar efforts primarily to collecting, preserving, and publishing the documentary evidence of Jewish life under the Nazi occupation, particularly in the Warsaw ghetto. He ultimately published a monumental compendium of documents in English translation from Emanuel Ringelblum's secret Oyneg Shabes archive (*To Live with Honor to Die with Honor!*, 1986); a six-volume annotated Hebrew translation of the publications of the underground press (1979–97); and the complete two-volume critical edition of Ringelblum's writings in the Warsaw ghetto (Yiddish 1985, Hebrew 1992–94).

Letters smuggled into the Warsaw ghetto from other Jewish communities were the principal source of outside information in the ghetto. Included in the Oyneg Shabes collection were letters from a leading cultural figure in the Vilna ghetto, Zelig Kalmanovich (see also the article by Kalmanovich in Selection 43 below). The letters were addressed to Isaac Giterman (1889–1943), who served as director of the American Joint Distribution Committee in Poland before World War II and continued to coordinate aid work in the Warsaw ghetto.

The sentiments expressed by Kalmanovich illuminate his place at one end of the spectrum of Jewish reactions to Nazi subjugation—that of eternal optimism and belief in the power of cultural resistance, in contrast to other literary and political figures who were less resigned and more combative. He was considered the "prophet of the Vilna ghetto" by his admirers, including Vilna ghetto survivor and historian Mark Dworzecki,[1] who is credited with originating this phrase by Nachman Blumental (one of Kalmanovich's detractors), who decried Kalmanovich's attitude in an article titled "No Heroism and No Spirit."[2]

The following article,[3] in which Kermish published four letters by Kalmanovich, is an example of his use of the "unknown letters" genre as a documentary historian. First, he sketches the general historical context of the letters. Second, he allows the letters to speak for themselves (without commenting on the psychic horrors they tacitly convey). Third, he provides explanatory notes (much greater in length than the letters themselves). His general introduction and the fourth letter, which is the longest and most informative, appear below.

Introduction

A significant place in the Oyneg Shabes archive (Ringelblum Archive) is occupied by several hundred letters—originals and copies—that were sent to Warsaw from tens of cities and towns, as well as labor camps. One can single out a specific group of letters from community leaders, intellectuals, writers, and rabbis to the director of the Joint [American Jewish Joint Distribution

Committee], Isaac Giterman—the great friend of modern Jewish culture, one of the most devoted builders of YIVO [Yiddish Scientific Institute], executive member of YIVO in Vilna, supporter of various communal cultural undertakings, in particular HeHalutz [Zionist pioneering youth movement].

This collection of letters is an exceedingly important and interesting source of facts and events about almost three years of Nazi occupation. We present here four unknown letters from Zelig Kalmanovich that were sent from the Vilna ghetto to Isaac Giterman in the Warsaw ghetto. The letters were transmitted by secret emissaries of the Jewish underground movement in the months of February to April 1942.

After the war broke out on the first of September 1939, Isaac Giterman, together with refugees, arrived in Vilna and immediately began welfare work. For example, a special dormitory was established for Jewish writers and journalists, in which Polish writers and journalists also took refuge.

At the end of 1939, Giterman decided to travel to Paris on business for the Joint. He left on a ship for Stockholm, from which he was to fly to Paris. But the Germans captured the ship before it arrived in Stockholm and interned the more than eighty Polish citizens, including Isaac Giterman, in a prisoner-of-war camp in Stargard (Pomerania, Germany), where he became acquainted with thousands of Jewish prisoners. He was freed in March 1940 and came to Warsaw, where he commenced work at once to help the tens of thousands of refugees and exiles who found themselves in difficult circumstances. He was also concerned with the tens of thousands of homeless persons who wandered from one place to another throughout the province. [Giterman was killed by SS soldiers in the Warsaw ghetto in 1943.]

The letters from Zelig Kalmanovich to Isaac Giterman were preserved in the second section of the Oyneg Shabes archive, in one of the two milk cans unearthed on December 1, 1950.

★ ★ ★

Hirsh-Zelig Kalmanovich (1881–1944), one of the leaders of YIVO, particularly the scholarly and organizational leadership of the institute, and also the editor of its most important publications; a learned man, at home in all branches of ancient and modern Jewish culture; a collaborator in Yiddish scholarly literature; a researcher of Yiddish philology (he worked for many years on a Yiddish dictionary; fought for the purity of the Yiddish language; demanded the use of more Hebrew words; was among the strongest opponents of adopting Soviet orthography); was very active in the Vilna ghetto as one of the central figures of

Jewish cultural life. He was a cofounder and the director of the literary union in the ghetto, in which Jewish intellectuals of all political persuasions were concentrated: Zionists, Bundists, Communists, and others. He was also very active in the cultural field in the ghetto; he led the "Culture House" at 6 Strashun Street and the People's University at 12 Szawelska Street.

Z. Kalmanovich's visit to the Land of Israel just before the war (1939) was deeply etched in his heart and memory. He became strongly attached to the country—where, at Kibbutz Merhavia, his son Shalom lived. Understandably, as a result, his Zionist attitude became still stronger in the ghetto; he believed still more in Zionism and was a loyal friend of the Halutz [Zionist pioneering youth] movement. In his public utterances, he expressed his regret at having wasted his efforts to build Jewish culture where destruction awaited it. Nevertheless, a great optimism prevailed in Kalmanovich during that dreadful time, and he did not want to believe that total ruin would occur. He constantly tried to lift his own spirits and to encourage others as well. In the worst of times, he continued his creative work and wrote a great amount. Among his writings from that period remain large fragments of works of literary criticism that he wrote in the ghetto, such as a work on Y. L. Peretz ("Y. L. Peretz's View of Yiddish Literature"),[1] a treatment of Ahad Ha'am's opinions about Hebrew literature (he wrote both works in Hebrew), and the essay "The Fundamental Problems of the History of Literature." On the last theme, he also gave public lectures several times in the ghetto.

His diary, written in Hebrew (only certain passages in Yiddish) and covering the period from June 1942 to August 31, 1943, as well as his essay "The Spirit in the Ghetto,"[2] were found soon after the liberation by [famed Yiddish poet] Abraham Sutzkever and, along with other valuable materials, shipped to YIVO in New York.

In the diary, he recorded events, notes about the fate of people and institutions, and his thoughts about problems of existence of the Jewish people. The author, who strove to record personal experiences and community actions, emphasized the broad, strong creative spirit of the Jewish people, which revealed itself in the ghetto—one of our greatest and most distinguished events.[3] He believed in the strength of creativity, that it would sustain us after the liberation to construct a new culture on the ruins of our people and be united with the liberated in the Land of Israel.

The letters that I. Giterman received from Z. Kalmanovich he handed over, like other letters of historical value, to the Oyneg Shabes archive. In Ringelblum's diary, there are echoes of Kalmanovich's letters, for example the entry about the Vilna ghetto that Ringelblum wrote on May 7, 1942: "Community work blossoms in Vilna—evening concerts—a teachers union created. Literary union, lectures twice a week . . .YIVO—Kalmanovich and twenty people—sort the archive of YIVO—Strashun Library, lies in the university library."

In his testamentary letter to the Yiddish Scientific Institute—YIVO, to the Yiddish PEN Club, and to writers Sholem Asch, H. Leivik, Y. Opatoshu, and Dr. Raphael Mahler of March 1, 1944, "in a moment when 90 percent of the Polish Jews are already murdered," Ringelblum dwelled on the cultural work in the Warsaw ghetto and also emphasized the accomplishments of the clandestine Oyneg Shabes archive. In that connection, he mentioned his contact with Z. Kalmanovich, who, "under the supervision of the Germans, systemized the YIVO materials and hid a significant portion of them."

The letters by Z. Kalmanovich bear witness to Jewish vitality and the strong will for life, as well as the ability to adapt to the worst and most extreme conditions of the ghetto that include vestiges of a murdered community, over which hung the sword of death the entire time. His allusions in the letters to the increased strength of cultural work in the ghetto, whose purpose was to immunize the conscious portions of the population in the ghetto, particularly the youth, against the methods of dehumanization and moral degradation applied by the Nazis to the Jewish population, are an additional demonstration of the spiritual resistance produced by the multi-branched cultural work in the ghetto.

And last but not least, Z. Kalmanovich's letters allude to the close ties between the Jewish underground in the Warsaw and Vilna ghettos and are a paean to the heroic emissaries ("The young people who have a special place in our heart"), who risked their lives and maintained these ties between the ghettos and brought to the remnant in Vilna words of encouragement and financial assistance.

For purposes of concealment in writing names, Z. Kalmanovich gave only the first name; the same was also true in the references to organizations and institutions. We completely deciphered the letters, which were difficult to read, and added explanatory notes.

We express a special thank-you to our friend Shalom Luria [1920–2011], the son of Zelig Kalmanovich, for deciphering several words in the manuscript that were difficult to read.

[To integrate Kermish's explanation with the narrative, his notes have been inserted into the letter by Kalmanovich below {in curly brackets}. Paragraph breaks have been added for clarity.]

Letter of April 21, 1942

Dear Friend Isaac. This time I will try to be somewhat more expansive, share with you a few characteristics of our life, some constructive, happy—it is not only that the sun is shining, and that the world has the scent of spring. On the contrary, it is possible that the people confined here perceive this more negatively than winter. Only the one who is doing something and has the illusion of accomplishing something is content and thanks the One on High that the miracle happened to him and that he can now sit with a certain calmness of soul and write a letter to a good friend.—{About this state of mind among the surviving remnant in the Vilna ghetto, Z. Kalmanovich expressed himself similarly in his essay "The Spirit in the Ghetto," saying: "Those who remain—they have no alternative, they must generate from within the elixir of life that will sustain themselves."[4] Similarly, Herman Kruk also recorded in his diary for February 10, 1942: "In the ghetto a caricature of life has taken hold—everyone tries to keep busy and not have any free time. Better not to be alone.[5]}

The impression arises that the soul is smoothing itself out a bit. There remain, it is true, only a few of the many, and those who remain are not the very best. But our father Jacob's grandchildren have demonstrated here once again the mighty, literally superhuman strength to adapt and to force the cruel angel to say amen against his will.—{While Z. Kalmanovich was being deported, on the last day of August or at the very beginning of September 1943, to Estonia, where he was murdered in a German slave-labor camp in Narva, he sent a letter from the camp, saying: "I am fortunate that I am with our father Abraham's grandchildren."[6] Regarding "superhuman strength . . . ," see the related notes in the diary of Zelig Kalmanovich, for example the entry of July 23, 1943, where he repeats these words, in a manner of speaking: "Through work we will force the evil angel to yield to our will."[7]}

The workshops are accomplishing remarkable things,—{Herman Kruk also provides a series of facts about how "the ghetto is producing in various fields, and it displays marvels in every field of activity."[8] The technical workshops conducted a broad, multibranched effort, as did the light-industry workshops, which included brush-making, braiding, wrapping, and packaging sections. In the beginning, for example, the braiding section produced various types of footwear from manila hemp and later, because of a shortage of raw materials, turned to braiding for other uses. The technical laboratory instituted production of an entire series of new, useful articles. A washing liquid was developed in the technometric laboratory that received a great many orders.⁹}

And soon a sort of technical class was created for twenty-five young people (in fact, one hundred remained outside);—{From the beginning, the labor section followed the course of disseminating ever more knowledge of trades among the ghetto dwellers to help the old workers improve their skills and the young people prepare for their future work lives as quickly and as early as possible.¹⁰ In charge of the technical school in the ghetto, the so-called "ghetto technicum," was the director, engineer Matisyahu Shreiber. The first graduation of the technical school took place in the ghetto on the first of September 1942. Nineteen young people received diplomas from the completed course for metalworking and electrotechnics.¹¹ During the six-month course, the technical school graduated tens of electrotechnics and metalworkers.¹²}

Some forty teachers were occupied with schoolboys in traditional religious education, in Yiddish and also in Hebrew.—{At the beginning of September 1941, a group of teachers undertook to create a section for childcare. A registration of teachers and children took place, in which 3,000 children were enrolled. The *Judenrat* approved forty positions for teachers. Because of the German *Aktionen* [round-ups], the number of children continuously decreased. The number of teachers who were working when the passes were distributed was forty-three. Instead of the thirty that were promised, a total of ten passes were distributed. Only later was the problem of passes solved in the form of "protective passes." In the meantime, tens of teachers were gone.¹³ As the ghetto residents gradually began to get back on their feet, the teachers, after instituting the literary-artistic meetings, also organized themselves. Every Friday, a meeting of teachers took place, where reports were read on popular scholarly themes. In the afternoon hours, gymnastics courses were instituted.¹⁴}

There is a choir . . . ,—{In April 1942, two choirs were created in the ghetto, a Hebrew one, under the direction of the musician Wolf Durmashkin [1914–1944], and a Yiddish one, directed by the old director of the *Vilbigkhor* [Vilna Jewish Education Society Choir], Avrom Sliep [1884–1942]. The program of the Hebrew choir, of more than 100 persons, organized by Brit-Ivrit [Hebrew Union], included chiefly Zionist pioneering youth songs, Yemenite, Hasidic, chapters of the Tanach [Hebrew Bible], "songs of the people" by Bialik and others. Both choirs were constantly preparing as-yet unheard folksongs, as well as oratorios, chorales, and operas. The public appearances of the choirs were accompanied by the symphonic orchestra of Wolf Durmashkin.[15]}

. . . every week concerts.—{On January 18, 1942, the first concert in the ghetto took place, in which the singer Liuba Levitska, [pianist] Sonia Rekhtig [d. 1945], and [actor] Shabse Bliakher [Shabtai Bleicher, 1906–1943] took part. Most students (70%) were Jewish policemen with their families, members of the *Judenrat*, and others. The organized Jewish workers—according to Herman Kruk—resolved to boycott the concerts because, "although art in the ghetto is a mitzvah, in the sorrowful situation of the Vilna ghetto, however, under the shadow of Ponar, where, out of 75,000 Jews in Vilna, only 15,000 remain, organizing a concert is literally a disgrace." In the street, leaflets were posted urging people to boycott the concerts.[16] Nevertheless, the first appearance of the symphonic orchestra was—as A. Sutzkever writes—a popular holiday in the ghetto. The orchestra managed to produce seven premieres (approximately thirty-five concerts). On August 19, 1942, for example, the third concert took place under the direction of W. Durmashkin and was, in the conditions of the ghetto, an accomplishment of a high level. Besides the concerts of the symphony orchestra, special cabaret concerts were also presented. From time to time, concerts of chamber music took place.[17] In this way, the ghetto was also not lagging in the area of music.}

People quarrel at the Saturday night events of the literary union, as 200 want to attend, but there is only space for half.—{On Saturday, the 7th of February [1942], the founding meeting of the union of Jewish writers, literati, and artists took place. Eighty literati, writers and artists, stage artists, singers, musicians, and sculptors participated. The union set for itself the task of self-help and encouraging artistic creation in the context of the ghetto, preparing a chronicle of the displaced Jewish writers, artists, and intellectuals, gathering the lost creations of those displaced and preparing materials for a literary-artistic collection from the ghetto. Selected to lead the union were Zelig Kalmanovich, Herman Kruk, Hersh Gutgeshtalt, Avrom Sutzkever, and others. The literary-artistic union, headed by Zelig Kalmanovich, quickly made a name for itself in the ghetto.[18] Its evening events in the ghetto theater, on Mendele, Sholem Aleichem, Y. L. Peretz, H. N. Bialik, and Yehoash, enjoyed a large response.[19] The union also announced contests in three areas of art: literature, music, and painting. Tens of poems, dramas, compositions, and pictures, all created in the ghetto.[20]

On May 6, 1942, at one of the evening events, in the presence of fifteen of the most distinguished literati and artists, A. Sutzkever read his newly written poem, "Dos keyver-kind" ["The Grave-Child"], a dramatic chronicle. The work elicited great enthusiasm and, above all—a long debate.[21] At the ensuing meetings that the union organized, an attempt was made to give a series of stimulating literary-artistic and community events: for example, on July 25, 1942, the sixth literary-artistic meeting took place, dedicated to *Yung-vilne* [the Young Vilna artistic-literary group]. At the event, where there was also an exhibit of drawings, pictures, and reproductions by the group of painters, documents and publications of *Yung-vilne*, an audience of 200 people attended.[22]}

In addition, a Brit-Ivrit event attracted a hundred-person audience, mostly young people.—{In winter 1941, in the period between the German *Aktionen* of the "yellow passes" and "pink passes," the Brit-Ivrit was created. The purpose of Brit-Ivrit was to create in the ghetto, through the living Hebrew word and the vision of a free life in one's own land, a forum that would contrast with ghetto life. The Brit-Ivrit gatherings (evenings on H. N. Bialik, Ahad Ha'am, as well as Benyamin-Zev Herzl, on the young Hebrew poetry, etc.) would draw a crowd of listeners that numbered as many as 600.[23]}

About the fact that people are reading a lot, I need not bother to say.—{The Jewish reader is a unique page of history. Already in fall 1941, the reading room had begun to function. Even in November 1941, during the great German *Aktion*, when the population decreased systematically by approximately 30–40 percent, the number of books being read increased, however, by almost a third. The winter months diminished the functioning of the reading room. But after a break and renewal, it reopened on May 5, 1942. In November 1942 the ghetto library lent more than 100,000 books for reading.[24] In December 1942 the number of books lent for reading was 140,000.[25]}

For Passover, there were seders, greatly impoverished, but still seders.

Statistics are being kept.—{The statistics office dealt first of all with the first three months of the ghetto, the fateful months of September–November 1941, the difficult ghetto experiences during the sadly well-known *Aktionen* during which 47,447 Jews were killed.[26] The statistics office thereafter dealt with the materials collected about all the ghetto institutions and published them in the statistical bulletins.[27]}

An archive is being collected.—{In accordance with the initiative of H. Kruk, an archive of the ghetto activities was instituted by the *Judenrat* at 6 Strashun Street. With time, the archive, in which old valuable documents and manuscripts were also held, assembled a mighty treasure of documents from the ghetto and city, among them eyewitness accounts by people who escaped from Ponar and other *Aktionen*.[28]}

A museum is being created.—{With great difficulty and risk, Herman Kruk succeeded, under the nose of the Nazis, in assembling a large number of artistic works. Among them were rare, one-of-a-kind items, in terms of artistic and historical value. On July 31, 1941, Zelig Kalmanovich wrote in his diary about a meeting of the "committee for the museum of the ghetto, to erect a monument to events and people." Only much later, a year later, did the ghetto leaders and police chief officially announce that "a ghetto museum has been organized," and that H. Kruk was nominated as a leader of the committee to create the museum.[29]}

People are doing gymnastics.—{On August 2, 1942, Zelig Kalmanovich wrote, among other things: "From the 5th to the 7th, ballplaying took place in the square. A thousand or so people came to see the playing, mostly younger people. There were also older people . . . [ellipsis in original] The onlookers applauded and yelled in honor of the winners, even though their voices could be heard in the street of our enemies."[30]}

—Worse is the situation with making a living; the small amount of household goods is running out. The assistance [received from you] is a great matter, altogether invaluable. On account of the second third [of three aid payments], the entire family is seated. And there was complete peace in the home. The benefits were enjoyed by 25, 5 to 100, 20 to 50. We will now wait for the third third. I am not able to be the giver; the receiver stares and extends his hands and hopes.—{At the end of 1941, the Jewish underground in Vilna sent a secret delegation to Warsaw, consisting of Edek Boraks ([1913–1941], Hashomer Hatzair), Shlomo Entin ([1915–1922], HaOved HaTzioni), and Yisrael Kempner ([d. 1943], Betar) [as well as Yehuda Pinchevski, d. 1943, Betar]. This delegation brought to Warsaw the first competent information about the murder of the Jews in Vilna, as well as the news about the beginnings of resistance, and requested money and weapons for resistance purposes. These emissaries were also the first to bring words of encouragement and support for the survivors in Vilna. In his letters to Isaac Giterman of March 23 and April 21, 1942, Kalmanovich confirmed the arrival of two portions of the financial aid for the Jewish writers and intellectuals in the Vilna ghetto.³¹}

The emissary told about fears that supposedly hung in the air. Let us consider that this is a false fear and that *shluchei mitzvah einam nizokim* [emissaries for a mitzvah are not harmed]. We are praying, and the merits of the survivors will be a protection. I have here three-four people who were in administration, two specifically. I could not include them in the number of twenty-five. Perhaps it would be possible to put in a good word for them separately on an occasion soon. In YIVO we are working every day, twenty people, and order is being established, and Jewish treasures are being brought together here. Many things are found; what the lords [the Germans] have in mind to do with them we do not yet know. But they are friendly and do not hurry.—{By that time, the most important of the lost archival materials had been found, among others: about T. Herzl's visit to Vilna in 1903, a folder with correspondence from the World Zionist Union with the Central Committee in Lithuania, many letters from [Rabbi] Chaim Ozer Grodzinski to well-known Jewish personalities.³²}

There should just be a source of income, and people would be able to endure. We hope that you will have us personally in mind, like the first time. I will mention to you again that Miriam is here, the wife of Zalman [Reisin, prominent Yiddishist intellectual], and I am sure that Zalman's relatives will help you, if only they receive word. The emissary will tell you more orally in any event. The best greetings and wishes to you and your Libe, and Menachem [Linder, prominent young Jewish economist and demographer] and his family and the other Isaac—{Isaac (Ignacy) Shiper, Jewish historian and builder of modern Jewish historiography, simultaneously political leader, also active in Jewish communal life during the war.}

Introduction Notes:

1. Mark Dvorzhetski, "Der novi fun vilner geto" [The prophet of the Vilna ghetto], *Idisher kemfer* (New York, September 24, 1948): 4–5. Reprinted from his *Yerusholayim d'lite* (Paris, 1948), 260–64. Reprinted in *Shriftn* 99–100 (Buenos Aires, August–September 1950): 125–27, 152.

2. Nakhman Blumental, "Nisht keyn gvure un nisht keyn gayst!," *Arbeter vort* (Paris, March 6, 1953): 3; (March 20): 3; (April 3): 3; (April 17): 3–4; (April 30): 3–4.

3. Yosef Kermish, "Umbakante briv fun zelig kalmanovitsh, fun vilner geto, tsu itsik giterman, in varshever geto," *Di goldene keyt* 110–11 (Jerusalem, 1983): 17–30; Hebrew version, *Massuah Journal* 14 (April 1986): 191–203.

Article Notes:

1. The principal part of the work was printed in *Di goldene keyt* [The golden chain] 2 (Spring 1949): 114; supplements to the work were published in *YIVO bleter* XXXI–XXXII (1948): 49–64.

2. The essay "Der gayst in geto" was printed in *YIVO bleter* XXX, no. 2 (Winter 1947): 169–72.

3. The diary was printed for the first time, in Yiddish translation, with comments by Yudl Mark in *YIVO bleter* XXXV (1951): 18–92. In the year 1977, it appeared in the original Hebrew: *Yoman be-geto Vilna u-ketavim min ha-`izavon she-nimtse`u ba-harisot* (Sifriyat Po`alim, Tel-Aviv; 1977), with an introduction and comments by Kalmanovich's son, Shalom Luria [or Lurya]. [An additional portion was published in *YIVO bleter* N.S. 3 (1997): 43–113.]

4. Zelig Hirsh Kalmanovich, "Der gayst in geto," *YIVO bleter* XXX, no. 2 (Winter 1947): 172.

5. Herman Kruk, *Togbukh fun vilner geto* [Diary of the Vilna ghetto] (New York: YIVO, 1961), 161.

6. Mark Dvorzhetski, *Yerusholayim d'lite in kamf un umkum* [Jerusalem of Lithuania (Vilna) in struggle and extermination] (Paris: Yidishn natsyonaln arbeter-farband in amerike / Yidishn folksfarband in frankraykh, 1948), 264.

7. Dvorzhetski, 76–77.
8. Kruk, 255, 329.
9. Kruk, 417, 422, 453; Kalmanovich, 54, 57, 63, 75.
10. Kruk, 422.
11. Kruk, 337.
12. A. Sutskever, *Fun vilner geto* [From the Vilna ghetto] (Moscow, Der emes: 1946), 103.
13. Kruk, 202.
14. Kruk, 235.
15. Kruk, 235, 359; Dvorzhetski, 246.
16. Kruk, 130, 133–39.
17. Sutskever, 106–7; Kruk, 329.
18. Kruk, 140, 141, 254.
19. Sutskever, 108.
20. Sutskever, 109.
21. Kruk, 253, 254.
22. Kruk, 319–26.
23. Dvorzhetski, 246–47.
24. Kruk, 255–57, 415.
25. Kalmanovich, 50.
26. Kruk, 258–64.
27. Sutskever, 171.
28. Kruk, 219; Sutskever, 111; Dvorzhetski, 219.
29. Kruk, 328.
30. Kalmanovich, 30–32; see also 63, 68, 70, 87.
31. [Various citations; omitted here for reasons of space.]
32. Kruk, 161; Emanuel Ringelblum, *Ksovim fun geto* [Writings from the ghetto], vol. 1 (Tel Aviv: Y. L. Peretz, 1985), 345 [with introduction by Joseph Kermish].

35

Inscriptions on Walls, Sacred Texts, and Other Books during the Holocaust

by Nachman Blumental, 1966

NACHMAN BLUMENTAL (see Selections 28 above and 49 below) was uniquely qualified—and positioned—to fulfill his interest in collecting items created by Jews under Nazi occupation. In prewar Poland, he had specialized in Yiddish literature and Jewish folklore, and after the war he served as a researcher, and later director, of the Central Jewish Historical Commission in postwar Poland. Between the liberation of Lodz in early 1945 and the reconstruction of Warsaw in 1947, the commission was located in Lodz. Nearly all the inhabitants of the Lodz ghetto had been deported and killed by the Germans, but unlike the ghettos in Warsaw and other cities, much of the Lodz ghetto was left intact by the Germans as they fled the advancing Soviet army in January 1945.

The somber distinction of the Lodz ghetto is that after the war it was possible to enter Jewish homes that looked as if their inhabitants had just stepped out. The few survivors of the ghetto were able to return to search for meaningful belongings, often bringing these to the commission, and researchers like Blumental were able to search the ghetto themselves for historical materials. As a result, the commission soon became a repository for physical artifacts. From Lodz, the commission expanded its efforts to all of liberated Poland and assembled a collection of thousands of books, manuscripts, photographs, and artworks.

Among these were items that carried urgent personal messages, whether to family members or posterity. In the following article, Blumental describes some of his more poignant discoveries, together with the details of daily life in the ghettos that they illuminate.[1] The article appears here unabridged; the many ellipses (. . .) are original to the writing.

Inscriptions on Walls, Sacred Texts, and Other Books during the Holocaust

We do not know what community is spoken of here. We do not know who the author is—but what difference does it make whether this took place in Worms, Speyer, or Mainz? And what difference does it make who wrote it? For, among us Jews, it was—as we know—a story of all times and places! And that which happened yesterday in such-and-such holy community could recur tomorrow or the next day in another place that lies nearby or thousands of kilometers away . . .

In the margin of a *Chumash* [Pentateuch] that was miraculously saved from the surrounding turmoil, a Jew, who was also miraculously saved, inscribed the following brief words during the time of the Black Plague:

> For this is a survivor of the fire on the day of fury and wrath which God raged down in his anger on the holy community of Melamna De'shatron [probably Sisteron on the river of Durance in Southern France], for they are all martyrs of the Lord, children and women in one day, in our many sins, in the year 5108 from the creation (1348), on Friday during the week when "and let them shave all their flesh" [Num. 8:7, of pericope Beha'alotcha] is read, and this Pentateuch was brought to me in the city of Igish [Aix in Provence] in the year 5109 to the creation (1348), on Shabbat during the week when "I will certainly return unto thee" [Gen. 18:10, of pericope Vayera] is read, and only I alone remained since I was invited and summoned ten days before the persecution to come to Avignon before our mistress the queen [Queen Jeanne], and there I have sat and cried the bitterness of my soul.[1]

From an entire community of Jews, there remained only one, who by chance during that hasty moment—as our old-time chronicler explains—was not in that place. And of all those who once created the lively existence of the community, of the entire community, of all their possessions—which were accumulated with so much effort over the course of years and with so much love and perseverance protected for "coming generations"—there remains one half-destroyed *sefer* [holy book] that was brought to the only heir, a townsman of this community. And in the margin of the *Chumash*, he recounted the story with simplicity, terse and dry, and ended: "I returned and cried in the bitterness of my soul." Woe is to the survivor!

So it was in the past, in the dark period of the "cruel Middle Ages," in an old faraway city . . .

And so it remained—but much worse!—until the recent years of our time (1939–1945).

At the beginning of 1945, searching and rummaging in the emptied-out houses of the Lodz ghetto, from which, at the last moment—in the summer and fall of 1944—those Jews still living were sent to Auschwitz, I noticed a *normal*, simple, undistinguished little book with a very simple binding, a remnant of the earlier good old times. It did not even seem worthwhile for me to bend over and lift it from the dusty pile on which it lay. This was not what we sought in the ruins of a Jewish life, when it appeared to us that the owner of the house and his family had just left their home for a while and would return in a short time. Everything was still standing and awaiting their return; even the family photographs were still hanging on the walls; even the eating utensils were still sitting on the table with the remains of a meager breakfast . . . In the room, one could still feel the breath of the owners who had just been here—and were delayed in their return. Where could they be?

Looking around for a long while in the neglected, orphaned home, which still hid and preserved everything from the former life—apart from life itself—I nevertheless unwillingly took this mute book in my hand: Aha, Broder Christiansen's *Philosophie der Kunst* [Philosophy of Art] in Yiddish [New York, 1920] . . . A very fitting instructor for the people and time that interest us, precisely current affairs! For what should and could interest a Jew in the ghetto if not the philosophy of art, philosophy of life in general?!

What our Jews in the ghettos and camps found of interest, what they read and studied if any time or possibility for it remained—would also be worthwhile to investigate sometime. It would be an interesting and informative subject. And we will still surely have occasion to undertake this problem. But let us return to the matter at hand.

I hold the book in my hand, but it tells me nothing about how and where its owner met his fate, and I want to put it aside. For *our historical research on the recent khurbn*, it certainly has no significance.

And when I am already about to toss it aside, the cover opens and on the white pages of the inside endpapers—I notice something written with a pencil: from the right—in Yiddish, from the left—in Polish. There—this can indeed tell us something, if they are not just "empty" thoughts and one-time reflections about the book that was read, which one ordinarily—being unable to tear oneself away from the book, pours out on paper kept near the text that was read, which either inspired us or called forth anger—experiences, that must be expressed in an unmediated reaction.

And I read first in Yiddish: "Freyde! Take the *burke* [hooded fur cape] in the package, with the blankets. Lock the door and give the keys to Mendele in care of the porter Hirshberg. Stay well, Jacob Rotheim—Also take the cooking pot in the package."

The Polish text—the man was apparently not sure whether his wife would be able to read the Yiddish easily, so he added the same in Polish as in Yiddish. The same was true among us in Poland in the interwar years: the men *still* read in Yiddish (and Hebrew), as well as to a lesser extent in Polish, whereas women of the younger generation *already* read almost exclusively in Polish. The Polish text, however, contained two more very important details: "I am on Czarnieckiego," "And join me."

This clarifies everything for us: on Czarnieckiego Street is the central ghetto prison in Lodz. From the start, Jewish "criminals" were held here; later, all the people who were to be deported for "work" were assembled here; they were held until a complete group was gathered to be taken on a "transport" (usually 1,000 or 1,500 people).

From there the transports were sent, in summer 1944 . . . to Auschwitz. Jacob Rotheim was apparently also captured, or was summoned together with his department for "work," so as not to lose track of him, in case he might fail to return? He makes use of the opportunity and sends his wife a parting letter by means of an acquaintance, probably a Jewish policeman (among them one could also occasionally find a decent person). He, the man, gives her, his wife, practical, useful instructions about what to take with her. A deportee from Lodz has the "right" to take along twenty-five kilograms of hand baggage, which he would supposedly need later for his work in the new place. That the Germans considered this package to be their property (*Statsvermögen*) [state property] and would take it from the Jew as soon as he entered the camp—the Jews in the ghettos could not know. On the contrary, they *rightly* argued that, if they were ordered to take with them personal baggage, it was a sign of life: having no suspicion that this was nothing more than a diabolical means of deceiving them.

So Jacob Rotheim did indeed want his wife to take with her all that was needed most.

And on what did Jacob Rotheim write to his wife Freyde? On a book that he apparently had with him and was reading, and perhaps he was caught on the way to the library—illegal, of course, because the Germans disallowed this too—while he was going to borrow it, or return the book after reading it? This, too, our Jews also encountered . . .

Illegal libraries existed in almost every large ghetto and often conducted their work in hazardous circumstances. Also a chapter in itself.

We do not know whether the wife read the note from her husband, whether she was able to take with her the indicated items, whether she was able to lock the door and hand over the key by means of the porter (of the department?), a relative, or cotenant of their dwelling. Usually, the Jew who was sent to death had to turn over the dwelling in order, lest someone later break in the door, heaven forbid, and damage . . . German property . . .

We do not know whether the wife Freyde found and read her husband's last note. We also do not know whether she was able to join her husband, whether they went together to the gas chamber at Auschwitz, or each separately? . . .

The only desire of a Jew in that time was to *go* (in the specific ghetto sense) together with those closest; not alone, forlorn . . .

And if Freyde had indeed at that moment been able to avoid the deportation and run away or hide herself, after reading the note from her husband—surely she abandoned everything and ran to Czarnieckiego to join her husband . . . Oh, the cursed faithfulness to family members among Jews . . . And in death, they did not separate . . .

And perhaps even both had no thought of death, believing that they were indeed going to work, of which there is a sign: the husband tells his wife to bring the cooking pot, which was, as the murdered writer of the Lodz ghetto, Joseph Zelikowicz, expresses in one of his numerous notes, a symbol of life in the Lodz ghetto. In this pot would be the well-known daily (watery) soup that was the chief component of the "nourishment" in the Lodz ghetto for fortunate *working* people . . .

We know nothing about all of this, just as we do not know whether another Jew—who took leave of his wife on the endpapers of a volume of *Kol Kitve Frishman* [All the Writings of David Frischmann] and asked naively, "Will we still see each other again?"—did or did not see his wife again before his death. But what difference does it make? A single fate united them both.

Such silent witnesses, witnesses of an exterminated people, witnesses who correspond with the name of our people—the People of the Book—were preserved for us from the once great Jewish community of Lodz.

But from other cites here and there—one in a thousand—such silent witnesses were also preserved, who tell us much, very much . . .

In a little book of Daniel (Lemberg: Pesil Balaban publishers, 1877), which a peasant handed to a Jew in Radom shortly after the liberation—a Jew writes on the last page:

> I left the Pionek factory and stayed in the attic of a Christian. I can only tell you that the front is near. I hear shooting from cannons, and it lasts so long. We are but a few Jews who want to save our lives, but it is hard because the non-Jews in the village do not let any Jews live. Only almighty God can help [so that] we should remain the few Jews of all Poland.

Read this testament once and again, word by word! It deserves it. A few dry sentences from a simple, ungrammatical Jew, and yet sounding like a masterful poem that shakes the reader. No artist in the world could express it so!

Who is the author? On another page of the book we find a name—apparently of the author of the note, Abraham Isac Kestenberg, Kfar Shtuduv." We are most probably dealing with a Jew from Radom who was sent to work in the ammunition factory in Pionki [Poland]. From there, he and a few other Jews succeeded in escaping and hiding in the attic of a peasant in the town of Sztutowo [site of the Stutthof Concentration Camp]. The Jew gives a detailed account of what awaits him. In compressed language, he conveys everything that has a connection to the life of a Jew on the so-called Aryan side at that time. *The good* Christian (singular!), who sustained him, and the *evil non-Jews* (plural!), who lie in wait to take his (their) life—these two forces: the good and the evil that eternally fight each other and which change only their form over time.

And how poignant—almost like a fictional literary situation, hearing from the Jew about the cannon shots "that last so long." At that time, at the end of 1944, the front was already at the line of the Vistula, just twenty kilometers from the Jew's hiding place.

And at the end of the tragic poem (the introduction, the exposition of the poem is the first sentence, which sounds like an epic beginning of a story: "I left the factory." A positive development of the action is contained in the sentence: "I hear shooting from cannons." The effect of the counteraction: "The non-Jews do not let them live"—this is the tragic conflict, the confrontation of the contradictory forces)—the finale: a prayer to the Master of the Universe, that only he—as the Jew writes—can help. But the Master of the Universe, as the reader inherently understands—did not help . . . The writer could not admit it. Moreover, what is unsaid has greater effect—this is what every experienced writer knows.

A purely individual matter—the life or death of a single person—is transformed in this poem into a general, national question: "We are the few Jews in all of Poland." In that moment, in the last minutes of his life, the Jew was also conscious of the fate of the entire people of Israel here in the countries occupied by the Germans.

The Jew does not complain about his own fate—does not weep. If the entire people is murdered, he too can be no exception. Rather, he thinks of himself as a vestige of the former people. It would therefore be right for these few Jews to remain alive so they could at least tell the world what happened to them. "The few Jews," "The last Jews"—this is the style of that time; not "literature" but reality. The Jew, the author—we sense—also accepted the edict against him with love and left a testament for the world—he left the world a true Jew, in accord with himself and with his God . . . And the counsel of the Lord shall stand [Psalms 33:11].

How these few Jews were killed we do not know. We can only surmise on the basis of similar events in other places. But this is not, after all, important: the subject here lies not, after all, in the detail, but in the general, and with such Jews a large nation was killed, far more than six million, indeed perhaps a full seven million?! There remains only a silent witness, the inscription on a holy text . . .

And when we leaf through the pages of this little book of Daniel, an old worn-out little book, we find another notice: "Dina daughter of Gershom passed away 22 Tevet 5646 [1881/82]." This is an older inscription that still comes from peacetime. A normal death.

Such were the typical inscriptions on the covers and title pages of holy texts, to which we were accustomed since time immemorial . . . A simple family chronicle that was recorded in the margins of holy texts . . . When born, when died . . . in order to keep the mitzvah [commandment] of observing the *yortsayt* [death anniversary] . . . Only in a time of cruelty, of great events, in times when the fate of the entire people totters, do the inscriptions on the holy books become different. From a brief family note, the family chronicle expands to become a memorial for a murdered community, a grave marker for a slaughtered people.

From the first note, from 1348, written somewhere in Western Europe—to the last note, from 1944, written in Eastern Europe—has anything changed in the history of the Jewish people here in exile?! The same transformations, the same fate.

★ ★ ★

Another Jew, in the Kovno ghetto, writes in the margin of a Russian book by Lermontov a parting letter and a call to take vengeance.[2]

Of course, we can find more and more such examples, but—and in that event, this must also be emphasized—what we have discovered after the war is only a small fragment of what was created in that time, and most of it is probably lost. And will something more of it perhaps be found? One must never lose hope, and one must search and search forever, and never will we be certain whether somewhere there still lie treasures that we have not yet recovered; and the thought will forever gnaw at us that *we* all together and each of us separately—have not fulfilled our duty to the very end, and that, if a portion of what is missing was destroyed, the fault is ours.

The inscriptions on the covers of the booklets, however tragic they may sound, are still an expression of a certain—what should one call it?—*heymishkeyt* [hominess, familiarity]; the person is still in a human setting, he is still in his home, he still has something of his possessions, something familiar . . . but, for the Jew, endlessly varied is the way to the abyss, to destruction . . .

More frightful than these inscriptions (on paper!—what a luxury!) are the inscriptions that are written with pencils, with coal, scratched with nails, with pieces of wood; and if those were lacking—with one's own fingernail—on the walls of the cells where they were locked away without even the ability to move, and from which a straight and short path led to the gas chamber or gas van. From the last stage of life, which often preceded death by only a few minutes, we have an entire group of inscriptions of the most varied sorts and in various languages (but mainly in Yiddish).

To these belong the inscriptions on the walls of the church in the Chełmno death camp, where the people were held so long, until the gas van would come for them; the van had so much work that one sometimes had to wait for it an entire night.

To these belong the inscriptions from the synagogue in Kovno, where the assembled congregation waited to be sent straight to their death . . . and the inscriptions on the walls of the basement from which the convicted were led to their death—in Częstochowa.

And from many, many other places.

The content of the inscriptions is varied. Some are purely informative: the condemned gives his name and nickname, where he comes from, sometimes even his age—this applies to boys and girls who thereby express their protest and sorrow that, at such a young age, it is already their lot to be killed, without any fault and for no reason.

Here is an inscription of this type in the Kovno synagogue: I am twenty years old. Oy, how beautiful is the life all around . . . Why must I be killed, while my entire being aspires to live? Are these indeed the last minutes of my life? Vengeance! May everyone who reads this take vengeance; that is my last wish.—Roza Fridman.[3]

In other inscriptions the condemned calmly state that they know what awaits them: to be killed on the spot, to be shot or killed in a gas chamber.

But there are also those who believe, in accordance with the deceptive German propaganda, that they are being sent to work. (Inscription on the wall in Chełmno church: "We are going to Leipzig.")

But occasionally the inscriptions convey a leave-taking, and sometimes we find the expression of suffering on account of one's own fate and concern for the fate of those close, who are still alive in a German camp or are in hiding from the enemy's eye.

Here is one of the many inscriptions: "Rubinku—Feldman, I am leaving you, son, take care of yourself!—Your mama H(annah) Feldman." And when this mother's life was prolonged for a few more minutes, she wrote on the wall again to her son, about which she did not stop for a minute to consider—her parting poem, part two: "Dear Rubin, I am going away calmly, I kiss you—Your mama Hannah" (Częstochowa).

In order to calm her—probably only—son, she conveys a thought about herself, too, that her son should not worry about her, his mother; that he should not have any sorrow that she suffered before her death. No, she has no fear of death but is entirely calm and indifferent to her own fate; she suffers only for his, the son's, fate—only for that is she afraid . . .

Her last thought, her last wish—is for her son; of herself, she did not think for a minute. All that is hers belongs to the child . . .

A *Yidishe mame*!

And the Jews working in the Tomaszew factory hall write their last wishes and their testaments on the walls; here is such a testament: "Gedalia Erenberg, born September 10, 1907, in Kraśnik [Poland], sends this last message to Jan Papirose in Kraśnik, for him to take my child to the Land of Israel after the war."[4]

Of all that was once possessed, of the entire family, what remains for Erenberg—or so he believes remains—is one child hidden with a Pole. The last thought of the Jew is for his child, for whom he wants security after the war. And nothing else remains for him but to convey his last wish to the silent wall. How tragic for a Jewish father!

★ ★ ★

Here, on the soil of Polish Jews, hundreds of thousands of Jews brought from the western regions were also murdered: chiefly, German Jews. Regarding their coexistence—better said, non-coexistence—with the local Jews, there is much to recount: the struggle between "East" and "West," between East European Jews and West European Jews, unfortunately continued to the very end, to the doors of the crematoria.

Who is right? We will not enter into this tragic dispute at the moment, particularly because both East European and West European Jewry shared a common, tragic fate.

Permit me, however—here indeed—in the name of our shared fateful history and to equalize the accounts of Eastern and Western Jews, also to cite an inscription from a Western European Jew, found not in any holy text, nor in any booklet printed with Jewish letters, but in a notebook, written in German. A Jew, a German, who was thrown into the Lodz ghetto in 1941 to traverse the path to death in Chełmno or Auschwitz, together with the local Jews, left behind in the Lodz ghetto his private notebook, which was like his life's companion—not apart from him his entire life. This notebook is here, but what became of its "owner"?

And what do we find in the German notebook? A copy of *Anthrosophischer Seelenkalender* [The Calendar of the Soul, 1925 (weekly meditations)] by Dr. Rudolf Steiner [1861–1925], namely, thoughts and poems by the well-known theosophist. The owner of the notebook was apparently an adherent of his. We find here a great many very lofty and wise thoughts about human morality, about love for humanity, animals, and even plants; for God and for nature—thoughts removed from the world; his voice is spiritual! And among the thoughts jotted down, as it appears from the indicated date, in the year 1930, suddenly appears a later addendum that stabs the eye with its outrage and truth . . . A sentence from the occupation period, very likely already from Lodz, and here it is: "They are all splendid poems, but the ghetto taught us everything about life."

Only here in the ghetto, among Jews, did the German Jew tumble from his imaginary worlds: only here did he sense the difference between "poetry" and "reality"; only here did he become truly familiar with "living," so to speak; only here did he have a taste of being an ordinary Jew among other Jews. Only in his own last note, which outlived the author himself, do we sense the same familiar character as in reading the testaments of the East European Jews.

Introduction Notes:

1. Nachman Blumental, "Oyfshriftn oyf vent, sforim un bikher" in his *Shmuesn vegn der yidisher literatur unter der daytsher okupatsye* [Chats on Yiddish literature under German occupation] (Buenos Aires: Tsentral-farband fun poylishe yidn in argentine, 1966), 139–52; revised and expanded version of his "Oyfshriftn oyf vent, ksovim un bikher," *Lebns-Fragn* 145 (January 1964): 10; 146 (February 1964): 7–8.

Article Notes:

1. Shimon Bernfeld, *Sefer haDema'ot* [Book of tears], vol. 2 (Berlin: Eshkol, 1923), 89. [The English translation and bracketed insertions are taken from *The Bezalel Narkiss Index of Jewish Art*, "French Liturgical Pentateuch" (Obj. ID: 26162) at https://cja.huji.ac.il/browser.php?mode=set&id=26162.]

2. See Meir Yelin and Dimitri Gelfern, *Partizaner fun kaunaser geto* [Partisans of the Kovno ghetto] (Moscow: Emes, 1948).

3. *Yalkut Vohlin* [Volyn anthology] (Tel Aviv: Irgun Yotse Vohlin 1946 or 1947), 29; back-translated from Hebrew to Yiddish [in Blumental's article].

4. *Sefer Radom* [Book of Radom] (Tel Aviv: Irgun Yotse Radom b'Yisrael / Ramomer landsmanshaftn in amerike, 1961), 331.

Part Six

EDUCATION

36

Joseph Perl as a Pedagogical Leader and His School in Tarnopol 125 Years after Its Founding

by Philip Friedman, 1940

PHILIP FRIEDMAN (1901–1960, see also Selections 41 and 47 below) was born in Lemberg, Austrian Galicia (today Lviv, Ukraine), and received his doctorate in Central and East European history from the University of Vienna in 1925. His dissertation and early work pertained to the Haskalah period in his home region of Galicia. But Friedman's adopted home of Lodz, where he taught history at the humanistic Hebrew gymnasium, became the focus of much of his work during the 1930s in both Polish and Yiddish. He was also a teacher in YIVO's *Aspirantur* (graduate) program in Vilna. He founded the Academic Circle of the Friends of YIVO in Lodz as a counterpart to Mahler's and Ringelblum's Young Historians Circle in Warsaw and in 1938 published the first volume of a new Yiddish historical journal on the Lodz region, in which he advocated for regional studies and against the Marxist interpretation of Jewish history.

In late 1944, Friedman emerged from the German occupation to head the newly founded Central Jewish Historical Commission in liberated Poland, and he became the acknowledged leader of the first Jewish historians of the Holocaust.

Before the Holocaust, Friedman focused his research principally on Jewish economic and cultural history. The former found expression in his studies of Jewish agriculture in Galicia and Jewish occupational structure in Lodz. An example of the latter is his study of the school founded by Joseph Perl (1773–1839), the pioneering educational reformer and Hebrew novelist of the Haskalah period. Yet the extensive literature on Perl and his writings generally overlooks his school.

Friedman prepared a comprehensive study of Perl's school that appeared in Yiddish in the YIVO journal of psychology and education in August 1940 but which received only a token press run of forty copies during the Soviet occupation of Vilna. Alone among the journal's articles, it was reprinted in the 1948 volume of *YIVO bleter*, yet it remains unknown outside of Yiddish circles. A series of excerpts appears below, comprising approximately one-tenth of Friedman's seventy-page monograph.[1]

Perl's Personality and His Attitude Toward the Education Problem

Joseph Perl was born on November 10, 1773, to his father Todros and his mother Miriam. He was the only boy in the family and had a sister by the name of Perl (married name, Atlas). His father had a robust, passionate, and stubborn nature. After the death of his first wife (January 26, 1828), being an old man of eighty-three years, he married a fifty-year-old woman (February 25, 1829),[1] although his grown children (Joseph Perl was then already fifty-six years old) were against it. This match became an open scandal, and Joseph Perl suffered greatly because of it.[2]

From his father, Joseph Perl inherited his character—he had a robust nature that did not reckon with opponents when he needed to execute his plans, both for the founding of the school and in his fight against Hasidism, as well as in his wanting to seat ShI"R [Rabbi Shlomo Yehuda Rapoport, 1790–1867] as rabbi in Tarnopol [today Ternopil, Ukraine]. His father was a wealthy lumber and wine merchant. Joseph intended to become a rabbi and in his younger years studied a great amount of *Gemara* and *poskim* [rabbinical commentaries and decisors]. Then he became a fervent Hasid and traveled from one rebbe to another. For the sake of his father's business, he undertook distant travels to Leipzig, Vienna, Budapest, and Danzig, coming in contact with various people, and "acquired the sickness." At the age of twenty, he was already a *maskil* [adherent of the Haskalah, the Jewish Enlightenment] and aspired to secular education. In the summer of 1794, he attended lectures by the teacher at the main Jewish school in Lemberg [today Lviv, Ukraine], Joel Turnau.[3] Thereafter he brought to Tarnopol the famous *maskil* from Brody, Ber Gintsburg, and for three entire years studied with him German, French, Latin, mathematics, history, and natural science.[4] Soon after, Perl acquired another esteemed teacher and friend. This was Mendl Lefin [1749–1826] who, around 1802–3, came to Galicia, spent time at first in Brody, and later settled in Tarnopol where he lived until his death.[5]

In the first years of the nineteenth century, Perl also made himself independent in the field of business. He conducted widespread trade in wine and became a building contractor, constructing various official offices for the Russian and Austrian authorities, thereby making many acquaintances and forming important connections. In his correspondence, we find many letters to various Polish and German nobles and Austrian officials. In the Russian period, he had already acquired an important position in communal life in Tarnopol. In the Austrian period his influence increased still more. The Austrian government would ask his advice on various Jewish matters. He was often received in audiences by the Galician government in Lemberg and by the ministers in Vienna. On the other hand, he had very broad acquaintanceships in the Jewish world, corresponded with many Jewish scholars, communal leaders, and rabbis in Poland, Austria, Germany, and Russia, gathered around himself a circle of the best Galician writers and scholars, was a patron of Haskalah literature in Galicia. He himself began to write around 1812–13. His first literary appearances were connected with his activity as the founder and leader of the school. He wrote announcements and memorials about the school, prepared curricula and instructional books, and edited a folk calendar in which most of the articles probably came from him. After that time, Perl wrote a great number of works in Yiddish, Hebrew, and German, but only a portion of them appeared in print.

Like all *maskilic* writers and activists, Perl strove for reform of Jewish life. He believed that the only means of achieving this reform was to reeducate Jewish young people, create new schools for them. Perl reiterated this standpoint in his different memorials, as we will later see. The same was believed by Mendl Lefin and Perl's younger friend Yehuda Leib Mieses [1798–1831].[6] Perl had a strongly negative attitude toward the educational system that had prevailed among Jews until this time and (in his memorials to the Russian and Austrian governments) gave such a sharp, comprehensive and systematic, exhaustive critique of it as no Haskalah writer had yet published before this time. And here is the summary of Perl's critical conclusions. . . .[7]

[In subsequent paragraphs, Friedman summarizes the following topics: 1. The traditional religious schools; 2. The subjects of study; 3. Study of religion and morals; 4. Place and time of study; 5. Who is engaged in teaching and what does he receive for it?; 6. Is there supervision of the education of Jewish youth?; 7. How does the Polish Jew benefit from this education, and for what practical result does he send his son to be educated?]

The Founding Period

Perl sent the governor a long memorial in which he thoroughly developed and described the entire school plan. From this first document about Perl's school plan, we find the first written concept, so it appears, from Perl's own hand, with many improvements. From this very interesting document, we learn the fundamental outline of Perl's pedagogical plans. *The Memorial to the Russian Government*—written around 1812—begins with an exhaustive critique of traditional Jewish education, which was already known to us from Perl's conclusions cited above. But following this critique of Orthodox Jewish educational methods comes a sharp critique of the radical, enlightened circles among the Jews, of the "anus-enlightened," as Perl called them. In this way, Perl reveals to us how the adherents of the middle course avoided the radical fanaticism of the right and the left. And perhaps in this way he wanted to improve his standing in the eyes of the Russian government, inasmuch as to them the radical enlighteners were—since the Paris Sanhedrin of 1806–1807—a bit suspect of having quiet sympathies toward Napoleon. In any event, it is a little puzzling that in his numerous later writings and memorials to the Austrian government, this sharp critique of the radical *maskilim* is missing.

Perl dwells further on the question of whether it would be possible to reform the traditional Jewish schools by forcing the Jews to introduce a better method of instruction. It would perhaps not be difficult to force them to do so—contends Perl—but it will accomplish nothing because Jews are highly stubborn people. By force, this stubbornness—which is a historical product of age-old persecutions—becomes still stronger. "If one wants to prevail in something with this nation, one must be extremely cautious not to awaken its stubbornness, which has become a habit. . . . [ellipsis in original] One need only make the means of enlightenment easier, bring it closer to the people, but in a manner that they do not sense any coercion along the way."

After these general observations, Perl offers the following practical conclusion: "In the schools where the Jewish youth are studying, . . . children must learn Hebrew. . . . [ellipses in original] Everything must have the appearance of holiness."

Perl begins his concrete school plan with a description of the school building. The building must have at least four comfortable rooms for instruction, "each in itself, so that each has no connection with another." The director ought to live in the school to have the necessary supervision over everything. In the school there must be a spacious synagogue. This is necessary "because it gives everything in the eyes of the children and of the parents an appearance of holiness and reverence. . . . Second, by this means the parents will have more opportunity to be present for instruction . . . [ellipses in original] because each Jew comes three times a day to pray." In truth, the founding of a synagogue at the school was a very clever step and a clear demonstration of how practically and entrepreneurially Perl calculated the whole matter. Besides the virtues that Perl mentions in his memorandum, the synagogue had far greater significance to him than many other attractions. First, the income produced by the synagogue supported the school. In his history of the Tarnopol school, the director Jacob Neuman observed that "constructing the school building, which cost a great deal, was supported by the sale of seats in the synagogue."[8] From the budgets of the school, one can see that the income from the synagogue played a great part in it, in particular in the first years. Besides this, the synagogue popularized the school and gained it the sympathies of various circles that no longer wanted to pray in the old synagogue, which was small and located in "the bad part of the city." To attract the congregation, it was arranged that the official rabbi of the region would give a sermon in the new synagogue a few times in the year. And one hoped to achieve another pedagogical goal by connecting the school and the synagogue—says Neuman in his report—namely, that the schoolchildren would pray under the supervision of the teacher and learn to pray quietly and properly, without raised voices and shouting, as that is the custom "in our country." . . .

Of exceptional interest is the first *curriculum*, as it was developed by Perl for the Russian government: in the first class, one would teach reading German, "to the point of being able to understand the German reading book," reading and understanding the prayer book, elementary Hebrew grammar. In the second class would come orthography and calligraphy, the beginnings of *Russian*, mathematics, and *writing in Yiddish*. The chief subject in the second class was called "the interpretation of the Tanach [Hebrew Bible] according to the best and most suitable Hebrew translation, with German translation" (the name Mendelssohn was not mentioned). But, in the third class, one would study *Mishnah* with a simple commentary and begin learning *Gemara*, "religion and ethics, taken for the most part from the Tanach and Talmud." In the general subjects—besides those already mentioned—is also added bookkeeping. The curriculum of the fourth class is very broad and interesting. Here, one will also learn "the most important foundation of the art of running a household and of agriculture, historical foundations of the arts and handcrafts, something of natural history and natural science, of history and geography, in particular of the fatherland . . . [ellipsis in original] something of aesthetics, of rhetoric, but in particular the students will need to be prepared for that by means of brief monologues." As we see, this is a very rich curriculum. But in addition to this, Perl already decided in 1814 to introduce the study of *Polish* and *French* language, and he also offered some of the parents that, if they wished, their children could also learn *Italian* and *music*. . . .[9]

Girls—Perl contended—need not learn as much as boys. They will attend the school only from 5 to 10 years of age and will study only German, Russian, a little religion and ethics, writing and reading Yiddish, "main principles of the art of conducting a proper home," and agriculture, counting, and female endeavors. . . .

[Ensuing sections describe the school's operations, the teachers and other school personnel, pedagogical methods, publishing activities, further plans by Perl, and, at length, the opposition to Perl by Orthodox rabbis and Hasidim, and Perl's plans for a trade- and craftwork-school, among other topics.]

The Significance of Perl's School and Its General Characteristics

Perl's school was the first Jewish Haskalah school in Eastern Europe. It was the first time that a Jewish pedagogical initiative arose among Jews themselves and not through pressure from above, whether by the government (the Homberg School in Galicia) or by the non-Jewish community. It was also the first community Jewish school. The Tarnopol school strove for the first time to create a deeper synthesis between Jewish and general education. In addition, the introduction of craftwork for girls and the study of various crafts for boys was a novelty in Eastern Europe. Because of all these virtues and because of its high pedagogical level, the Tarnopol school had great influence and served as a symbol and example for the founding of almost all other Jewish schools in Eastern Europe up until the 1840s.

Perl's creation of the school was not an entirely original matter. It was the expression of the ideals and intellectual trends that prevailed among the Jewish *maskilim*. In the pedagogical goals and tasks of the school, one clearly recognizes the influence of the French rationalists (in particular the encyclopedists who so strongly emphasized the importance of craftwork and practical art), of Rousseau, of the French pedagogue Rolland, of the Austrian pedagogue Felbiger. It is difficult to determine whether those were direct influences. Rather, we can infer an indirect influence—by the Jewish schools in Germany, which were imbued with the spirit of rationalism and whose influence on Perl we recognized at every turn. . . . Perl was not a pedagogical theoretician. His school was not an example of theoretical consistency but was a practical attempt to create a certain compromise, or, if one wishes, one could also say, a synthesis between general and Jewish educational ideas.

This synthesis is Perl's greatest service and most original accomplishment. The Haskalah-schools generally tended to reduce and narrow the Jewish studies relative to the general studies. Perl went in an entirely opposite direction from the Jacobson School, the Philanthropin, the Berlin Freischule, etc. He saw the very essence and the true purpose of the Jewish school in a harmonious synthesis of Jewish and general education. Perl cultivated and realized in his school a very broad program of Hebrew studies, and—as we saw [in paragraphs omitted above]—he was considering how to further broaden and deepen the Jewish fields of study, whether in the form of a higher institute, a teachers seminary, or an actual rabbinical school. His attitude toward Yiddish studies was not clear, purely utilitarian, and without consistency, although Perl himself was—as we now know—a brilliant Yiddish writer, who wrote novels and satires in Yiddish, letters, and at times also gave Yiddish sermons in the synagogue. In addition, in the area of "temple reform," he was not nearly as radical as the German *maskilim* and did not find favor with the radical wing of the Galician Haskalah. For him, the radical *maskilim* were "the new Jew-haters" and "anus-enlighteners." He was ready to deal with Rabbi [Jacob Meshullam] Ornstein and make still further compromises. This was not because of weakness but political calculation and cleverness on his part. Perl was after all a powerful man, and when he saw that he could achieve more with strength than with fine speech, without any hesitation he made use of the strength of . . . [ellipsis in original] the Austrian emperor: he forced Jewish communities to pay taxes for his school; he fought against the enemy of his school, Rabbi Hirsh Zydaczower [1763–1831], with means that would not generally be considered proper.[10]

Perl saw in his school, above all, a community institution. For him, the new education of Jewish youth was the most important means in the struggle by the Haskalah to win over the Jewish masses for its ideals. The school needed to disseminate the ideals of the Haskalah in a direct manner: it should produce folk writers, and it should concentrate around itself and around its library the elements friendly to the Haskalah in a sort of folk university. In the founding of a teachers and rabbinical seminary, a new, great reservoir of fighters for the Haskalah would be created. In fact, the atmosphere of the school was such that, in the first years, it produced many teachers, *maskilic* writers, and activists. Perl was proficient at assessing and dealing with people and knew how to select from among his students young collaborators who, with time, acquired a reputation as important pedagogues and Haskalah activists. Perl gave his teachers the possibility of living fruitfully; the relatively high pay freed them from worries about income and allowed them to devote themselves entirely to pedagogical and communal literary activity.

After Perl's death, his school met the same fate as many similar creations of the Haskalah period. The tragic fate of the Haskalah movement, which carried within itself the seed of its own downfall, also had to materialize in its school creations. We know how quickly the Jewish schools in Germany lost every sparkle of Jewishness. Perl's school maintained its Jewish character much longer. But after Perl's death the Jewish content was much reduced. The further development of the school did not go in the direction envisioned by its founder. The spirit of the time and the conditions of the time were stronger than the spirit of the founder.

[The last section of Friedman's article discusses the later years of the school until the time of his writing, in the late 1930s.]

Introduction Notes:

1. Filip Fridman, "Yosef Perl vi a bildungs-tuer un zayn shul in tarnopol (125 yor nokh ir grindung)," *Shriftn far psikhologye un pedagogik fun yivo* II (Vilna, 1940): 128–87; photo-reproduced in *YIVO bleter* XXXI–XXXII (New York, 1948): 131–90 (excerpted here).

Article Notes:

1. The dates originate from the registers of deaths and marriages of the Jewish community in Tarnopol.

2. This is evident from Perl's letters of that time to his sister, copies of which are in Perl's archive.

3. Regarding Joel Turnau, see M. Balaban, "Herz Homberg" in *Z historji Żydów w Polsce* [From the History of the Jews in Poland] (Warsaw: B-cia Lewin-Epstein i S-ka, 1920), 204, 223.

4. For specific details about Perl's biography, see Yisroel Vaynlez, "Yoysef perls lebn un shafn," in *Yoysef perls yidishe ksovim* (Vilna: YIVO, 1937), VII–LXX.

5. More specifically on the relationship between Joseph Perl and Mendl Lefin, see Yisroel Vaynlez, "Mendl lefin-satanover," *YIVO bleter* II (Vilna, November–December 1931): 334–57.

6. M. Lefin, in his French memorial (see Vaynlez, 339; Lefin's memorial was discussed in detail by Dr. N. M. Gelber, *Aus zwei Jahrhunderten: Beiträge zur neueren Geschichte d. Juden* (Vienna: R. Lowit, 1924), 45–49); Y. L. Mieses, in his well-known book, *Sefer Kin'at Ha-Emet* (Vienna: Anton Schmid, 1828); see Dr. Y. Tsinberg, *Geshikhte fun der literatur bay yidn,* vol. VIII, part 1 (Vilna: Tomor, 1929), 52.

7. According to Perl's memorial to the Russian governor von Tails in 1812, and in particular his memorial to the Austrian education minister in 1819 (both manuscripts are in Perl's archive).

8. The indicated manuscript, written in German, is in the Tarnopol Perl Library and Archive and is titled: *Über die Entstehung und Einrichtung der Tarnopoler Israelitischen Freischule nebst einer genauen Erwägung der Ursachen, warum un wie der Unterricht in allen hebräischen Gegenständen mit dieser Lehranstalt vereinigt worden sey. Vom Direktor der Freischule (Neuman.).* There is no date of completion for the manuscript; from the content, one can deduce that it was written in 1815 or 1816.

9. Perl's letter to Abraham Teitlboym in Mada (Hungary) of September 11, 1814 (Perl's Archive in Tarnopol). Perl's rich language curriculum is somewhat reminiscent of the Jacobin School, where at first one also studied six languages at once! His plans about introducing agriculture, artisanry, handicraft and other practical subjects apparently also arose under the

influence of a few German Jewish schools (Jacobson's School [in Seesen, Lower Saxony], Philanthropin [in Frankfurt a. M.], the schools in Hamburg, Breslau, and Dessau).

10. In any event, the fight against the Hasidim with denunciations was an altogether ordinary matter among the *maskilim*. Rabbi Nachman Krochmal, Rabbi Yehoshua ben Levi, Shmuel David Luzzatto, Yehuda-Leib Gordon, Mieses, and other major figures of the Haskalah saw no sin in this. See . . . F. Friedman, "Di ershte kamfn tvishn haskole un khsidis [The first fights between Haskalah and Hasidism]," *Fun noentn over* [From the recent past] I, no. 4 (Vilna, October–December 1937): 259–74.

37
Yehuda-Leib Gordon as a Fighter for the Haskalah in Jewish Schools in Lithuania in the Mid-Nineteenth Century
by Nadzieja Jaffe, 1938

NADZIEJA JAFFE (in Yiddish, Dina Yafe; née Gershun, 1895–1943) was born in Vilna, Russian Lithuania (today Vilnius, Lithuania), and received her doctorate in history from the University of Vilna in 1936, when she was already past the age of forty and a wife and mother. Among writers of Jewish history in Yiddish, she is apparently the only woman to have received a doctorate before World War II. During the Nazi occupation, she was one of the group of scholars forced to work in the YIVO building to sort valuable materials for the Nazis. She was sent to Treblinka where she died. The page of testimony in her name at Yad Vashem, completed in 1955 by her son, Aryeh Jaffe, lists her occupation as "historian."[1]

Jaffe and her writings are largely unknown in the scholarly literature. Nevertheless, from 1937 to 1940, she published at least nine articles, most on specific topics in the history of the Jews of Vilna. All appeared in local Yiddish newspapers, except two that were published in historical journals: one in YIVO's *Historishe shriftn* and the other in the independent journal *Fun noentn over* (From the recent past), edited by lay historian Moyshe Shalit (see Selection 44 below), which also published articles by Friedman, Ginsburg, Kon, Niger, Ringelblum, and others. The latter article by Jaffe (overlooked in her entry in the *New Lexicon of Yiddish Writers*) discusses the famed Hebrew writer Y. L. Gordon and his early attempts at Jewish educational reform. The subject may also have attracted her attention because of his pioneering insistence on providing education to girls as well as boys. The article appears below.[2]

The archival documents of the Third Department [tsarist secret police] in the former Vilna Educational Region are especially relevant to Jewish matters. For the 1850s and 1860s, this is the best source material on the history of the conflict within the Jewish community for and against the Haskalah [the Jewish Enlightenment].

The dead documents also hold living tragedies. One of these tragedies is the fate of Yehuda-Leib Gordon, the famous poet and publicist who wandered during the 1850s and 1860s through the faraway Lithuanian towns.

At first, Gordon was employed as a teacher in a state Jewish school in Ponevezh [today Panevėžys, Lithuania]. Here he wrote his collection of parables, *Mishle Yehuda* [Parables of Judah, 1859], and the correspondence regarding this composition was preserved in the archives.[1] Gordon lobbied for publishing his compositions at state expense and for distributing his collection in state Jewish educational institutions. The education curator submitted Gordon's manuscript to the "learned Jews" Shemu'el Yosef Fünn and Jacob Tugendhold for expert opinions.

Tugendhold strongly praised Gordon's composition "in the Hebrew mother tongue" and found that the author had mastered it extraordinarily well.

Fünn also praised Gordon's language as simple—and aside from a few Germanisms—pure and close to the language of the Hebrew Bible. In only four fables was Fünn of the opinion that the "author is so full of enthusiasm for the Haskalah that he expresses himself too aggressively regarding that manner of thought for the folk masses."

Gordon's manuscript was sent farther, however, to the education ministry, and there it was sent to the Jewish censor Iosif Zeiberling. In accordance with the spirit of the time, he saw "free thoughts" in the composition and in his report wrote "that some expressions ought not be shown to children and people who are in such a civil situation as the Jews."

"Thus, for example," wrote Zeiberling, "we find in the adaptation of La Fontaine's fable 'Le dragon á plusieurs têtes' ['The Dragon with Many

Heads']—which stresses the virtues of autocracy over representative government—in the start, also a certain justification for the latter, which can put unnecessary thoughts in young and inexperienced minds, and the very subject of this fable is not suited for the book *Fables of Judah*."

In the translation of La Fontaine's "La Génisse," which was known by [the famous Russian fabulist Ivan] Krylov under the name "The Lion on the Hunt," the teacher Gordon reiterates La Fontaine's stanza too clearly in the moral, which he himself appends in this manner: "Because lawgiving and laws / exist only for weak people, / and not for the cunning, like snakes / or the strong, like lions."

By contrast, Krylov conveyed La Fontaine's stanza very artfully and gently: "I am entitled to all this because I am stronger than everyone."

In his imitation of La Fontaine's fable, "The Town Mouse and the Country Mouse," the author sets the house mouse with the priest, and in his chat with his friend, the field mouse, he says: "He (the priest) steals the property of his coreligionists, and I take from him."—"In the indicated fable by La Fontaine, there is no character who is a priest." Besides this, Zeiberling contends that "the author uses too many sharp, cutting words in some fables against Jews who still hesitate about Haskalah matters."

On the basis of Zeiberling's assessment, the ministry refused to give Gordon a stipend to print his work. In 1860, he printed the fables at his own expense, but he revised them according to Zeiberling's directions, and, for 95 rubles and 40 kopeks, the ministry bought 116 copies from him for the libraries of the Jewish schools.

But the principal struggle that Gordon had to endure in Ponevezh was with the conservative Jewish circles.[2] On September 22, 1860, the director of the Ponevezh gymnasium, who also had supervision of the Jewish school, writes to the curator: "Most Ponevezh Jews have no loyalty to Gordon because he does not observe their customs and laws of dress and in general does not demonstrate any religious fanaticism and therefore the number of students in the local school is very small. This cannot be said of the supervisor Kostka, who carries out his duties with diligence.[3] And therefore, considering Gordon a good teacher and a thoroughly educated person, I nevertheless believe that it would be better to transfer him to Shavel [today Šiauliai, Lithuania] because the local Jewish school would benefit from this."

And so Gordon was transferred to Shavel. Already in Ponevezh, together with another teacher, Rumshen, he had wanted to open a Jewish school for girls.[4] Now, in Shavel, he lobbied further for opening such a school.[5] At first, he was refused because he had included the Polish language in the curriculum. Gordon was required to renounce Polish, and on September 9, 1869, he received permission to open the school. The curriculum includes the Hebrew, Russian, and German languages. In accordance with the progressive ideas of the school proprietor, it indicates that the chapters of the *Chumash* [Pentateuch] that were not suitable for children would not be read. For those who had the desire, a time was set when the students could learn music, dance, and elementary knowledge of French, studies that appeared to be necessary at that time in Shavel for women's education. The tuition was 2 rubles a month. The students numbered about eighteen. The director of the elementary school writes that "Gordon's pay is extremely low and that, in maintaining the school, material reward was not his chief motivation, but his zeal and concern for spreading education among his fellow believers." In March 1864, the school had to close for financial reasons, but in 1865 he lobbied again for it to open because he had invested a great amount of expense in it.

But the Shavel Jews were not at all satisfied with Gordon's work. On May 10, 1869, they sent a request to the curator [director of the educational district].[6] The Jews write that they will happily send their children to the state Jewish school, that they are satisfied with the school supervisor, Zagorski (a Christian), with the Jewish teachers Epstein and son, but that Gordon is a skeptic and that there is a danger that he will influence the youth and lead them away from the path of righteousness. They request that in Gordon's place a Russian Orthodox teacher be appointed who would teach them Russian and not lead them astray in their faith.

By order of the curator, the director of the elementary schools in Shavel attempted to resolve the matter. The Jewish deputies were not able to provide any facts against Gordon; they just complained that Gordon violates the Sabbath, carries his watch and handkerchief on the Sabbath, does not wear a hat while eating, goes about in a uniform, eats from the same vessels as Christians. There were also, as the director informs the curators, educated Jews in Shavel who sent their daughters to Gordon's school and lobbied for Gordon to remain in Shavel. The director writes that this has nothing to do with Gordon's character but with the struggle of the Orthodox against the progressives, and he considers it necessary to keep Gordon in Shavel so that the first will not gain an advantage over the second.

But in the fall of that same year, 1865, a position became free for a supervisor in a state school in Telz [today Telšiai, Lithuania].[7] Gordon begins lobbying for the position. The curator inquires of the director of the Shavel elementary school about Gordon. Although, as the curator writes, only those who have completed the school for state rabbis are appointed to positions of leadership in Jewish state schools, and Gordon had not completed it.[8] Nevertheless, information about his education and his pedagogical activity interested the curator. The Shavel school director writes a reply on November 15, 1865, about Gordon:

> I know Gordon as a teacher who is conscientious and entirely devoted to his work, about whom I am convinced, visiting his classes not only in the state Jewish school but also in the private girl's school, of what he has endured. Despite many unfavorable conditions, Gordon did not cease teaching young girls Haskalah and conducted his work with energy and without stopping. Besides this, he is sufficiently educated and looks with sympathy on reforms.
>
> But I cannot remain silent to your excellency about the fact that in Gordon's character there is a streak that cannot be considered a virtue in a rising teacher-administrator: he is sharp with regard to his fellow religionists who belong to the old generation and even treats them with contempt. In this one sees the source of the bitterness evinced by the majority of local Jews toward Gordon. Perhaps, receiving a position for which he is qualified, he will change and become more cautious.

On December 3, 1865, the curator appointed Gordon supervisor of the state Jewish school in Telz, but he asked the school director to impress on Gordon that, for the sake of the good of the work, he be cautious, not overstep, not engage in any extreme, or else another supervisor would be appointed.

In Telz, Gordon again opened a school for girls,[9] and as the director informed the curator, he gave it not only moral but financial support. Upon opening the school on October 12, 1866, Gordon gave a speech in which he said, among other things: "Since ancient times, the Jewish people distinguished itself among the Eastern peoples with its humanitarian attitude toward women. Women had complete freedom among Jews, and they participated in all matters of family and civic life. Just such a tolerance is demonstrated by Jews of our time with regard to the education of women. Whereas their sons occupy themselves entirely with Talmud, Jews do not think for a minute about sending their daughters to school. In the areas where schools for Jewish girls exist, they are overflowing."

But in Telz, stronger persecutions awaited him than in Shavel. At the beginning of July 1867, Gordon had the carelessness to punish the student Nisn Pres, for impudence, with five lashes.[10] What was permissible for a teacher was not allowed to Gordon. There was a commotion. The nearest government authorities ruled that Gordon should not be tried because, on the basis of the rules of the education ministry, the supervisor had the right in such cases to impose that sort of punishment.

But then a group of Jews sent a request to the curator in which they write that Gordon's teaching was having no results and that, in addition, he deals so brutally with the children that many Jews are afraid to send their children to school, although they strongly regret not being able to do so. Therefore, these Jews request the appointment of a Russian Orthodox supervisor in the school instead of Gordon. The request had fifteen acknowledged signatures.

Exactly such a request was sent to the governor-general. Telegrams were sent to the Kovno governor and the curator. The *maskilim* were also not silent—the state rabbi Chazanovich, the regional doctor Mapu, and some merchants; they also telegraphed and sent requests; called their opponents "a negligible heap of fanatics." They wrote that "all of Gordon's means and actions were correct and with results."

To clarify the fight in the Telz Jewish community, the director of the elementary school in Shavel forwarded to the curator Gordon's letter to him, which painted the entire picture. The copy of the letter was preserved in the archives. We present it here, translated in its entirety. *Copy of the letter from the supervisor of the Telz state Jewish school, Leib Gordon. Addressed to the Shavel school director Matvey Vasilievich Fursov, August 8, 1867:*[11]

[Following this appears a long letter from Gordon, in which he ascribes his difficulties to an unprovoked campaign organized by local and outside reactionary groups opposed to his progressive steps in educating boys—and especially girls—in the spirit of the Haskalah.]

The director writes with regard to this letter:

> From the petitions for and against Gordon, a deep although clumsy intrigue by the fanatical party among Jews against the conscientious work and honest execution of his duty on Gordon's part becomes apparent. His letter, which clarifies the matter, leads to other, not entirely pleasant facts.

> First of all, there is no basis for doubting that Gordon's lines breathe with truth and that in them one hears no anxious notes of complete despair in the victory of truth, and finally, that the fight with fanaticism broke Gordon's energetic nature.
>
> Second, there are clear reasons to believe that the constant intrigues and the shameless false accusations do harm not only to individuals but also to the Jewish Haskalah in general.

The director maintains "that the Jews themselves do not know what and toward what they strive. The Shavel Jews, who got rid of Gordon, now cry loudly that the level of the school has fallen since Gordon left. The same Jews complain that the director is Russian Orthodox. And the intrigues do not stop increasing."

The director himself decided to go to Telz to investigate the matter, and he was there on August 25, 1867. In the archives about the matter is his report of September 15, 1867, for the curator. Everywhere, from both Christians and educated Jews, the director heard the best opinions about Gordon, and he concluded that he was not only appreciated but honored. The signatures on the petition against Gordon appear, according to the words of an expert, to be written by one hand. It is also not conceivable how the signatures could be verified; some of the undersigned did not know how to write. The accusers were afraid to identify themselves to the director; they even responded to his invitation coarsely and sharply. Eventually, a deputation appeared that was prepared to bring its chief accusation against Gordon: that he said one may eat meat with dairy.

From that conversation—writes the director—he understood what Gordon had to do. He advised him to demand legal redress against the slanderers—but the Jews did not rest. With broken and anonymous writing, a denunciation was sent on September 11, 1867, to the curator and education minister. Here, there was also a denunciation against the director's investigation, in which he called the informers fools. The boy, Pres, who had been punished, was portrayed as sickly as a result of his suffering. Doubt was also expressed about Gordon's political correctness; he is a heretic, he does not pray in the synagogue; he has food cooked for him for Sabbath lunch, and he writes and smokes on the Sabbath. Besides this, Gordon was accused of stealing government money and lumber. The informer finished by saying that Gordon dominated the Telz community organization and held it under his yoke like Pharoah held the Jews in Egypt. The government ought to see to saving the Telz Jews from this demon.—Despite all of this, Gordon remained in Telz. In 1868, he lobbied for a position as a director in the Grodno Jewish school; he was motivated by his wanting to give enlightened education to children in a regional capital city. He did not receive this position. In 1872, he was struck by the hope—a possibility to leave for St. Petersburg. His powers did not let go of him so easily, and his letters to the school district were despondent.[12] "I must be in St. Petersburg at the start of the coming week," he writes to the school district on May 31, 1872. "For me, this is a question of 'to be or not to be.'"

As is well known, Gordon ultimately succeeded in escaping from the hinterland and beginning a new life in St. Petersburg.

Introduction Notes:

1. https://collections.yadvashem.org/en/names/929740.

2. Dina Yafe, "Yehuda-Leyb Gordon vi a kemfer far der haskole (loyt di materyaln fun vilner melukhe-arkhiv) [according to materials from the Vilna state archive]," *Fun noentn over* [From the recent past] II, no. 3–4 (Vilna, July–December 1938): 224–33 (abridged).

Article Notes:

1. Archw. Państw. w Wilnie, Okr. Szkolny, st. III r. 1858, Nr. 56 [verbatim].
2. Arch. Państw. w Wilnie Okr. Szk. st. III r. 3 1860, Nr. 55 [verbatim].
3. Kostka was a Christian.
4. Wil. Arch. Państw. st. 3 r. 1860, Nr. 34 [verbatim].
5. Wil. Arch. Państw. st. 3 1860, Nr. 464 [verbatim].
6. Wil. Arch. Państw. Okr. Szk. st. 3 r. 1865, Nr. 47 [verbatim].
7. Wil. Arch. Państw. Okr. Szk. st. 3 r 1865, Nr. 80 [verbatim].
8. Did not graduate as a state rabbi but did pass the examinations as an unmatriculated student of the rabbinical school as a teacher.
9. Wil. Arch. Państw. Okr. Szk. st. 3, 1865, Nr. 15 [verbatim].
10. Wil. Arch. Państw. Okr. Szk. st. 3 r. 1867, Nr. 80 [verbatim].
11. [At the end of the letter, the article lists the date as August 6, 1867; the letter does not appear to have been published elsewhere, for verification of the date.]
12. Wil. Arch. Państw. Okr. Szk. st. 3, 1[8]67, Nr. 4 [verbatim].

38
The Rise of Yiddish Secular Schools in Poland during World War I
by Chaim-Solomon Kazdan, 1947

CHAIM-SOLOMON KAZDAN (1883–1979) was born in Kherson, Russian Ukraine (today in Ukraine), and without university training became a leader of the secular Yiddish school systems in Eastern Europe. As a teacher, he was among the first to introduce Yiddish instruction into Jewish schools in Ukraine in the early twentieth century. In Kiev, during the short-lived period of Ukrainian independence after World War I, he was coeditor of the first pedagogical journal in Yiddish, *Shul un lebn* (School and life). In 1920 he relocated to Warsaw and became one of the founders of the Central Yiddish School Organization (TsYShO), which created the principal network of secular Yiddish-language schools in prewar Poland. Historian Isaiah Trunk, also a teacher in the TsYShO schools, described Kazdan as "a pioneer and veteran of the secular sector in the Jewish school system, one of its most prominent builders."[1] He published widely on topics in Yiddish pedagogy and Yiddish literature and culture. He escaped from Poland in 1939 and settled in New York in 1941.

After the Holocaust, Kazdan continued to write about Yiddish education but came to accept that the high period of the Yiddish secular school movement had passed. Whereas other leading figures in Yiddish pedagogy (such as Hyman Bass, Abraham Golomb, and Zalman Yefroykin) redoubled their efforts to keep alive an increasingly marginal secular Yiddish school system in the United States and Latin America, Kazdan turned to writing the history of the Yiddishist school movement in Eastern Europe before the Holocaust. He published two major monographs, *The History of the Jewish School System in Independent Poland* (1947) and *From Traditional Religious Schools and Secular Schools to TsYShO* (1956), as well as the *Yizkor book of the Murdered TsYShO Teachers in Poland* (1954), and he edited the *Medem-Sanatorium Book* about the Jewish Labor Bund's school for tubercular children in Poland (1970), all in Yiddish. Portions of the opening chapter of the first-named book, in which he describes the initial growth of the Yiddish schools, appear below.[2]

During the last few years before the First World War, Warsaw—the capital city of what was then Russian Poland—was an exuberant center of new Yiddish secular culture. In the years 1907–1908, a multifaceted activity was conducted here by the Jewish section of the Warsaw "University for All" (five departments). The first speakers in Yiddish here were Y. L. Peretz, Dr. G. Levin, and L. Hersh. The average number of attendees at the Yiddish public readings of the folk university section was 758 persons; the total number of attendees at the 27 courses in Yiddish in the first year was 15,812, and in the second school year—8,335 (for political reasons, the course was shortened). Peretz's lectures alone were attended by 4,742 persons. On March 1, 1908, the Society to Combat Illiteracy began its activity. In its six evening schools, there were as many as 500 students.

In the same year, Yiddish was introduced as a subject of study in the high school of the well-known Warsaw [woman] pedagogue Ravich (later taken over by Mrs. Z. Kalecka), and the Yiddish teacher there was David Herman, who later gained fame as a director of Yiddish theater.

In the circles of the Jewish Labor Bund in Warsaw in those years, people circulated plans for organizing a day school for working-class children in the Yiddish language. But because of the police regime of the time, the plans were never realized.

In 1911, a Yiddishist group was created within the Warsaw Jewish Teachers' Society, which began to conduct an organized and systematic struggle for introducing the Yiddish language into the existing communal schools. . . . The group organized several reports . . . The reports and the debates about them drew a large audience of intellectuals and workers. Two new projects arose at that time: 1) to create courses for teachers with a broad curriculum of Yiddish, Yiddish literature, and economic science; the curriculum was sent with a memorandum to the school authorities, but permission for the courses was not received; 2) inasmuch as the kindergartens were under the control of the administrator and not the school authority, and in the permission for a kindergarten no language was specified for the institution, the Warsaw Yiddishists therefore decided to open a kindergarten in the Yiddish language.

Fundraising was begun, and a teacher was invited—but because of insufficient funding and also political difficulties, this project was not realized.

But the Yiddishists in Warsaw could not rest. Y. L. Peretz and his circle, Peretz's agitation for Yiddish theater, the practical activity of Ha-Zemer [The Song; music society] with its *kestl-ovntn* ["box evenings" at which young people would pull discussion questions out of a box], the representatives of Yiddish literature, and, principally, the Jewish labor movement—all created an atmosphere in which the desire to create a school in Yiddish became ever stronger and more mature. And in 1912, this striving was realized in one niche in the following manner: in Warsaw there existed at that time an "Education for Children" society that maintained its own school—half *Talmud Torah* [traditional religious school], half *nachalne uchilishche* [official Russian government school]—a beginning school in Russian. So this school, which was under the control of an assimilatory leadership, succeeded in pressing for the local pedagogue and Yiddishist Shloyme Gilinski [1888–1961] to be hired as director. Supported by the group of Yiddishists, Gilinski conducted a quiet "revolution" in the school; the first class was held entirely in Yiddish; later, natural science, geography, and history started to be taught in Yiddish.

The school became popular with the parents and among the faculty. This three-class high school of the Society for Children's Education was, therefore, the *first school with Yiddish-language instruction in the territory of Poland.*

When the war broke out, the school was left hanging in midair. Out of seven teachers, only two remained, and later even only one. The teachers were forced to work illegally and dedicate their free time to the school . . . It was possible to maintain the school—with a budget of 15–18 rubles per month . . . [ellipses in original] Five months after the start of the war, the OPE (Society for the Promotion of Enlightenment among the Jews of Russia) and OZE (Health Society) came to their aid. The school continued normally.

The newly erupted World War simultaneously opened new possibilities and perspectives for educational work in the Yiddish language. In almost the first months of the war, the problem arose of caring for the children of the homeless who appeared in Warsaw in great numbers. The Zionists opened *gan-yeladim*(s) [Hebrew: kindergarten(s)] for the homeless children, the assimilationists—*Ochranke*(s) [Polish: nursery]. The Yiddishists began a fight for Yiddish in the institutions for children of the homeless. The fight took on sharper and sharper forms; the St. Petersburg societies (OPE, OZE, etc.), who financed the institutions, supported the adherents of Yiddish [a major shift away from support of Russian, which Kazden documented elsewhere]. In the Zionist camp, the fight was led by H. Farbstein, Levin-Epstein, Sh. L. Gordon, Yitzhak Grinbaum; on the Yiddishist side, the newly arrived Jacob Lestschinski, A. Strashun, Katzenbogen, L. Bramson, and the local M. Birnbaum and Sh. Gilinski. A compromise was agreed upon regarding the schools that were supported by communal funds: general studies should be conducted in Yiddish; in return, in the first class, Hebrew would be introduced first and, only toward the end, Yiddish. In fact, in the newly opened schools, all the classes were conducted in Yiddish. There were five such schools. Some 30 percent of the students were local Warsaw children. During the German occupation, these schools were without means, but they continued their existence little by little.

Parallel to the several compromise-schools, there were also purely Hebraicist institutions, on the one hand, and purely Yiddishist institutions on the other. Children's homes, which developed from the charitable children's kitchens, were established and functioned in Yiddish. One such kitchen on Eisengas Street, created by a group of young women—former students from Kalecka's gymnasium—attracted Y. L. Peretz to their work, and from it arose *the first Yiddish children's home* [orphanage]—which officially opened on March 23, 1915, at 7 Gensze Street. Y. L. Peretz opened the children's home and signed in the minute book his famous motto: "Do not say to anyone: remain as you are; rather, develop from what you are." In the minutes of the children's home, it says clearly: "The language of the home is Yiddish." . . . Later, from among the older children of the children's home, an advanced class was assembled that served as the foundation of the Yiddish high school in Warsaw, at 49 Mila Street. . . .

On October 29, 1915, the official opening of the children's home named for [Bundist leader] Bronislaw Grosser took place. Beginning with 40 children, the children's home soon moved to new premises, and the number of children there was 80. The institution grew quickly and soon moved again (in July 1916) to new, larger quarters, and here there were already 160 children. At the beginning of the 1917–18 school year, one grade was opened, and a year later, a second grade. In this way, the children's home was transformed little by little into a normal elementary school. The same Bundist school leaders opened a children's home (with two teachers) in 1917–18, a year later—another children's home (with three teachers), and the children's homes were gradually transformed into schools. In 1920–21 a new school was opened with two grades—by this means, in 1920–21, the Grosser schools and children's homes already had four locations with twelve sections. . . .

At the beginning of the 1916–17 school year, the Zionist-Socialist Workers Party founded a labor children's home in the name of Y. L. Peretz.

The Poale-Zion were also very active in the school field. During the German occupation, they also founded a number of children's homes, which were transformed thereafter into normal elementary schools.

In total, in 1920, the Yiddish secular school system had already created a multibranched school network of various political movements, which had [2,000 children, according to a table in the article].

We can establish, therefore, that in this period various strata of the Jewish population actively undertook the creation of modern Jewish schools. In the first rank was the Jewish working class. Both in pace and number of institutions, the schools created by the Jewish labor movement took first place, but strong school activity was also demonstrated by the Jewish democratic-bourgeois elements. In no period of the subsequent years did the Jewish bourgeoisie fail to demonstrate as much energy and ability for organizing Jewish schools as in this period under discussion.

The same process took place in the entire province. Schools and children's homes of the Grosser type (Bund) were established, for example, in Lodz, Bialystok, Brisk [today Brest, Belarus], Chelm, Kalisz, Kałuszyn, Siedlec, Piotrków, Tomaszów-Mazowiecki, Pinsk [today in Belarus], and others. . . .

The Rise of Yiddish Secular Schools in Poland during World War I 311

Together with the process of continual growth of the school systems, the idea began to mature that the schools of the various Yiddishist political movements ought to unite. Each group of schools had, until then, worked on its own alone. Even the teachers had not shared their experience, but now life forced the teachers and leaders of the Yiddish secular schools to draw closer to each other, hold joint conferences, begin common pedagogical work, etc. . . .

Nearly at the start of the German occupation, attempts were made to confer with the bourgeois elements of the Jewish community that did not support Yiddish as the language of instruction. One such large conference took place at the premises of the Jewish teachers union, and the Zionist lawyer Abba Olshvanger was the president of the conference.[1]

This was the conference of representatives of teacher groups, trade unions, community leaders, and writers of various movements. The conference was called by the leaders of the Jewish Teachers' Society—to consider the issues of Jewish elementary schools in connection with the decision of the General Civic Citizens Committee (in place of the City Council), which had entirely ignored the Jewish population. Among the representatives of the trade unions was Vladimir Medem, who had just recently been released from prison; he was ill and physically exhausted.

A passionate debate was conducted about the question of the language of instruction. The Zionists put forth a demand that the language of instruction for the school should not be specified but be satisfied with the formula "Jewish school." The Yiddishists demanded that Yiddish be required as the language of instruction. The relative balance of forces at the conference was almost exactly equal. At the end, two general speakers appeared: H. Farbstein and V. Medem. Medem's arguments, his manner of speaking—won the majority of those present. The result of the vote was: Farbstein's resolution (on behalf of the Zionists) received 35 votes, Medem's 44.

Medem's resolution was the first public declaration during the German occupation about Yiddish as the language of instruction in the Jewish elementary schools. For the first time in a resolution, the demand was made of the Polish public for an autonomous agency that would organize and direct the Jewish schools. [The remainder of Kazdan's 579-page book details the rise and growth of each branch of the Yiddishist school movement in interwar Poland, as well as the opposition to it by Zionist, assimilationist, and Orthodox Jews.]

Introduction Notes:

1. Yeshaye Trunk, "A pyonerish verk in unzer historish-pedagogisher literatur" [A pioneering work in our historical-pedagogical literature], *Unzer tsayt* [Our time]11–12 (181–82) (November–December 1956): 51.

2. Kh. Sh. Kazdan, *Di geshikhte fun yidishn shulvezn in umophengikn poyln* [The history of the Jewish school system in independent Poland] (Mexico, D.F.: Gezelshaft "Kultur un helf," 1947), 19–27 (abridged).

Article Notes:

1. See Sh. Gilinski, "Medem baym boyen undzer shul" [Medem in the creation of our school] *Shul un lebn* [School and life] 20, nos. 1–2 (February 1923).

39
Jewish Schools in the Vilna Ghetto as Spiritual Resistance
by Mark Dworzecki, 1948

MARK DWORZECKI (see Selections 12 and 33 above, 42 and 48 below) began writing his history of the Vilna ghetto while still in the ghetto. Within a year of his escape from a forced march in Germany, in April 1945, he had established himself in Paris as a leader of the survivor community and began publishing advance chapters of his ghetto history. As his first step toward becoming a professional historian of the Holocaust, it blends objective narrative with personal observation in a manner not usually found in historical writing.

The first major portion to appear was "The Cultural System in the Vilna Ghetto," published at the early date of March 1946. In Dworzecki's order of priorities, cultural life in the ghetto began with the unified system of schools created immediately after the ghetto was imposed by the Nazis. Included were general schools at all levels, as well as religious and vocational schools operated by each cultural element in the ghetto, including clubs, holiday events, and sports—as described in the article below.[1]

Two months later, Dworzecki would write: "And perhaps the writer of Jewish history will say: It is madness to . . . teach children facing death—And perhaps he will say: This is how the Jews produced cultural resistance against the German intent to break them spiritually before their murder" (Selection 12 above). For the duration of his postwar career, Dworzecki resolved to be the latter voice in writing Jewish history of the Holocaust.

One of the brightest chapters of Jewish life in the Vilna ghetto was the cultural system.

If the Vilna Jewish community carried the name *Jerusalem of Lithuania* over the years, the Vilna ghetto is worthy, in the cultural respect, of carrying the name *Jerusalem of the Ghettos*, as a symbol of Jewish spiritual resistance under the Nazi regime.

Despite the danger of death, of deportations and exterminations, despite want, hunger, and suffering, the Jewish community of the Vilna ghetto considered it its mission to continue within the ghetto walls the old, beautiful, long-lasting Jewish cultural tradition of Vilna, to create a multibranched school system, theater, choir, Hebrew and Yiddish cultural institutions, libraries, reading rooms, to continue creating Yiddish and Hebrew literature. People wrote poems in bunkers, collected books in cellars, and children lived in old ruins; the insanely chaotic living conditions did not break the Jewish spirit of creativity in the ghetto.

How the School System in the Ghetto Was Established

On the third day of the ghetto, the teacher Moshe Olitski, former long-time director of the Vilna Hebrew teachers union,[1] convened a meeting in the building of Rabbi Shaulke's *kloyz* [prayer hall][2] (on Shavelska Street) with teachers Rachel Broida (Communist), Mira Bernstein (Communist), Miriam Gutgeshtalt (Bundist) and proposed an initiative to create a united school system of all the former Vilna school movements. They signed a memorandum to the *Judenrat* in which they pointed out the necessity of creating institutions to supervise the children, where attention could be given to the children while their parents went to work, playing with them, teaching them to sing, educating them, as well as a certain sum for school-teaching. It was reported that Jacob Gens, the chief of the ghetto police, who was nervous about the difficult situation in the ghetto and the constant threat of Nazi *Aktionen* [round-ups], answered the delegation: "Don't disturb me, but find some places and do with the children what you want."

Later, Gens [when he became head of the *Judenrat*] demonstrated great interest in the matter of the school system. He would visit the studies, the school holiday events, as well as express opinions about the school curriculum.

With time, the number of certificates for teachers increased, and eventually compulsory school attendance was introduced in the ghetto.

The first premises of the ghetto schools were a ruined synagogue on Szawelska Street, a crumbling butcher shop on Yatkever Street, and a ruined house at 12 Strashun Street. Some sixty men, former teachers of various political orientations, soon began carrying out the debris, stones, and broken windowpanes of the ruins, making doors from small pieces of boards, and washing the floors. The teachers, with the help of nurses, conducted a registration of children. In a whole series of places in the ghetto, placards were hung calling for the enrollment of children in the childcare institutions. The parents were initially a bit afraid in case this was a trick by the *Judenrat* to know how many children there were and to know their addresses. But seeing who was in charge of the school system—teachers, who had raised generations of students in Vilna—the parents gained confidence and took their children to the registration. In September 1941 more than 2,700 children from 6 to 14 years of age were then registered. A certain portion of the children were, for various reasons, still not registered; both because the children needed to care for smaller abandoned children and because in the ghetto there was a large number of children completely without parents and defenseless (*Bezprizornici* [in Russian]), who themselves needed to seek their living. . . .

When the so-called white *Judenrat* passes, which at first gave protection to their owners from being captured for work, were issued by the *Judenrat*, all sixty men who were busy creating the school system received these white passes. When the time came for the yellow life-passes, it was the fate of the school system to receive only ten yellow passes. . . . The rest of the sixty teachers did not receive yellow passes. Some succeeded in going outside the ghetto to work and receiving passes there, some hid in bunkers, and a large portion were expelled to Ponar.

The *Kultur-kamf* in the Ghetto

A culture struggle in the united school system in the ghetto developed in the first period regarding the character, nature, educational style, and composition of the teaching personnel and the curriculum—with which social and national ideas should the young people emerge into the wilds of the ghetto—what place should be held, in creating a united school system, by Yiddish and Hebrew, the Land of Israel, Tanach, Jewish history, general history—which periods and heroes should serve as examples, etc. Consequently, there were times when a clear ideological influence from one group would prevail, and times when the influence would pass to another. Mainly, the Zionist "roof" [umbrella organization] fought ideologically against the overwhelming influence in the school system held at first by the Bund, thanks to the accident that the culture department of the *Judenrat* was led by a member of the Bund.

As a result of the so-called *kultur-kamf*, parity was introduced between Hebrew and Yiddish teachers, changes took place in the officials of the Jewish cultural department of the ghetto and of the school section—and a *synthetic* curriculum was created for the ghetto school system. . . . [Subsequent paragraphs name eight leaders of the school system, indicating their affiliations with the Zionists, Bundists, Communists, etc., plus forty-seven teachers.] Both after and before instituting the synthetic ghetto curriculum, as well as during the various changes in the school system, the faculty from all groups worked together with great devotion to the children and, with enthusiasm for the subject and true dedication, built the school system.

The Synthetic Curriculum of the School System

I will devote a few words here to the curriculum of the school system, which was adopted after the so-called *kultur-kamf* in the ghetto and which presented an interesting attempt at a synthesis of national and social ideas and evoked approval by the parents' circle and extraordinary enthusiasm among the children. I will try to give an outline of the curriculum and "synthetic ideology" of the school system, just as they remain in my memory.

The Principles of the Curriculum

- The school system is a synthetic one. The faculty is constituted from all former school movements.
- The language of instruction is *Yiddish*. In one kindergarten, the studies were conducted in such a way that the children could transition over time to Hebrew as the language of instruction.
- In all schools and in all classes, a great measure of *Hebrew* and Hebrew literature was taught, with the emphasis on their important role in the life of the people and its age-old culture.

- *Jewish history* is an integral subject of the school system. Simultaneous with teaching about various periods of Jewish history, parallel similar periods of world history were taught.
- Tanach [Hebrew Bible] is one of the fundamental areas of study in the school system.

The Principles of the Education

- Sense of national *Jewish worth*.
- Love for the *people's past*, with special attention to the period of national sovereignty and to the fighters for the *people's freedom*: the Hasmoneans, Bar-Kochba, and Masada.
- Knowledge of the *people's present*: Jewish life in all Jewish communities.
- Faith in the *people's future* (at the time it was understood: the people's future—a Jewish free people in a sovereign Land of Israel as a part of a free humanity).
- Love for *work and freedom*.
- Love for humanity, of work and of struggle against oppressors, sense of *international partnership* of all peoples in the fight for a better and more just world.

Knowledge of the Land of Israel (Palestinography) was taught as a special subject.

Religion was taught as a nonobligatory subject for the children who wanted to acquaint themselves with the principles of the religion.

The Ghetto Schools, Teachers, and Children

Vilna had always been famous for the dedicated faculty of its school systems; a teacher from Vilna had a reputation in Poland as a person in whom pedagogy and communal activity were intertwined, a person who considered his calling not as an occupation but as a mission to which he devoted himself, heart and soul. I worked for a number of years as a school doctor in Vilna Jewish schools belonging to various movements. I was always inspired by the devotion of the teachers. But such enthusiastic, fervent, self-sacrificing devotion as the Vilna ghetto teachers displayed toward the building of the school system and toward the children I did not see even in the illustrious years of Jerusalem of Lithuania. Teachers and children had a shared will to build the school system and became one family—together they carried debris, stones, and bricks out of battered ruins that were to be converted into places for learning, together collected a door from one ruin, a board from another, a broken piece of a window from a third, to assemble from all of them something that would resemble a schoolroom. Female teachers and schoolgirls stood together washing the floors of the schools. Male teachers and students jointly cut wood to be able to warm the cold rooms where people sat and froze in the harsh ghetto winters.

In the first period of the ghetto, there were also no school benches. The children sat in clusters on the ground and listened to the words of the teachers. Only later did school benches begin to appear in the ghetto.

When the children would be asked to write on "open themes," they would adjust themselves to the reality of the ghetto. I recall names of children's written works: "How I Saved Myself from Ponar," "The First Day in the Ghetto," "My Parents Were Taken Away to Their Deaths," "Hiding in a Bunker," etc.

Once, when an *Aktion* broke out in the ghetto and a teacher without a pass was in the middle of a lecture, she did not stop the course but spoke further to the children about the better world that was yet to come. The teacher did not have time to hide. Her fate was—to Ponar.

Very often the children would gather in school a full hour before the start of studies and barely wait impatiently until the teacher would begin to speak. They held their notebooks steady on a friend's shoulders and took notes about the lectures in this way. With a capacity for fantasy, they would transport themselves to another world, where there was no ghetto and no *Aktionen*, and to heroic, Hasmonean, Masada-like Jews. During the breaks, children whose parents had just recently been taken away would dance a circle-dance and sing: We are young people, we are young people . . . [ellipsis in original]

I often had occasion to be in the lectures. I recall a lecture when Moshe Olitski told about the destruction of the First Temple and the Jewish wars. Children's eyes flamed with insatiable fantasy; they did not let him finish his course hour: "Teacher, tell more about Jewish fighting! Teacher, tell more . . ." [ellipsis in original]

School Institutions in the Ghetto

There were the following school institutions:
Elementary School No. 1—at 12 Strashun Street. Director Yosef Leykin; secretary, Rokhl Gershteyn. Thirty-six teachers, men and women, taught

there. This was the largest ghetto school. The daily attendance would often exceed a thousand children, and the number of classes more than fifteen.

Elementary School No. 2—at 1 Szawelska Street. Director Gedalia Bushl, assistant Yisrael Magarshak. Actively participated: Moshe Olitski. Nearly eight hundred children. With some ten classes.

Elementary School No. 3—at 21 Daytshe Street. Some hundred children, temporarily as many as four hundred. With seven classes.

High school courses—fifty, eighty, as many as one hundred children in four classes. . . . [in the same location as Elementary School No. 3]

[The subsequent section describes the school holidays and how they were celebrated with student presentations at enthusiastic gatherings of teachers, parents, and students.]

"Graduations" would take place movingly in the schools at the end of the ghetto school year, when the children received their certificates and were promoted to a higher grade. The graduates of the school went on to attend either the technical school or the technical workshops to receive their own work-booklet [authorizing employment]. Remaining for another year was regarded by the children as a great tragedy . . . [ellipsis in original]

The graduating children would read aloud reminiscences about experiences in school, give parting greetings to their young classmates and their class teachers and school directors, and at the same time remember their school directors with presents—each gift accompanied with a parting speech, with a specially prepared poem, and often with a live flower (how did the children succeed in obtaining the flowers?). Such gifts, I recall, were received by the teachers Moshe Olitski, Baruch Lubatski, Yosef Leykin, Turbovich, Gedalia Bushl. . . .

A large, general graduation of all the ghetto schools took place in spring 1943 in the ghetto theater with the participation of all the representatives of all the communal and political circles in the ghetto. The teacher Yisrael Dimentman recounted to the audience the accomplishments of the children in the course of the school year and about the educational ideals of the ghetto school system. Dr. Kaplan-Kaplanski, the well-known former school leader, greeted the children in the name of all the Jewish labor brigades and recalled former school graduations in Vilna. I had occasion, in the name of the school medical center, to speak about the health condition of the children and how infectious diseases among them were fought. Jacob Gens, in his grammatically poor speech and in a militant tone, commanded the students: Be comradely, brotherly, take care of your parents, love the people, work for the ghetto. Be proud and courageous Jewish children. . . .

The Religious Schools

Religion was taught in the ghetto school system as a nonobligatory subject, but in a very interesting and informative form by Rabbis Marcus and Slodzinski and yeshiva student Nieboshtshik-Naborshtshik, so that in fact all the children would receive religious studies. Nevertheless, religious parents decided to create special schools where an exclusively religious education would be given to the children.

Religious School No. 1, Religious School No. 2, and a small yeshiva were created. The studies were set mainly at such times that an entire group of children could simultaneously attend the general schools.

The faculty and the communal circles did not consider the religious school system a competitor to the general ghetto school system that divided their efforts—but a supplementary school system. On the contrary, if separate secular and separate religious schools had been created in the ghetto, in those conditions it would have been considered a split in the school systems.

Religious School No. 1—located at 1 Szawelska Street in Yogiches's *kloyz*.

Religious School No. 2—on Yatkever Street in the butchers' *kloyz*.

Small Yeshiva—at 1 Szawelska Street in Yogiches's *kloyz*.

Great Yeshiva—under the name of Rabbi Ḥaim Ozer Grodzenski, at 5 Szawelska Street in Reb Shaulke's *kloyz*.

Children studied in Religious Schools No. 1 and No. 2 until the age of twelve: Hebrew, *Chumash* [Pentateuch], Tanach [Hebrew Bible], some mathematics; in the Small Yeshiva—children from 12 to 16 years of age: *Mishnah, Gemara*; in the Great Yeshiva—students from just before the war. Altogether, the religious school system numbered nearly two hundred men. [Dworzecki then names the rabbis and advanced students who led the classes.]

I recall that I was in Religious School No. 1, in Yogiches's *kloyz*, to conduct a medical examination of the children. Naborshtshik began teaching the children the first chapter of Joshua and interpreted it for them thusly: "And it was after the death of Moses; Moses carried the light of the Torah in a dark world, and we also carry it in the ghetto, for which the world pursues us." I encountered Nieboshtshik-Naborshtshik later in the Stutthof and Dautmergen concentration camps. There were always circles of yeshiva men around him, who would snatch a chapter of Mishna in the concentration camp before going to sleep. A few months before the liberation he perished in Dautmergen from general bodily weakness.

From time to time, the religious schools would stage a public "examination." The children would be seated around tables, with the rabbi in the center. He examined them on what they had learned, and the guests posed questions to the children. Afterward, a *sudes mitsve* [festive religious banquet] would take place. . . .

The "Ghetto Technicum"

Great pride was felt by the grown children of 15 and 16 years of age who attended the technical school, the "Ghetto Technicum," of which the director was engineer M. Shrayber (former director of the Vilna Jewish Technicum "ORT"). Among the teachers: engineer Yanov and engineer Yisrael Kunitski.

In the technicum there were a couple of sections: metalworking and electromechanics. In the course of several months of intensive work, the children learned a trade as an assistant metalworker or assistant electrical technician and could then go to work as professionals outside the ghetto and have the advantage of a work-booklet of their own.

At the first graduation from the technicum, there was a large celebration in which the ghetto leaders participated. The children received beautiful hand-printed Yiddish diplomas. Simultaneously, an exhibition was held of various technical instruments that the children had learned to produce in the course of their studies at the technicum.

[Subsequent sections discuss the music school, youth and children's clubs, vocational school dormitories, sport activities, and teachers union.]

Introduction Notes:

1. Mark Dvorzhetski, *Yerusholayim d'lite in kamf un umkum* [Jerusalem of Lithuania (Vilna) in struggle and extermination] (Paris: Yidishn natsyonaln arbeter-farband in amerike / Yidishn folksfarband in frankraykh, 1948), 222–34 (quoted here, abridged); slightly revised version of "Dos kultur-vezn in vilner geto" [The cultural system in the Vilna ghetto], *Parizer shriftn* 2–3 (March 1946): 28–40.

Article Notes:

1. [Dworzecki's own first Hebrew teacher.]

2. [The synagogue established in honor of Rabbi Shaul Katsenelenbogen, a student of the Vilna Gaon.]

40
The Jewish Vocational and Higher School System in the Warsaw Ghetto, 1940–42

by Esther Goldhar-Mark, 1949

ESTHER GOLDHAR-MARK [Estera/Edwarda Mark, 1908–1991, née Goldhar] was known chiefly as the wife, and then widow, of Ber Mark (director of the Jewish Historical Institute in Warsaw from 1949 until his death in 1966). She was, however, a historian herself, who worked at the Institute for Party History until her departure for Israel in 1969.[1] She had been a public elementary school teacher in Warsaw from 1929 to 1939. During the 1939 German invasion, she and her husband fled to Bialystok in the Soviet area of occupation, where she served as the principal of a Yiddish-language high school.[2] They then fled to the Soviet interior in 1941 before returning to liberated Poland.

She was the author of "a number of documentary works on the Polish resistance movement and of a series of monographs on Jewish heroes of the anti-Nazi resistance movement in occupied Poland," all in Polish. Subsequently, in Israel, she worked "as a historian, researcher, and archivist for the Society for Historical Research of Polish Jewry."[3] She wrote at least one *yizkor* book article in Yiddish on prewar Jewish history.[4]

Her most enduring contribution to Jewish historical writing came in assisting her husband during his years of illness and near blindness with his final work, a history in Yiddish of the resistance movement in Auschwitz *The Scroll of Auschwitz*, which she completed and published in Israel in 1977. From the description of her activities in the foreword to the book, only modesty and duty prevented her being listed as coauthor.

She was also the author of the early, unique, and valuable work of Yiddish historical research that appears below on the educational programs in the Warsaw ghetto.[5] Her introductory note about documentary sources concludes: "In collecting the materials about the vocational school system in the Warsaw ghetto, I tried above all to obtain testimonies from individuals who participated actively or passively in the educational process. The testimonies acted like cement that made it possible to fill the voids in the documents to create a relatively complete picture of our topic."

This article belongs to the brief period in which Poland descended from liberation to Stalinism. It appeared in 1949 in the officially sanctioned journal of the Jewish Historical Institute in Warsaw, *Bleter far geshikhte* (Pages for history). On the one hand, the volume concludes with an article obligingly devoted to "The Most Important Dates in J.V. Stalin's Life." But, at this last moment before the imposition of Soviet revisionism (evident in much of the Institute's work in the 1950s), it was still possible for her to name the Jewish organizations "ORT" and "Toporol" as sponsors of education in the ghetto and to give credit for funding the classes to the American Jewish Joint Distribution Committee (which was expelled from Poland later that year in the campaign to end western influence in Poland).

The Jewish community in the Warsaw ghetto fought with all means against the violent assault by the German occupier on all aspects of life. In this defense, the Jews demonstrated great dedication, energy, organizational ability, and stubbornness. One of the most important and interesting phenomena of this passive resistance, of the stubborn will to endure, to hold on to a certain cultural level, and also to care—in those frightful conditions of isolation—about continuity, about future cadres of occupational intelligence, was the creation in the Warsaw ghetto of a broad network of courses of vocational training. These courses were created with great effort and sacrifice by progressive representatives of the Jewish working intelligentsia and by "ORT"[1] and "Toporol."[2]

The idea and the initiative to establish vocational courses in the ghetto already signified a violation of the German policy that was intended to morally crush the Jewish youth and deprive them of education and knowledge. Therefore, of course, the initiators could not propose the matter themselves. They needed to seek various figures who enjoyed the trust of the German occupation authority. In this way, the actual creators of the vocational school system in the ghetto had to make use of the *Judenrat* as an intermediary who would intercede with the enemy to obtain permission to open such courses.

Later, starting in September 1940, the Jewish Social Self-Help obtained the right—through its district and city watch committees—to intervene, among other things, about the details of founding short-term courses for the Jewish population.[3]

The enemy, although its general policy was directed entirely toward forbidding education in the occupied country overall and in the ghetto in particular, especially humanistic education, overlooked temporarily, however, a certain crack in this general policy, namely: inasmuch as the German authorities at that time, in the first phase, still counted on meeting their own needs for a workforce with certain technical qualifications, they also allowed the creation of vocational schools for Jewish youth; the students of these courses were even freed from forced labor in the camps. . . .

It was not only the general policy of the Germans that had a specific tendency; the exception, the tactic of allowing certain vocational courses in the ghetto, also had specific, limited bounds. The occupying authority had no interest in the matter of occupational intelligence for Jews—if it permitted the creation of vocational courses, it did so only and exclusively because it considered the needs of German industry at a given moment. But it also dealt in a one-sided manner with the guidelines of the general policy regarding the Jewish population and allowed no driving courses. According to the German plan, the Jewish vocational courses should turn out only artisans, laborers, and technicians of a certain level of qualification so they could be used by industry in the capacity of assistants, totally dependent on the German technical leadership.

The occupier had a similar policy regarding the Polish system in general. The level of the Polish vocational school system was lowered sharply by the German authorities; for example, courses in history, geography, physics, chemistry, and natural science were relegated to the business schools, and in this way, education was reduced to purely vocational subjects.[4]

This tendency in the Polish school system is evidenced by the following words of Governor-General Hans Frank at the meeting of the "government" on March 8, 1940: "We will place the vocational school system at such a level that, at the highest, it will reach the lowest level of the German vocational schools."[5]

The Jewish vocational pedagogues and the Jewish youth very nimbly and skillfully made use of the tiny crack left a bit open by the German authorities. The communal elements of the ghetto attempted—with true dedication—to widen the narrow possibilities, for their own benefit, given by the enemy.

The courses they created quickly became very popular among the ghetto youth. Enrollment in the courses was tremendous. It indicated a truly great desire for these very limited fields of vocational training.

What explains this desire?

First, the courses were the only form of a legal school at that time.[6]

Second, they made it possible to learn a trade quickly and perhaps find work.

Third, they freed one from the labor camp; participation in such a course already meant—being employed; and it was well known how strong the fear was in the ghetto of the word "unemployed."

The last point explains the relatively greater participation of children of the well-to-do strata in the vocational courses; before the war, most children from such homes avoided the vocational school system.

It was not only young people who enrolled in the courses. Older people also attended, with the hope that they would be considered "working Jews" by the Germans. And here we come to a painful matter.

For the Germans, in tolerating the vocational courses, no small part was played by their perfidious policy of creating the illusion among the Jews of survival and the delusion that working Jews would be privileged and would remain. These illusions were supported by the *Judenrat*. Another false delusion was encouraged by certain bourgeois communal leaders, adherents of the productivization idea, which consisted of contending that in the framework of the ghetto it was possible to realize this idea. This was precisely incorrect—the false idea that in the ghetto national Jewish culture could flourish; in truth, the ghetto was an impediment both to a true flourishing of culture and to realizing the productivization idea. . . .

But the communal forces in the Warsaw ghetto, which saw in the courses one of the expressions of self-defense against the hunger tortures and barbaric assaults of the occupier, made use of this possibility and, under the cloak of elementary technical courses, violated the framework that was established by the Germans, in fact raised these courses to the level of middle and higher education. By this means, the vocational courses were partly converted into a form of opposition to the will and goals of the German authorities and from this standpoint were illegal.

Origin of the Courses

During the 1939–40 school year, the Jewish institutions for vocational education in Warsaw were not active. In fact, on October 8, 1939, orders appeared permitting the educational institutions that were active before the war to open,[7] and the schools even prepared for student registrations on this basis, but a few days later a new order was issued, on the basis of which all learning institutions were closed in the vicinity of the "disease-prohibited area" of that time with the excuse that it was necessary to resist the spread of infectious diseases.

As a result of longstanding efforts, the *Judenrat* received permission on August 15, 1940, from the head of the city of Warsaw to open courses for vocational preparation.[8]

On August 31, 1940, an order was issued about the Jewish school system in the Government-General of Poland; the order said that the *Judenrat* was obligated to undertake school systems for Jews, that it should create and maintain the necessary number of general schools and, in addition, also establish vocational and occupational schools.[9]

But this promise remained only on paper. The prevailing type of vocational school system in the ghetto was not the school, but vocational courses or short-term occupational training. . . .

On September 3, 1940, the first men's courses were already active in the fields of metalworking and electrical installation, both for boys from 15 to 18 years of age and for adults, and also women's courses for tailoring at the premises of the ORT society.[10]

At the request of the *Judenrat*, the German authorities approved a set of newly created curricula for further courses. One should say that, in general, these curricula were used by the teachers as a legal cover under which they taught much broader subjects than the officially tailored guidelines allowed.

The legal agency for vocational courses was the Commission for Handicraft Training, which consisted of twenty persons. This commission divided its work among subcommissions. . . . The commission members were assigned to various courses for the purpose of watching over the economic and hygienic conditions. The chairman of the commission was Y. Yashunski, the director of ORT.

It is clear that these vocational courses are something entirely different from the occupational school system from before the war. Here is what was said about them by engineer Yosef Yashunski in his report on three terms of activity, which was published [by the *Judenrat*] in the *Gazeta zhidovska* [Jewish gazette] no. 45, June 6, 1941: "The authors of the curriculum of the courses considered above all the fact that the altered living conditions did not favor continuation of the tradition of two- or four-year vocational schools, that the curriculum must therefore be synthesized for more modest and more practical time requirements, which would be suited to the framework of courses lasting for a few months."

In practice, this was indeed the approach taken.

The number of instructional hours in these courses reached an average of 42 to 46 per week; of these, about 30–40 hours were dedicated to workshop studies, the rest to theoretical topics.

And only such purely practical courses were approved by the German authorities, who would not allow a larger number of theoretical topics. They required practical assistants for German masters, and because of this they tolerated purely vocational education. . . . But, as much as possible, the teachers brought in ever more theoretical topics. In the later months they were successful in broadening the framework of certain courses.

Statistics of the Courses

The network of the courses and their structure were not static but developed and changed. Most characteristic of this is that, in the first period, the number of students grew quickly.

From September 1940 to May 15, 1941, 3,649 students attended the courses. In February 1941, 26 groups, i.e., 1,046 students, completed the studies that began in September 1940. In the month of May 1941, the number of students in all the courses—for men, women, and coeducational—amounted to 2,500. . . .[11] [Subsequent paragraphs and tables give details about the topics, numbers of students, and structure of the courses.]

The courses required payment. The average tuition amounted to 30–40 złoty per month. For many students this was a heavy budgetary burden.[12]

Only a small portion benefited from the help allotted by the security section of the Jewish Social Self-Help.[13] As a result, the courses were actually—with few exceptions—accessible mostly to children of well-to-do parents.

The language of instruction in the courses, according to their authorization, needed to be Yiddish, but this was theoretical; in reality, the studies were conducted in the Polish language.[14]

[The subsequent section discusses the "Evolving Conditions of the Courses" over time.]

ORT and the "Section for Vocational Training"

What was the nature of the joint effort between the Commission for Vocational Training and the ORT society?

It is clear that ORT, as a society with longstanding experience, played the most important role, both in founding and in conducting the courses. The actual initiator, organizer, and operator of the courses was ORT. But this society had no right to appear before the occupying authority. Officially, ORT had ceased its activity in vocational training. As a result, the ORT leaders needed to come to the Jewish administrative agency recognized by the occupier, the *Judenrat*, and also to the official Jewish agency for social assistance, the Jewish Self-Help, for them to be the external lobbyists and the front for the vocational courses.

The *Judenrat*, which had a legal existence, did not want, however, to remain only a front. In order to be able to watch over what took place in the courses, the *Judenrat* created the abovementioned Commission for Vocational Training.

As a result, the burden of the practical work was laid above all on ORT, which prepared the curriculum and placed at the disposal of the courses its entire apparatus together with the physical premises and facilities.[15]

Furthermore, even the financing of the courses was not undertaken by the *Judenrat*; in December 1940, an agreement was made between the *Judenrat* and ORT according to which ORT undertook to finance the courses; ORT obligated itself to secure the regular payment of wages to the course personnel and also the costs of investments. At that time, ORT still received certain funds from the "Joint."[16] . . .

[The subsequent sections are: Agricultural Courses (offered by Toporol), and Secondary and Higher Vocational School System (covering the medical education courses, which have been the subject of much later research).]

Termination of the Courses

The occupation authority, which, early in 1942 started vigorously preparing for the great expulsions from the Warsaw ghetto, had at the beginning of March of that year already put a stop to the further development of the courses, the head agencies of the Government-General issuing an order on March 9, 1942, according to which the committees for social self-help and the *Judenräte* were forbidden to establish short-term courses for training in the field of handicraft and agriculture.[17]

This order had no immediate effect on the life of the already existing courses. The Germans did not control the courses directly. The work meanwhile continued, but misfortune soon arrived suddenly. The cruel *Aktion* [round-up] that began on July 22, 1942, also dragged away, together with the masses of Warsaw Jews, the students and lecturers of the courses. The life of the courses was immediately cut short.

In such a manner, the efforts in the bitter ghetto conditions to create some form of possibilities for school-age youth to continue their education suddenly ended. All the accomplishments and dreams were discontinued and suppressed.

The courses fulfilled a certain important social mission. They wrested a portion—in truth, a small portion—of the youth from demoralization and spiritual decline. The courses also played a role in circumventing the decrees of the occupier.

But the story of the courses in the Warsaw ghetto demonstrates simultaneously that goodwill and stubbornness count for little when there must also be the necessary free conditions for it to be truly possible to create cultural value. Despite all the positively great and important efforts, it was still an illusion in the abyss of the ghetto, in isolation from the world, that one could create truly valuable culture and science.

Introduction Notes:

1. Joanna Nalewajko-Kulikov, "The Diary of Bernard Mark (December 1965–February 1966)," *East European Jewish Affairs* (2024): 182–34.
2. "Testimony of Esther Mark, regarding her experiences in hiding in Bialystok, in the Saratov area, and Moscow," https://collections.yadvashem.org/en/documents/3558287.
3. Yuri Suhl, *They Fought Back* (New York: Crown Publishers, 1967), 77.

4. Ester Mark, "Di kompartey in falenits" [The Communist Party in Falencia], *Sefer Falenitz* (Tel Aviv: Orly, 1967), 93–98.

5. Ester Goldhar-Mark, "Dos yidishe fakh un hekhere shul-vezn in varshe in der tsayt fun der daytsher okupatsye," *Bleter far geshikhte* II (1949): 175–206.

Article Notes:
1. "ORT"—the initials [in Russian] of "Society for Handicraft and Agricultural Work" among the Jews of Russia [founded in St. Petersburg in 1880].

2. "Toporol"—the initials [in Russian] of "Society for the Promotion of Agriculture" among the Jews of Russia [founded by the American Jewish Joint Distribution Committee in 1933].

3. Archives of the Jewish Historical Institute, records of the Jewish Social Self-Help [hereafter JSSH], folder 180, circular no. 4.

4. Wacław Jastrzębowski, *Gospodarka niemiecka w Polsce w 1939–1944* [German economy in Poland] (Warsaw 1946), 248, 249, 251.

5. *Biuletyn Głównej Komisji Badania Zbrodnic Niemieckich w Polsce*, cz. II, *Okupacja hitlerowska w Polsce w świele "Dziennika" Hansa Franka I protokółów osiedzeń rzadu GG*, wybrał I zestawił Eugeuniusz Szrojt str. 13 [Bulletin of the Main Commission for the Investigation of German Crimes in Poland, part II, Nazi occupation in Poland in the light of Hans Frank's "Diary" and the minutes of the General Government's meetings, selected and compiled by Eugeuniusz Szrojt, page 13].

6. In the Warsaw Ghetto, the most widespread form of education consisted of the so-called *komplet* [set] for students of elementary and mid-level schools. The sets numbered several or at most ten students, men and women. The study courses of the sets were held secretly in private homes, often in very difficult technical conditions. At the end of April 1941, the Warsaw *Judenrat* received permission to operate private elementary schools, but the illegal sets continued to exist.

7. Announcement from the chief commander of the invading German army. (Dziennik Urzędowy m. st. Warszawy, 8. X. 1939 [verbatim].)

8. JSSH, ORT, folder 189.

9. Weh: Prawo G.G. A. 420. Rosporządzenie o szkolnictwie żyd. W G.G.

10. JSSH, ORT, folder 189, also: *Gazeta zhidovska*, August 28, 1940; and Bulletin of the Statistical Section of the *Judenrat*, no. 8, September 4, 1940, p. 12.

11. JSSH, ORT, folder 189, report of Y. Yashunski, May 5, 1941.

12. The average wage of a white-collar worker in the ghetto varied from 200 to 250 złoty per month: information from Magister H[ersh] Wasser [a surviving member of Emanuel Ringelblum's Oyneg Shabes project].

13. JSSH, folder 411.

14. JSSH, Ringelblum Archive, folder 74 "School System." Also: testimony of Makarewicz-Rajcher, protocol 4263.

15. JSSH, ORT, folder 189.

16. Ibid.

17. [A long note citing information from Joseph Kermish about the dates on which this order took effect in various places in Poland, as well as temporary exceptions.]

41

The School System and Education for Holocaust Survivors in the Displaced Persons Camps in Germany

by Philip Friedman, 1948

PHILIP FRIEDMAN (see Selections 36 above and 47 below) was described by Salo Baron as "the chief founder of a new discipline of Jewish studies" for organizing the early study of the Holocaust—particularly as a field of *Jewish* studies in contrast to *Nazi* studies. He published early studies of Auschwitz, the leaders of the Jewish Councils in the ghettos, social relations within the ghettos, and on the processes of Holocaust research, among many other topics.

In November 1944, Friedman founded the Central Jewish Historical Commission in Poland and guided its development until impending Stalinization led to his departure for the West in 1946. His goal was to settle in New York, where Baron would open the door to teaching at Columbia University and where he could resume his prewar connection with YIVO in New York as chair of its Historians Circle. His principal employment from 1948 until 1957 came as dean of the Jewish Teachers Seminary and People's University in New York, the only college in America for advanced Yiddish studies and training of Yiddish teachers and the only institution to grant doctoral degrees for dissertations written in Yiddish and Hebrew.

During the interval between Friedman's Polish and American periods, he served as director of the Education Department of the American Jewish Joint Distribution Committee in the

Displaced Persons camps in the American zone of occupied Germany. In this position, he oversaw the creation and operation of schools for surviving children and adults. (He also oversaw the publishing of memoirs, histories, fiction, poetry, and textbooks for the survivors.[1])

Friedman's account of the education program, written at the end of his period of service, appears below.[2] Not surprisingly, the work is more reportage than historical synthesis, but it preserves the details of a transient episode of Jewish history in its historical context. Among all of Friedman's writings, it is exceptional for discussing a historical topic in which he himself was involved (although he does not mention his own role) and for the uncharacteristic passion of his conclusions.

Origins and Development

Among the rescued Jews in Germany, there were almost no children. There are no reliable statistics about the age and sex of the Jews who were liberated in Germany in January 1945. The number of these liberated Jews was estimated overall to be about 30,000 to 40,000 souls. The greatest portion of them were liberated directly from the concentration camps. In the camps, the Germans generally kept alive only the able-bodied young men and women who were fit for labor. Only as an exception did they tolerate here and there a few Jewish children.

The number of Jewish children was therefore altogether minimal. And it appeared that setting up a normal Jewish school system was not a burning issue.

The situation changed quickly, however. As early as the second half of 1945 the so-called infiltration (illegal immigration) of Eastern European Jews (particularly from Poland, Hungary, and Czechoslovakia) into Germany began. Not only adults but whole families with children emigrated from these places. In this way, by the end of December 1945, there already numbered, among the 40,000 Jews in Germany (American zone), 680 children up to the age of 6 and 1,200 children from 6 to 14 years old. (The numbers come from the first statistical count, conducted by the Jewish Central Commission in Germany.)

In spring 1946, the great wave of immigration to the American zone began. In the main, these were Polish, Russian, Hungarian, later also Romanian, Jews. The Jewish population increased by a factor of three or four, but the number of children rose tenfold. Families with many children came from Russia, Hungary, and Romania. Entire colonies and children's homes with rescued Jewish children were brought from Poland on the theory that it would be easier to bring them from Germany to the Land of Israel or to their relatives in other countries. The result was that, at the end of 1946, the population of 142,000 Jews in the American zone included about 28,000 children, of whom 16,700 were from 6 to 17 years old.

Consequently, the problem of children's education came to the fore in 1946. But not only the question of children's education. Simultaneously, a burning need appeared for intensive educational work among the adults. . . .

In the life of the survivors, it is possible to distinguish certain chronological phases of development:

Soon after the liberation, the first problem was to satisfy the most pressing material needs: healing, eating, clothing, living places; after this, new problems arose: searching for relatives in the farther reaches of the liberated countries, searching for relatives and friends in the neutral and allied countries and asking them for help and emigration possibilities. Only when these most primitive necessities for life were satisfied to some degree, when the heartfelt emotional demands (family, friends) were more or less answered (most did not find their lost families), when the possibilities for emigration appeared for the most part to be a seductive mirage, and it became understood that life in diaspora Germany would stabilize for at least a few years—then, the desires of the survivors turned to matters that, in the hierarchy of human needs, are on the higher rungs of the ladder.

The hunger for culture, the longing for the printed and spoken Yiddish word, for the creative revelation of one's own long-fettered spiritual forces, the impulse for giving literary and artistic form to their experiences was as intense as their earlier hunger for bread, human living conditions and health. Among some of the adults and particularly among the youth who spent long years in the ghetto, camp, forest, and bunker, with the partisans, collectives, etc.,—there was a relapse into illiteracy (particularly in the field of Yiddish and Hebrew). The children, moreover, in regard to schooling and Jewishness, were mostly a blank page.

A multibranched school organization, to help with these cultural needs and to solve such difficult problems, cannot be created overnight. Whole mountains of difficulties and impediments had to be overcome before it could be realized. We will only illustrate these difficulties with a few examples:

1. Despite the weak emigration outlook, the survivors strongly believed that the day of the new Exodus from Egypt was not far off. They had absolutely no desire to build something stable on that abominable, hateful ground and to invest any amount of their forces in constructive work in Germany.
2. The Jewish community in Germany was not unified. It was not an organically developed historical community. The historically well-established German Jewish community had been destroyed, and the survivor element from that community was very small and played no active role in Jewish life in Germany. The new Jewish community in Germany was an accidental gathering of Jews of Polish, Russian, Hungarian, Romanian, Czech, and German Jews, with entirely different cultural traditions, different languages, mentality, and habits of living. To create a unified school organization for this babel of languages and mixtures of tribes was not an easy matter.
3. The economy of the survivors was not normal. It was built entirely on financial assistance, in its functions therefore completely dependent on the pace and size of the support that was promised by independent, external factors. In those conditions, it was very difficult to administer the well-planned construction and financing of so great an undertaking as organizing the school system and cultural work.
4. The Nazi regime destroyed the Jewish intelligentsia with special zeal. A result of this was, among others, also the great lack of pedagogical forces and cultural leaders among the survivors.
5. Most of the children had never attended a school or were unaccustomed for long years to normal school study. The youth were demoralized by their experiences under the Nazi regime and unaccustomed to every school discipline. A portion of the youth were raised in a foreign spirit (for example, on the "Aryan" side, in churches, in the Soviet schools).
6. In what language should the studies in the new schools for the survivors be conducted? A multicolored mixture of Polish, Russian, Hungarian, Romanian, German, Czech, etc., prevailed in the children's world. A small percentage of the children understood and spoke Yiddish, a still smaller—Hebrew.

7. How should the individual classes be organized? According to age, or according to the knowledge level of the children who came from altogether different school systems or who, in general, had attended no schools? According to the knowledge level of the children, one would need to seat, for example, 6- to 8-year-old children together with 16- to 18-year-old boys and girls and give them the same elementary studies. The appropriate means and pedagogical forces to solve this problem by individual study or through special classes were lacking.
8. Despite all the difficulties, schools were founded. The first creations of schools (end of 1945, start of 1946) were spontaneous. They were founded by the camp and city committees, parents committees, even the parties and youth organizations. There was still no central, guiding authority. The chaotically blossoming school network called forth a large variety of curricula, systems, organizational forms, and types of schools. But the impulse for learning was so strong that it overcame all obstacles.

At the end of spring 1946, the first teachers conference in Camp Feldafing (Upper Bavaria) created a provisional curriculum for the first four elementary school classes. But even this minimal curriculum was very difficult to put into practice. The situation improved when the central Jewish organizations in Germany, understanding this new development, founded special school- and culture-sections. . . .

School System

Statistics

Approximately a year and a half after the liberation, on January 1, 1947, 10,400 Jewish children studied in 62 camps and cities in the American zone. There were approximately 600 teachers.

On April 1, 1948, the school network of the directorate for education and culture encompassed 75 schools with 595 teachers and 7,107 children, as well as 46 kindergartens with 150 female children's teachers and 1,700 children (in total, 121 school institutions, 827 teachers, 8,707 children, of whom there were 4,450 girls and 4,257 boys).

As may be seen, the number of children with regard to January 1 declined, contrary to the number of schools and teachers. This indicates that more pedagogical intent and energy were employed for the individual child than previously.

The smaller number of children is explained by a series of causes, namely, by the larger child-emigration of the survivors in 1947, particularly to the Land of Israel (first in priority, the orphaned children from the so-called "children centers"); in their place in the school came the newly immigrated children, but their number was not so large as to fill the available spaces. All the numbers should be accepted with great caution because the fluctuation of the children and teachers was very great. On account of the permanent emigration (overseas and to Western Europe) and immigration (from Eastern Europe), the numbers changed from day to day.

Structure of the School System

The majority of schools (circa 75 percent) had 6 grades. Just 10 percent of the schools had only the first and second grades. Another 10 percent had only 4 grades. More than 6 grades (seventh and eighth grade) were found in only a few schools. There were also schools that had a ninth and tenth grade. These higher grades were mostly treated like a pre–high school (for example, in Landsberg, Föhrenwald, Zeilsheim, Ulm, etc.); a complete high school with 8 grades existed only in Munich, where in May 1948, the first celebratory graduation examinations took place.

The curriculum was a normal elementary school curriculum (except for the Munich high school and the pre–high school). The language of instruction was Hebrew. The majority of children, particularly in the younger classes, very quickly mastered Hebrew. Conversely, the higher classes were very often taught in Yiddish. English was taught mostly in the fourth and fifth grades. The question of introducing the study of Yiddish language and literature as a separate subject evoked a passionate debate at that time in Germany and outside Germany. The Education Department did not take any position in principle. In a small number of schools, where the parents requested it, or where there were appropriate conditions for Yiddish studies as a subject for instruction (qualified pedagogical forces and a warm attitude to the question on the part of the parents and the students), Yiddish language and literature were taught as required subjects. Conversely, in the majority of schools, Yiddish was used solely as an instrumental language in the higher grades because some of the students came from schools where instruction was in a foreign language, such that they did not know Hebrew well enough.

The education was conducted in a national-Jewish and Zionist spirit. In general, the ideological position of the school system was the expression of the entire attitude and political orientation of the survivors, which moreover was expressed in the explicit and clear instructions and ideological declarations of the Central Committee [of liberated Jews in the US zone], i.e., of the elected representation of the survivors in Germany.

The Teachers

A great difficulty for the school system was obtaining the appropriate pedagogical forces. Of the circa 600 elementary school teachers, at most 200 (33 percent) were teachers before the war, the rest being amateurs. Circa 60 percent of the teachers were capable in Hebrew, the rest teaching in Yiddish. Of the more than 100 women who were children's teachers, only a few were qualified; fewer than half of them knew Hebrew to a sufficient degree. It was difficult to obtain new or more highly qualified teachers. On the contrary, the existing cadre of teachers continuously diminished in number. . . .

The continuous reduction in the number of teachers through *aliyah* [immigration to the Land of Israel], emigration, and transfer to other occupations was impossible to stop, and it was necessary to deal with the fact that in the new school year of 1948–1949 the school system had to struggle mightily on account of the shortage of teachers. . . .

Religious Instruction

The schools of the department for education and culture corresponded approximately with the prewar Tarbut type of school that was widespread in Eastern Europe (i.e., secular schools with Hebrew as the language of instruction, in a Zionist spirit [in which Friedman had been a student and then teacher before the war]). Besides this, in the department's school system, there were schools of the Yavneh type (Mizrachi [religious-Zionist]). In the American zone there were three Yavneh schools with 550 children. The religious needs of the Tarbut school children—where the parents requested it—were met by afternoon courses where Jewish laws and customs were taught, *Chumash* [Pentateuch] with Rashi and other commentators, at times also *Mishnah* and *Gemara*. This afternoon instruction was conducted by traditional religious-school teachers. Approximately 1,500 to 2,000 children were served by this.

But this did not satisfy the strictly Orthodox circles—particularly the circles around Agudas Yisroel—which desired for their children the traditional Jewish education in *cheder, Talmud Torah,* and yeshiva. In the Agudas communities, a series of attempts were made to create such purely religious schools. Thus, for example, in the "Ohel Sarah" communities: to found schools of the Beis Yaakov type. In the Chofetz Chayim communities and other religious communities, yeshivas were founded for boys of various traditions: the Tomchei-Temimim yeshivas of the Lubavitch Hasidim, Polish yeshivas according to the example of the Yeshivas Chochmei Lublin, yeshivas of Lithuanian *misnagdim*, yeshivas of the Hungarian Orthodox, etc. The Orthodox school system was supported materially by the Va'ad Hatzalah and the Joint [American Jewish Joint Distribution Committee]. . . .

Educational Work for Youth and Adults

As mentioned, this was an especially difficult task. The voids in the upbringing and education among semi-adult youths and adults did not lend themselves to being filled as quickly as those among children. Adults are no longer as receptive to educational work as children. They cannot be forced to attend school. And other means of giving them a desire to learn have little effect. A purely theoretical subject without direct practical application seldom has an attractive force for adults. Other matters, above all, possibilities for earning and all sorts of pastimes, have a greater and more attractive influence on them and pull them away from the influence of an educational framework.

All of this greatly complicated the educational work for adults. Besides this, educational specialists were lacking. Nevertheless, a certain number of evening schools were founded in the camps. Conversely, in the cities the difficulties were still greater, especially where fewer Jews lived. It must also be borne in mind that the largest cities gave many opportunities for further education, pastimes, and social life in a non-Jewish spirit and a non-Jewish environment than the concentrated, purely Jewish camp.

The educational work for youth and adults had the following purposes: 1) instilling in them elementary knowledge, 2) further education for the more advanced, 3) cultural pastimes and occupations in their free time, 4) instilling Jewishness and Jewish subjects. The courses included: Hebrew, Yiddish, English, Jewish history, Palestinography, Tanach [Hebrew Bible], natural science, and mathematics. The maximum was 16 hours per week, but most evening schools managed with 3–5 hours per week. The language classes had the largest attendance. Each course lasted a maximum of one year. Many evening schools had to be closed after a short time for various reasons (emigration of students, shortage of teachers, insufficient attendance, etc.). At the beginning of spring 1948, in the American zone there were 112 evening schools with approximately 100 teachers and 2,200 students. . . .

The Vocational Schools

Vocational training was conducted by "ORT." The first five vocational schools were founded as early as 1945; the oldest of them was the vocational school in Landsberg (August 1945); on January 1, 1947, there were already 43 vocational schools with 5,200 students, 440 instructors, and 39 trades; on January 1, 1948, there were 60 schools with 8,412 students (of whom 2,060 graduates), 721 instructors, 53 trades, and 496 courses.

Young people and adults from 16 to 40 years of age participated in the courses. To a certain degree, this affected the rate of attendance, which was not as great as among the children in the normal schools. Theoretical and practical studies occupied an average of 40 hours per week. Recently, an inspectorate was created, and seminars and a press for publishing vocational literature were founded. On the basis of an agreement with the Education Department, ORT organized 5 to 8 hours of instruction in its schools for Jewish studies (Hebrew, Jewish history, Palestinography). This reform was just now instituted: up to March 1948, Jewish studies were introduced into 123 ORT schools.

On the other hand, however, in a number of general schools, vocational training was introduced in the higher grades by ORT instructors. This innovation is also just now being slowly introduced.

It is interesting to see which vocational courses are the most popular. Of the 53 trades that ORT introduced, the greatest interest was evoked by groups connected with tailoring: 41.6 percent of all ORT students attended these classes. In second place stands light-metal industry and fine mechanics (locksmithing, automechanics, watchmaking, typewriter repair, galvanoplastic—20 percent), in third place, technical trades that give an opportunity for individual employment (electrician and radio technician, cinema technician, photography, techno-chemistry—11 percent), after which haberdashery (8 to 10 percent) and finally textile industry, dental technician, carpentry, and shoemaking (approximately 3 to 5 percent of students for each trade).

Publishing Work

The lack of schoolbooks constituted one of the greatest difficulties in the school effort. Since 1946, by means of the Joint and other agencies, books arrived from the Land of Israel and America, but their number was not sufficient, and they were often obsolete books and unsystematic, haphazard gifts. It was not possible to create a unified course of study on this basis.

The Jewish organizations among the survivors soon began printing books. New, original books were not created because that would have required long preparation by specialists, and the technical possibilities were lacking. It was almost impossible to organize Jewish presses with Hebrew type for this purpose. Therefore another way was chosen. Books were selected that were considered most suitable for the survivors, and they were printed by a special photo-technical system. In this manner, by March 1947, the Joint had printed 11 schoolbooks with a pressrun of 70,000 copies, the cultural office of the Central Committee 4 books (16,000 copies), and the Jewish Agency 3 books (10,000) copies.

Since the founding of the Education Department, in the course of one year (from March 1947 to March 1948), 52 books were printed with a pressrun of 151,000 copies. Besides this, certain parties and youth organizations published a quantity of textbooks and youth literature (12 books, of unknown pressrun).

This book production can be characterized according to their language and type in the following manner:

By language: 68 books in Hebrew, 8 in Yiddish, 4 in Yiddish-Hebrew (periodicals and dictionaries), 2 in English, 1 in Russian (geographic atlas); in total 83 books.

By type: 55 textbooks, 23 readers for school and youth, 3 pedagogical publications for teachers, 2 dictionaries; in total 83 books.

In addition, the Va'ad Hatzlahah printed a number of religious books for the religious schools (*Chumash* with Rashi and other holy books, *Kitzur Shulchan Aruch* [Jewish lawbook], some *Maseches* [tractates of the Talmud]).

Conclusion

Educational work among the survivors in Germany is a transitional phenomenon. It will be, in largest part, liquidated in the immediate coming years. The schoolchildren among the survivors are an even more mobile element than the adults. They are the first and chosen candidates for *aliyah*. Several thousand orphaned children have already been transferred to the Land of Israel. The Jewish Agency has a special department, the Youth Aliyah Department, that deals exclusively with this problem.

To the superficial observer, it would seem therefore that it was not worthwhile to invest so much energy and expenditure in a structure that cannot be something that endures.

But this is not so. The children who were brought to Germany from every corner of the world, who had behind them the wild and strange experiences of wartime, who for long years could not benefit from normal education, who spoke in every possible language and mixture of languages from Europe—could not and should not be brought in this intellectual and moral state to the Land of Israel or other agreed-upon countries. They must above all become capable again of habituating themselves to human and Jewish society. They must undergo a certain reeducation; they must be restored spiritually and morally before they travel farther. Besides this, one could not allow children who have lost so many years of their development to lose another one or two years in the "waiting room" in Germany.

In addition, still another important issue must be taken into consideration. The educational work not only reconstituted the children in a wonderful manner and made them into a vanguard of the survivors, but it also had a great influence on the survivors *in general*. The school in the camp became something more than just an educational institution for the children. In its activities and holidays, in the mere fact of its existence, the school became the cultural center of the camp. In the continuous provisionality and hopeless chaos of camp life, it is the only solid point. Very often, the school is the only place in the camp where culture, "Oral Torah," so to speak, is taught systematically by a large human community. This systematic cultural activity also has an educational influence on the other people in the camp and illuminates the gray reality.

Contrary to the prewar period, the survivors' school seldom expects help in its educational activity from the parents. The pitiless Nazi era destroyed the Jewish home. Father, mother, and child had to wage their struggle with the brown beast with their own forces and mostly separated from each other. After the liberation, they did not always find their way back, not in unity of soul, nor in intellect or feeling. The experiences of the war years tore the parents away from any interest in culture. They became estranged and skeptical regarding the benefits of education and culture after the representatives of a highly cultured people, the "people of thinkers and poets," treated them in a manner that is so well known to us. As a result, in this spiritual atmosphere, an entirely strange and new phenomenon revealed itself in the camp life of the survivors: the school did not draw upon the parents as in former times, but the parents benefited from the school. In a manner of its own, the school demonstrated an influence on the family life of the camp residents. The children were a host of savage people when they came to school for the first time after their horrible experiences and years-long life of wandering. They were full of fear and mistrust, skeptical. Yes, the camp children were even cynical. Now, after a year and a half, they have become normal schoolchildren, with an inner, unforced discipline, with a great desire for knowledge, with a thirst for nicer and better forms of living, elevated by an idealistic and national-Jewish spirit. From old-wise, burdened creatures they again became childish and young; they learned again to laugh and to play. This transformed child brings into his home new ideals and sunshine, and before one notices it, the child transforms the raw atmosphere of the camp barrack into the proper atmosphere of a Jewish home, as we know it from before the war. The child opens the way to a new and warm family life that was lost in ash and flame in the difficult, terrible time of estrangement and forced separation of man, wife, and child in so many fateful moments. [Friedman's own wife and daughter were killed by the Germans.]

From the school, rays of life and hope penetrate through the darkness of the camp life that is so lacking in consolation.

Introduction Notes:

1. Filip Fridman, "Dos gedrukte yidishe vort bay der sheyres hapleyte in daytshland" [The printed Yiddish word among the survivors in Germany], *Di tsukunft* [The future] (February 1949): 94–97; (March 1949): 151–55.

2. Filip Fridman, "Shul-vezn un dertsyung in der sheyres hapleyte in daytshland" [The school system and education among the survivors in Germany], *Kiem* [Existence] (September–October 1948): 557–65 (abridged).

42
Four Years of the Chair for Holocaust Studies, Bar-Ilan University, Israel
by Mark Dworzecki, 1948

MARK DWORZECKI (see Selections 12, 33, and 39 above, 48 below) lobbied government and university officials in Israel during the state's first decade to create a university curriculum in Holocaust studies. He ultimately succeeded in establishing the world's first chair in Holocaust studies, which opened in 1959 at the recently founded Bar-Ilan University, and to which he himself was then appointed. In January 1960, he wrote to his colleague Philip Friedman in New York with news about his first class of students: "There are 32 students enrolled; 6 former camp inmates, 2 from Tripolitania [Libya], 1 new immigrant from America, 1 new immigrant from Soviet Russia, all the rest *sabras* [native Israelis]."[1]

As both a Holocaust survivor and historian, Dworzecki innovated in his teaching techniques. At a time when the relatively young Israeli academic community sought legitimacy through scholarly rigor, he was criticized for such "unprofessional" practices as having students interview Holocaust survivors—something that would, of course, become universal in Holocaust education for as long as survivors would be available (and then through interactive digital recordings). He also focused on training future teachers in the subject of Holocaust history, rather than on training academic successors in Holocaust research. In 1963, he published the following first-person account of his experiences in Holocaust education.[2]

Friends from Israel and the countries of the Diaspora often ask me about the Holocaust chair at Bar-Ilan University: What is taught there? What is the composition of the students? What sources do they use? How many have already graduated from these studies? What was the general course of development of the chair?

I understand the spiritual sources of these questions. There ought to be *bearers of memory* filled with scholarship about everything that happened to the Jews in the frightful years of the Nazi regime: carriers of memory who would transmit the facts and perhaps also their conclusions to the young generation in the elementary and middle schools in Israel and abroad; I would say that in all these questions I sense an unconscious echo of the words of the poet-partisan Hirsh Glik: "Like a watchword this song will go from *generation to generation*" [from the "Partisan Song" of the Vilna ghetto].

How to Reach the Young People?

In this short article, I will give answers to all these questions.

First, a bit of history. Since their liberation from the camps, the writers and intellectuals among those rescued have been occupied unceasingly with telling about those years of destruction and struggle that are seen so indistinctly—both at *yizkor*-events and ordinary meetings, as well as in newspaper articles and memorial books. The meetings—for the people of today; the books—for people of all generations. But a painful phenomenon is always discernible: the students at the *yizkor*-gatherings are—adults; the readers of the books—also adults. How then to reach the young people, the schoolchildren? These questions pain every writer among the survivors; they also pain me without cease.

At a Meeting During the Zionist Congress in Jerusalem, 1951

At the first Zionist congress that was held in Jerusalem after the creation of the State of Israel, delegates from all the Zionist streams were sitting around the tables in the congress café. It happened that I was sitting near Rabbi Dr. Mordecai Nurock and Prof. Pinchos Churgin. Dr. Nurock was known in Israel as *the thinker*, as the parliamentarian, for whom every problem of the survivors was close to his heart; Prof. Churgin had just organized and built the new Israeli university, Bar-Ilan.

Prof. Churgin and Dr. Nurock asked me what I was currently writing about the Holocaust years and what I thought might be done to deepen that memory. I suggested to them the idea of founding a chair on the Holocaust years at the young university that had just been founded, Bar-Ilan. "I know," I said, "that there will be many who will say: we are still too close to the years of destruction; how can we teach objectively about those years? And who could be the teacher? Those who did not see the *khurbn* themselves know too little about it, and those who saw the *khurbn* eye-to-eye—are not after all objective . . . [ellipsis in original] and they will also say: how can a young university create a chair that does not yet exist, so far as I know, at any university in the world?"

Three Who Departed

A short time later, Professor P. Churgin telephoned me: We are going to establish the chair. Professor [Samuel Shraga] Bialoblocki became an enthusiastic supporter of the chair idea. A brilliant scholar of Tanach [Hebrew Bible] and Talmud, himself a Lithuanian Jew; in his young years he was called the "Genius of Pilvishok" [today, Pilviškiai, Lithuania]. When the chair was inaugurated, Professor Churgin was already no longer living; the introductory speech to my first lecture was given by Professor Bialoblocki, and at the head table sat Dr. Nurock. Today—Professor Bialoblocki and also Dr. Nurock are also already gone. I want to mention their names here with veneration as the chief co-builders of the *Khurbn-* and Resistance-Chair.

Racist Antisemitism—the Foundation of Nazism

To understand how the Jewish *khurbn* was prepared, we are forced to study abominable Nazism; we must also dedicate a cycle of lectures to antisemitism in Europe in general and in Germany in particular. We must learn how ideas about antisemitism arose in Europe, the ideas that peoples are not equal, and that, from the racial standpoint, there are "superior peoples" and "inferior peoples." We must learn how racist antisemitism became a principal foundation in the Nazi way of thinking.

At the same time, tens and tens of names are brought forth of philosophers, historians, sociologists, theologians, writers, and thinkers—who, in the course of hundreds of years, spread hatred of Jews in their works. I normally expect that the students will read the texts of those writers. A tremor runs through the study hall when the students recite antisemitic texts by the world-famous German poet Goethe. Nietzsche lived before the start of Nazism, but sorrowful thoughts dominate the students when someone reads Nietzsche's words about *Übermensch* and *Untermensch*—and when one sees what those ideas led to—in Hitler's *Mein Kampf.*

In the German camps, Jews were sterilized. A shudder runs through the lecture hall when the students read the texts by German scholar Hundt-Radowsky, who, 150 years ago, proposed sterilizing the Jews.

Through these texts, it becomes clear to the students that Nazism and bloody antisemitism were not an accident in German history, but that they were a consequence of intellectual thoughts and processes which took shape over hundreds of years.

Often, during the breaks between classes, students ask me: "What is the assurance that these racist, antisemitic, and Nazi ideas have disappeared permanently from present-day Germany? How do we know that they will not be revived again?" To this, I answer: "My task is to teach you about the *recent past*; regarding *today*, look in the current press; in light of the experience of yesterday, it will also be easier for you to understand the processes of the present."

The Various Ways of Jewish Resistance

We learn about Jewish life in the ghettos and camps, about the stages in which the Nazis prepared the "Final Solution," meaning the total liquidation of European Jewry; we tell about the SS, about the *Reichssicherheitshauptamt* [Reich Main Security Office], about the Gestapo, about the Eichmann office. We cover the psychological problems of the Nazi murderers and the psychological problems of the Jewish and non-Jewish victims. We learn about hunger in the ghettos and camps, about the plagues, about "natural mortality."

Much attention is given to all manifestations of Jewish resistance in all countries occupied by the Nazis, and when I speak about Jewish resistance, I mean both spiritual resistance and also moral, economic, sanitary, and political resistance. We also discuss how the underground movements arose in the ghettos and Jewish participation in the partisan fight in the forests. The students are always instructed to look in the *yizkor* books for individual Jewish heroism in the ghettos and camps.

This means that they learn both about *historical events* and also about *spiritual and biological processes* of the *khurbn* period.

Something About the Students

In a few months, 50 students will complete their studies. In total, this means that 200 have taken the *Khurbn*-chair courses. The majority of them want to be *teachers* in Israel and abroad. They want to bring knowledge of the *khurbn* to their students. Most of them are *sabras* [native Israelis] for whom it is difficult to imagine a Jewish Warsaw, a Jewish Vilna, Jewry from Paris or from Amsterdam. Each year there are also students from America and Europe (France, Belgium, Switzerland, etc.). In the middle of the year, the students must compose written works, and at the end of the year there is a written examination that lasts three hours. One cannot receive a diploma in Jewish history without taking the *Khurbn*-chair courses. A group of students prepare still broader scholarly research, which is made possible by stipends from Yad Vashem. Each year a special learning day takes place at Yad Vashem, where they acquaint themselves with the "*Khurbn* Library" that was created by the chair and which already numbers nearly 500 books (among them a group of French books, sent by the friends of the chair in Paris, under the leadership of Professor [Henri] Baruk). I observe how from year to year the number of "bearers of memory" becomes larger and larger.

Introduction Notes:

    1. Letter from Dworzecki to Friedman, January 31, 1960: YIVO archives, Papers of Philip Friedman, RG 1258, F 57.

    2. M. Dvorzhetski, "4 yor katedre fun khurbn un vidershtand in universitet bar-ilan, yisroel" [4 Years of the Chair for Destruction and Resistance at Bar-Ilan University, Israel], *Undzer kiem* [Our existence] 28 (Paris, May 1963): 9–10, 16.

Part Seven

BOOK REVIEWS

43
The History of the Jews in Russia (1914)
Reviewed by Zelig Kalmanovich

The preeminent forerunner to the use of Yiddish as a language for Jewish historical scholarship was a volume on the history of the Jews in Poland and Lithuania by a group of forward-looking historians, published in Russian in 1914.[1] It was to be part of a projected fifteen-volume *History of the Jewish People* that was cut short by the start of World War I. One of the editors, Mark Wischnitzer, referred to it often in his later writings and considered it the culmination of previous efforts to advance the study of Jewish history in Russia.

Among its innovations was a collective approach to writing Jewish history, which had previously been the purview of solitary authors such as Graetz and Dubnow. But its principal innovation was to focus on the internal social, cultural, economic, and political history of the Jews, rather than on the Jewish religion or sacred texts—as was typical in Western Europe—or on the external forces that affected the Jews—as was typical in Eastern Europe.

The volume includes studies by twelve historians, nine of whom would later make significant contributions to modern Jewish historical scholarship in Yiddish. (Each appears in the present collection of translations.) Their work inspired an enthusiastic review essay by the young Yiddish-oriented intellectual, Zelig Kalmanovich, in the leading Yiddish literary journal in the

Russian Empire, *Di yudishe velt* (The Jewish world), published in Vilna.[2]

Kalmanovich (1881–1944; see Selection 34 above) was a linguist who had previously translated Dubnow's *Jewish History* (1909) and Josephus's *Jewish Wars* (1914) into Yiddish. His review, titled "A New Work on the History of the Jews," is unknown in the field of Jewish or Yiddish studies, yet it is unique for conveying—in Yiddish—the new spirit of East European Jewish historiography that would soon animate Yiddish historical writing.

The introductory portion of Kalmanovich's review is presented here. The remaining portions summarize each of the studies in the volume (and continue into the following issue of the journal), thereby also subtly demonstrating that Yiddish could serve as a capable vehicle for serious historical writing. Indeed, the emergence of Yiddish historical scholarship occurred in two phases: the first was the new perspective that placed the Jewish people at the center of their own living history, and the second was a natural progression toward presenting that history in the people's own language.

The need for a Jewish history constructed according to modern scholarly methods has long been felt. The modern-day Jew who wants to know the history of his *people* can by no means be satisfied with the attempts so far to create a general history of the Jews. The science of Jewish history was born in the countries of Western Europe, where there are no Jewish folk masses and where there could be no interest in the social and cultural life of those folk masses in the present or past. Jewishness in these countries exists only in the form of a faith, and so the only scientific interest could be on the part of theologians and rabbis. They were more interested in the system of dogmas, opinions and beliefs, and the many customs and habits known by the name of Judaism than in the community of living people who were the bearers of that Judaism. If these theologians touched not only on the Jews' theological ideas but also on the life of the Jews themselves, they did so only to the extent that religious ideas were embodied in the life of the community. The external conditions under which the Jews live, the governmental system of the countries in which they live, and the historical fate of the neighboring peoples come into consideration only to the extent that they provide the possibility for free exercise of the Jewish faith or to the extent that Jews have suffered persecutions and restrictions because of their faith. The internal organizational forces receive consideration and understanding just to the extent that they act to support or disrupt certain beliefs and customs. The spiritual creativity of the people is considered only from the standpoint of whether it leads forward or backward in the development of abstract monotheistic religion. Regarding the entire remaining social life of the Jewish community, whether in ancient times or the Middle Ages, Jewish theologians have no interest and no understanding. The works that we have in this field so far are either mere fragments or, when whole treatments are available, they cover only the history of a single country and are usually the result of research by non-Jewish historians who have written the history of their country and must therefore consider the role and significance of the Jewish community.

The result of this phenomenon is that the works of Jewish history provided to us by Western European Jewish scholars are, for the most part, no more than the history of Jewish literature, religious philosophy, and synagogue worship. The social development and general cultural history of the Jewish people remain, for the broad range of readers, concealed in darkness, and there is still to come the large and difficult work on sources, which, even if known to the theologians, are not utilized.

We find an entirely different picture when we turn to the Jewish historical scholarship that has been carried out in Eastern Europe. Here, the object of Jewish history, the Eastern European Jewish community, has already grouped itself as a more or less compact mass for five hundred years; here, even the most superficial observer has available a life of the masses and communal form of organization; in this community, the specific economic, social, and general cultural interests are already clear, and here the religious element is only one recognized factor among many other factors. The life of this community must be of interest not only to rabbis but also to true writers of history, statisticians, economists, sociologists, and political scientists. The Eastern European community and its offshoot in North America increasingly demonstrate a tendency to free itself from the authority of the synagogue and religion and to adopt the appearance of a modern secular nation, which intensifies the desire to trace the secular aspects of its past, as well as the pasts of all other Jewish communities. Specifically, the present socioeconomic structure of the Eastern European Jewish community must have its roots in the people's past. As a matter of course, it is also necessary to adopt modern historical methods for the history of the older Jewish communities in order to transform and construct Jewish history anew, this time as the actual history of the Jewish *people*. It is sufficient to compare, for example, the old, honored historical journals: the German *Monatsschrift für Geschichte und Wissenschaft des Judentums* [Monthly Journal for History and Science of Judaism] and the French *Revue des etudes juives* [Journal of Jewish studies] with the young Russian journal *Evreiskaya Starina* [Jewish Heritage, edited by Simon Dubnow] or with the anthology *Perezhitoye* [Our Past, edited by Saul Ginsburg] to see the complete difference between West and East in one aspect: the former are concerned largely with literary-historical themes and, in particular, are conducted according to literary-historical methods. The latter draw fully from living sources. Their purpose is to embrace the historical life of the Jewish people in its entire scope, and they strive to employ historical-sociological methods.

It is therefore no surprise that the *first* attempt to construct Jewish history on these new scholarly foundations has been made just now in Russia. In Western Europe, the goals and methods of Jewish historical scholarship since the time of Graetz have nearly been canonized. When something new is accomplished—and a great deal has actually been accomplished in the details—it is nothing more than partial improvements to the basic work, to Graetz's work, in the manner of his splendid work. This is because the basic principle, the point of departure, and the purpose remain the same as for the honored old historian. Entirely different are the purposes and methods of the Eastern European Jewish historians: before them lies the problem of a national, not a confessional, community, and so they must learn not from Graetz, but from the modern historians of other peoples. And this task of creating a new Jewish history that will occupy the appropriate level of modern scholarship has been taken up by a collective of Jewish scholars in Russia. A year ago, we received the prospectus for this work, the *History of the Jewish People*. The work consisted of two parts: 1) the *Worldwide History of the Jews* in ten volumes, which included the history of the Jewish people from the oldest times to the most recent generation, outside of Russia, and 2) *The History of the Jews in Russia* in five volumes. This work set for its goal, according to the prospectus, to "show the actual life of the people, as the true creator and transmitter of its history." To the publishers, it was clear that "the Jewish people were not only an object of mercy or wrath of the surrounding peoples; they dealt not only with abstract ideas and accumulated religious and philosophical values, but they also lived, accommodated themselves to the changing political and socio-economic conditions of their surroundings, fought for their specific national culture, and took part, as an entire people, in the material and intellectual evolution of humanity." This is the new concept innovated by the young Jewish historical science in Eastern Europe.

Before us now lies the first volume of *The History of the Jews in Russia*, the eleventh volume of the *Worldwide History of the Jews*. [This volume alone appeared before the project was ended by World War I and the Russian Revolution.] Proceeding from the primary difference between the old Jewish historical science and the new, it is clear why just now the history of the Jews in Russia was singled out. The trend toward secularism, toward purely national organization, was most clearly expressed in the community that lives at present under the rule of the Russian state. Therefore, modern scientific methods can more easily and surely be applied to researching and writing the history of this community. Because of the importance of this community in the present Jewish cultural movement, its size (together with the present Austrian lands and the branch in North America comprising nearly 75 percent of the entire Jewish people) earns it a special place and special consideration. Just as in its current life, there must be features in its past that distinguish it from other Jewish communities. In accordance with their general view of historical scholarship, the publishers set themselves the task to "clarify and illuminate the evolution of the cultural life of the Jews in Russia, their legal and economic way of life" (from the introduction).

The multifaceted nature of the issues that must be considered makes it impossible in the present state of historical science for such a task to be undertaken by a single individual. Setting aside worldwide Jewish history, which would truly require writing a history of the world—a task at which no one has so far succeeded—even the history of the Jews in Russia must at present become a collective work when it amounts to using much unexamined raw material, most of which is not yet even printed. Therefore, the publishers have rightly applied the method that was adopted in such cases by German scholarship: the entire work consists of a series of monographs, each of which considers a separate problem and is prepared by a specialist. This manner of organizing the history of a people, which is itself a fundamentally unitary process, also contains a drawback that the publishers often acknowledge: the large number of authors makes it difficult to maintain a unity of viewpoints. But this drawback is turned to advantage by means of the richness of the material and the specificity of its presentation, which is possible only with such a system of monographs. Of course, a place remains for a history of the Jews in Russia by one author, written from a single point of view, and the present publication would certainly help a great deal in his work.

The first volume of the work treats the history of Jews in Poland and Lithuania until the time these countries came under Russian rule, namely, until the end of the eighteenth century. We find here the following works:

The introduction to the work, written by P. S. Marek. Here is presented a short overview of the general aspects of the fate of the Eastern European Jewish community in the course of the thirteenth century until the nineteenth century. It sets forth the chief sociological principles of the methods of constructing a Jewish history. It would be worthwhile to discuss these principles, especially in their application to the most recent history, but that must await another occasion.

[Kalmanovich then devotes one or more pages to each of the chapters, on the following topics:]

1. Mark Wischnitzer, General overview of political and social history of Jews in Poland and Lithuania.
2. Ignacy Schiper, Jewish settlements in Poland and Lithuania from earliest times to the end of the eighteenth century.
3. Meir Balaban, The internal organization of the Jewish community in Poland.
4. Wischnitzer, The internal organization of the Jewish community in Lithuania.

5. Legal Systems:
   a. Balaban, The organization of the Jewish law court (*beth-din*).
   b. Ben-Zion Katz, The Jewish *beth-din* and rabbinic responsa.
   c. Stanisław Kutrzeba [prominent Polish historian], Trials between Jews and non-Jews.
6. Economic Life:
   a. Wischnitzer and Schiper, Commercial businesses, leasing and estate-leasing (*arenda*).
   b. Wischnitzer, Jewish craftsmen and their guild organization.
7. Schipper, The taxes on the Jews.
8. Dubnov, The internal way of life of the Jews in Poland and Lithuania in the sixteenth century.
9. Azriel-Nosn Frenk, Internal way of life of the Jews in Poland and Lithuania in the seventeenth and eighteenth centuries.
10. Rachel Bernstein-Wischnitzer, Jewish art in Poland and Lithuania.
11. Literature and Religion:
    a. Israel Zinberg, Development of rabbinic literature, Yiddish folk literature, mystical movements.
    b. Wischnitzer, The Frankist movement.
    c. Saul Ginsburg, The beginning of Hasidism.
12. Wischnitzer, Bibliography of the history of Jews in Poland and Lithuania.

Naturally, this brief review of the contents can give only the barest introduction to the entire work. We have before us, as noted above, for the first time a work of Jewish history constructed according to a truly scientific method. If perhaps specialists discover that in one or another detail it is possible to hold opinions different from those of the authors of the work, the entire work nevertheless gives us an altogether correct picture of Jewish folk life in all its aspects, starting with the economic and finishing with the religious. The present first volume gives us the full right to hope that in further portions, where the historical sources are much richer and more varied, the picture of Jewish life will be presented still more distinctly and clearly, and we will have the *History of the Jewish People* in the full sense of the term.

Introduction Notes:

1. *Istoriiā evreiskago naroda*, vol. XI: *Istoriiā evreev v Rossii* [*History of the Jews*, vol. XI: *History of Jews in Russia*] (Moscow: Izd-vo T-va "Mir," 1914).

2. Zelig Kalmanovitsh, "A nay verk iber der geshikhte fun yuden" [A new work on the history of the Jews], *Di yudishe velt* 1, no. 2 (February 1915): 199–207; 1, no. 3 (March 1915): 338–54.

44
Saul Ginsburg. Historical Works (1937)

Reviewed by Moyshe Shalit

MOYSHE SHALIT (1885–1941) was born in Vilna [today Vilnius, Lithuania] and became a prolific journalist and editor of Yiddish newspapers and journals, as well as administrator of Jewish charitable and educational organizations. At the start of the German occupation of Vilna in 1941, he refused to serve on the first Jewish Council and was arrested and murdered in Ponar.

Shalit was also an amateur historian who edited the quarterly "cultural-historical journal" *Fun noentn over* (From the recent past), which appeared in Warsaw from 1937 to 1939 with the assistance of the Anski Historical-Ethnographic Society of Vilna. It carried articles by several of the scholars translated in the present volume, including Friedman, Ginsburg, Jaffe, Kon, Niger, and Ringelblum.

Shalit was a frequent contributor himself, at times drawing on his circle of acquaintances for material. One of these was historian Saul Ginsburg (see Selections 19 and 30 above). Shalit greeted the publication of Ginsburg's three-volume set of collected works with a celebratory review of the historian and his work—emphasizing Ginsburg's accessible style and focus on the internal history of the Jews.[1]

שאול גינזבורג

היסטארישע ווערק

ערשטער באנד

פון אידישען לעבען און שאפען
אין צארישען רוסלאנד

ערשטער טייל

•

ניו יארק
שאול גינזבורג 70-יאהריגער יובילעי קאמיטעט
תרצ"ו

To celebrate Saul Ginsburg's seventieth birthday (seventh day of Passover—April 13, 1936), a committee was formed in New York for the purpose of publishing at least a part of his historical works in *book form* and thereby "pay a debt of public gratitude to this scholar and cultural leader, who has already served the Jewish people for more than forty years with his works in the field of Jewish history, educational systems, and publicity."

Saul Ginsburg, the scholarly publisher (together with P. S. Marek) of the groundbreaking collection *Jewish Folksongs in Russia*, the founder of the first modern Jewish daily newspaper in Russia, *Der fraynd* [The friend], the editor (together with I. Zinberg) of the well-known new *historical* anthologies *Perezhitoye* [Our Past, in Russian], and afterward *he-Avar* [The Past, in Hebrew], and a whole series of others—published many tens of valuable historical works about the life of the Jews in Russia in the last two centuries, on the basis of official and private archival materials, which have, however, until now (other than a few exceptions, books published in Russian) been spread across various journals and newspapers and are now, for the first time, *newly reworked*, partially gathered together in the abovementioned edition in *Yiddish*.

This edition of Saul Ginsburg's historical works is without any doubt the most *interesting* and *characteristic* phenomenon in Jewish historical literature in recent times.

These are not simply articles on historical subjects or various more or less important investigations and speculations—but masterworks of great scholarly-literary and especially cultural-historical value.

In these works, Ginsburg is revealed to us not only as a historian but also as an artist. His style, his language, his tone, his *manner of description* have no equal in our historiography and make him beloved and understandable for the broadest circle of readers—and create exemplars for us of invaluable *historical folk literature*, a new type, which we have not had until now.

Many of Ginsburg's works can (and should) be used with great success in the higher grades of our schools as an authentic Yiddish reader with a group of the most dramatic moments in our history in modern times.

A series of works—thanks to their power of attraction, simple and clear narration and suspenseful (in the best sense of the word) content, and simultaneously highest historical value—should be disseminated in small booklets in tens and hundreds of thousands of copies among the people as healthy spiritual sustenance (and at the same time as antidote) in the fight against the plague of inferior works and falsification.

Ginsburg's greatest service from the purely scholarly perspective is that he laid the trope for the study of our *inner* life in former times. He was the first to make *wide* use of, besides official—also private archives, letters, family documents—and, in the official sources, as in the private ones, he researched and studied above all the *lifestyle, character, cultural phenomena, social factors*—and presented the entire factual material strictly in accordance with historical truth but simultaneously inspired with the *breath* of the epoch and with the *spirit* of the heroes.

In the first two volumes the author treats Jewish life and creativity in tsarist Russia, and, in the third volume, Jewish suffering in tsarist Russia.

In the first volume, we find thirteen articles on the cultural history of Russian Jews in the nineteenth century. We have here new materials about the Decembrists and the Jews; about David Luria in Shlisslburg Fortress; Rabbi Menachem Mendel of Lubavitch and the government; Rabbi Israel of Ruzhin and his wayward son; a group of historical-literary studies, such as Y. L. Gordon's arrest and exile, Mendele Moykher Sforim in his letters, Israel Aksenfeld, the *Voskhod* [Russian Jewish periodical *Sunrise*] and its founding, the ban on Yiddish theater, etc.—further articles discuss Jews in the Franco-Russian war period of 1812, and following this, extraordinarily interesting and, in theme, entirely new studies of ordinary life in bygone times, such as: the old-time Jewish post [see Selection 30 in this volume], old-time daring Jewish youths and bandits, Jewish informers in former times, the bandit Boytre,[1] and how our great-grandparents fought the cholera epidemic.

In the second volume is a group of studies of old-time family life under the general title "Individuals and Generations," which are also entirely new, both in their content and in being constructed with the use of archival materials—further pieces discuss "guests": Moshe Montefiore in Russia; Isaac Alteras, the forerunner of Baron Hirsch; Dr. Herzl's visit to St. Petersburg—then eight historical miniatures portraying various pictures, events, and episodes. The book begins with two splendid studies about Jewish recruiting.

The third volume provides a long, very interesting, and, in terms of content, exceptionally important work, based on primary sources, about the Jewish cantonists [see Selection 19 in this volume]. As a complement to this, it continues with three articles from the series "Kiddish Hashem" and then four larger studies under the general title "Libels and Decrees," such as the blood libel in Velizh, the Decree of Amtslav [today Mstsislaw, Belarus], attacks on Jewish clothing, Jewish ghettos in old-time Russia.

The secretariat of the New York "Saul Ginsburg 70-Year Anniversary Committee," which consists of Dr. Herman Frank, Jacob Krepliak, and Isaac Rivkind (treasurer is Louis Rimski), perfectly executed its task—and deserves genuine congratulations for enriching our literature and especially our historiography with a so very important, first-class edition.

The three volumes of Saul Ginsburg's historical works, which together have more than 1,650 pages, are excellently published in accordance with the best modern methods of book technology, each provided with tables of contents and indexes, portraits, facsimiles, and pictures—and, at the end, also with a thorough, very well-assembled "Saul Ginsburg Bibliography" by Isaac Rivkind.

The bibliography encompasses the years 1892–1937, chronologically, each year separately, with all the necessary commentary and precision: 260 entries for Saul Ginsburg's writings, 7 entries for Ginsburg as editor, and 35 entries about Ginsburg.

In all three volumes, there are attachments of important documents and materials. Saul Ginsburg's historical works should become a book for reading in every Jewish home.

Introduction Notes:

1. Moyshe Shalit, "Shoyl ginzburgs histor. verk, 3 bender, nyu-york 1937" [Saul Ginsburg's Historical Works, 3 volumes], *Fun noentn over* I, no. 4 (Warsaw, 1937): 339–42 (339–41 quoted; order of paragraphs revised according to importance).

Article Notes:

1. [Also the subject of Moyshe Kulbak's well-known 1936 play, *Boytre the Bandit*, about a Robin Hood–like figure.]

45
Isaiah Trunk. The History of the Jews in Płock (1939)
Reviewed by A. Valdman

"A. VALDMAN" was apparently the pen name of a politically astute writer who chose to remain unknown to the authorities in late interwar Poland. Only the present article from March, 1939, and another the previous month on the causes of Jewish emigration from Poland appear with this name in the available indexes. Both stress the anti-Jewish acts from which Jews suffered in Poland during the years before World War II.

Valdman's review of this work on the Jews of the old Polish city of Płock (pronounced "Plotsk" in Yiddish) by Isaiah Trunk (see also Selections 7, 15, 21 above) is titled "700 Years of Jewish Settlement in Poland."[1] He recognizes, and makes explicit, the instrumental value of the work (as Trunk intended) for defending Jewish rights in Poland by proving the antiquity of Jewish settlement and the value of Jewish contributions to the Polish economy and state.

A historical book has been published that is far more than history and scholarship: it is a historical testimonial to the Polish Jews, a documentary eyewitness to their services and accomplishments for the Polish state. *The History of the Jews in Płock* is the title of the book, and it was prepared by one of the youngest but most important Jewish historians, Sh. Trunk. The book was published by the Historical Section of the Yiddish Scientific Institute [YIVO] with the help of the Committee to Celebrate the 700-Year Anniversary of the Jewish Community in Płock. Indeed, in the introduction to the book, the anniversary committee [in fact, Emanuel Ringelblum] writes: "This book appears at a time when the rights of the Jewish population in Poland are being denied—at a time when Polish Jews, who have lived in the country for centuries, are considered foreigners by reactionary forces. This book demonstrates that Jews in Poland are not foreigners who arrived yesterday. It demonstrates that the thread of Jewish history in Poland extends across long, long centuries."

The book encompasses the period from 1237 to 1657, namely, from the birth year of the Jewish community in Płock to its ruin and decline. The author introduces us to the community life of the first Polish Jews, and shows us their economic and political-legal situation.

The Jews, writes Trunk, were *servi camerae* [servants of the chamber] of the duke, and certain individuals even enjoyed extraordinary rights on the basis of the duke's privileges. The duke was the supporter of the Jews, and his court defended them against the violent acts committed by the Christian population.

At the end of the fifteenth century, the Duchy of Płock was incorporated into the Polish state (Crown Poland). From then on, the Płock Jews were subject to the same laws as the Crown Jews, and their legal situation changed radically. The role of Jews in the economic life of the city was colossal. At that time, Płock was an important commercial stop along the Vistula riverway to Danzig. In Płock, the Jews therefore had a broad field for their commercial interests. The Płock Jewish merchants traded in wool, leather, fish, and sweets and exported herring, tar, and down to Danzig.

But the strong participation of the Jews in Polish commerce evoked opposition on the part of the rising Polish bourgeoisie. Already in the second half of the fifteenth century, the Polish bourgeoisie entered into a fight against Jewish commerce. The non-Jewish urban petit bourgeoisie demanded that the king limit the rights of the Jewish merchants. Their lobbying did indeed achieve the desired result: King Zygmunt I issued an entire group of decrees against Jewish merchants—among them three regulations for the Jewish merchants in Płock. With time came new anti-Jewish decrees, which however had certain "exceptions" that, to a certain extent, softened the sharpness of the laws and created a possibility for a broader interpretation of the regulations.

Besides credit operations and leaseholds of public revenue, Płock Jews were occupied with craftwork. Among Jews, there were many weavers, tailors, furriers, and shoemakers.

One of the most interesting chapters of the book is the treatment of the legal situation of the Płock Jews. It tells about a Jewish court that consisted of Jewish trustees [wealthy community leaders] and had the right to judge and punish with the "highest punishment"—with the "pillory." The Jews had to pay nine different types of taxes and besides them also various communal payments, such as for the city clock and others.

The ritual [murder] trials that led to the death of three innocent Jews, a father and two sons, form a special chapter in the history of Płock. The most interesting part of the book is without doubt the chapter: "The Jews in the Christian Environment" [see Selection 15 in this volume], which relates facts and episodes that are strongly reminiscent of present-day relations between the Jewish and Christian populations. Cases of individual and collective violent attacks (pogroms) were not rare events. Płock itself experienced five frightful pogroms (in the years 1534–1656), besides a great number of individual attacks. For the most part, the participants in these attacks were the so-called "Jacques's," i.e., Polish school youths who studied in the clerical schools.

Nevertheless, "we must say," writes Trunk, "that the Jews were well able to defend themselves."

There are also chapters at the end of the book about the private life of rich and powerful Jews in Płock, and, although this work is not yet finished, and further volumes are yet to come—we must already say that this first volume of the history of the Jews in Płock is an important entry in Jewish historiography. Until now, in the Jewish history of Poland, the accepted starting point is the end of the thirteenth century. According to the well-known Jewish historian Dr. Y. Schiper (*The Economic History of the Jews in Poland During the Middle Ages*), the very oldest information about an organized Jewish community is about Kalisz, where in 1287 the community heads purchased a hill to establish a cemetery there. But Trunk shows, on the basis of archival sources, that the first Jewish community in Poland dates its beginning much earlier, as early as 1237, and one of these "firstborns" is indeed Płock.

Trunk's book is a clear repudiation of the recent "achievements" of official Polish historiography, which attempts to reduce and obscure the role of Jews in the economic history of Poland. The energetic historian and university professor Roman Rybarski writes, for example, in his book *Commerce and Commercial Policy in Poland in the Sixteenth Century*,[1] that the Jews in Poland only destroyed the old economic organization, but they did not create any new economic positions. Yet it is sufficient to leaf through the book by Sh. Trunk to be convinced of the falseness and hypocrisy of this clearly antisemitic theory, which predominates ever more in Polish historical scholarship. It is also a great service of the author of *The History of Jews in Płock* that he emphasizes the baselessness and falsity of the so very widespread antisemitic theory in Polish historiography, which is even accepted by such a liberal and democratic professor as Professor Włodzimierz Dzwonkowski—that the Jews helped the Swedes during their military invasion in Poland. The description of the pogrom that the Swedes conducted against the Jews in Płock is, it appears, a sufficient example to demonstrate the baselessness of this malevolent libel.

Finally, it would be an injustice to the Yiddish Scientific Institute if we did not also mention the exceptional technical and aesthetic virtues of the book. It is truly a beautiful, tasteful book, and the Historical Section of YIVO deserves a hearty congratulations for it.

Introduction Notes:

1. A. Valdman, "700 yohr idisher yishuv in poyln," *Haynt* [Today] (Warsaw, March 10, 1939): 10.

Article Notes:

1. [Roman Rybarski, *Handel i polityka handlowa Polski w XVI stuleciu* [Trade and trade policy of Poland in the sixteenth century], 2 vols. (Poznań, 1928–29).]

46
Jacob Shatzky. In the Shadow of the Past (1947)
Reviewed by Samuel Rollansky

SAMUEL ROLLANSKY (Shmuel Rozhanski, 1902–1995) was born to a Lithuanian family living in Warsaw. After a traditional Jewish education and graduation from a secular gymnasium, he left for Argentina in 1923, where, during a long and productive career as a teacher and writer, he became the leading face of Yiddish culture in Argentina. He was director of the Argentine branch of YIVO (Yiddish Scientific Institute) and published articles in its *Argentiner YIVO shriftn* and other journals worldwide. He is best known for his work as editor from 1965 to 1984 of YIVO's 100-volume series Musterverk fun der yidisher literatur (Exemplars of Yiddish literature, often mistranslated as "Masterworks")—which was the *second* notable series of Yiddish books to be published in Argentina after World War II.

The *first* series was Dos poylishe yidntum (Polish Jewry), consisting of 175 volumes published from 1946 to 1966 by the Central Union of Polish Jews in Argentina on Jewish life in Poland before the Holocaust. In 1947, the thirteenth volume of the series was devoted to historical writings by Jacob Shatzky, titled *In the Shadow of the Past*.[1] Rollansky reviewed Shatzky's book with enthusiasm in the local Yiddish press, and his review appears below.[2]

Many years later, Rollansky reprinted Shatzky's article on the *Tsene-rene* (see Selection 24 above) from this book in his own *Musterverk* series, in the volume devoted to the *Tsene-rene*.[3]

Dr. Jacob Shatzky's studies collected in the book *In the Shadow of the Past*—published by the Central Union of Polish Jews in Argentina as the thirteenth volume of the series Dos poylishe yidntum [Polish Jewry]—is a valuable contribution to understanding the relations between Jews and Christians. We see here strivings by Jews and tendencies of Jewishness, both in the shadow of their own healthy life and in struggling, whether as the partner or victim of evil.

The book depicts primarily how Jews felt as they wanted to identify with Polish patriotism and how Polish patriots, mostly friends, related to them in the fight for the independence or freedom of the country. Here are seen problems of assimilation and figures of famous assimilated Jews and converts. In contrast to them, however, are flashes of Jewish religious and popular romanticism. There is, in this way, a certain degree of balance. Opposite the sketches "In Pursuit of Total Assimilation" and "The Frankist Conversionary Movement," there is "Three Hundred Years of the *Tsene-rene*" [see Selection 24 in this volume]. Opposite the dark sides, we see the light sides. Opposite "An Extraordinary Characteristic of the Jewish Convert-Bourgeoisie," the historian shows us "The Oldest History of Yiddish Theater in Warsaw" and also "A Proposal to Found a School for Jewish Artisans in Warsaw in 1836" and "On the History of Jewish Colonization in the Kingdom of Poland (1840–1860)."

From one side—in the shadow of the life of the people; from the second side—the evil of assimilation and conversion.

You see here how the historian orients himself in life and his conflicts. Determined, practical, with a feeling for reality.

Dr. Shatzky considers this a task of the Jewish historian, and so he takes pride in being the son of Jewish Poland. "The Jewish historian in Poland," he writes in the introduction to the book, "was the ammunition supplier for the rows of Jewish fighting masses. The arguments and evidence that a historian excavated in dusty and dark archival cellars could attain the scholarly recognition they deserved only in books. In life, they were used in the fight for rights in the forum of the Polish Sejm [parliament], in the speeches of political and national leaders, in the passionate polemic in the press" (p. 7).

Blessed with the talent to express difficult matters in a light manner and simple language, our scholar conveys to us—with folksy clarity—figures and problems that pertain to great movements. Shatzky writes so simply that it would seem he intends to popularize this or that issue, this or that personality, while in truth he conveys many facts that, in the Jewish historical literature, are new and, with regard to their scope, thoroughness, and conceptions, bring new information to general history.

Much has been written, for example, about "Adam Mickiewicz [the Polish national poet] and the Jews," a subject with which Dr. Shatzky opens his book *In the Shadow of the Past*. Since this study was published for the first time (in *Di tsukunft* [The future, New York] in 1923), this subject has been discussed many more times. There was even a time when it caused a violent dispute, and it was involved with a great scandal and bitter trial. But the basic idea and the historical conception about the relation between the greatest Polish poet and the Jews was not changed by this entire dispute. Dr. Shatzky's study remains the only thorough depiction of that period, when Mickiewicz, in the thrall of mysticism, dreamed of entering Poland with a Jewish legion that was created in Turkey and would revolutionize Poland!, that the Poles themselves would be swept up in the fight for national independence (1855). This is a very important chapter, which the Polish historians and literary critics had no desire to present clearly. Symptomatic of this is that Józef Kallenbach [1861–1929], one of the most thorough Mickiewicz scholars, in his two-volume work about the poet, depicted everything clearly, but when he came to the Jewish legion with which Mickiewicz allied himself, lost his tongue, became nebulous and lacked even information . . . [ellipsis in original] It was not enough for the Christians that Mickiewicz was sure that the Jews, in an environment of tolerance and love, would assimilate, as the Jewish legionnaires who wanted to give their lives for Poland also hoped to "accomplish."

What could become of such assimilationist patriotism? To this, Shatzky gives an answer in the study with which he concludes the book: "In Pursuit of Total Assimilation." In this colorful portrait of Alexander Kraushar [1843–1931], rich in details that are extraordinarily characteristic of the development of this personality, we see the Jewish historian, who, in his pursuit of full Polishness, left through conversion, over time became a reactionary and a devout Catholic. "In Kraushar's life and in his literary activity," Shatzky says at the end of his study, which was published in the *YIVO bleter* in 1943, "we see a case of total assimilation, a history of one who began as a student of the Jewish past and ended as a denier of the Jewish present" (p. 228).

Dr. Jacob Shatzky appears before us not only as a historian who wants to tell us what was, just for the sake of telling! Rather, he arms us with evidence and arguments, both when he sets us under the shadow of the poor but sunny Jewish life with the *Tsene-rene* and when he sets us against the evil that leads to assimilation and conversion.

Introduction Notes:

1. Yankev Shatski, *In shotn fun over* [In the shadow of the past] (Buenos Aires: Tsentralfarband fun poylishe yidn in argentine, 1947).

2. Shmuel Rozhanski, review of *In shotn fun over*, *Yidishe Tsaytung*, April 27, 1947; reprinted in Sh. L. Shnayderman, *Tsvishn shrek un hofenung* (Buenos Aires: Tsentral-farband fun poylishe yidn in argentine, 1947), 363–65.

3. *Ivre-taytsh—Band I—Tsene Urene* (Buenos Aires: Literatur-gezelshaft baym YIVO, 1973), 324–29.

47
Philip Friedman. Auschwitz (1950)
Reviewed by Julien Hirshaut

JULIEN HIRSHAUT (1908–1983) was born in Drohobych, Austrian Galicia (today in Ukraine), and received a master's degree in law and political economy from Lemberg (today Lviv, Ukraine) University. He wrote widely for the Jewish press in Poland before and immediately after the Holocaust, then settled briefly in Paris and eventually in New York. Hirshaut was one of the best known and most accomplished of the lay historians who worked in Yiddish after World War II, writing on the Holocaust and Jewish history in Poland, as well as biographies of historians Balaban and Schiper.

Hirshaut also reviewed works by Yiddish historians for the postwar volumes of *YIVO bleter*, such as the history of Auschwitz by Philip Friedman (see Selections 36 and 41 above) that was published in the Argentine series Dos poylishe yidntum (Polish Jewry).[1] Friedman's book was the first comprehensive account of the operation of Auschwitz as a factory of death, and it became widely known. It is an expanded version of his earlier articles on Auschwitz, first published in Polish and then in English translation. In his own bibliography, Friedman lists twenty-four Yiddish and four English reviews of the Yiddish book. The review by Hirshaut that appears here is notable for its scholarly, rather than emotional, appraisal of Friedman's research.[2] It is a rebuttal to the minority of reviews, by survivors of Auschwitz, who contended that anyone "who was not there" could not write about it with authority.

The book and the review use the Polish name of the town, "Oświęcim," rather than the German name of the town and camp, "Auschwitz," as was common in the early postwar years, and this is preserved in the translation. As is well known, that name soon became outmoded in deference to Polish sensibilities about the false imputation of Polishness to a German camp on Polish soil.

Oświęcim (Auschwitz) was the largest death camp of Nazi Germany. For this death factory, the intellectual elite of the German people, professors, doctors, and engineers, collaborated hand in hand with executioners and, thanks to this "blessed" joint effort the most modern and best-regulated factory for mass murder was erected.

More than five million people were killed in Auschwitz by the Germans, among them more than three million Jews. This means that Oświęcim itself conducted more than half of the German death work, while all the other death camps (Maidanek, Treblinka, Belzec, Sobibor, etc.), along with the thousands of execution places, together did not reach the level of productivity at Auschwitz.

Although the role of Oświęcim in the German extermination *Aktionen* [round-ups] was so great, we have a very meager literature on this subject so far. Serious books about Auschwitz (not counting memoirs and newspaper articles) published by all the affected peoples can be counted on the fingers of one hand. In addition, the available eyewitness accounts and reports from those who returned from Auschwitz illuminate only a portion of the facts that played a part in that Gehenna in the course of its four-year existence. How much evidence of human suffering, how much evidence of heroism and martyrdom were lost!

Until a short time ago, there was no book in the Yiddish language about this largest extermination camp. Barely a year ago, the Argentine publishing house of the Polish Jews issued the first book about Oświęcim. The author, historian Dr. Philip Friedman, survived the horror of the Nazi occupation in Poland. He was miraculously able to save himself in hiding and avoid a personal encounter with the German places of extermination. Dr. Friedman first became acquainted with the Auschwitz camp when he visited there as a member of the Polish state commission that investigated the German crimes. That Dr. Friedman had not himself experienced the horror of Oświęcim was fortunate for carrying out the task he undertook in writing the book *Oświęcim*. A historical researcher and historical writer who wants to fulfill his task properly as an objective chronicler and honest evaluator must be free of any personal emotionalism.

The material that is in the book *Oświęcim* is organized in a well-considered order. After the first few chapters, which convey the general geographic and topographic information about the vicinity of Oświęcim, comes a short and matter-of-fact history of the death camp. The author conveys details not known until now about visits by high-ranking Nazi personalities to the camp. The author demonstrates, on the basis of documents, that not only the official Nazi political agencies participated in building the Oświęcim death camp but also German economic and even private companies that ultimately had no connection to the Nazi Party or the government. This revelation is very important. It is also an indication that not only the Nazi Party but all of German society bears the responsibility for the acts of killing.

The book continues with the organization of the death industry. All institutions of the camp (not only the gas chambers and crematoria) served the purpose of killing people. Establishing the camp in an unhealthy, muddy area, not providing it with water and keeping it in a thoroughly poor hygienic condition, starving the inmates and simultaneously driving them to labors that were beyond human strength, continuously torturing the inmates—all of this was premeditated as the means to an end: eradicating the inmates. The Germans succeeded. Hundreds of thousands of people were killed at Oświęcim outside the gas chambers. They were killed by hunger, weakness, illness, and torture.

The scientific experiments that German professors and doctors conducted on the Oświęcim victims form a special chapter in the history of German crimes. Dr. Friedman lists the names of a group of representatives of German medicine (Professor Schumann, Dr. Klein, Dr. Mengele, Dr. Rascher, etc.) who were involved. The histological institute in Breslau participated in some of the more important experiments. There were also many pharmacological institutes that would send their new and unproven preparations for testing on the Oświęcim inmates.

The gas chambers and crematoria can be described as the lowest levels of the Oświęcim Gehenna. In the period of greatest "prosperity," when the Jews from Hungary and the Lodz ghetto were liquidated, the "production" of the crematoria reached their highest level. On the basis of documents, Dr. Friedman indicates that June 28, 1944, was the record day. On that day the murderers gassed and burned 24,000 people.

It is well known that the Germans sought to make ever greater profits from their death industry. They would rob their victims of their last piece of clothing. Their diabolical extermination plan clearly anticipated the income that would arise from stealing the property of the victims. Of course, the Oświęcim death industry also had its commercial aspect. From a series of figures, assembled by the author, we get a glance at the balance sheet of this uncommon undertaking. The balance sheet was very active. The camp treasury received from German companies enormous sums of money for the work of the "loaned-out" campmates. A further source of income for the Germans was the goods of the victims. All of this was still too little for the plundering Germans. They robbed not only the living but even the dead. They tore out gold teeth from the corpses and cut off the women's hair, from which German factories made mattresses.

The last chapter of Dr. Friedman's *Oświęcim* takes us into the world of the underground struggle that the campmates conducted against their murderers. In Oświęcim there was an underground fighting organization in which Jews played a great part. Instances there of resistance and of escaping were no rarity. The human spark was not extinguished among the humiliated and tortured slaves; in many cases, they knew how to maintain their human worth.

Oświęcim is an important contribution to the research literature about the recent *khurbn*. The author assembled a great number of documents and eyewitness accounts and dealt with them systematically and with erudition. The numerous pictures and photocopies of original documents that appear in the book strengthen the reader's confidence and faith in the truthfulness of the author's conclusions. His work is supported by reliable and verified sources. The language is simple, without ponderousness or pomposity. The author deliberately avoids every strong expression. The colorfulness of the depictions and the truthfulness of the conclusions increase the value of this work.

Introduction Notes:

1. Filip Fridman, *Oshvyentshim* [Auschwitz] (Buenos Aires: Tsentral farband fun poylishe yidn in argentine, 1950).

2. Y. Hirshoyt, "Di natsishe mordvirtshaft in dem oyshvyentshimer gehenem" [The Nazi death-economy in the Auschwitz Gehenna], *YIVO bleter* XXXV (1951): 291–93.

48
Mark Dworzecki. White Nights and Black Days: Jewish Camps in Estonia (1970)

Reviewed by Israel Kaplan

ISRAEL KAPLAN (1902–2003) was born in Volozhin, Belorussia (today Belarus), and received a master's degree in history and philosophy from the University of Kovno (today Kaunas, Lithuania). Before World War II, he published articles and stories in Yiddish periodicals. During the Holocaust he survived the Kovno ghetto, forced labor camps, and Dachau. He became best known in Holocaust studies as the cofounder of the Central Jewish Historical Commission in the American zone of postwar Germany and editor of its journal, *Fun letstn khurbn* (From the recent destruction). Ten issues appeared from 1946 to 1948, in which he published many of the survivor oral histories he conducted and documents he collected. Kaplan settled in Israel in 1949, where he became a popular and prizewinning author of books and stories, many on Holocaust themes, in both Yiddish and Hebrew.

Kaplan was a contributor to the leading Yiddish literary journal in Israel, *Di goldene keyt* (The golden chain), which published the review that appears here of a book by Mark Dworzecki (see Selections 12, 33, 39, and 42 above). Dworzecki had been a medical doctor in Vilna before World War II and, after surviving the Vilna ghetto and several labor camps, turned to writing the history of the Vilna ghetto immediately upon his liberation.

He would later earn his doctorate in history at the Sorbonne with a dissertation on the Jewish camps in Estonia (which he had experienced firsthand), published in Yiddish, Hebrew, and French editions.[1] Kaplan's review of that later work discusses the evolution of Dworzecki's historical method and emphasizes his innovative use of survivor testimonies.[2]

Khurbn!

The destroyed Jewish life of Europe pursues us, does not release us, and demands and demands to know ever more precisely about that national *khurbn*.

We read a short story or novel from our most recent fine literature and delight in the deeply rooted life in our cities and towns: an idyllic life, a fresh life, a daily existence so real. And suddenly, with a start—already nothing remains! . . . [all ellipses in original] and nothing related to it. During the years of the Second World War, the age-old Jewish life there did not change in a natural way and rebuild itself. The trunk was cut off together with the branches, the roots severed, and the entire fertile soil gone. Everything was murderously destroyed.

Kollel Varsha [Warsaw Community] and more and more *kollelim* of the Old Yishuv in Israel [religious Jewish communities of the pre-Zionist period]. They bear the names of Jewish centers and communities in Europe. For generations, from there went not only material support for the Yishuv, the "Halukah money" [charity from Jewish communities in Europe]. Spiritual sustenance also spread here from these powerful Jewish places of creativity, and it molded the spiritual existence of the people here and, indeed, also organically blended with their own closely guarded lifestyle. Kollel Varsha and the other names quickly bring us to the wonderful communities that were destroyed . . . In the small Hasidic prayer houses, one also finds only remnants, which are a form of leftovers from that grand table of Hasidism in Eastern Europe. Gravestones are the congregations, the "Anshe Smargon," "Anshe Minsk" [People of Smargon; of Minsk], and other such *landsmanshaftn* [hometown associations]. And the "Lithuanian" yeshivas that call themselves today by the names of the famous places there—make us shudder at the names of those destroyed Torah centers. Alas, such a deeply learned world!

But names, gravestones and memorial tablets, and also *yortsaytn* and *haskores* [memorial anniversaries and prayer services], cannot come close to taking the place of the fundamental and comprehensive information that we want to know about the great *khurbn*. Here, our desire turns toward the few researchers whose writings, chronicles, and monographs lay a serious historiographical foundation for the national *khurbn*. Of great importance are the studies by authors who themselves also experienced the Nazi Gehenna in the ghettos and concentration camps. As a result, there is a special interest in each new work by Dr. Mark Dworzecki, who for years has been absorbed in research of the *khurbn* and has already enriched the historiography of that period with quite a few books.

Dr. Dworzecki's book *Yerushalem d'lite in kamf un umkum* [Jerusalem of Lithuania in struggle and extermination], is well known. It was published in 1948 and covers the life and suffering of the Jews in Vilna under the Nazi occupation. In the book that was published just now about the Jewish camps in Estonia, Dr. Dworzecki returns primarily to his Vilna Jews and describes the further fate of those who were deported and brought to the northernmost country of the Baltics. But in the more than twenty years that separate the two books, the author broadened and deepened his research and also greatly revised his method of approaching the entire subject. This is clearly noticeable in the latest work and gives it still more credence.

Besides his personal memories, in the new book Dr. Dworzecki relied very much on eyewitness accounts, which are of great significance in the study of the *khurbn*. The author himself conducted more eyewitness interviews of former inmates of Estonian camps. He also made wide use of published memoirs. As a result, it is difficult to understand the omission of the material from the journal *Fun letstn khurbn* [From the recent destruction, of which the reviewer was the editor] and especially the memoirs of Dr. L. Burzanski, in issue 9 [1948], about the liquidation of the Klooga camp in Estonia. The author found important information in the published proceedings of the trials of the war criminals. Included also are previously unpublished archival materials. Overall, Dr. Dworzecki is cautious about making conclusions and with expressing a strong opinion about many of the issues he discusses. As a scholar, he expresses his intent only to penetrate the details, to "attempt to study," "learn to recognize."

"Who was exiled from Jerusalem with the exile"—like the long-ago Mordechai Ha-Yehudi [in the Scroll of Esther], Mark Dworzecki lives and suffers together with those driven from his Jerusalem of Lithuania. In the Jewish camps, he was also together with those deported or driven from other cities and countries. He also weaves into his Scroll of Estonia the Jews who were brought from Kovno, from Latvia, and also from Bistriţa, Transylvania. And at the same time, short descriptions of the Kovno ghetto, of the Jewish troubles under the Nazis in Riga, and of the deportation from Bistriţa . . . A camp inmate together with the others who were rounded up, he accompanies them in the book, camp by camp, *Aktion* by *Aktion* [roundups], and through the other bizarre calamities. And in time the Russian front comes nearer, in summer 1944, and the liquidation of the camps begins, with the horrible mass slaughters in Lagedi and Klooga. And the evacuation to Germany. And again and again, mass victims. Until, in the first half of 1945, liberation arrives for the sparse, sparse remnants. The author covers nearly every step of their course of suffering with his personal memories and years-long investigations.

Chapters in the book recount in detail the living conditions in the camps. We read about the food supply, clothing, and shoes. And the work, the forced labor! . . . A separate chapter speaks of the children in the Jewish camps. During the deportations, as is well known, the Germans immediately took the children away from their parents. And yet a number of people used the most varied means and succeeded in bringing the children with them in secret. But they could not keep them hidden for long in the camp. And the Germans ordered special "children's groups" and other "concentrations." And the fate of these groups was already sealed—the children's *Aktionen*.

Himself a medical doctor, Dr. Dworzecki provides much information about illnesses, mortality, and the fight for health in the camps. As is already his custom, the author dwells more broadly on the communal life of the inmates, and in particular from the moral viewpoint. Spiritual resistance against the Germans was strong, against their attempt to turn the Jews into beasts, deaden every nobler feeling in them, and make them despair of any salvation. Death was indeed before their eyes, but the hope in the people's hearts flourished.

There was also an underground movement in the Jewish camps in Estonia. The chief goal—escaping to the nearby forests and there joining the red partisans and fighting together with weapons against the Germans. Those from the Vilna and Kovno ghettos already had a certain expertise in organizing themselves and forming secret cells. It was mainly the young people who were active, and under the drastic regime, a few struggled physically with the Germans in the camp itself. The book also speaks about death-defying escapes, but which very seldom ended with success.

"The system of deportations and the system of camps"—reads the subtitle of the book. Whether the author is actually successful in his attempt with this research to capture accurately the "system" remains in doubt. The German "Final Solution" to the Jewish problem is already clearly known. The system itself had its interpreters and servants—the commandants, camp leaders and their assistants, and other high officials, and the *Kapos*. Each of these demons was an authority in giving the system an interpretation—with the wildest persecutions and death. And the deeds of these types were indeed described in the book, and other murderers were also characterized. The book is also provided with a notable number of appendices, which help to orient oneself in this difficult subject.

The book, as stated, encompasses a complete set of camps across an entire country, and this is of special importance. In the main, the books of our *khurbn* literature are devoted solely to individual communities and ghettos or camps. But where are the monographs about Dachau with all its satellite camps? And Kaiserwald or Stutthof and still other centers and their branches? One would indeed wish to see Dr. Dworzecki's book as a portent of a series of further such monographs by him and also as a stimulus and guide for other authors of *khurbn* literature.

Introduction Notes:

1. M. Dvorzhetski, *Vayse nekht un shvartse teg (yidn-lagern in estonye)* [White nights and black days (Jewish camps in Estonia)] (Tel Aviv:Y. L. Perets, 1970). Hebrew, *Mahanot ha-yehudim be-Estonia* (Jerusalem:Yad Vashem, 1970). French, "L'histoire de la déportation et des camps en Esthonie" (PhD diss., Sorbonne, 1966).

2.Yisroel Kaplan, "Yidn-katsetn in tsofn" [Camps for Jews in the north (Estonia)], *Di goldene keyt* 72 (1971): 244–46.

49
Nachman Blumental. Words and Sayings from the Holocaust Period (1981)
Reviewed by David Shtokfish

DAVID SHTOKFISH (Sztokfisz; 1912–2008) was born in Lublin, Poland, and became a Yiddish journalist in Poland before World War II. During the Nazi period, he took refuge in the Soviet Union and then returned briefly to liberated Poland, where he helped to revive the Yiddish press. He settled in Israel in 1948, continuing as a Yiddish writer and editor, notably as editor for forty years of the Yiddish newspaper *Yisroel shtime* (Voice of Israel) and of his hometown survivor annual *Kol Lublin—Lubliner shtime* (Voice of Lublin). His most enduring work came as editor of more than a dozen *yizkor* (memorial) books on destroyed Jewish communities, published in Yiddish and Hebrew from 1955 to 1990.

Among Shtokfish's writings on Holocaust topics is his review of the best-known book by Nachman Blumental (see Selections 28 and 35 above), *Verter un vertlekh fun der khurbn-tkufe* (Words and sayings from the Holocaust period).[1] The book presents Blumental's thirty years of work collecting expressions used by Jews during the Nazi period, chiefly in Yiddish, but also in Hebrew, Polish, German, and Russian, that gave spiritual and moral strength to the will to resist. Shtokfish's review contends that, despite the many Holocaust remembrances already written, Blumental's collection fulfills an imperative that has not been exhausted and "will last forever and ever."[2]

Shtokfish laments in his postscript that publication of such a book required the sponsorship of many foundations and individuals. Yet, by the date at which the book and his review were written, the mass commercial market for (nonreligious) Yiddish books—paradoxically given renewed life by literature on the Holocaust—had also greatly declined. The only later book of Yiddish historical scholarship was the 1983 posthumous collection of writings by Isaiah Trunk.[3] And so, with this late review, the present volume of translations honors a closed canon of scholarly work—awaiting new readers.

נחמן בלומענטאַל

ווערטער און ווערטלעך
פֿון דער חורבן־תקופה

תל־אביב—1981

We remember the *piyyut* [liturgical poem] "Akdamut" that is recited on Shavuot before the Torah reading: If all the heavens were parchment, and all the reeds were pens, and all the oceans were ink[1] . . . Then, let us suppose (and paraphrase) that certainly a world of ink, pens without limit, and an immense number of parchments have already been used to describe the Shoah—nevertheless, there has not been a full exploration of the extent of the cataclysm, its complete horror, heroism, and ghastliness. The memoirs of the *khurbn* period, its prose, poetry, and journalism that have been published so far have still not exhausted the subject of Auschwitz, Maidanek, Treblinka, and Sobibor. And just as it troubles the mind that there are "unsatiated" readers of *khurbn* literature, there are also many, many who have "had enough already" of all the descriptions and depictions of the Second World War. And how much is indeed the limit?!

Nevertheless—I recommend wholeheartedly, both to those "who have had enough already" and, without any doubt, to those who have not yet touched a book on that period, that they should acquire Nachman Blumental's *Verter un vertlekh fun der khurbn-tkufe*—a collection of more than 2,500 characterizations, syllogisms, terms, and various expressions created by the people in the years 1939–1945 in the ghettos, camps, partisan groups, and in all the places where the Hitlerian murderer imprisoned our Jews. And they, the humiliated, insulted, tortured, persecuted, and murdered, even when the knife already lay on their throat, made use of the final, but not disappointing, weapon—*the word!* The joke, folk wisdom, aphorism, expressed in tragic circumstances, brought about a release from tension, and relief, brought forth a smile, possibly even laughter—and with that sort of weapon, one fought back against the enemy, whether by freeing those close from illusions or even by laughing at oneself. "A blow subsides and a word abides"—says a folk saying. There is no doubt that Blumental's collection of words and sayings will abide forever because it is a compact lexicon of the *khurbn*, an anthology of gallows humor.

And this is not only a collection of the spoken word but also of the written word—in hundreds of books in the Yiddish, Hebrew, Polish, German, and Russian languages, quoted from newspapers, journals, and other publications. Today, one can imagine how many years of labor had to be invested in such a book because each word "has a father": the source, i.e., the book from which the quote was taken, the author, the time and place in which it was created, as well as who the creator of the saying was.

Already in 1944, on the morning after the liberation, Blumental began collecting words, as he recounts in the introduction to the book (pp. 7, 9):

> When, in the middle of 1944, I was in Eastern Poland and encountered a small number of Jews, I could almost not understand their language. Such changes had taken place here in the course of the short period of my absence—three years. I wanted to know what happened here, every single detail. On the other hand, every one of them, "those who remained"

(only later did I become acquainted with the expression "Holocaust survivor"), spoke very willingly, as if to be rid of the great burden that weighed on him. The innumerable words that were used by the people and which I did not understand impeded the conversation. It was necessary to ask at length what the works meant—and the number of incomprehensible words was great. Among them were some that, after stripping them of their Yiddish trappings, appeared to be foreign words, taken from German, Polish, Ukrainian. In a smaller number—from other languages: Russian, Hungarian, etc. . . .

In 1943, in Warsaw, the Polish underground published a collection of anti-Hitlerian jokes and anecdotes. In the book, there is a chapter titled "Jewish Jokes." The underground—not only Polish—became convinced that nothing helped the fight against the Hitler regime like a simple joke. Against a joke, even a dictator like the almighty Hitler—is helpless. As a result, the comparatively large number of humorous books, journals, and fliers published in occupied Europe in various languages, including German. Even serious illegal publications had "humor corners." The same was true of the illegal Jewish press that appeared in occupied Poland, of which only a part was in Yiddish.

True and certain! Jews also joked in the ghettos and the death camps and in this way reacted to the decrees of the oppressors. The gallows humor encouraged, armed the victims spiritually and morally, and awakened them to the fight.

In September 1941, in the Ringelblum Archive ("Oyneg Shabes"), one such folk saying was recorded that Blumental lists in his book under the word "Hitler": "In Poland, Hitler conducted a total war; in France—a month-long war; in England—a fatal war; in Russia—a catastrophic war" (p. 77). This is a prophecy, permeated with true Jewish faith, issued just three months after the outbreak of the German-Soviet war when the Wehrmacht had won overwhelming victories on all fronts. But consider such folk wisdom, born in the Shavel ghetto (p. 80): "Hitler announced a contest for an inscription that would be engraved on his headstone. Many proposals were submitted, but not one pleased him. Inquiry was made of a Jew. The Jew, not thinking long, suggested: Beauty, Purity, Sacrifice. This pleased Hitler very much. The Jew was attacked by the Jews: How come?! What does this mean?! So he replied: The inscription means nothing more than "*a sheyne, reyne, kapore*" [a common Yiddish idiom that means, literally, "a proper, pure expiation," with reference to the biblical scapegoat sent into the wilderness, but meaning, "good riddance"]. . . .

One is tempted to offer more and more excerpts from this extraordinary book, but in a review one is not permitted such a "luxury." So let us end this portion with another story—from the Lodz ghetto and about Rumkowski [leader of the *Judenrat*] (p. 255): "In the Lodz ghetto there were Jewish firefighters. Rumkowski, in a public speech, strongly praised his firefighters: 'They stay awake day and night.' Someone called out from the community: 'And when do they sleep?' A second Jew answered him: 'When it's burning.'"

★ ★ ★

And now—something about the author, publisher, sponsors, and other matters:

Regarding the author, he is no new face in Jewish literature, and most especially in the field of Shoah research. Born in 1902, in Borszczów, eastern Galicia [today Borshchiv, Ukraine]. Graduated from the Philological-Humanistic and Philosophical Department of Warsaw University. From 1928 to 1939—teacher in the Jewish humanistic gymnasiums in Lublin, later—in Lodz. In Poland, after the liberation, his document collection *Obozy* ("camps") appeared in Polish, and methodological instructions for collecting materials about the *khurbn* period. Then—*Słova Niewinne* (Innocent Words) [on the Nazi German vocabulary].

In Israel, to which he immigrated in June 1950, Blumental edited periodical publications from Bet Lohame ha-Geta'ot [Ghetto Fighters' House] and the book *Pamiętnik Justyny* (Diary of Justina), published in Polish and Hebrew. Prepared for publication the editions from Yad Vashem: *Protocols of the Judenrat in Lublin*; *Protocols of the Judenrat in Bialystok* [both in Hebrew]. Together with Dr. Kermish, edited the documents of the uprising in the Warsaw ghetto. Published many articles and newspapers in YIVO publications and periodical writings. Edited some twenty *yizkor* books of destroyed Jewish communities.

The question arises: How does it happen that a person with such a high record of scholarly, literary, and journalistic work, after assembling in the course of thirty-some years the thousands of words and sayings of that period, had to appeal to the "private initiative" of journalist Ovadia Feld for the book to see the light of day? Where was Yad Vashem, YIVO, or the kibbutz Bet Lohame ha-Geta'ot—because it is fundamentally their task to undertake such a book and make possible its appearance? As many as seven organizations and institutions, and again that many persons (two from New York, two from Paris, eight from Frankfurt, and two from Israel) gave support for that purpose. But for how long will books of such scope and importance depend on the "good heart" and . . . [ellipsis in original] pockets of individuals?

But it seems that it is also to the credit of such broad-hearted Jews and organizations that valuable books are published. And one of them is, without any doubt, Nachman Blumental's *Verter un vertlekh fun der khurbn-tkufe*.

Introduction Notes:

1. Nakhman Blumental, *Verter un vertlekh fun der khurbn-tkufe* (Tel Aviv: Y. L. Perets, 1981).

2. David Shtokfish, "A leksikon vegn khurbn, an antologye fun galgn-humor" [A Lexicon on the Holocaust, an anthology of gallows humor], *Kol Lublin—Lubliner Shtime* [Voice of Lublin] 16 (November 1981): 21–22; reprinted in David Shtokfish, *In gang fun gesheenishn* [In the course of events] (Tel Aviv: Yisroel-Bukh, 1982), 717–20.

3. Yeshaye Trunk, *Geshtaltn un gesheenishn [naye serye]* [Figures and events [new series]] (Tel Aviv: Y. L. Perets, 1983).

Article Notes:

1. [Quoted from typical translations of "*Akdamut*" rather than the reviewer's inaccurate recollection.]